Laure Junot Abrantès

The Home and Court Life of the Emperor Napoleon and his Family

Vol. 2

Laure Junot Abrantès

The Home and Court Life of the Emperor Napoleon and his Family
Vol. 2

ISBN/EAN: 9783337350109

Printed in Europe, USA, Canada, Australia, Japan

Cover: Foto ©ninafisch / pixelio.de

More available books at **www.hansebooks.com**

THE
Autobiography and Recollections
OF
Laura, Duchess of Abrantès

(WIDOW OF GENERAL JUNOT)

WITH

*Reminiscences of her Life in Corsica, Paris,
and in Spain and Portugal*

*A NEW EDITION
IN FOUR VOLUMES, WITH PORTRAITS*

VOLUME THE SECOND

London
Richard Bentley and Son
Publishers in Ordinary to Her Majesty the Queen
1893

THE
Home and Court Life
OF
The Emperor Napoleon
AND HIS FAMILY

WITH

*Pictures of the most Distinguished
Persons of the Time*

BY

MADAME JUNOT (NÉE PERMON)
DUCHESSE D'ABRANTÈS

*A NEW EDITION
IN FOUR VOLUMES, WITH PORTRAITS*

VOLUME THE SECOND

London
Richard Bentley and Son
Publishers in Ordinary to Her Majesty the Queen
1893

CONTENTS

OF THE SECOND VOLUME

CHAPTER I.
1—6.
Presentation at Court—Conversation with the First Consul—Hortense de Beauharnais.

CHAPTER II.
7—14.
Preparations for Madame Permon's ball—A family visit to the Tuileries.

CHAPTER III.
15—27.
The ball at Madame Permon's—Important guests—The Minuet de la Cour—Conversation with Napoleon—Jerôme Bonaparte.

CHAPTER IV.
28—34.
Political career of Lucien Bonaparte—Kind act of his towards the Fléchelle family.

CHAPTER V.
35—45.
The customs of the New Court—The First Consul's reviews—The drummer of Zurich—The Diplomatic Corps.

CHAPTER VI.
46—50.
Anecdote of David—Gérard—General Moreau's pistols.

CHAPTER VII.
51—59.
Pauline Fourès—Napoleon's *liaison* with her in Egypt—She becomes Madame Ramchouppe.

CHAPTER VIII.
60—64.
General Junot's work in Paris—Chevalier's conspiracy—The Chouans.

CHAPTER IX.
65—77.
Gaiety of Madame Permon—Explosion of the infernal machine—Alarm at the Opera—Effects of the explosion in the Rue Saint Nicaise—Police investigation.

CHAPTER X.
78—85.
Visits to the Tuileries—Caroline Murat—M. Portalis.

CHAPTER XI. 86—92.	Breakfast with Madame Bonaparte—Visit to the lions—Napoleon and the Psylle—The snake found.
CHAPTER XII. 93—107.	Madame Junot's receptions—Cambacérès—The catastrophe attending M. de Souza—A second attempt upon his wig—General Mortier—César Berthier.
CHAPTER XIII. 108—122.	The First Consul on parade—M. de Latude—Visit from the terrible Santerre—General Charbonnier—His incompetence—The fiery Vandamme.
CHAPTER XIV. 123—128.	M. Charles and his friendship for the Empress Josephine.
CHAPTER XV. 129—134.	A tribute from General Kléber—The affairs of Egypt—General Damas.
CHAPTER XVI. 135—141.	M. Geouffre's mission to General Menou foiled—The painter Goubaud and his tricolour unwelcome.
CHAPTER XVII. 142—147.	Description of Malmaison—Insincerity of the Empress Josephine.
CHAPTER XVIII. 148—153.	Private theatricals at Malmaison—Arrival of two old soldiers—Alarm in the night.
CHAPTER XIX. 154—179.	Scene between the First Consul and Madame Bonaparte—Her jealousy of Madame Junot—Interviews with the First Consul at unofficial hours—Arrival of Junot—A hunting scene—Madame Junot's return to Paris.
CHAPTER XX. 180—190.	The Theatres—The Opera—A masked Ball.
CHAPTER XXI. 191—202.	Private theatre at Malmaison—Actors and their critics—The bootless dragoon—Anecdote of Isabey—Leapfrog with the First Consul—Punch of the Republic.
CHAPTER XXII. 203—215.	Gaieties in Paris—Career of General Brune—His murder—Junot's incomplete report.
CHAPTER XXIII. 216—222.	Count Louis von Cobentzel—Amusing scene with a special courier from Vienna.
CHAPTER XXIV. 223—230.	*La Comédie Française*—General Sprengporten—Madame Récamier.

CHAPTER XXV. 231—238.	Uneasiness of General Rapp—Junot's interview with the First Consul—Order of the day regarding the Battle of Nazareth.
CHAPTER XXVI. 239—248.	Hoax upon the Princesse Dolgorouki—M. De Lacépède—Perilous position of M. Robert.
CHAPTER XXVII. 249—257.	M. Brunetière—Visit to Mademoiselle Clairon—The Queen of Babylon without bread—Generosity of her friends—Her opinion of Mademoiselle Mars—The mysterious shot.
CHAPTER XXVIII. 258—278.	Admiral Linois's engagement—The flotilla at Boulogne—Scandalous pamphlets—The First Consul reproaches General Junot—General Junot's wound at Milan.
CHAPTER XXIX. 279—287.	General Lannes's freedom—An appeal for an audience—Certificate of examination.
CHAPTER XXX. 288—300.	Illness of Madame Permon—Madame Junot's confinement—A merry dinner-party—Poor Andoche—An impromptu visit to the Tuileries—Birth of Junot's eldest daughter.
CHAPTER XXXI. 301—312.	M. d'Offreville a terrible bore—Talma—Comic scene at the *Théâtre Montansier*—The runaway cabriolet.
CHAPTER XXXII. 313—328.	The King of Etruria—M. de Talleyrand—A Tuscan Fête—Œdipus at the *Comédie Française*—Regnault de Saint Jean d'Angely—Proposed creation of the Legion of Honour—Cardinal Consalvi—"Te Deum" at Nôtre Dame.
CHAPTER XXXIII. 329—342.	Death of Madame Permon—Departure of Madame Leclerc for St. Domingo—Her fondness for dress—Toussaint—Death of General Leclerc.
CHAPTER XXXIV. 343—355.	Peace of Amiens—Mr. Fox in Paris—Anecdote of Fox—His debts—The First Consul's coat—His well-shaped legs—Story of a Marseilles banker.
CHAPTER XXXV. 356—365.	Arrival of foreigners in Paris—The Duchess of Courland—Lady Conyngham—Lord Whitworth—"The Marquis of Steyne"—Count Philip von Cobentzel—Madame Demidoff.
CHAPTER XXXVI. 366—382.	The painter David—The Gobelin tapestries—The Museum of Painting and Sculpture at the Louvre—Cabinet of Medals—Story of M. de Sartine—Intolerance of the clergy—The curé of St. Roche and Mademoiselle Chameroi—Napoleon's dignified rebuke.

CHAPTER XXXVII.
383—394.
{ Cardinal Caprera — Baptism of Junot's eldest daughter—A little devil—Disappearance of Cardinal Caprera's biretta—The First Consul's godchild — General and the Countess Verdier—Madame Marmont.

CHAPTER XXXVIII.
395—408.
{ The First Consulship for life—Breakfast given by General Junot—Present from the First Consul—Little Josephine Junot—Illness of Junot—Unexpected visit from Napoleon.

LIST OF THE PRINCIPAL HONOURS CONFERRED BY THE EMPEROR NAPOLEON.

CONTEMPORARY RULERS.

CAMBACÉRÈS.

LIST OF PORTRAITS

CONTAINED IN THE SECOND VOLUME

GENERAL BONAPARTE, AFTERWARDS THE EMPEROR OF THE FRENCH AND KING OF ITALY - - *frontispiece*

JERÔME BONAPARTE, KING OF WESTPHALIA, COUNT MONTFORT (COUNT HARTZ), MARSHAL OF FRANCE IN 1850 - - - - *to face page* 26

JEAN VICTOR MOREAU, GENERAL, CONQUEROR AT HOHENLINDEN, AND AFTERWARDS SHOT FIGHTING AGAINST HIS COUNTRY AT DRESDEN - *to face page* 50

ELIZA MARIE ANNE BONAPARTE, GRAND-DUCHESS OF TUSCANY, PRINCESS OF LUCCA AND PIOMBINO (COUNTESS OF CAMPIGNANO) - - *to face page* 194

MARIE CAROLINE LOUISE ANNONCIADE BONAPARTE, GRAND-DUCHESS OF BERG AND CLEVES, AFTERWARDS QUEEN OF NAPLES (COUNTESS OF LIPONA, DUCHESS OF TARENTUM) - - - *to face page* 326

LUCIEN BONAPARTE, DUKE OF MUSIGNANO AND PRINCE OF CANINO - - - *to face page* 330

MEMOIRS OF MADAME JUNOT

DUCHESS OF ABRANTÈS

CHAPTER I.

My Presentation to the First Consul and Madame Bonaparte—Duroc and Rapp on the Steps—Eleven o'Clock—Politeness of Eugène de Beauharnais—Gracious Reception by Madame Bonaparte—Amiability of Hortense—Conversation with the First Consul—Bonaparte's Opinion of Mirabeau—The Rogue and the Tribunes—M. de Cobentzel and Singular Reserve of Bonaparte—Bonaparte upon the Society of the Faubourg Saint Germain—Portrait of Mademoiselle de Beauharnais.

My presentation to the First Consul and Madame Bonaparte was a great affair for my mother; she occupied herself upon my toilet with more minute care than I imagine she had ever bestowed upon her own in the highest tide of her vanity. One thing disturbed her much, no ceremonial. "Nevertheless, he acts the King," said my mother. The truth was that at this time the interior of the First Consul's family was like that of a very rich man, with no more etiquette; Madame Bonaparte had not even yet ladies in waiting.

We went to the Tuileries after the Opera, leaving the ballet of *Psyché* in the middle that we might not be too late, and arrived at ten o'clock. My heart beat as we alighted at the Pavilion of Flora, at the door which precedes that in the angle so long called the entrance of the Empress. As we ascended the five or six steps before the door on the left, leading to the apartments on the ground-floor, we met Duroc and Rapp. "How late you are!" said Duroc. "It is near eleven o'clock." "Ah!" added the brave Alsatian, "Madame Junot is a worker of marvels; she is about to make an infidel of our good Junot." And he burst into a loud laugh.

I was desirous of turning back; but Junot replied, "Madame Bonaparte desired me to come here after the Opera." "Oh!" said Duroc; "it is quite a different thing if Madame Bonaparte has appointed the hour."

At this moment the folding door of Madame Bonaparte's apartment opened, and Eugène de Beauharnais ran down. He was sent by his mother, because, having heard the wheels of a carriage within the Court, and finding that no one came up, she began to fear lest by mistake, arising from the lateness of the hour, I might be told that she could not receive me.

I was sensible of this attention, and the more so as the messenger was himself very fit to dispel apprehensions of a doubtful reception. M. de Beauharnais gave me his arm, and we entered the large salon together. This fine apartment was so obscure that at first entering I saw no one in it; for it was lighted only by two chandeliers placed on the mantelpiece, and surrounded with gauze to soften the glare. I was very nervous on entering; but an observation from Eugène de Beauharnais contributed wonderfully to restore my composure.

"You have nothing to fear," said he; "my mother and sister are so kind!" These words made me start; no doubt I might experience that emotion which a young woman is so liable to feel at a first presentation to strangers, especially when she has some reason to imagine that she may not be very cordially received ; but my spirits recovered surprisingly.

Madame Bonaparte was in the same place which she then occupied as mistress of the house, and where afterwards she was seated as sovereign of the world ; I found her before a tapestry frame prosecuting a work, three-fourths of which was performed by Mademoiselle Dubuquoy, whose ingenious hint that Marie Antoinette was fond of such employments had inspired Josephine's inclination for them. At the other side of the chimney sat Mademoiselle Hortense de Beauharnais, an amiable, mild, agreeable girl, with the figure of a nymph and beautiful light hair. Her gracious manners and gentle words were irresistibly pleasing.

The First Consul was standing before the chimney with his hands behind him, fidgeting as he had already the habit of doing ; his eyes were fixed upon me, and as soon as I recovered my self-possession I found that he was closely examining me ; but from that moment I determined not to be abashed, as to allow myself to be overcome by fantastic fears with such a man would be ruin.

Madame Bonaparte stood up, came forward, took my two hands and embraced me, saying that I might depend upon her friendship. "I have been too long Junot's friend," she continued, "not to entertain the same sentiments for his wife, particularly for the one he has chosen." "Oh, oh ! Josephine," said the First Consul, "that is running on very fast ! How do you know that this little pickle is worth loving ? Well, Mademoiselle Loulou (you see I do not forget the names of my old friends), have you not a word for me?"

He had taken my hand, and, drawing me towards him, looked at me with a scrutiny which for a moment made me cast down my eyes, but I recollected myself immediately. "General," I replied, smiling, "it is not for me to speak first." The slight contraction of his brow would have been imperceptible to any other person, but I knew his countenance well: he smiled almost instantly, and said, "Very well parried. Oh, the mother's spirit. Apropos, how is Madame Permon?" "She suffers much; for two years past her health has altered so seriously as to cause us great uneasiness." "Indeed! so bad as that; I am sorry to hear it, very sorry; make my regards to her. It is a wrong head —a devil of a spirit;* but she has a generous heart and a noble soul."

I withdrew my hand, which he had held during this short colloquy, and took my seat near Madame Bonaparte. The conversation became general and very agreeable. Duroc came in, and took part in it. Madame Bonaparte said little on subjects she did not understand, and thereby avoided exposing her ignorance. Her daughter, without saying more than is becoming in a young girl, had the talent of sustaining the conversation on agreeable topics.

M. de Cobentzel was expected at Paris, and his arrival was spoken of. Madame Bonaparte said that she had heard someone observe upon the astonishing resemblance between Count Louis de Cobentzel and Mirabeau. "Who said that?" asked the First Consul hastily. "I do not exactly recollect. Barras, I think." "And where had Barras seen M. de Cobentzel? Mirabeau! he was ugly; M. de Cobentzel is ugly—there is all the resemblance. *Eh, pardieu!* you know him, Junot; you were with him at our famous treaty, and Duroc, too. But you never saw Mirabeau. He was a rogue, but a clever rogue! he himself did more mischief to the former masters of this house than the States-General altogether. But he was a rogue." Here he

---

* I have already said that I shall preserve the turn of Napoleon's phrases and his manner of speaking; it was original, and at once Oriental and *bourgeoise*.

took a pinch of snuff, repeating, "He was a bad man, and too vicious to be tribune of the people; not but in my tribunate there were some no better than he, and without half his talent. As for Count Louis de Cobentzel———"

He took another pinch of snuff, and was about to resume his observations, but stopped as if struck by a sudden reflection. He thought, perhaps, that the first magistrate of the Republic should not so lightly give his opinion upon a man just named by a great Power to treat with him. He stopped then with a sentence half uttered, and, turning to me, said :

"I hope that we shall often see you, Madame Junot. My intention is to draw round me a numerous family, consisting of my generals and their young wives. They will be friends of my wife and of Hortense, as their husbands are mine. Does that suit you? I warn you that you will be disappointed if you expect to find here your fine acquaintances of the Faubourg Saint Germain. I do not like them. They are my enemies, and prove it by defaming me. Tell them from me, as your mother lives amongst them—tell them that I am not afraid of them."

This sentence, spoken with harshness, gave me uneasiness from two causes : it was disobliging both to Junot and to me ; it seemed to reproach him for taking a wife from a hostile society, and to hint that I came into his own with unfriendly dispositions. I could not forbear answering, perhaps hastily :

"General, excuse me if I cannot consent to do what is not in the province of a woman, and particularly in that of General Junot's wife ; and permit me to carry from you to my friends only messages of peace and union ; I know that they desire no others."

I would not interrupt the relation of this interesting interview to describe the person and manners of Mademoiselle de Beauharnais, but I think it would be an injustice both to her and my readers to omit to describe her as she appeared at my first introduction to her. Hortense de Beauharnais was at this time seventeen years old; she was fresh as a rose, and though her fair complexion was not relieved by much colour, she had enough to produce that freshness and bloom which was her chief beauty; a profusion of light hair played in silky locks round her soft and penetrating blue eyes. The delicate roundness of her figure, slender as a palm-tree, was set off by the elegant carriage of her head; her feet were small and pretty; her hands very white, with pink well-rounded nails.

But what formed the chief attraction of Hortense was the grace and suavity of her manners, which united the creole languor with the vivacity of France. She was gay, gentle, and amiable; she had wit, which, without the smallest ill-temper, had just malice enough to be amusing. A careful education had improved her natural talents; she drew excellently, sang harmoniously, and performed admirably in comedy. In 1800 she was a charming young girl; she afterwards became one of the most amiable princesses of Europe. I have seen many, both in their own courts and in Paris, but I never knew one who had any pretensions to equal talent.

She was beloved by every one, though, of all who surrounded her, her mother seemed to be the least conscious of her attractions. I do not mean to say that she did not love her, but certainly she did not express that degree of maternal affection which Hortense de Beauharnais merited. Her brother loved her tenderly: the First Consul looked upon her as his child; and it was only in that country so fertile in the inventions of scandal that so foolish an accusation could have been imagined, as that any feeling less pure than paternal affection actuated his conduct towards her. The vile calumny met with the contempt it merited, and is now only remembered to be confuted.

CHAPTER II.

The Wedding-ball—List of Guests—Swearing—Invitation to the First Consul—His Visiting-cards—Diplomatic Breakfast—Visit to the Tuileries, and Invitation to Madame Bonaparte—The *Monaco* and *Les Deux Coqs*—The First Consul's Closet—Charm of his Physiognomy—The First Consul accepts an Invitation to the Ball—The First Anniversary of the 18th of Brumaire, and the Ball deferred—M. de Caulaincourt's Indiscretion.

My mother had determined to give a ball on the fifteenth day after my marriage : it was an ancient custom, and though not now the fashion, she would by no means forego it. One evening when we had dined with her, she required our assistance in arranging her plans : " For this ball," said she, " must be one of the prettiest that has been given this long time past ; my house, it is true, is very small, but it must be turned into an enchanted parterre of flowers. Come, take your place at the desk, Madame Laurette, and make out our list of invitations, for all your husband's friends must be of the party." Junot thanked her, and kissed her hand.

"Oh ! surely," she replied, "your friends are my friends now, only they swear rather too much ; and you, I have been told, can do so, too, when you are angry. You must leave off that ugly habit ; it does not become a gentleman." Junot laughed, and held up his finger to me. " What, because she tells me that you swear?" said my mother. "No, I hope she will never cease to pour all her confidence into my maternal ear; besides, remember, she has not yet made acquaintance enough with your ear for it to supplant mine; but come, to work."

Junot took the pen, and wrote down all the names of the ladies, beginning with Madame Bonaparte and Mademoiselle de Beauharnais. He then waited for the name with which my mother would commence the list of gentlemen.

"The First Consul of the French Republic, One and Indivisible; is not that the style?" said my mother. "The First Consul!" we exclaimed together. "Yes, the First Consul; is there anything astonishing in that? I am tired of being on bad terms with anyone, and besides——" "And besides," said Junot, laughing, "you think that perhaps you were more in the wrong than he."

"No, no," said my mother; "that is quite another affair. He was in the wrong altogether; but I considered that, as Laurette might be daily in his society, these sort of quarrels might produce disagreeable effects for her, and I wished to prevent that—was I not right?" We embraced her. "But the invitation," she added, "is not all. Do you think he will accept it? do you think he will come?" "I am sure of it; only name the hour that will suit you best, and I will come to fetch you," said Junot, enchanted at this prospect of reconciliation between his mother-in-law and his beloved General.

My mother looked at him with an air of astonishment perfectly laughable. "Fetch me! to go where?" "Where!" returned Junot, as much surprised in his turn; "to the Tuileries, to tender your invitation to the First Consul and Madame Bonaparte." "My dear Junot," said my mother, with the utmost seriousness and sang-froid, "you are quite, nay, perfectly mad." "It seems to me that what I say is, nevertheless, very sensible ; that nothing, in fact, can be more reasonable," replied Junot, somewhat disconcerted by the apostrophe. "And I tell you, you are mad. Would you have me go to request General Bonaparte to come again to my house, after having forbidden his appearance there?"

"How, then, do you propose to invite him?" asked Junot, with an accent impossible to describe. "Truly, how should I invite him? Precisely in the same manner as I do everyone else, except that the card shall be all in writing, and I will write it all in my own neat hand, which he knows perfectly well."

Junot strode up and down the room, exclaiming, "But that cannot be! You had better not invite him at all! He will think that you intend him a disrespect." "He would be much mistaken, then. But he would think no such thing ; and you will see that, after having received my note of invitation, he will do as all well-bred men would ; he will call on me before the ball, or at least he will have a card left at the door." "Do you think, then," said Junot, in the utmost surprise, "that he keeps visiting cards?" "And why not? My dear child, because Bonaparte gains battles, is that any reason that he should not visit?"

For a long time my inclination to laugh had been suppressed with the utmost difficulty ; Albert, throwing himself back in his arm-chair, had given way to his from the first ; and this last observation, together with the stupefied astonishment of Junot, who, with his mouth half open, could not find words to answer, was altogether too much for my gravity, and I burst into one of those fits of wild mirth which one only enjoys at sixteen. My mother and Junot were still no less serious, my mother at intervals murmuring, "I do not see why he should not visit, and certainly I shall not go first."

My brother and I became by degrees more reasonable, seeing that she was perfectly in earnest, and certainly intended that the First Consul should come first to her. Now, it is true that not even a thought of royalty was yet attached to his name, but already for twelve months he had exercised the supreme authority of the State; and this power had placed him on an elevation which appeared quite natural and becoming to him; he was there because it was his proper place.

Albert knew my mother's character, and that by further opposition we should irritate without persuading her; he therefore sat down to the desk, and requested her to dictate her list, which she did with as much self-possession and composure as if the First Consul had never existed. The list consisted of seventy men and forty ladies — a large number for so small a house; but then, as now, it was a pleasure to be crowded, and the greatest approbation that could be expressed the day after a ball was, " What a charming *fête!* we were almost suffocated!"

The next morning Albert breakfasted with us, and it was resolved in our little council that we should all three proceed immediately to the Tuileries, and, in my mother's name, make our personal request to the First Consul and Madame Bonaparte to honour with their presence the ball my family were to give on the occasion of my marriage, taking good care to say nothing of the written invitations which had been entrusted to me for delivery.

Madame Bonaparte received us in the most gracious manner; it was in such cases that she appeared to the utmost advantage. She had already gone through all that a royal novitiate demanded, and it can scarcely be imagined with what ease she stepped into the station of Queen. She accepted our invitation for herself and Mademoiselle de Beauharnais: the latter, she said, was absent from the

Tuileries. She seemed, however, by no means willing that we should extend our invitation to the First Consul. "He has been," she said, "but to two *fêtes* since his entry upon the Consulate—the one at Morfontaine, where policy led him to meet the American envoy; the other was the fête given him by the Consul Cambacérès on his return from Marengo; and besides," added she, "he dances but little."

"My sister," said Albert, with his natural mildness of manner, "will not readily admit that; the First Consul has often, *very often*, danced the *Monaco* and *Les Deux Coqs* with Laurette, to the sound of my eldest sister's piano. Do you know, madame, that we may claim almost the rights of fraternity with General Bonaparte?" "Yes, he has often told me so," she replied, with an affectation of friendliness. But this was not true, for I know that the First Consul never spoke of my mother to Madame Bonaparte, except when she herself led to the subject, which she was not fond of doing.

After taking leave of Madame Bonaparte, we proceeded by the staircase of the Pavilion of Flora to the apartments of the First Consul. The aide-de-camp in waiting observed that the hour of admission was past. "But I have an appointment," said Junot. "And madame?" asked the aide-de-camp. He was the unfortunate Lacuée, killed at Austerlitz, nephew of the Comte de Cessac, and cousin of M. de Beausset.

"We are too recently married, my friend," replied Junot, "to be more than one and the same person; therefore announce me, if you please; and though ladies do not often come to trouble your hermitage, show that you know how to be gallant, and give my wife your arm." When the door was opened, and the First Consul saw me, he said, smiling very good-humouredly, "What means this family deputation?—there is only Madame Permon wanting to its completion. Is she afraid of the Tuileries, or of me?" "General," said my husband immediately, "Madame Permon would gladly have joined us, but she is very ill, and finds it impossible to leave her chamber to come to request a favour of you, which she is very desirous to obtain. My wife is charged to address to you her petition in form."

The First Consul turned towards me with a smile, saying, "Well, let me hear. What do you wish for?" It is difficult, if not impossible, to describe the charm of his countenance when he smiled with a feeling of benevolence. His soul was upon his lips and in his eyes. The magic power of that expression at a later period is well known; the Emperor of Russia had experienced it when he said to me, "I never loved anyone more than that man!"

I told the General what had been agreed upon, and had scarcely ended my little harangue, when he took my two hands, and said, "Well, I shall certainly be at this ball. Did you expect I should refuse? I shall go most willingly." Then he added a phrase which he often repeated: "Though I shall be in the midst of my enemies; for your mother's drawing-room, they tell me, is full of them."

Junot now made a sign to us to take leave; we accordingly made our parting salutations, and the First Consul, after pressing my brother's hand with as much cordiality as if we were still in my father's house, inquired on what day this ball should take place. "Next Monday, General; it is, I believe, the 10th of November."

"What! the 10th of November," said the First Consul, going to his escritoire; "that seems to me to be some particular day; let me see;" and as he spoke he found the calendar he was seeking. "I thought so," he added, on consulting it. "The 10th of November is the anniversary of the 18th Brumaire, and I cannot join a party on that day. Your mother will have no company;

your acquaintance of the Faubourg Saint Germain will certainly not quit their retreats to make a festival of the anniversary of the re-establishment of the Republic. What concerns me personally," and his countenance as he spoke assumed an expression serious and severe, "is of little consequence, but I must see the Republic respected; it would not, therefore, be suitable that the anniversary of the day which restored it to us entire should be celebrated otherwise than as a family festival. I do not refuse Madame Permon's invitation if you will name another day."

The change was immediately resolved upon, and he himself named the 12th of November. "Do you receive Josephine?" he inquired. I answered that Madame Bonaparte had accepted for herself and her daughter the invitation which my mother, to her great regret, had not been able to give in person.

"Oh, I have no doubt but Madame Permon is ill," said the First Consul; "but there is idleness, if not some other motive, which I will not mention in her absence. Is there not, Madame Loulou?" And so saying, he pulled my ear and hair till he made my eyes water, which I was not sorry for, as it furnished an excuse for not answering this blunt interpolation, and for the colour which flushed my cheeks. While this was passing between us and the future master of the world, another scene took place in the apartments of Madame Bonaparte below-stairs.

M. de Caulaincourt paid his court very attentively to Madame Bonaparte; an old friendship or relationship between them was connected with a remembrance of protection on his part, and of gratitude on hers. She was, in consequence, on very good terms with my adopted godfather, and almost every morning the pony, with its velvet saddle and gilded bridle, trotted from the Rue des Capuchins to the Tuileries.

Here it arrived on the morning of our visit, just as we had left Madame Bonaparte, and the conversation naturally falling upon the invitation we had brought, M. de Caulaincourt, to whom my mother had related all that had passed on the preceding night, glorying in the firm stand she had made in favour of a written invitation, unceremoniously accused me of having mistaken my instructions, and very innocently repeated to Madame Bonaparte all that he had learned from my mother, of whose plans he perfectly approved. This unlucky incident produced a rather awkward dénouement on our return to the salon ; but our apologies were graciously accepted, and whether or not the truth ever reached the ears of the First Consul it produced no visible result.

My mother easily perceived that it would be ridiculous for her to celebrate the anniversary of the 18th Brumaire ; the change which we had made in the day consequently received her perfect acquiescence, and passed off without any observation.

CHAPTER III.

The Ball and the Flowers—The First Country-dance—Mademoiselle de Beauharnais, Mademoiselle de Perigord, Mademoiselle de Caseaux and myself—The Minuet de la Reine and the Gavotte—The fine Dancers—Madame Leclerc and the Toilet of Madame Bonaparte—Noise of Horses and the Arrival of the First Consul—The Dance interrupted—The First Consul's Gray Overcoat—Long Conversation between the First Consul and M. de Talleyrand—M. Laffitte and the Three-cornered Hat—M. de Trénis and the Grand Bow—The First Consul listening to a Dancing-lesson—Bonaparte not fond of Long Speeches—Interesting Conversation between Bonaparte and my Mother—Jerome, his Debts, his Beard, and Superfluous Travelling-case.

ALL was preparation in my mother's house for the expected ball, which she intended should be one of the most agreeable to be given this year in Paris. Our friends also looked forward to it with impatience. My mother had already refused the requests of above forty men and twelve women for tickets. She was delighted when such requests were made to her. The arrangements for ornamenting the house were perfect; and when at length all the trees, plants, and flowers assumed the places her taste appointed them, and innumerable lights shone among them from lamps of every colour, the staircase and hall perfectly resembled an enchanted palace.

Madame Bonaparte arrived about nine o'clock, accompanied by her son and daughter, and led by Colonel Rapp. My mother met her in the middle of the dining-room; the other ladies she received at the door of the salon. She was polite and gracious to everyone, as she so well knew how to be. She conducted Madame Bonaparte to the arm-chair on the right of the fireplace, and begged her, with the hospitable grace of the South, to make herself perfectly at home. She must have appeared to her, what she actually was, a very agreeable and charming woman.

My mother was, perhaps, the prettiest woman in the room, after the First Consul's two sisters. She had been for some time in better health, and the respite from suffering had restored to her features that harmony and regularity in which her beauty consisted. She wore on this evening a dress, made by Madame Germon, of white crape, trimmed with bunches of double jonquils. Its form was Grecian, folding over the bosom, and fastened on the shoulders with two diamond clasps. Her head-dress had a degree of eccentricity in its composition which became her admirably.

As she could not, or rather did not, choose to appear on the occasion of my marriage with her hair wholly uncovered, she had a toque of white crape (made by Leroi, who then lived in the Rue des Petits-Champs, and had already acquired some reputation), through the folds of which her fine black hair appeared, resembling velvet, intermingled with bunches of jonquil, like those which trimmed her gown. She wore in her bosom a large bouquet of jonquils and natural violets, furnished by Madame Roux, but exhibited neither necklace nor jewels of any kind except two very fine diamond drops in her ears. This attire was set off by a person whose elegance of figure and manner were at least her most striking ornament.

At a quarter before nine o'clock Junot went to the

Tuileries to be ready to attend the First Consul to my mother's, but found him so overwhelmed with business that it was impossible for him to name the hour at which he could arrive; but he was desired to request as a favour that the dancing might commence, the First Consul giving his assurance that he would certainly come, however late he might be compelled to make his visit.

The ball, then, was opened at half-past nine. Junot danced with Mademoiselle de Beauharnais, Eugène de Beauharnais with me, Hippolyte de Rastignac with Mademoiselle de Caseaux, and Mademoiselle de P—— with M. Dupaty. M. de Trénis was not yet arrived, nor M. Laffitte. These gentlemen were at this time in the extreme of everything that is inconceivable; and to join a party at two or three o'clock in the morning was nothing unusual with them.

I had this evening, in the opinion of my mother and all our old friends, an important duty to fulfil: it was to dance the *minuet de la cour* and the *gavotte.* For three weeks Gardel's long lessons had been renewed, that this minuet, which with my whole soul I detested, might be executed in perfection. I had entreated my mother to spare me this painful exhibition, but to no purpose. Not to dance the *minuet de la Reine* at a bridal ball would have been a dereliction of all established customs, which she could not by any means sanction.

M. de Trénis belonged to our society: he was a worthy man, and far from meriting the character which he gave himself of being nothing but a dancer. He possessed much information and some wit; natural good sense and a correct judgment, very capable of appreciating the ridiculous extravagance of his own words; that of his dress, though in the height of fashion, was by no means so exaggerated. As of all the fine dancers of the day, he was the one with whom we were the most acquainted, I had engaged him to dance the *minuet de la cour* with me, hoping to be less timid with him than with M. Laffitte or M. Dupaty.

At half-past ten General Bonaparte was not arrived; everyone else was, and the five rooms in my mother's suite of apartments were much more than conveniently crowded. All the Bonaparte family except Joseph, who, I believe, was then at Luneville, came early.

Madame Leclerc, always beautiful and elegant, had taken her seat at a distance from her sister-in-law, whose exquisite taste in dress never failed to put her out of conceit with her own appearance, how carefully soever her toilet had been performed. "I do not understand," said she to me, "how a person of forty years old can wear garlands of flowers!"

Madame Bonaparte had a wreath of poppies and golden ears of corn upon her head, and her dress was trimmed with the same. I was afraid that she would foolishly make the same compliment to my mother, and unwilling that a stupid remark should spoil the pleasure of the evening, I answered that my mother, who was older than Madame Bonaparte, had also flowers on her head and round her gown. Madame Leclerc looked at me with an air of astonishment. "But it is quite different—quite a different thing," said she.

At a few minutes before eleven the trampling of the First Consul's horse-guards was heard. Very soon afterwards the carriage drove up to the door, and almost immediately he appeared at the entrance of the dining-room with Albert and Junot, who had received him in the hall. My mother advanced towards him, and saluted him with her most courteous obeisance, to which he replied, with a smile:

"Eh, Madame Permon, is that how you receive an old friend?" and held out his hand. My mother gave him hers, and they entered the ballroom together. The heat was excessive. The First Consul remarked it, but without taking off his gray overcoat, and was on the point of making the tour of the room, but his searching eye had already observed that many of the ladies present had not risen at his entrance; he was offended, and passed immediately into the bedroom, still retaining my mother's arm, and appearing to look at her with admiration.

Dancing had been discontinued as soon as he appeared, and Bonaparte soon perceived it by the stillness of the salon, from whence issued only the murmuring sounds produced by the observations made upon him in an undertone.

"Pray, Madame Permon," said he, "let the dancing be resumed; young people must be amused, and dancing is their favourite pastime. I am told, by-the-by, that your daughter dances as well as Mademoiselle Chameroi.* I must see it. And if you will, you and I will dance the *Monaco*—the only one I know."

"I have not danced these thirty years," replied my mother.

"Oh, you are jesting. You look to-night like your daughter's sister."

M. de Talleyrand was of the party. The First Consul, after having spoken to us all in the most agreeable manner, entered into a conversation with him in my mother's bedroom, which lasted without interruption for three-quarters of an hour. Towards midnight he returned to the salon, and appeared determined to make himself perfectly agreeable to everyone.

How great soever my reluctance to dance this unfortunate

* Mademoiselle Chameroi was the finest dancer at the Opera. At this period Eugène Beauharnais much admired her. It was on the occasion of her funeral that the singular history of the refusal of the Curé of St. Roch to bury an actress took place, which is related further on. She died very young.

minuet, I had no choice but to answer to the summons of my mother, who, without concerning herself whether I was maid or wife, expected me to be always obedient to her commands. For a moment I thought myself safe. M. de Trénis was called for, but could nowhere be found. I went to tell my mother, but gained nothing. M. Laffitte was requested to supply his place. He had no hat; my mother soon found him one.

All these difficulties removed, I at length went through the dreaded minuet, having whispered to Gardel not to allow the gavotte to be played, and reckoned my last courtesy a real happiness. M. Laffitte was reconducting me to my seat, holding in one hand an enormous three-cornered hat that he had borrowed of I know not whom, and leading me with the other, when we met M. de Trénis. He looked at me with so terrible an air that I became uneasy for the consequences of having danced the minuet with another person. I told him mildly that I had waited till past midnight, and that my mother had at length required that I should dance with M. Laffitte. "I hope, my dear sir, that you will forget this non-observance of my engagement, and particularly as your absence was its sole cause."

He acquiesced in his disappointment, and, seating himself between my friend Mademoiselle de Merigny and myself, commenced a most ludicrous harangue upon the regret he experienced, which was the greater on account of my share in the loss; "for I shall never, never forget the spectacle I saw," added he. I was alarmed, and entreated an explanation, which, after listening to most high-flown compliments on the excellence of my own dancing, I obtained at length in the following terms:

"That you should dance a minuet with a man—a good dancer, no doubt; yes, he dances well, but if he dance a country-dance well—he never, never in his life, knew how to make the grand bow with the hat—he cannot make the grand bow."

Mademoiselle de Mérigny and I could not help laughing. But M. de Trénis was too deep in his subject to attend to our merriment. "That seems to surprise you," he continued; "I can easily believe it. Not to know how to put on one's hat!—for that is the science—it is not difficult to explain—stay—give me leave." Then, taking us both by the hand, he led us to my mother's room, where there were but few persons, and, placing himself before the pier-glass, hummed the close of the minuet air, and began the salute with the most perfect gravity, putting on his cocked hat with all the effect so important an affair demanded.

The laughing fit returned with redoubled force; but the comedy was not yet complete. Junot had joined us, and the First Consul, whose presence had not as yet caused us any constraint on account of his close conversation with M. de Talleyrand, now stepped gently behind M. de Trénis to share the amusement with which this original was providing us. He made a sign to Junot to engage him in conversation, which was easy, if dancing were the subject, provided, however, that it were seriously treated. For he never laughed, he said, unless the air of a country-dance was very gay, and then the orchestra compelled him to smile. "How do you agree with M. Laffitte?" said Junot, with as serious a countenance as he could command.

"Why," replied he, "as well as two men of talent can be supposed to agree when so nearly upon an equality. But he is an honest fellow, not at all envious of my success. It is true that his own may well render him indulgent. His dance is lively and powerful. He has the advantage over me in the first eight measures of Panurge's gavotte. But in the jetés! oh! there he has no chance: he has nerve, but I have grace."

The First Consul opened his eyes and ears, altogether unaccustomed to such rant. "It is prodigious," said he at length; "this man is much more irrational than many who are confined in mad-houses. Is he a friend of yours?"

"Not exactly; but he is an intimate acquaintance—that is to say, we see him twice a week. But, except at a ball, he never talks of dancing, and can reason cleverly upon the manners of ancient Greece; it is a portion of history he has very much studied. He speaks several languages, and, Albert says, is worth more than his reputation."

Bonaparte never listened to so long a discourse; I have learned that it never answered to make long speeches to him. He had returned to his place near M. de Talleyrand; I saw by the direction of his eyes that he was speaking of M. de Trénis. He met my eyes fixed upon him, and called me to him, to make me a compliment on my mother's ball; his praises seemed almost a reproach. My mother had been perfectly polite to him; but it appeared to me that she should have been more cordial.

I went to her, and, persuading her to walk with me, led her towards her own chamber, where I found the First Consul on the spot where I had quitted him; but Junot and M. de Villemanzy had replaced M. de Talleyrand. As soon as the First Consul saw my mother, he went direct to her, and said, "Well, Madame Permon, what have you to say to one of your old friends? It seems to me that you easily forget them. Do you know, I thought you very hard the other evening, and at the very time one of your friends held his knife in readiness?"

"Oh, horrible!" exclaimed my mother; "how can you, Napoleon, say such things?—*Per Dio tacete! tacete!*"

"But why would you not return my friendly salute? I took the first moment of recognizing you to make it."

My mother alleged the weakness of her eyes, and not

without cause, for they became very useless in the last years of her life; but General Bonaparte would not be put off with this excuse. "What am I to think?" said he; "are we no longer friends?"

"*Non posso dimenticare, caro Napoleone, che siete figlio dell'amica; fratello del mio buon Giuseppe, del caro Luciano, e di Pauletta.*"—The First Consul made a movement, which I noticed, and replied with a bitter accent:

"So, then, if I still hold a place in your regard, I owe it to my mother and my brothers. It may well be said that to expect friendship from a woman is to expect the sands of the desert to remain fixed."

This discussion gave me pain; it seemed that my mother remembered that unfortunate quarrel excited by one of our cousins, who never could indemnify us for the affection which we lost through his means. The First Consul walked in silence towards the fire. My mother was seated upon a sofa opposite to him, her arms crossed upon her bosom, and shaking her foot in the fashion which usually preceded a violent scene. Albert, going to and fro between the chamber and the salon, at this moment approached General Bonaparte to offer him an ice.

"I assure you," said he, "that neither Madame Permon nor myself require ice—indeed, I believe we are petrified; I knew very well that absence deadened remembrance, but not to such a point as this." He touched an unlucky string.

"Truly!" said my mother, with a constrained smile, but with her lips sufficiently opened to show her two-and-thirty pearls (on which General Bonaparte cast his eyes; he spoke of them to me the following day);—"truly! one may be permitted to forget after an interval of some years. Did you not wish to persuade me that it was difficult to remember, after a few days, an action which affected the fate of an entire life?"

"Ah!" exclaimed the First Consul, and his countenance darkened in an instant. He knit that brow, the movement of which already agitated the universe; his under lip pressed strongly against the other; and, joining his hands behind him, he walked a few paces without speaking; but all this was scarcely visible, as Junot and my brother told me, when I returned from joining in a country-dance. The First Consul promptly resumed his air of serenity, and, seating himself beside my mother, looked attentively at her hand, which he had taken to kiss.

"It seems to me that you do not correct any of your faults, Madame Permon?" and he pointed to the bitten nails of her fingers.

"No," said my mother, "they and I have grown old together. Leave all in its place; it is only you who are forbidden to remain as you are; you have still so many steps to climb before you reach the summit of your glory that to wish you repose would be to wish harm to ourselves."

"Do you really think as you speak?"

"You know my sincerity. I do not always say all I think; but I never say what I do not think. Have you forgotten my frankness?"

Bonaparte took my mother's hand and pressed it affectionately. At this moment the clock struck two. He asked for his carriage.

"Will you not stay supper?" asked my mother.

"I cannot possibly," said he, with an accent of regret; "but I will come and see you again."

My mother smiled, and shook her head gently.

"Why that smile? do you doubt me, Madame Permon? If in this evening either of us has doubted the friendship of the other, I do not think it is I who should be accused of having caused that suspicion. Yes, I shall come and see you again. The Signora Lætitia shall bring me, since I must rest my claim to your regard upon her, or upon Joseph, or upon Lucien, or even upon Paulette; who knows? perhaps upon Jerôme. Speaking of that brave little citizen, you brought him up well while I was far off. I find him wilful, and wilful in bad things. The Signora Lætitia spoils him so totally that I much doubt whether he will mend where he now is."

To speak of Jerôme was to touch another chord which vibrated very sensibly on my mother's ear. "He is an excellent lad," said she—"all warmth of heart, and good sentiments. Jerôme is a true sailor; let him tan himself in the sea air, and he will return to you a Duguay-Trouin, or at least a Duquesne."

This was not the only time in the course of the evening that my mother had advanced an opinion with which she was not perfectly satisfied; but she loved Jerôme, I believe, almost as well as she loved me, and her partiality really went a great way. The First Consul was right when he said that at his return he found his brother singularly educated. The seniors of the family had taken care that everything should be in good order—that is to say, Jerôme was at the College of Juilly, and was frequently visited there by his family; but he still more frequently visited Paris himself to offer the respects of a young gentleman of fourteen to Mademoiselle Emilie and Mademoiselle Hortense de Beauharnais; then believing himself a man, the studies went on as they might.

Jerôme and I were of the same age; my mother, who coupled with his birth the unhappy circumstances of the death of M. Charles Bonaparte, loved him so much the more. In general, she had a warm affection for all the brothers, but had her preferences amongst them as amongst the sisters. Madame Leclerc was her favourite, and to such a degree that I, who could not share her prejudice, often had warm discussions with her on the subject, in which perhaps jealousy might have its share.

At that time I loved Madame Murat the best of Napoleon's sisters, and Joseph and Lucien were, with the First Consul, those of the whole family whom I preferred. Jerôme had been very much loved, very much spoilt, not only by my mother, but by my brother, and, indeed, by all of us. I did not find that when he advanced in life, and consequently when his sentiments might be expected to develop themselves, he was to my mother in particular what he ought to have been. I do not accuse him, but I shall have future occasion to prove that I was not mistaken. But this, after all, is no crime.

The First Consul told us, while speaking of Jerôme, that he had contracted one of the oddest debts that could be imagined for a youth of fifteen. The First Consul was at Marengo: his brother was already in the service, but, being too young to take part in the campaign, was left in Paris. On the return of the First Consul, Bourrienne was presented with a number of bills, amounting in the whole to a considerable sum, the payment of which was pressing. Amongst others Biennais figured for eight or ten thousand francs. Great inquiries were made, and many reports were spread, as to how so large a debt could have arisen?

At length it was discovered that M. Jerôme Bonaparte had purchased of M. Biennais, Rue Saint Honoré, at the sign of the Singe Violet, a magnificent travelling-case, containing everything that could be invented by elegance and luxury, in gold, mother-of-pearl, silver, and ivory, the finest porcelains, and the most beautifully executed enamels; in short, the whole was a jewel. But one very essential thing was wanting to this dressing-case, and that was a beard to make it useful; for whatever it contained would

JERÔME BONAPARTE,
KING OF WESTPHALIA,
COUNT MONTFORT (COUNT HARTZ),
MARSHAL OF FRANCE IN 1850.
1784—1860.

admit of no other application. Razors, shaving-pots of all sizes in silver and china; combs for the moustaches; in short, every article of convenience for shaving, but the beard was wanting; and, unfortunately, the young man who was but fifteen had some long years to wait for it. The First Consul told this little history in a very entertaining style.

CHAPTER IV.

The Tribunes and Long Harangues—The Consular Court and the Roman Forum—M. Andrieux—Lucien, the Author of the 18th Brumaire—Depression of Lucien, and Remarkable Visit—Lord Malmesbury—Madame Bonaparte and her Brother-in-law—Embarrassment of the First Consul—Lucien announces his Departure—*The Road to the Throne*—Lucien's Children—Secrecy of Lucien's Journey—The Little Beggar—Portrait of Lucien—The Fléchelle Family and Injustice repaired.

AT the period of my marriage the Consular Court was rather singularly organized. Its arrangement was somewhat affected by the strong prejudices of the First Consul. He wished it to be in a grand style, yet was fearful of incurring the reproach already directed against him by several tribunes, who, mistaking the *Palais Royal* (where equality no longer existed) for the Roman forum, delighted in making long harangues in which Cæsar, Brutus, Pericles, Solon, Aristides, and Lycurgus all found a place, but which had no more reference to the unfortunate French Republic than if its locality was beyond Tobolsk.

Lucien, immediately after the 18th Brumaire, was appointed Minister of the Interior.* It is unfortunate that a

---

* M. de Laplace preceded him, but only for a few days; his pursuits in science and those of the administration could not possibly advance together. When he was nominated, an acquaintance of mine made, with two strokes of a pencil, a charming little drawing of an astrologer falling into a well; the resemblance to M. de Laplace was perfect.

prejudice, for it was certainly nothing else, prevented his being elected Second or Third Consul.

At first sight, the participation of two brothers in the Consulate would naturally lead to the conclusion that but one would direct the Executive; whereas, in reality, the national interest would have been far better defended than by a man such as the Consul Lebrun, who, unquestionably honest himself, was, nevertheless, too readily disposed to affirm every proposition, even of his second, and still more of his first colleague.

In accomplishing the events of the 18th Brumaire, at which he had laboured with an influential activity, whose remembrance should never have deserted Napoleon, it cannot be doubted that Lucien believed his brother would confer on France a Government that should render her at once happy at home and great and formidable abroad. As for war, it was then looked upon merely as a party of pleasure; in its prosecution, not only the glory but the good-fortune of the French was calculated upon as certain.

In the interior, on the other hand, misery was at its height: although not in the Consulate, as Minister of the Interior much was in Lucien's power: the choice of prefects and of mayors; new municipal laws to be given to the communes; the whole mode of election to be reformed; manufactures to be protected, which at that time were everywhere rising; new discoveries to be turned to account: and misery to be relieved by employment, the only alms which should be bestowed on the people—all this he foresaw, and undertook with courage and success. But he soon appeared sad and unhappy. Obstacles multiplied around him; he had spoken of them to my brother-in-law; my mother, who tenderly loved him, perceived it before he opened the subject. Lucien was unhappy, and doubly so through the means of his brother.

But in justice to Bonaparte, I must declare that he was unworthily deceived with respect to his brother; he was persuaded of the existence of facts entirely false. He was even inspired by someone with uneasiness for his personal safety. He never yielded to these suspicions, but the voice which accused his brother was one very dear to him. It was evident that he sought with avidity everything that could afford him a ray of consolation amidst that perplexing obscurity with which others endeavoured to fill up the distance that fate had just established between the two brothers—an interval which Lucien always respected, even when refusing to acknowledge it, but which the First Consul should have overlooked. A violent animosity had, however, arisen between Madame Bonaparte and her brothers-in-law, which not only interrupted the domestic happiness of this numerous family, but proved in the end a source of the greatest misfortune to herself.

I visited my mother every day, and frequently dined with her. One day that we had dined alone, Albert and M. de Geouffre being both absent, we had scarcely risen from table when Lucien arrived. He was mournful, very serious, and appeared in deep thought. My mother remarking it, he admitted it, and told us he was on the eve of departure; upon which my mother uttered an exclamation. "Did not you know it?" said he; "I take Geouffre with me."

"If you wish to let me know your affairs by my son in-law," replied my mother, "command him to communicate them, for when you are in question he is a true Malmesbury."*

---

* Lord Malmesbury was sent on a special mission to the Directory from England in the year vii., while M. de Talleyrand was Minister for Foreign Affairs. It is to be presumed that Lord Malmesbury's instructions were not very extensive, for at every word hazarded by Talleyrand —who, it may be observed, did not himself waste many—Lord Malmesbury uniformly replied: "Allow me to write home respecting that."

"Yes, I am going," said Lucien, crossing his arms over his bosom, and contemplating the fire with that sombre abstraction which indicates deep grief; "I am going! my counsels displease; and, moreover, there is at present a barrier between Napoleon and me which can never be removed, because it is beneath my character to justify myself, and thereby to recognize the legality of a tribunal which, on the contrary, I challenge. My brother believes the perfidious insinuations of a woman, with whom he ought to be too well acquainted to sacrifice his family to her; he suspects the fidelity of a brother whose devotedness has been the sole means of opening to him the road to a throne."

"To a throne!" cried my mother.

Lucien replied only by a smile, at once melancholy and expressive. "Always remember, Madame Permon," rejoined he, "that I certainly had no such thoughts on the 18th and 19th Brumaire."

It may be well supposed that, in speaking afterwards of Lucien to the First Consul, I was careful not to repeat this part of the conversation.

"Are you going far?" inquired my mother.

"I must not tell you; I ought not to have announced my departure. I request of Madame Junot not to speak of this conversation before her husband."

Some days afterwards Lucien quitted Paris. A carriage, containing Arnaud, a miniature-painter named Chatillon, and M. Felix Desporte, preceded him, and took the road to

---

(*Permettez que j'en écrive à ma cour.*") And as we seldom fail to take advantage of the ridiculous, a caricature was exhibited, in which Talleyrand, stepping up to the English Ambassador, inquires how he is; and Lord Malmesbury shows him, according to the custom of caricatures, a long paper inscribed with the words, "*Permettez-moi d'en écrire à ma cour.*"

Amiens, while Lucien, in his berlin, with my brother-in-law, set out towards Bordeaux. He had with him his two little girls, the youngest of whom was still in arms; and on these two little beings he lavished all the cares of the most attentive woman.

My mother, learning that he was going to take his children, advised him to leave them with the kind and excellent Madame Joseph; but at the first word Lucien, starting from his chair, exclaimed: "No, no; I will not leave my children here; do not talk to me of separating from them! I may be accused of levity, of easy morals, but, at least, neither mother, brothers, children, nor friends, shall ever have occasion to reproach my heart." He was much agitated; my mother embraced him and said, "Well, you are right: take these poor little ones; they are no longer blessed with a mother, and a fond father can alone supply her loss."

A messenger was despatched after the carriage, which was journeying towards Amiens; it changed its course, and rejoined Lucien near Bordeaux. I know not the cause of all this mystery; perhaps it was designed to conceal from Austria, with whom negotiations were being carried on, the mission of the First Consul's brother as Ambassador to Spain. This could not, indeed, be kept secret above seven or eight days, but that is much in diplomatic relations; I state the facts as they occurred: Lucien arrived at Madrid, and replaced there two men whose abilities, when compared with his, made a very *médiocre* appearance; these were Berthier and Alquier.

Some time after the departure of Lucien an affair was much talked of, and his enemies would fain have misrepresented it: but the following is the exact truth. The ages of the children are particularly accurate, a matter of some importance to the good or evil aspect of the story.

A boy, eleven years of age, neatly dressed, was standing in the Rue Des Petits Champs, near the Place Vendôme, and asking alms of persons in whose physiognomy he could descry a more than common share of humanity. A young man, wrapped up in a large blue greatcoat, with knit pantaloons of gray silk, a round hat, and gold spectacles, casually looked upon the child as he passed. There was kindness in his countenance, and his smile emboldened the poor little importunate to hold out his hand ; the gentleman frowned, yet gave him a coin of *douze sous* (sixpence).

"Why do you beg, child?" said he in a severe tone. The poor child began to cry, pointing with his finger to a woman and two little girls, the eldest of whom was ten, and the other nine, seated on the stone bench of the house which then stood in a little recess, where the passage to the Jacobin market now is.

"These are my mother and sisters," said he, sobbing. "My father is very ill, and I have a little brother younger than my sisters ; I cannot work, and we must eat, and give my father his barley-water : how can this be done if I do not beg?"

The gentleman, overcome with such a tale of misery, approached the woman, asked her some questions, and, having taken her address, left her a louis-d'or.

On his return to the Home Department, Lucien, who has no doubt been recognized in the portrait I have just drawn, charged a confidential person to make inquiries respecting the Fléchelle family. The result of these inquiries was not only satisfactory, but of a nature to extort a blush from the Government, had it been possible for the Directory to blush for its evil deeds. Fléchelle had been employed in the grant office, where his conduct was irreproachable, but in consequence of one of those intrigues too common under a venal Government he was dismissed without pension or indemnity; and, as security against his complaints, was calumniated to the Minister of the day, who refused even to see him.

This man had four children, and from an easy competence his family were suddenly plunged into absolute destitution. Overwhelmed with grief, the vigilance of his wife alone defeated an attempt at suicide, and soon remorse occasioned an illness. Lucien the next day sent them, through his confidential agent, a hundred francs, and an abundant provision of sugar, coffee, candles, oil, etc., a cartload of wood, and a sack of coals: he also conferred on Fléchelle, as a just indemnity, the brevet of a place at the *barrières*, worth two thousand francs.

The agitating joy of the news proved too much for the father, enfeebled by long illness; he died, and left his family again exposed to misery. Lucien, immersed in cares at the moment of his departure for Spain, was unable then to assist them, but the excellent Mrs. Anson, meeting with this desolate family, became a second consoling and succouring angel to them.

Attempts were made to report the story at Malmaison in a very different light: I took the liberty of representing the truth. "The young girls are not sixteen or seventeen years of age," said I to Madame Bonaparte, "for I have seen them." "Then I have been deceived," replied she; "but you have much affected me by the misfortunes of this poor family; give me Madame Fléchelle's address, for I will send to her to-morrow; I wish to have my part in the good work." She sent them, I believe, forty francs. Madame Bonaparte was often compassionate, but the indiscriminate nature of her protection and her recommendations often made her ridiculous, even in the eyes of those to whom she was benevolent.

CHAPTER V.

Madame Bonaparte's Apartments—Functions of M. de Benezeck and the Republicans—The Aides-de-camp—Chamberlains—The Grand Dinners at the Tuileries—Improvement of Morals—The Ladies of the Emigration—Installation at the Tuileries—The Two Processions—General Lannes' Broth—The Fortnightly Parades—Intercourse of the First Consul with the Soldiers—My Cashmere Shawl, and my Father-in-law's Watch—The Swedish Minister and the Batiste Handkerchief—Bonaparte, a Drummer, and the Sabre of Honour—The Baron d'Ernsworth—The King of Spain's Horses—The Diplomatic Corps in 1800—M. de Lucchesini and the Italian Harangue.

MADAME BONAPARTE occupied the whole ground-floor of the Tuileries, which was afterwards her residence as Empress, and also that of Maria Louisa. Adjoining her dressing-room was the small apartment of Mademoiselle de Beauharnais, consisting of her bedchamber, and a study scarcely of sufficient dimensions to render the smell of her oil paints endurable, when she this winter* painted her brother's portrait. The apartments of Madame Bonaparte were furnished tastefully, but without luxury; the great reception-salon was hung with yellow draperies; the movable

---

* This same winter of 1800 the Tuileries caught fire, and Mademoiselle Beauharnais's portrait of her brother, which was a speaking likeness, was consumed. The fire was falsely imputed to incendiaries, but was occasioned by ill-constructed flues.

furniture was damask, the fringes of silk, and the wood mahogany. No gold was to be seen. The other rooms were not more richly decorated; all was new and elegant, but no more. The apartments of Madame Bonaparte, however, were destined only for private parties and morning visits.

The larger assemblies were held upstairs. As yet there was neither Chamberlain nor Prefect of the Palace; an old Counsellor of State, formerly Minister of the Interior, M. de Benezeck, was charged with the internal administration of the palace, which was at first a little difficult to introduce amongst what remained of true Republicanism. The functions of M. de Benezeck embraced those afterwards divided between the Grand Chamberlain and the Master of the Ceremonies. The *maîtres d'hôtel* and ushers performed the subaltern offices, and the *aides-de-camp* supplied the place of chamberlains.

The First Consul was in the habit of inviting two hundred persons every ten days to dine with him. These dinners were given in the Gallery of Diana, and the guests were of all ranks and classes, always including the Diplomatic Body, which at this time was become tolerably numerous. The wives of civil functionaries, of generals and colonels, formed the society, for as yet no one ventured to say the Court, of Madame Bonaparte. The General was rigid in the choice he made, not for his quintidian routs, but for the private and frequent invitations to Malmaison, and afterwards to Saint Cloud. It is a fact, which only prejudiced minds will dispute, that the First Consul wished to perpetuate, as far as lay in his power, the amelioration of morals produced by the Revolution. This will perhaps excite a smile in the perusal; nevertheless, it is certain that the morals of the existing generation have been retempered by the Revolution.

In 1800, when the Court of the Tuileries was formed, society wore an appearance of morality and domestic virtue which it had never before displayed in France. The Noblesse, or what was at length by common consent denominated the *Faubourg Saint Germain*, was constrained to follow the general current, although here again some exceptions were known in ladies who founded their fame on the importation of follies from Brussels, Coblentz, etc., and afterwards from England.

Eventually, the Imperial Court, like all else pertaining to sovereignty, spread its malign influence. It was, however, comparatively but little open to censure, as the Emperor exercised a magical sway over every woman admitted to his Court.

When the different powers had adopted the new Constitution proposed after the 18th Brumaire, and which I believe was the fourth they were called upon to sanction, the Government quitted the Luxembourg for the Tuileries. It may be observed that the First Consul, who had at first lodged the Third Consul in the Pavilion of Flora, soon retook sole possession of it, and M. Lebrun, like Cambacérès, retired to the occupation of a private house.* The whole Consular Triumvirate, however, was present at the reception of ambassadors or of national bodies. The 30th Pluviose, in the year viii. (19th February, 1800), the First Consul took possession of the palace of the kings, which, indeed, from the commencement of the Revolution, had been occupied

---

* Cambacérès lived at the Hôtel d'Elbœuf, in the Place Carrousel, opposite the Tuileries. The Consul Lebrun had the Hôtel de Noailles, Rue Saint Honoré. This appropriation was made for the family convenience of the two Consuls. Lebrun had his mother-in-law and five children with him (his eldest daughter, who soon afterwards married M. de Plancy; the youngest, now Madame de Chabrol; and his three sons, Charles, Alexander, and Augustus Lebrun); he required, therefore, a more spacious dwelling than Cambacérès, who lived alone.

by the National Representatives. At this time the Constitution of the 18th Brumaire exalted the Consular power above all other national authorities: it represented in itself the French people; and such an authority required a suitable abode.

Anyone who had witnessed the removal from the Luxembourg to the Tuileries on the 30th Pluviose of the year viii., if he had then fallen asleep to the sound of military music, playing all our patriotic airs, and had been awakened by the thunder of cannon on the morning of the 2nd December, announcing that the Emperor Napoleon was about to be crowned by the Pope in Notre Dame, would have discovered a curious contrast between the two processions. In the first, on account of the scarcity of private carriages at that time in Paris, it was necessary to engage for councillors of state and senators hackney-coaches, whose numbers were covered with white paper, producing an effect far more ludicrous than if the numbers had remained visible.

On the day of his installation at the Tuileries, scarcely had the First Consul arrived before he mounted his horse and held a review in the court of the palace, which was not then surrounded by a railing, but enclosed by ill-jointed boards; and the Place du Carrousel was then small and very irregular. The change was rapid; a word from Napoleon was sufficient.

The First Consul admitted that he was happy during his reviews. "And you, too, I am sure, are well content while I am with your conscripts," said he one day to General Lannes. "You do not grumble because the parade retards our dinner for an hour." "Oh dear no!" replied General Lannes, "it is all alike to me, whether I eat my soup warm or cold, provided you will set us to work at making a hot broth for those rascally English."

He had an aversion for the English that I have never

observed in any other general of the Emperor's army, even of those who had fought under the Republic.*

The quintidians (for we must speak the language of the period) were chosen for reviews, or rather for parades, in the court of the Tuileries. These parades were a spectacle worth seeing, especially during the Consulate. Under the Empire they might be more magnificent; but in 1800 their splendour was wholly national. It was the glory of France that we contemplated in those squadrons and battalions, which, whether composed of conscripts or veterans, equally impressed with fear the foreigner who surveyed them from the windows of the palace; for the ardour of the young troops was fostered by constantly beholding the old musketeers of the Consular Guard covered with scars.

The First Consul took pleasure in these reviews, which would sometimes occupy him for five hours together, without a moment's interval of repose. All the regiments in France came alternately to Paris and passed in review with the Guards every fortnight at noon. The First Consul was on these occasions always attended by the aide-de-camp on duty, the Minister of War, the General commanding the First Division, and the Commandant of Paris, the Commissary-General, the Commissaries of War attached to the city of Paris; in short, all persons to whom orders must be immediately transmitted, in case the First Consul should, in the course of the inspection, find any alteration or improvement requisite. By this means no delay could arise in the communication of orders: everything was done instantaneously

---

* It is singular that the eldest son of the Marshal was married to an Englishwoman, and it was reported that a younger son was about to follow the example. This proves that sentiments are, happily, not always hereditary. It seems, however, strange to see the affections of a family thus take a direction diametrically opposed to those of its head. His daughter-in-law might have cured him of his prejudices; she was a beautiful, amiable, and charming person.

and satisfactorily, for it was well understood that the eye of the chief closely superintended all, and that if punishment were awarded to negligence, punctuality would be duly appreciated.

Sometimes he galloped along the ranks, but this was rare; he never, indeed, sat his horse unless the troops had already passed in review and he was satisfied that nothing was wanting. Even then he would address a few questions to two or three soldiers casually selected; but generally after riding along the ranks on his white horse (*le Désiré*) he would alight, and converse with all the field-officers, and with nearly all the subalterns and soldiers. His solicitude was extended to the most minute particulars—the food, the dress, and everything that could be necessary to the soldier, or useful to the man, divided his attention with the evolutions. He encouraged the men to speak to him without restraint. "Conceal from me none of your wants," he would say to them; "suppress no complaints you may have to make of your superiors. I am here to do justice to all, and the weaker party is especially entitled to my protection."

These words he one day addressed to a demi-brigade (I believe it was the 17th), aware that the regiment before its removal to Paris had suffered deprivations in the department where it had been in garrison. Such a system was not only attended with immediately beneficial results, but was adroitly adapted to answer a general and not less useful purpose. The Army and its Chief thus became inseparably united, and in the person of that Chief the army beheld the French Nation. Thus the State, through him, dispensed both blame and commendation. Besides, Paris by this means became acquainted with the army; and the troops, in turn, visiting the capital, ceased to regard it as another world, and themselves as foreigners in it.

My husband, who invariably attended the First Consul on these parades, communicated to me everything remarkable; and in reporting the achievements of a day, which to other men would have comprized the labour of a month, would add: "All this proceeds with magic mechanism; this man is a supernatural being." Junot, it is true, might view his favourite General with prejudiced eyes; but not on these occasions, for he was at this period of his life truly admirable.

The Diplomatic Corps showed great eagerness to witness the parades, a privilege usually enjoyed by foreigners from the windows of General Duroc, who already occupied that part of the ground-floor at the end of the Empress's apartments. From the same place I saw the first parade after my marriage, on which occasion an amusing adventure happened to my father-in-law. Junot's attendance being required on horseback, he could not escort me to Duroc's, but entrusted me to his own family, who themselves had never seen a parade.

Arrived at the railing of the Pont Royal, we alighted, and, crossing the garden, endeavoured to gain on foot Duroc's door, which is situated at the right corner of the vestibule; but it was late, and we were compelled to make our way through a dense crowd. My mother-in-law, always happy and always merry, only jested on the pommellings she encountered; but her husband, quite unaccustomed to such things, was in terrible ill-humour, and railed particularly at the carelessness of young Parisian ladies, who would risk handsome cashmere shawls in such a crowd, repeatedly assuring me that I should lose mine, and at the same time boasting his own prudence in securing his watch by guarding it constantly with his hand.

His cautions and vaunts were of course alike overheard, and as the most effectual means of momentarily eluding his vigilance, a dexterous twitch was given to my shawl; the manœuvre completely succeeded—I screamed, the shawl was saved; but, alas! that moment sufficed for the abstraction of the carefully-guarded watch; and its unfortunate master, on discovering his loss, clamorously lamented over an old and valued servant of thirty-five years' standing, till reminded by Madame Junot that it stopped about once a week, and had within the last year cost him fifty francs in repairs.

Meanwhile we had reached Duroc's door, and were placed at a window. The parade had not yet commenced. The officers were silently promenading in the ranks of their respective regiments, speaking occasionally, but only in a whisper, to a soldier or subaltern, when the carriage of a weapon or the position of a hat seemed to demand rectifying.

Junot, who knew the passionate enthusiasm of my patriotism, had warned me that I should be much excited; he kissed his hand to me in passing, and, smiling to see my handkerchief at my eyes, whispered to Duroc, when both again looked at me, and I observed that my emotion affected them.

A foreigner sat near me whose admiration of the scene before him was so profound and so worthy of the occasion that it struck me, and he wore a badge so singular that I could not resist the impulse of curiosity, and inquired the meaning of it. It was a batiste handkerchief of extraordinary whiteness, tied round his arm like the scarf of an aide-de-camp. "It is a memorial of my Sovereign and of a glorious day, madame," answered he, and announced himself as Baron d'Ernsworth, the Swedish Minister.*

* A revolution took place on the 18th of August, 1772. The partisans of Guiland adopted as a rallying-sign a white handkerchief tied round the arm; and the King, after his final success, granted, as

I introduced to him the parents of General Junot, to whom he was as polite as he could have been to the Montmorencies and the La Tremouilles of France; he was near fifty years of age, and of a fine figure, perhaps somewhat too much *embonpoint* for the elegance of the military costume which he wore. He spoke, with an expression which went to my heart, of the reputation of him whose name I bore. "So young," said he, "and already so famous; but with such a Captain how can the lieutenants, though but children, be otherwise than worthy sons of their country!"

At this moment the First Consul stopped under our window, and said to a drummer of about sixteen or seventeen, "So it was you, my brave boy, who beat the charge before Zurich." The countenance of the young soldier was suffused with crimson, but it was not timidity which called the flush to his cheek. He raised towards the First Consul his large black eyes, sparkling with joy at being thus publicly distinguished, and replied in a half-tremulous, half-confident tone, "Oui, mon Général."

"It was you, too, who at Weser gave proof of the most gallant presence of mind by saving your Commander."*
The youth blushed still deeper, this time from modesty, and answered, in a lower voice than before, "Oui, mon Général."

---

an honorary recompense to his faithful adherents, permission to wear for life a white handkerchief round the left arm, in commemoration of the service they had rendered to the Crown.

* I was particularly struck by this fact, because all the occurrences of this first parade made a deep impression on my mind; but the military annals of the period are filled with similar anecdotes, too frequent to obtain insertion in *The Moniteur*, or other journals. Speaking of the above the same evening to the First Consul, as comparable to the noblest deeds of antiquity, he replied, "Bah! ask your husband; he will tell you there is neither regiment nor demi-brigade in the army that could not cite ten such. He himself would be the hero of several."

"Well, I must discharge the debt of the country; it will be paid you not in a ring of honour, but a sabre of honour; I appoint you a subaltern in the Consular Guard; continue to behave well, and I will take care of you."

As the First Consul ceased speaking he raised his eyes to the low window at which we were seated, and, touching his hat, saluted us all with a gracious smile. My mother-in-law's eyes filled with tears, "How ought we to love this man!" said she, crying and laughing together; "see how the poor boy is overpowered." The young drummer was leaning on the shoulder of a comrade and following Bonaparte with his eyes. He was pale as death, but how eloquent were his looks!

I know not what may have become of him, but I will answer for it if his life were sacrificed for Napoleon it cost him no regret. He was in the evening the subject of my conversation with the First Consul; he listened with interest, and addressing Berthier, who was just arrived from Spain, to take the portfolio of Minister of War, desired him to take down the young man's name, and provide him with an outfit for his new rank. He may be at this day either a general or of the number of the dead; one or other he most assuredly is.

This parade was selected for my first attendance because some spirited horses sent to the First Consul by the Spanish King were then to be presented. The ceremony was said to recall the equestrian present made to Cromwell by a German prince. I know not what the Mecklenburgh horses might have been, but the Spanish were sixteen most beautiful creatures, both in coat and form; fourteen were from the royal stud, and two of them from the studs of the Count of Altamira and the Duke of Medina Cœli; and these latter were the tallest and finest of the troop; the first, El Jounalero, a really superb animal, and the other of equal size and younger, showed the fire, the slight fetlock, and arched neck of the Arabian breed.

The Diplomatic Corps was at that time composed of the Spanish and Roman Ambassadors, the Ministers of Denmark, Sweden, Baden, and Hesse Cassel; the Dutch Ambassador, M. Schimmelpening, celebrated for his beautiful and most courteous wife; Ambassadors from the Cisalpine and Ligurian Republics, and a Swiss Minister.

Prussia, still desirous of an accommodation with us, had, in October, 1800, despatched M. Lucchesini on a special mission, but his credentials as Minister-Plenipotentiary were not presented till 1801 or 1802; he remained but a few years with us, and after the campaign of Jena returned no more to France. The First Consul disliked him, and accused him of intriguing.

"Not that he entraps me," said Bonaparte; "but he willingly would, and that offends me. If those who negotiate with me did but know how much more surely their tortuous path tends to ruining themselves than to misleading me, they would choose a straighter road."

An attention which M. Lucchesini hoped would work wonders was, on the contrary, displeasing to the First Consul, and threw the foreign diplomatist into a dilemma from which he could never recover, because he was long unconscious of it; this was haranguing the First Consul in Italian on delivering his credentials. Bonaparte had a strong objection to being addressed in Italian; he was, and chose to be, a Frenchman.

Soon after this the Congress of Luneville gave us peace with Austria, and that of Amiens with England. Russia also became our ally, and all this within less than a year. These are delightful recollections, and again I exclaim, Oh, what a time was that!

CHAPTER VI.

Revival of the Public Prosperity—Destruction of the Bands of Robbers—M. Dubois, Prefect of Police—The Exhibition of 1800—David and the Picture of the Sabines—Girodet, and the Vengeance of an Artist—The Satirical Picture of Danaë—Gérard—Belisarius and the Portrait of Moreau—The King of Spain's Pistols given to General Moreau— Remarkable Words of Napoleon — Moreau's Distrust of him—Napoleon's Popularity.

I HAVE already observed with what rapidity General Bonaparte had succeeded in consolidating a corps, which every day acquired new strength and stability. All who surrounded him, it must be acknowledged, lent their aid with a persevering ability, of which he could thoroughly appreciate the advantages. Every day brought news of the seizure of some fresh band of brigands, robbers of diligences, forgers, or false coiners; the latter especially were very numerous.

Dubois, the Prefect of Police, was extremely zealous and active in discovering the guilty, and such as under futile political pretexts disturbed the public tranquillity; he was inestimable in his place, and Napoleon, who undoubtedly knew how to discern and to employ the men who would answer his purpose, took care not to remove him from his office till after the fire at Prince Schwartzenburg's ball.

Not only were all the interior wheels of the State machine beginning to play, but even the arts, that more silent and centrical spring, afforded striking proofs of the reviving prosperity of France. The Exhibition was this year particularly good. Guérin, David, Gérard, Girodet, and a powerful assemblage of talent, excited by that emulation which the fire of genius always inspires, produced works which will hereafter raise our school to an elevated rank. The picture of the Sabines and of Marcus Sextus, besides several portraits, adorned the list of paintings for the year 1800.

I will here notice some circumstances connected with them worth preserving, and not recorded in the journals. The first is somewhat unworthy of the talent of David. On some frivolous pretence, instead of sending his "Rape of the Sabines" to the Salon, he privately exhibited it on payment of a franc, to the peril and danger of Parisian mothers, who, as was observed in a pretty little vaudeville which appeared at the time, dared not take their daughters with them.

Girodet was then in the full vigour of his genius, and united with it a mind of a superior order; but he was irascible and passionate, of which this year afforded an instance capable of tarnishing his high character.

He had painted the portrait of a female celebrated for her beauty and dramatic talents, and some discussion arising respecting the payment, the husband imprudently indulged in some very disparaging expressions, which were repeated to the enraged artist, who, disfiguring the portrait with a knife, returned it with an intimation that the lady might dispose as she pleased both of it and its stipulated price, as he should pay himself in his own way. If Girodet had confined himself to the threat, which was intended no doubt to alarm the parties, all would have been well, but he went further, and was wrong in so doing.

The Salon was to be open for some days to come; with a rapidity difficult to conceive, he painted and caused to be placed at the Exhibition a picture of extraordinary merit, representing the interior of a garret. In one corner was a miserable bedstead, covered with a wretched mattress and a blanket full of holes; on this lay a young and beautiful maiden, with a head-dress of peacock's feathers, having no other clothing than a tunic of gauze, through which were seen a pair of legs of gigantic thickness. She held this dress with her two hands to catch a shower of gold that fell from the roof of the garret. Near the bed was a lamp, whose dazzling brightness attracted a crowd of butterflies, who all found their destruction in the traitorous light. Beneath the bedstead was seen an enormous turkey, stretching forth one of his feet, on the toe of which was a wedding-ring. In an obscure corner of the room was an old woman, dressed like a beggar, resembling perfectly a decrepit wretch who was often seen asking alms at the gate of the Palais Royal, and who, it was said, was the mother of the original in the cut picture, and of whom there was a striking likeness in the recumbent Danaë. Other allusions in the picture were equally remarkable, amongst them a frog swelling itself to an unnatural size, etc.

From the first moment of its exhibition this picture attracted the undivided curiosity of the visitors; but whether Girodet (who afterwards testified some regret for the extremity to which his resentment had been carried) relented, or whatever the cause, the picture was in a few days withdrawn.

A piece of a different kind, and the principal ornament of the Salon, was Gérard's portrait of General Moreau. The hand which portrayed Belisarius and Psyché was there distinctly traceable. It was a *chef-d'œuvre*. Not only was the resemblance perfect, but it seemed to possess a soul. It was not colour laid on canvas, it was animate: it was General Moreau himself who looked upon you.

The position, too, was admirably chosen. It would have been easy and natural to represent him in full action, with all the splendid appendages of military costume, for assuredly Moreau has more than once headed his troops in the hour of danger; but he was habitually calm and reflective; this, therefore, was the expression Gérard judiciously selected, and the dress and attitude were in keeping. Judging by other works of Gérard, this will probably always retain the beauty of its colouring.

Independently of his professional talent, Gérard was eminently gifted, and all his compositions are full of mind. His Belisarius is admirable; there are but two persons, an infant and an old man, but no circumstance is omitted that can excite interest in favour of the old Roman general. In the background of that gray head, stamped by Justinian with the anathema of mendicity, is seen only a desert, and a scorching yet stormy horizon. The features of his youthful guide already exhibit the livid paleness of death. Belisarius is thus alone with the agony of death on a narrow path, at the brink of a precipice: one step and he must fall. His arm, which advances a useless staff, seems to start from the canvas; he is abandoned by all Nature.

The portrait of Moreau reminds me of an anecdote concerning him, which occurred at that time, and was afterwards related to me by Junot, who was an eye-witness. When the rupture of the armistice in Italy and Germany was foreseen, General Moreau came to Paris to receive the orders of Government. He arrived at ten in the morning of the 17th October, and instantly, without even changing his boots, went to the Tuileries. The First Consul was at the time in the Council of State, but as soon as he heard of General Moreau's arrival he hastened to hold a conference with him.

While he was in the salon, the Minister of the Interior,

Lucien Bonaparte, happened to enter, bringing a pair of pistols of extremely fine and curious workmanship, which Boutet had just completed by order of the Directory as a present for the King of Spain. They were valuable, both for the skill the artist had applied to their construction and for a great quantity of diamonds and precious stones with which they were embellished. "These arms come very àpropos," said the First Consul, presenting them to General Moreau with that smile which could win hearts of stone— "General Moreau will do me the favour to accept them as a mark of the esteem and gratitude of the French nation."

"Citizen Minister," added Bonaparte, turning towards his brother, "have some of the battles of General Moreau engraved on the pistols, but not all; we must leave some room for diamonds. Not because the general attaches much value to them; I know that his Republican virtue disdains such baubles, but we must not altogether derange the design of Boutet."

Methinks, after such expressions, Moreau might have placed confidence in the friendship Bonaparte offered him. Why should the First Consul have flattered him? Why, especially, should he at that time have offered him a hand which was not sincerely friendly? Was it to flatter the popularity of Moreau? At this period the popularity of Bonaparte was far superior to his. Hohenlinden was not then gained, and even after that brilliant victory Napoleon had no cause to dread a rival in the hearts of Frenchmen; at this period he was really beloved.

JEAN VICTOR MOREAU,

GENERAL,

CONQUEROR AT HOHENLINDEN,

AND AFTERWARDS

SHOT FIGHTING AGAINST HIS COUNTRY
AT DRESDEN.

1763—1813.

CHAPTER VII.

The Eastern Queen at the *Comédie Française*—Pauline and her Portrait—The Young Sempstress of M. de Sales—Marriage of Convenience, and the Army of Egypt—Cavalcade of Asses—Dinner at General Dupuy's, and the Wife without her Husband—The Cup of Coffee and the Orange—Bonaparte, Berthier, and the Husband Ambassador—An English Tour—*Gallantry* of Kléber—Goodness of Desgenettes—Return to France, and the Divorce—Dread of Scandal, and the Wife with Two Husbands—Saint Helena, and Admirable Conduct.

I was one day at the *Comédie Française* with my husband, attentively listening to Talma in the part of Orestes, when Junot, touching my arm, told me to look attentively at a young woman he was about to salute, and who was seated between Berthier's box and our own.

My eye followed his salute, and I saw a woman of about twenty-two or twenty-three years of age, florid as a young girl of fifteen, and of a gay and agreeable countenance. Her flaxen hair formed the only ornament of her head. She was wrapped in a magnificent white Cashmere shawl, with an embroidered border, and appeared to be *en négligé*. She returned Junot's salute with an air of acquaintance which surprised me, and I inquired her name.

"It is Pauline," said he, "our Eastern Queen." He had already mentioned Madame Fourès to me, to caution me against the indiscretion of naming her before Madame

Bonaparte. "This, then, is Madame Fourès," said I, and instantly put to him all the inquiries one woman will make concerning another whom she sees for the first time. He told me she had natural wit, and a desire of distinction, but a total ignorance of the manners of the world, that is to say, of good and elegant manners.

"I like her much," said Junot; "she is kind-hearted, simple, and unaffected, always disposed to join in mirth, and still more ready to oblige. I have a friendship for her, and hope to prove it; but there are, about the person of the First Consul, men who were at her feet in Egypt, and have since refused to know her, and repulsed her in the little intercourse she has been obliged to hold with them. Duroc, who has honour and a feeling heart, told me that the poor young creature knew not what would have become of her had she not opportunely met with him to convey a letter for her to General Bonaparte. She is no longer in want of anything, and this is no more than a debt which the First Consul owes to a woman whom he has sincerely loved."

I afterwards learned a variety of particulars relating to Madame Fourès, and as she was long attached to the fate of Napoleon, and gave him in adversity proofs of gratitude and interest, I think it best to insert here all that I know of her.

Pauline was born at Carcassone. Her father was a gentleman, but her mother either a chambermaid or cook. The education of the young daughter partook of the mixed rank to which she owed her birth: she received some instruction, and finally went out to work. She was one of the prettiest girls in the town, and perfectly virtuous. My friends, M. and Madame de Sales, showed her a kindness, which her conduct justified, and treated her more like a child of their own than a workwoman, for her conduct was most exemplary.

She recited M. de Sales's verses, and sang with taste, and it was here principally that her beauty acquired her the surname of *Bellilotte*.

The son of a retired merchant named Fourès was charmed by that pretty Hebe face and the fame which attended it; he paid his addresses to her, but as he was far from agreeable she hesitated for some time; an accidental introduction to the table of M. de Sales, to entertain his guests with her singing, and the impression she was sensible of having made there, induced her to consult M. de Sales on the subject of the marriage. "M. Fourès offers me the advantage of a fortune," said she, "moderate, it is true, but independent. I think I will accept him," and shortly after she married him.

The intended Egyptian expedition was soon announced at Carcassone, and Fourès, who had seen service, willing to answer the national appeal to all the retired officers capable of bearing arms, set out for Toulon, the general *rendezvous*. He tenderly loved his young bride, and made her the companion of his journey, while her adventurous spirit wished for nothing better than to share all danger and fatigue with her husband. She put on male attire therefore, and they arrived in Egypt; it is not true that Napoleon had seen her in France, or that he had dressed her as a naval aspirant on board the *Orient*, as I have read in a foolish book, whose author has collected together all the most absurd falsehoods respecting Napoleon.*

When at Cairo, the General-in-Chief was one day riding, followed by a numerous staff, to attend a sort of fair about a league from the town, when the party was detained on the

---

* This book appeared in 1815, and is entitled *L'Amour et l'Ambition, ou la Vie d'un grand Homme*, par Louis Frederic Reisberg. To give an idea of its accuracy, it is only necessary to say that the author makes Madame Bonaparte (Josephine) daughter of Louis XV.

road by a troop of asses, commonly used for the saddle in that country. They were mounted by officers and some of their wives. General Bonaparte, who is well known to have had a quick eye, was struck by a passing glimpse of a female face, yet he pursued his route without a hint of the circumstance.

The next day Madame Fourès received an invitation to dine with General Dupuy, Commandant of the city, who had with him a Madame Dupuy, and the invitation was sent in her name as well as his. "It is singular," said Fourès, "that I am not invited with my wife, for I am an officer." He was a lieutenant in the 22nd Chasseurs à Cheval. He, however, allowed his wife to go, strongly recommending her to make it understood that she had a husband, a fact already but too well known. Madame Fourès was most politely received. The dinner-party was select, and everything passed off quietly, and without the smallest indication of what was to follow; but at the moment coffee was about to be served, a great commotion was heard in the house, the folding-doors hastily opened, and the General-in-Chief appeared.

Dupuy made many apologies for being found at table, and pressed a cup of coffee upon Napoleon, which he accepted. He was taciturn, and fixed his attention on the young Frenchwoman, who, blushing crimson, dared not raise her eyes, and grew momentarily more and more dismayed at finding herself so obviously an object of attention to a man whose great name was already the theme of the world. The General-in-Chief refreshed himself with an orange and a cup of coffee, and then took his leave, without having addressed a single word to Madame Fourès, but also without having once taken his eyes off her.

A few days after Fourès was sent for by Berthier. "My dear Fourès," said the Chief of the Staff, putting into his hands a voluminous packet, "more fortunate than any of us, you are about to revisit France. The General-in-Chief has had reports of you which inspire him with such perfect confidence that he sends you to Europe as the bearer of despatches to the Directory. You are to set out within an hour; here is an order to the Commander of the port of Alexandria. Adieu, my dear fellow; I wish I were in your place."

"But I must go and apprize my wife, that she may make her preparations," said Fourès, recovering at length from the stupefaction he had been thrown into by a favour which he received with instinctive doubts. He was, however, dissuaded by unanswerable arguments, from carrying his wife with him; and Berthier affected sympathy with his distress at the necessary separation.

Fourès, amidst his grief, was tolerably self-satisfied; for, inconceivable as were the singular favours which had sought him out in his obscurity, we all have a reserve of vanity to assist us in comprehending what is incomprehensible; and before he reached his lodging Fourès had discovered within himself many reasons to explain the General's choice. His wife, who understood them rather better, took leave of him, "with a tear in her eye," and the good lieutenant, embarking, sailed for France. At that period it was more easy to embark for France than it was to land there. The English were on the alert, and no sooner was a sail descried on the surface of the ocean than twenty grappling-irons fell pounce upon it, and it was carried—God knows where.

Fourès's small vessel shared the common fate of those which left the ports of Egypt; it was taken, and himself searched even to his shirt for the important papers he was supposed to have concealed; but on examining those which his utmost address could not withhold, the English captain found them to contain nothing but well-known particulars which he remembered to have seen ostentatiously published in the *Moniteur*, from a previous despatch that had had the good fortune to escape.

This gentleman, vastly polite and accommodating, inquired of the lieutenant-ambassador where he would choose to be landed. He was himself bound for Mahon; from thence he sailed to the Molucca Islands; thence on a grand tour in the Pacific, or towards the Pole, depending on the instructions he might find at Macao; finally, he would very probably revisit the waters of the Nile; and if M. le Lieutenant preferred a residence on the coast during this little tour, he, a captain in the service of his Britannic Majesty, was quite at his command. Poor Fourès timidly asked if he could not return whence he came.

"For," observed he, very judiciously, "now that I am but an empty mail, what end would it answer to absent myself from my wife? Let me return to Cairo." The English captain, who, amongst other circumstantial intelligence from the interior of Egypt, was pretty well acquainted with the affairs of Madame Fourès and the General-in-Chief, landed the good lieutenant according to his desire, with great politeness and apparent cordiality, and wished him good luck. Fourès hastened to embrace his Bellilotte, but Bellilotte was no longer beautiful for him; he found his lodging deserted, and, his affection being sincere, the poor fellow's consternation and misery were proportionate. His wife was easily found; she inhabited an hotel close to that of the General; and being persecuted with his entreaties to return, she obtained a divorce pronounced by Commissary-General Sartelon.

Napoleon was much attached to Madame Fourès, who possessed every qualification calculated to attach him— qualifications still more brilliantly attractive in a distant and barbarous country, where the rest of her sex within reach were of a station and character from whom Bonaparte would not so much as have thought of seeking a companion. In Pauline he found an active and ardent imagination, an affectionate disposition, abundance of native humour, and a mind cultivated without pedantry.

Perfectly unaffected and disinterested, she was all tenderness and devotion. Combining with so many attractions a captivating exterior, Bellilotte could not fail of being beloved by a man to whom pretension, affectation, and self-interest were odious in women.

She was as full of fun and gaiety as a girl of twelve, and Napoleon often joked her upon this gaiety, and upon the laughing he had heard in the donkey adventure on the road to Boulac. Her situation threw her into frequent contact with the inferior agents of the commissariat and military treasury, and Bonaparte would often laughingly joke her upon her intimacies with them; but had he believed such things, he would never have mentioned them, even in jest, and she gave him in reality no cause of complaint.

When Napoleon determined on quitting Egypt she alone was apprized of so important a resolution. With much grief she was convinced of the impossibility of following him through the chances of a dangerous journey. "I may be taken," said he, when in tears she petitioned to attend him, promising to brave every difficulty, a promise she would religiously have observed—"I may be taken by the English; my honour must be dear to you; and what would they say to find a woman at my elbow?" After his departure, Egypt was to her but a vast desert. Napoleon left orders with Klèber to ship off, with as little delay as possible, certain persons whom he named. I have already reported how these orders were executed with respect to my husband and brother-in-law. Poor Bellilotte met with no better fate, and, being a woman, felt it more acutely.

Klèber, who in spite of a stature of six feet, and great military talent, was sometimes mean and pitiful in his notions, delighted in the power of tyrannizing over a woman who had been the mistress of Bonaparte, and in preventing his friends from joining him; but Desgenettes, ever ready to assist the unhappy, conceiving the distress of Madame Fourès, deprived of her defender, and exposed to the vengeance of a man who loved her, and whose jealousy must produce vexatious, perhaps dangerous consequences, came to her assistance, and interposed so effectually with Klèber for the delivery of the passport that Madame Fourès immediately obtained it and sailed for France, where she found her Egyptian friend in circumstances which gave him new claims on her affection.

Napoleon was, however, but newly reconciled to Josephine, and was too deeply immersed in serious and important labours to admit of any distraction. Though indifferent to Josephine, his attachment for her had once been sufficient to enable her to replace, in his imagination at least, a connection that might have afforded him happiness. Bellilotte was therefore discarded: from Duroc, who was especially charged with the disposal of her fate, I know the internal struggles which this decision cost Napoleon; but her name was Josephine's most effective weapon in all her domestic quarrels, and she would have allowed him neither peace nor respite had she once learned that Madame Fourès had a house in Paris. Napoleon, anxious above all things to avoid publicity, recommended a house out of town. And Pauline, ever resigned to the wishes of him she loved, hired or purchased a cottage at Belleville near the Pré-Saint Gervais, where she lived at the time Junot pointed her out to me at the *Comédie*.

Fourès also returned from Egypt, and the divorce pronounced abroad being invalid at home unless confirmed within a limited time, which had now elapsed, he reclaimed his wife, who refused his demand; and long and angry debates arose, which, reaching the ears of the First Consul, he with some harshness ordered the unfortunate wife to marry again. An opportunity offered in the person of M. Ramchouppe, who was enamoured of her; and Bonaparte promised a consulate on the conclusion of the match. She consulted her old patron, M. de Sales, who was now practising with credit as an advocate at Paris, and who still entertained a warm friendship for Bellilotte as well as for Fourès. She finally determined, contrary to his judgment, to marry M. Ramchouppe, and set out with her new husband for his consulate.

For many years nothing was heard of her; but on learning the captivity of Napoleon, the noble and exalted soul of Pauline rose superior to fear and prejudice. She realized part of her remaining property, and sailed from port to port, anxiously watching an opportunity to go to Saint Helena and to attempt the deliverance of him who had ever been dear to her as her best friend, and who personified the glory of her country.

Her plan was some time organizing, and no sooner was it completed than Napoleon's death crushed all her hopes. Pauline was in Brazil when the news reached her; where she may be now I know not, but in whatever quarter of the globe, should this book meet her eye, I could wish that it may convey to her the expression of my admiration and gratitude for a feeble woman, whose courage and feeling prompted an undertaking which men had not heart enough even to attempt.

CHAPTER VIII.

Awakening and Nocturnal Sally of Junot—The Adjutant Laborde—Chevalier's Machine — Accomplices and Informers — Attempts against the First Consul's Life—Difficult Arrest—The Madmen—Conspiracies—Secrets imparted to Caffarelli—Lavoisier—Poverty a Bad Counsellor—The Rule and its Exceptions—Description of the Machine—Maxim of the First Consul—The Military Family.

SOME days after my marriage I found Junot depressed and abstracted, visiting the Prefect of Police several times a day, often awakened in the night by an old adjutant called Laborde, who came to make reports, which seemed to be of great importance; he once got up at three o'clock in the morning, dressed himself, and sallied out on foot with this man, although the cold was excessive, and he had been suffering all day with a violent headache, which had entirely deprived him of appetite. But the interests at stake were very dear, and all else was forgotten.

At length, on the 7th November, he appeared more calm, and told me that the First Consul had just escaped a danger which must have been followed by the most disastrous consequences; for not only must the plan, if executed, have succeeded, but all the neighbouring inhabitants would have been its victims. This was the infernal machine of Chevalier, a prelude to the conspiracy of the 23rd December. Chevalier, whose name is almost the only one connected with this affair, was far from being its sole contriver. Men named Bousquet, Gombaud-Lachaise, Desforge, Guérauld, and a Madame Bucquet, were arrested at the same time, and, with Chevalier, confined in the Temple. This machine, which Chevalier was constructing, was seized in a chamber which he shared with a man named Veycer, in a house called the house of the Blancs-Manteaux. He had left his former lodging because the police were in search of him.

Veycer, his fellow labourer, was at first his comrade, and afterwards, whether through remorse or by means of bribery, was induced to assist in his arrest. It was apprehended that Chevalier, finding himself lost, might in a moment of despair set fire to the combustibles around him, and blow up with himself the house and all that it contained. Veycer's business was to prevent this, but Chevalier, as was natural to the part he was playing, was extremely suspicious. On retiring to rest he fastened his door with an oaken bar, and had always at hand a pair of excellent and well-loaded pistols; all this his bedfellow was aware of, and was not unmindful of his own safety.

On the eve of Chevalier's arrest the progress of his machine was at a standstill for want of money; and Bousquet, who appears to have been hitherto the banker of the diabolical enterprise, was equally without funds. Veycer was despatched in quest of money, which, of course, was not difficult to procure, as only six or eight francs were wanted. He brought them late at night, so that nothing could be undertaken till the morning.

Chevalier's confidence in his comrade (whose real name was not Veycer, and whom I shall simply call his comrade) was strengthened by this new service, and he slept amidst fusees and cartridges as tranquilly as if surrounded by roses.

The comrade had little difficulty in persuading him not to

burn a light, so that the room was in perfect darkness, and to this circumstance he owed his safety ; for, on hearing the first shake of the door by the police agents, he sprang forward to remove the bar that opposed them, and Chevalier, perceiving that he was betrayed, fired a pistol, which lodged its contents in the wall, but would not have missed his comrade had there been a light.

This arrest took place at two in the morning of the 7th November, a date impressed on my memory by the circumstance that, had my mother's intended ball that evening taken place, with so many of those wretches about the town, who went by the name of the *madmen*, and had been agitating for three months past, the probable consequences of their learning that the First Consul was about to spend a part of the night, unguarded, at a private house, where, on entering or returning, his person was so much more accessible than amidst the crowds that surround a public spectacle, could not but make both my mother and myself shudder.

The sect called the *Enragés* was composed of the very dregs of the worst days of the Revolution. The cleverest of them, and their ringleader, was one Moses Bayle, formerly a Conventionalist, who headed the attempt on the vaults of the Tuileries, opposite the *Vigier* baths, when the first grating yielded ; but the second, having a stronger lock, set force at defiance. The same party, under the same leader, attempted to assassinate the First Consul before the affair of Ceracchi and Aréna. This conspiracy, which had been framed almost unknown to the police, so completely were its authors protected by their insignificance, was discovered by an honest man whom they would willingly have made an accomplice ; but, revolting at the enormity of the project, he sought out General Caffarelli, aide-de-camp to the First Consul, and revealed to him the whole affair.

This man's name owes its preservation chiefly to its similarity to one of great celebrity, Lavoisier.

Paris was at this time infested with swarms of pardoned Chouans, and other vagabonds of all descriptions, who conspired against the First Consul's life, not for the sake of liberty, but because so terrible a catastrophe would throw all Paris into confusion, and enable them to repeat the horrors of the 10th of August and 2nd of September. But it was the opinion both of Junot and Fouché, who agreed on this point alone, that other heads controlled, and other counsels animated the machinations of which these illiterate and half-armed banditti were made to appear the sole contrivers. Since the First Consul had been in power more than ten obscure conspiracies had been discovered, and he, with the same greatness of mind which never afterwards deserted him, enjoined the authorities not to divulge them.

"They would lead the nation to suppose that the State is not tranquil, nor must we allow foreigners this momentary triumph; they would easily take advantage of it, and it shall not be."

I heard the whole history of Chevalier's affair from the old adjutant Laborde, who came the next morning to relate it to Junot; and also from Doucet, Chief of the Staff of Paris. The little machine was brought for Junot's inspection. It was a small cask filled with squibs, and balls containing seven or eight pounds of powder. It was bound at each extremity with two hoops of iron, and near the middle was introduced a gun-barrel, having the trigger strongly attached to the cask with pieces of iron. This infernal machine was to have been placed in the road of the First Consul. Fireworks were to have been thrown in all directions to increase the disorder; while *chevaux-de-frise*, manufactured by a locksmith, who was taken into custody, being placed in the adjacent streets, were to prevent the arrival of troops, and thus give time to men, capable of so diabolical a conception, to commit their meditated crimes.

Junot especially directed me not to mention this affair to any of my mother's associates; and so well did I obey his instructions that my mother knew nothing of the matter till the 23rd December. I soon, indeed, accustomed myself to hear almost mechanically matters of the utmost importance discussed; a habit that was common to me as well as to all the young wives of my time, whose husbands were continually about the Chief of the State, or engaged in highly confidential transactions.

The first time that I dined at the Tuileries, I was placed as a bride next to the First Consul; the Duchess de Montebello, then Madame Lannes, was seated on the other side; it was about a week after this discovery; he asked me if I had mentioned it to my mother. I answered, "No, for I was unwilling to give her uneasiness; and besides," added I, "Junot tells me such things must be talked of as little as possible." "Junot is right," added he; "I myself have recommended it to him. It is now no secret, as beyond a doubt the arrest of Chevalier is pretty generally known; but I do not wish explanations, sought for more from curiosity than interest, by persons so nearly connected with me as Junot." And he added, "As for you, Madame Junot, now that you make a part of the family of my staff, you must *see, hear, and forget* (vous devez *tout voir, tout entendre, et tout oublier*). Have this device engraved on a seal. But I remember that you can keep a secret." (He alluded to the affair of Salicetti.)

CHAPTER IX.

Garat, and the Ridiculous Cravats—Haydn's Oratorio—Brilliant Assemblage at the Opera—Junot's Dinner with Berthier, the 23rd December—General Security and Extraordinary Noise—The First Consul at the Opera, and Duroc at the Door of my Box—The Infernal Machine—M. Diestrich, Aide-de-camp to Vandamme—Return from the Opera—My Presence at the Tuileries the Evening of the 23rd December—Remarkable Scenes—Danger of Madame Bonaparte—Involuntary Tears—Correct Details relative to the Infernal Machine—Exaggeration of the Number of Victims—Junot's Coachman, and the Danger avoided—Agreement of Fouché and Junot—Junot's Nightmare—My Life in Danger.

My mother's health was strikingly improved since my marriage. Contrary to my brother's inclinations, as well as mine, she had called in a new physician, named Vigaroux, the son of a skilful surgeon of Montpellier, and he seemed to work wonders. He engaged to cure her in six months, and she was surely enough relieved from pain. She dined with me, went to plays, was going about on visits the whole morning, and, far from feeling fatigued, she was the better for all this exertion.

Garat, one of my mother's oldest and most assiduous acquaintances, came one day to entreat our attendance at the Opera on the 23rd December to hear Haydn's fine oratorio of the "Creation," which he, jointly with Steibelt, had arranged, and in which he was to take a part. My mother, who was passionately fond of good music and of Garat's singing, readily promised a compliance. She was to sit in my box; and as Junot dined with Berthier, the new Minister of War, it was settled that I should dine with her ready dressed, and Junot would join us after dinner.

My toilet completed for the evening, I entered the carriage with my brother-in-law, and we found my mother beautiful, gay, and enchanting. She was splendidly dressed in black velvet and diamonds, and no one would have supposed her of the age of sixty-two.

We dined early; my mother ordered her horses while we took coffee, and we set out immediately afterwards. It was seven when we arrived at the Opera. The house was crowded, and being well lighted, and the ladies in full dress, the spectacle was very brilliant.

We distinguished Garat with his opera-glass in his hand earnestly surveying the boxes to recognize his acquaintances; and though eight o'clock at night, he sought to catch a gleam of *Aurora*.* He was more ridiculously dressed than usual; no very easy matter. His coat collar stood higher than his head, and his rather monkeyish face was difficult to discern between ells of muslin by way of cravat below and a forest of curls above.

The instruments were tuned, and this immense orchestra, more numerous than I had ever seen it before, was pre-

---

* Garat was particularly intimate with Madame Aurora B——, and was always in company with her and her sister. Both parties frequented Talleyrand's house, and the valet-de-chambre, accustomed to announce them together, would cry with a loud voice, " *Mesdames de B—— et M. Garat.*" But all things change in this world: so that later these ladies and M. Garat were announced separately; but the habit was so established that more than two years afterwards, Courtiade, when ushering in the two sisters, still called out mechanically " *Mesdames de B—— et M. Garat.*"

paring to render Haydn's *chef-d'œuvre* more perfectly than he had ever the gratification of hearing it himself.*

Junot found my mother and me in high spirits, occupied in looking round this magnificent house, and returning the friendly and smiling salutations of our acquaintance. He was himself in a peculiar state of mind. Berthier had been repeating to him a conversation he had held with the First Consul respecting Junot; and his words were so full of kindness and friendship that Junot was sensibly affected, and his eyes watered, while happiness played in smiles on his lips.

Scarcely were thirty bars of the oratorio played before a violent explosion was heard, like the report of a cannon.

"What means that?" said Junot with emotion. He opened the box door, and looked about for one of his officers or aides-de-camp. "It is strange!" said he. "How can the guns be fired at this hour? Besides, I should have known it! Give me my hat," said he to my brother; "I will go and see what it is." Instantly Chevalier's machine occurred to me, and I seized the flaps of Junot's coat, but he looked angrily at me, and impatiently snatched it from my grasp.

At this moment the door of the First Consul's box opened and himself appeared, with General Lannes, Berthier, and Duroc. He smilingly saluted the immense crowds, who mingled frantic yells of pleasure with their acclamations.

Madame Bonaparte followed in a few seconds, accompanied by Colonel Rapp, Madame Murat (who was near her confinement), and Mademoiselle Beauharnais. Junot was re-entering the box to convince himself of the First

---

* Haydn was leader of the music at the chapel of Prince Esterhazy at Vienna; he wished much to visit Paris, but the Prince refused him permission to travel.

Consul's serenity, which I had just remarked upon, when Duroc presented himself with a discomposed countenance and an excited air. He spoke in whispers to Junot, and we heard nothing of his communication; but at night Junot repeated it to me. "I love Duroc; he is almost as much attached to the First Consul as Marmont and myself."

Duroc's words sufficiently explained the disturbed condition in which he appeared. "The First Consul has just escaped death," said he hastily to Junot; "go to him; he wishes to speak to you, but be calm. It is impossible the event should remain unknown here a quarter of an hour; but he wishes to avoid being himself the means of spreading such intelligence; so come with me and let me lean on your arm, for I tremble all over. My first battle agitated me less."

During the short conference of the two friends the oratorio had commenced; but the fine voices of Mesdames Branchu and Walbourne, and that of Garat, could not absorb the attention of the audience. All eyes were turned towards the First Consul, and he alone at this moment occupied our attention. As I have before observed, I had said nothing to my mother of Chevalier's infernal machine; but my brother-in-law knew the whole affair, and I whispered a word in his ear, to despatch him in search of news. I felt a presentiment of some misfortune.

The moment Duroc spoke to Junot the latter turned pale as a spectre, and I perceived him raise his hand to his forehead with a gesture of surprise and despair; but, being unwilling to disturb my mother and the people in the adjoining boxes, I contented myself with whispering to Junot to ask for intelligence. But before his return we had heard all. A subdued murmur began to spread from the stage to the orchestra, the pit, and the boxes. "The

First Consul has just been attacked in the Rue Saint Nicaise."*

The truth soon circulated throughout the theatre, when simultaneously, and as it were by an electric shock, one unanimous acclamation was heard. How tumultuous was the agitation which preceded the burst of national resentment! for in the first quarter of an hour the nation was represented by that crowd, whose indignation against so foul an attempt no words are capable of expressing.

Meanwhile I was engaged in observing the First Consul's box, which, being immediately below me, enabled me to see and hear nearly all that passed in it. He was calm, and appeared only warmly affected when the general murmur conveyed to his ear any strong expression of the public feeling. Madame Bonaparte was not equally mistress of her feelings. Her whole frame was agitated; even her attitude, always so graceful, was no longer her own. She seemed to tremble, and to be desirous of sheltering herself under her shawl—the very shawl which had saved her life. She wept: notwithstanding all her efforts to repress her tears, they were seen trickling down her pale cheeks, and when she looked towards the First Consul her shivering fit returned. Her daughter too was greatly upset. As for Madame Murat, the character of the family shone in her demeanour; although her situation might have excused the display of anxiety and distress so natural in the sister of the First Consul, she was, throughout this trying evening, perfectly composed.

Junot, having received the orders of the First Consul,

---

* This street no longer exists ; and the Opera-house was destroyed after the assassination of the Duc de Berri, to make room for the chapel intended to be erected in commemoration of this last murderous act ; the chapel was nearly finished, but has, since the Revolution of 1830, been pulled down, and the materials sold.

returned to desire we would not wait for him, and immediately left us upon duty. The Prefect of Police, whose box was next to mine, had long since quitted it and hastened to the Prefecture. When Junot was gone, my mother, who was now acquainted with the whole affair, told me that a young man of a military appearance, in the box beside me, had just told the ladies who occupied it that the conspirators had at first intended to lay their train at the door of the Opera, in which case the entire theatre would have been blown up; and she desired me to look at him, and tell her whether he were deserving of credit.

It was M. Diestrich, aide-de-camp to General Vandamme, and the ladies in the box were his mother and sister. I had once seen him at my own house on Junot's reception-day, and had met him two days before at General Mortier's. I begged him to tell me whether there was any new misfortune to be dreaded. "It is difficult," said he, "to answer that question. Death has been averted from the whole assemblage within these walls only by the observance of a general regulation that no carriage of any description shall be suffered to remain at the door of a theatre the first night of a new piece. But," added M. Diestrich, lowering his voice, "none of the authors of this infamous crime are yet arrested; who can answer that a second blow may not be prepared against the First Consul at the moment of his leaving the theatre, the first having failed? As for myself, I am come to fetch my mother and sister, and when I have seen them safely home I shall return, for the arm of a man is always necessary in a tumult." "I will go too," said my mother, "this gentleman is perfectly right; give me my shawl, put on your own and let us go;" and she continued urging my departure, and even wrapped me in my furs.

I knew that my mother would go, but for myself I would

fain know Junot's proceedings and keep him in sight. I thought the First Consul's side his most probable station at such a moment. It was not his duty to be running through the narrow alleys of Paris hunting the conspirators from their lurking-places, and I might reasonably suppose he would not be far from the Opera-house. While I lingered, Junot opened the box-door, and hastily said: "Go with your mother; after setting her down, borrow her carriage to convey you to Madame Bonaparte's; I shall be there, and will take you home;" and away he ran. In spite of the excessive cold he was covered with perspiration.

My brother-in-law accompanied us, and having set down my mother we proceeded to the Tuileries. The First Consul was returned from the Opera, and everything appeared as calm as if nothing had happened; but in the salon things wore a different aspect. Several of the authorities were assembled, the Ministers, the Consuls, the Commandant of Paris, General Mortier, Commandant of the Division, etc. The First Consul, who had hitherto appeared indifferent to all the attempts against him, showed this time no indulgence, and he had good reason.

Madame Bonaparte was quite overpowered; she cried incessantly. Independently of the danger the First Consul had so narrowly escaped, she had herself nearly fallen a victim to the explosion. As she was stepping into the carriage, General Rapp, who was not usually so observant of the perfect agreement of colours in a lady's dress, observed to her that her shawl matched neither her gown nor her jewels. Her perfect elegance in the adjustment of all the accessories of the toilet is well known, and she returned to repair the oversight. Scarcely did it detain her three minutes, yet these sufficed for separating her carriage from that of the First Consul, which it was to have followed close. This delay saved her!

The explosion took place just as Madame Bonaparte's carriage reached the Carrousel : its windows were broken, and pieces of the glass fell on the neck and shoulders of Mademoiselle Beauharnais, who sat on the front seat of the carriage, and her shawl did not protect her from some slight cuts.

It is well known that the barrel containing the powder and charge (and which resembled those borne by the water-carriers) was placed on a crazy little cart, drawn by a mare, and so stationed as to impede the road. It was intended, while in the act of removal by the guards, to explode by internal machinery, and destroy everything within reach. It was afterwards said that the rapidity of his carriage alone had saved the First Consul, and no doubt this circumstance had its share in his deliverance ; but the real cause of it was the result of mere chance. The piquet of chasseurs escorting the First Consul preceded and followed the carriage.

One of the foremost, perceiving that an old cart obstructed the way, called to the driver to get on one side ; but seeing no one (for Saint Régent, who lighted the train, was concealed behind a palisade),* he struck the mare smartly on the haunches with the flat of his sabre, which set her in motion, and advancing three or four steps she seems to have deranged the packthread, which, by opening a valve, was to admit air and cause the explosion.

The consequent delay was but momentary, yet it sufficed

* At the period of this tragic event the Place du Carrousel and the adjacent streets were totally different to what we see them now ; improvements were then going on, and palisades of lofty boards were at every corner. It was behind one of these palisades that the poor little ignorant chimney-sweep had hidden himself in order to set fire to the train of powder ; his name was Saint Régent. By the explosion of the machine he received some violent contusions, and was thrown across the street : the surgeon who picked him up immediately afterwards and dressed his wounds was arrested, and suspected of being a party concerned in the infernal attempt.

to ensure the safety of the First Consul, whose carriage had meanwhile turned through the Rue de Malte into the Rue Richelieu, instead of passing through the Rue Saint Nicaise, where the machine was. The mare was killed, but without any external mark of injury, so that a description of her was everywhere placarded, and the body deposited at the Prefecture of Police in order that the public might see and examine it, and perhaps be able to say to whom she formerly belonged.

Such was the violence of the explosion, so terrible the impulsion, that a part of the wheel and one of the iron bands that encircled the cask, darting across the intervening space from the Rue de Malte to the Hôtel d'Elbœuf, and unarrested even by the lofty height of that hotel, were hurled some distance beyond it.

Curiosity proved fatal to many inhabitants of the Rues Saint Nicaise and de Malte. Madame Léger, mistress of the Café Apollo, at the corner of the two streets, running to the door, according to her custom whenever the First Consul was to be seen passing, had both her breasts carried off by one of the hoops of the barrel, and survived but three days.

One of the waiters at the same café was killed, and the other wounded. The number of the victims has been much exaggerated. I have proofs that on that day the deaths did not exceed nine: they may, including the consequences, have afterwards amounted to twenty-nine or thirty. Great, no doubt; but far less frightful than if we had had to deplore the loss of two thousand people, as would have been the case had not the sentinel peremptorily resisted the placing of the cart at the door of the Opera-house.

It was not till my return home at night that I was informed of Junot's share in the danger. On his road to the

Opera from the Ministry of War, which was then at the Hôtel d'Avray, Rue de Lille, passing under the arch of the Carrousel, he recollected that it was only seven, and the First Consul would not have set out. He therefore ordered his coachman to stop at the Tuileries; but the restiveness of his young and spirited horses (we drove at that time the finest in Paris) frustrated this scheme. They were going with tremendous rapidity, and the coachman found it impossible to stop them till it would have become necessary to make a very awkward turn, and to again pass a narrow part of the street. Junot, therefore, with some signs of impatience, relinquished his design, and again gave the word "to the Opera." Had he alighted at the Tuileries, Napoleon's carriage being full,* he must have followed in his own; and the train of guards, the last of whom had his horse killed, would most certainly have been blown up. No one, however, appeared sensible of the danger he had escaped but myself and the coachman, who for more than a year could not pass the Place du Carrousel without a shudder.

All the authorities, the corporations, the tribunals,— everything that could call itself constituted, or wore the appearance of a body,—congratulated the First Consul and entreated him as a favour to pay more attention to his personal safety. The Council of State, with Boulay de la Meurthe at the head of its deputation, demanded especially that he would take measures for the maintenance of public order. But the most remarkable address was that of the City of Paris. This unfortunate city saw her interests at stake, exposed as she was to become the victim of miscreants, who cared not if, in the accomplishment of their own criminal views, they brought destruction on thousands of unoffending citizens.

* Lauriston, aide-de-camp on duty; Lannes, commanding the guards, and Berthier, Minister of War, were with Napoleon.

It was Etienne Mejean, Secretary-General of the Department of the Seine, at the head of the Mayors and of the General Council, who spoke, instead of Frochot, then Prefect, who was too ill to exercise his functions. Contemporary memoirs have made the Prefect present the Mayors to the First Consul, and have quoted his speech on the occasion. The question may or may not be an important one; but knowing the truth, I report it.

The next day, the 24th December, the agitation of Paris was extreme. The heinous nature of the plot was known overnight, but its details were not generally understood till the morning; and I cannot too often repeat, that the indignation they excited was universal, and the interest manifested for the First Consul beyond expression.

It may be well imagined that all the authorities, civil and military, were at once in a state of activity, requiring no other stimulus. Opinions differed upon the direction the researches should take. Junot and Fouché, who did not usually agree on police measures, could not convert the First Consul to their persuasion that all these frequent atrocities had their mainsprings both in France and at a distance from it. Napoleon was of a different opinion. "They are the work," he said, "of those same *Enragés*, who embrace in their number a multitude of *Septembrisers;*" and nothing could shake this idea. Yet it was notorious that these men were but the foreposts of a party, and the cat's-paws of their secret instigators.

" Do you believe that the cut-throats of the 2nd and 3rd of September, or that the executioners of the Republican marriages at Nantes, or the men who filled the ditches of Avignon with corpses, the assassins of the prisoners at Versailles, those wretches who for two years waded ankle-deep in blood, signing decrees of death against the aged, such as the Abbess of Montmartre at ninety,* or young victims of sixteen, such as the maids of Verdun—do you believe, sir," and he advanced a pace or two nearer to Fouché—"do you believe that all these men love liberty and the Republic? Can you answer YES? If you do, I for my part shall say NO. I tell you that they are men determined on licentiousness—men who, on the very eve of the massacres I have enumerated, had not wherewith to pay for a loaf, and six months afterwards were living in opulence; because they could, without a symptom of remorse, wear the clothing and sleep in the beds of their victims. You will tell me, perhaps, that some amongst them are still poor: it may be so; but for the most part they have long feasted on blood. I know what I know," added he, shaking his head.

"A handful of wretches, who have calumniated Liberty by the crimes they have committed in her name, are the guilty parties," said the First Consul. Dubois would not contradict him, though it was evident he thought with Junot and Fouché. Fouché replied, "These are fellows incapable of conceiving. They execute as the horse did who drew the machine, but can go no farther. It would be useless were I to run after these men of the Abbaye-aux-Bois.† Only leave me time, and I will unravel many things."

* This was Madame de Montmorency, who was so bent with age that the inhuman executioner could not perform his office without first straightening her body by force.

This unfortunate lady was both blind and deaf; when interrogated, Fouquier Tinville was obliged to scream to her, as she had been deprived of her ear-trumpet, and failing with all his exertions to make himself heard, she was condemned for having *conspiré sourdement* (conspired privately or *deafly*). When she was in the cart, and breathed the fresh air, she sang with a faint voice the "*Salve Regina*," believing herself restored to liberty.

† The Abbaye-aux-Bois, situated in the Faubourg Saint Germain, was the principal place for the meetings of the conspirators at that time.

For two days Junot scarcely allowed himself an instant's repose. He would not entrust to subalterns a commission so important as the pursuit of the agents in so atrocious an enterprise. He rose almost before daybreak, and from the headquarters of the garrison directed everything that fell under his jurisdiction. The activity, intelligence, and honourable devotedness of his coadjutor M. Doucet, Chief Adjutant-General of the garrison, cannot be too highly praised.

At ten o'clock on the evening of the 5th Junot came home, overcome with fatigue, and though he had promised to fetch me from my mother's, could not rally his faculties from the drowsiness which oppressed them.

On my arrival, my maid told me he was gone to bed, and had requested I would wish him good-night. Accordingly, I entered my chamber, and, finding him in a deep sleep, leaned over him and said, "What! already asleep?" His nights, generally restless, were at this anxious period disturbed by frightful dreams; and at the moment I spoke he was dreaming that he was in the Cabinet of the First Consul, which was filled with conspirators, one of whom was in the act of firing a machine. My words had partly roused him, and the fire-light favouring the illusion of his dream, he mistook me for the assassin, and with a furious kick drove me to the farther extremity of the room. My cries awakened him, and, becoming sensible who had been the object of his attack, he was much agitated.

CHAPTER X.

My Visits to the Tuileries after the 23rd December—Conversation with the First Consul—Inutility of an additional Victim—Bonaparte's Opinion of my Mother's Drawing-room—His Condemnation of the Emigrants—"M. Roger de Damas," a Synonym for Bravery—The Horse and the Cloak—Madame Murat at the Hôtel de Brionne—Promenade to Villiers—M. Baudelocque and Madame Frangeau—"We are not Rich"—The First Consul's Character—Portalis at Malmaison—The Preamble of the Civil Code.

WE were more than commonly assiduous in our attendance at the Tuileries after the explosion of the infernal machine; my mother herself pressed it upon me, and often, when desirous of my company, would sacrifice it to send me to the Palace. "Be very particular," said she, "to express to General Bonaparte the distress which this horrible affair has occasioned me. No set speeches, such as you would address to a Tribunal or a Council of State, but depict in its true colours all that I suffered on the evening and night of the 23rd December."

The attempted assassination made her shudder: she wept violently on her return home, and in the night had a violent access of fever, which made her very ill for two days.

When I acquitted myself of her commission to the First Consul, his answer was of a nature to have confounded anyone less acquainted with his character than I was. He looked me steadily in the face, fixed on me that piercing and fiery eye, which, by its quick and earnest expression, magnetized those it encountered, and desired me to repeat my mother's message.

"I have had the honour, General, of expressing to you, in my mother's name, the lively anxiety she felt in the incidents of the 23rd. She hopes you do not doubt her sincerity."

"Yet she ran away, and you, too, before the end of the oratorio."

I made no reply, but looked at General Bonaparte with an expression which he probably interpreted literally; for he added, withdrawing his gaze from me, and turning towards the window, although it was night, and nothing could be seen in the Palace court, "To be sure it would have availed nothing towards my safety, had any peril awaited me, that one more victim should have exposed herself to it."

"Let me add, General, that in the eyes of my mother it was her daughter who was in danger; in mine, it was my mother. We mutually owed regard to each other's safety: for myself, I do not exaggerate when I affirm that I left the Opera with the greatest reluctance; for I knew that Junot must partake the danger that threatened his General, and this idea was painful to me; but I could not suffer my mother to run the risk without being in some degree criminal."

"Yes, yes; undoubtedly, undoubtedly," answered the First Consul, with an inflection of voice it would be impossible to describe; "I am altogether ridiculous to have spoken so thoughtlessly, for you must call it so. I know in your mother's circle everything is acceptable that may make me appear in an unfavourable light."

"General," replied I, much hurt that he persisted in the belief that my mother's drawing-room was a centre for the dissemination of hatred against him, "how can I convince you? It can be accomplished only by one means, and that is in the power of God alone—it is, that the accent of truth may reach your heart. I have the honour to tell you, Citizen Consul, that never has a word to your prejudice been uttered in my mother's drawing-room but either she or my brother has instantly imposed silence on the holders of language which my mother's friendship for you, and for all your family, would interdict, even though it were the language of truth."

"Ah!" said the First Consul, "you admit, then, that persons inimical to me are received in your mother's drawing-room?"

"I have spoken with frankness, General, and shall continue to do so. Unquestionably, among my mother's acquaintances are some who are unfriendly to the present Government; I pretend neither to blame nor absolve them. I know that they are suffering the consequences of a long exile, that their property is confiscated, that most of them are in indigence, that many still groan under the proscription; but all these evils are not ascribable to you, and to resent them upon you would be equally unjust and absurd. But, on the other hand, I believe also——"

I stopped, and, half smiling, looked at the First Consul, who continued my sentence—" That I should be unjust in my turn if I obliged them to cry, *Vive la République!* Is not that your meaning, Madame Junot? But if they do not like that word, why do they return to France? Who recalls them? They are not wanted in any branch of the Administration. Fouché and Chaptal will be quite as good Ministers as M. le Comte d'Entraigues, and Junot and Lannes will command my soldiers as well as M. Roger de Damas, brave as he is."*

* Whenever the bravery of the emigrants was Napoleon's topic, M. Roger de Damas was always the example. He related a certain story,

"But, General," answered I, "is not our native soil the property of all her children? Cannot a Frenchman return home without the inducement of a place? Is there not an attraction infinitely more powerful? I know there is, by the experience of my own family; my uncle, M. de Comnèna, is returned to France, to live in peace and in the hope of a better future. And he certainly did not want confidence in your generosity, for he re-entered France without a passport, without even an encouraging word; and as he was far from expecting to find his niece the bride of one of your Generals, he reckoned only on the magnanimity of the Government towards a man who surrenders himself."

"Your uncle does not like me, and I may add he does not like the Republic; besides, he emigrated, and I consider all emigrants in the light of parricides. Nevertheless, I have complied with Junot's demands in favour of M. de Comnèna; for," added he, "Madame Permon carefully avoids presenting a petition to me, even in favour of her brother."

This was true; my mother had said, "If he be so disposed, he will do it for Junot: and if not, what good can my interference effect?"

My mother was, however, mistaken; the General would never have refused to Madame Permon what the First Consul

---

which I never heard but from him, about the head of a horse enveloped in a cloak, and a leap into the sea, horse and rider; Quiberon was the theatre. But as it was neither easy to follow Bonaparte in his narrative, nor to extract from him a repetition, I never exactly understood the particulars of this anecdote. All that I could gather from it was, that M. Roger de Damas, seeing himself on the point of being taken, had wrapped his horse's head in his cloak, that the animal might not be sensible of his danger, and striking the spurs into his sides, had made him leap into the sea. I made inquiries of a person who had served in Condé's army, and he assured me the circumstance was true, but had not happened at Quiberon. I give it as I heard it, and that was from Napoleon.

VOL. II.

of the Republic might perhaps have thought it inconsistent with his duty to grant to General Junot.

I remember that the same day the First Consul talked to me of all my family; inquired whether my grandmother was still living; what was become of my uncle, the Abbé de Comnèna; he also spoke of my brother, and his friendly intentions towards him. Junot's relations were not mentioned; he spoke only of my own.

As I have before said, I went often to Madame Bonaparte; Madame Murat, who was expecting her confinement, was also a frequent visitor, and I never met her without pleasure. She was unaffected, a dutiful daughter, a fond wife, and every way interesting.

One day I visited her at the Hôtel de Brionne,* where she was then living; she occupied the ground-floor, and M. Benezeck, with all his family, the first. I found her getting into her carriage for a ride to Villiers (Neuilly), which the First Consul had just given her, and she proposed my accompanying her, to which I acceded, and we set out, having the precaution to take her nurse, Madame Frangeau, with us.

Madame Frangeau was the favourite of Baudelocque, and could recount the minutiæ of the youth, maturity, and declining age of her patron, with commentaries and additions which each recital magnified by half; will not the simple mention of her name recall to the Queen of Naples, the Queen of Holland, the Duchesse de Frioul, and to all the young mothers of that day, who, like myself, were subjected to her six weeks' thraldom, her gown of the fashion of the Regency, and her whimsically antiquated head-dress, oddly contrasted with finery in the style of 1800?

* This house has since been pulled down. It was situated in the old court of the Tuileries, opposite the entrance leading to the Pont Royal. Maret occupied it after Murat.

This little ride to Villiers dwells on my mind, because so excessive was our mirth at Madame Frangeau's stories that at one moment I had fears for Caroline. She, however, thought not of accidents; she was better engaged in devouring ten or twelve large bunches of grapes and two rolls à la Duchesse, which Madame Frangeau had ordered to be put into the carriage. I never saw such an appetite! "Will you have some?" said she, recollecting at last that all the way from the barriers she had been eating without a companion.

After driving round the park of Villiers, and laying in a fresh stock of provisions (for the basket was emptied) we returned home. "The First Consul, in the gift of this country seat, has been most generous to us," said Caroline. "We are not rich, and if my brother had not added the means of furnishing and supporting the house it had been useless to us." In aftertimes, when Murat, returning from Italy, undertook the government of Paris on Junot's departure for Arras, no impossibility of this nature prevented his furnishing and inhabiting the Hôtel de Thelusson.

Our evenings, even after the play, if it were not too late, were spent at Madame Bonaparte's. There we enjoyed the happiness of meeting the First Consul.

His conversation, always attractive by its depth of thought, and the air of originality reflected from his rich and brilliant imagination, acquired increased interest from the consciousness that at such a moment all he said was of importance. For this reason I seldom missed the quintidian dinners. In spite of crowd, noise, and bustle, it was easy to hear the conversation of the First Consul with the men of talent and learning of France. The most profound civilians, the ablest financiers, the most subtle diplomatists, thronged around to hear him, and appeared to be rather taking lessons from him than imparting their knowledge to a young man, whose pale complexion bore witness to watchings and fatigues far exceeding theirs, though the superiority of years was greatly on their side.

For a just appreciation of the First Consul's character, he should have been listened to at Malmaison, or in Madame Bonaparte's salon at Paris; but never was he so interesting as at the period I am sketching, imperfectly, indeed, considering the strong and vigorous colouring required, when designed for eyes which cannot by the aid of personal recollection fill up the mere outlines of the picture.

It was when surrounded by the first men of the day that the First Consul should have been seen and heard; he then exhibited a fire which diffused life and warmth on all around him: I had never before seen him in so splendid a light, and I was more than astonished at it. Its effect upon me was at once seducing like an attractive charm, and strongly agitating from the conclusive and perfectly convincing brevity of his eloquence.

On M. Portalis arriving, the First Consul met him, and, taking his hand, led him to Madame Bonaparte. He had a great esteem for him. Portalis was not then afflicted with blindness; his sight was painful, but he did not yet require a guide. The First Consul spoke to him as soon as he entered about the preamble of the Code, which had been entrusted to him.

"You are idle, Citizen Portalis," said the First Consul, laughing. "You must make more haste; all the world is crying out after our Code; we must move fast where business is concerned."

"Ah! General," answered the worthy man, laughing in his turn, "you give others credit for your own gift of magic. As for you, you were endowed at your birth; but we, poor simple mortals, must feel our way soberly. Besides, do not you know, General, that our Code has only been a year concocting; and that a code of laws is an immense national monument, which requires time to erect? You have worked at it as well as we, and you know it is a skein not easily unravelled."

"Yes, certainly, certainly," said the First Consul; "but we must advance," he repeated still; "we must advance: is the preamble ready?"

"The First Consul is well assured that I shall always fulfil, not my duty merely, but far more than my duty, to second his great and noble projects for the happiness of France," replied M. Portalis; "the preamble is completed."

"Ah, you are a good and excellent Frenchman!" said the First Consul—"well and good! I like such men as you and the brave Duveyrier. I am happy when I see such around me; and so seconded, I cannot do otherwise than well."

CHAPTER XI.

Female Breakfasts at the Tuileries—Madame Vaines—The Lioness *en Couche,* and Visit to the Ménagerie with Madame Bonaparte—Marengo, the eldest of the Lions—The First Consul joins us at the Botanical Gardens—Bonaparte and Félix the Keeper—The Liar caught in the Fact, and the Crocodiles of the Bosphorus—Reminiscences of Egypt by the First Consul—The Psylli and the Serpents.

I WAS engaged to breakfast with Madame Bonaparte at the Tuileries. Her custom of inviting young married women, too timid to make themselves agreeable in the society of superior men, was delightful to me. Chatting with Madame Bonaparte, during the perfectly unceremonious repast, upon fashions, and all the little interests of society, these young ladies acquired confidence, and threw off that reserve which the presence of the First Consul was calculated to inspire.

Madame Bonaparte did the honours with grace and vivacity; we were generally five or six, and all of the same age, the mistress of the house excepted. At Malmaison the number was sometimes twelve or fifteen, and the breakfast was served in a small circular salon looking into the court, and which is now present to my imagination, though I have not entered it these sixteen years.

One day, at the Tuileries breakfast, I met Madame

Vaines, who was high in favour both with the First Consul and Madame Bonaparte, and another person, whose name I forget; all I remember is, that it must have been a female, for men were never admitted to these morning *fêtes*, the First Consul positively prohibiting it. Madame Bonaparte told us she was going to make a visit to a lying-in lady, and inquired if we would accompany her. We acceded, but begged to know in our turn who was the object of our visit. She answered, that to be sure it was a personage who might eat us, but that at present she was in a gentle mood; in short, it was the lioness of the Botanical Garden, who had been delivered at her full time of three whelps, all living.* The First Consul had been already there; but as Madame Bonaparte had informed him of her proposal, he had promised to join us if his engagements would permit.

The lioness was doing well, but was, as Madame Bonaparte had told us, in a languishing mood. Félix Cassal, her keeper, entered the cage, took the cubs from her, and the poor beast, without moving, turned her eyes on him with an expression of softness and affection. She was extended in her cage on a good litter, and her little ones lay rolled in thick coarse carpets, as warmly as in the African sands.

Madame Bonaparte took one of the cubs in her hands, which drew forth a growl from the mother; but Félix spoke to her, and acknowledging his voice by a momentary glance of more fierceness than the former, she again turned to the offender, and renewed her growl. Madame Bonaparte was alarmed. "Oh! never fear," said Félix; "she is behind a strong grating, and, besides, she has not yet recovered her

---

* While we are on the subject of beasts naturalizing themselves in France, I will add that the first monkey born there saw the light of day in a semicircular gilded boudoir to be seen from the Quai, belonging to the Hôtel Labriffe.

strength; she would not hurt much." "Oh!" said Madame Bonaparte, "I can dispense with the trial of her strength; there would be quite enough remaining to make me repent having caressed her son."

This Cassal was an extraordinary man in his way. He was a great traveller, and had made interesting observations, even on the common habits of the country he had passed through; and though he pretended to have seen marvels altogether incredible, yet all he said was not false, and both amusement and instruction might be extracted from him. He had himself purchased the lioness of some Arabs, who had taken her in the environs of Constantinople. While she was *enceinte*, a child having wounded her in the eye with a stone, she threw herself into so violent a passion as to produce abortion; and as she brought forth the present litter a hundred days afterwards, that must have been the utmost extent of her parturition, which disproves the conjectures of Pliny and Buffon; the latter, I believe, asserts that the lioness is six or seven months with young.

She littered on the 18th Brumaire, and Félix named the first-born whelp Marengo. "Was not I a good godfather?" said he to Madame Bonaparte.

He made me touch one of the whelps; but the lioness, who had turned away and appeared to think no more of the matter, suddenly started up to her full height, and uttered a roar that shook the very walls.

Félix soothed her, and took the cub himself. He told us that the First Consul, on his visit to the lioness, had caressed her, and was very well received. "He inquired the hour of her delivery," said Félix; "the nature of her food, and especially of her beverage; and the General who was with him gave me a bright piece of gold, that the lioness might drink to the health of the Republic, a direction I have obeyed. Oh, he thinks of everything, the

Citizen Consul!" While he spoke, I was meditating on the fortunes of this extraordinary man, which seemed to be mysteriously linked with all the wonders of his age.

The First Consul met us on horseback before we had quitted the gardens, and Félix no sooner perceived him than he hurried forward to report the bulletin of the lioness; assuring him that she had drunk to his health, and that she was wonderfully well. Napoleon caressed her, and talked with Félix of all his beasts, with as much ease, and as perfect a knowledge of their properties and habits, as if this branch of science had been his particular study.

Félix, finding such encouragement, entered upon one of his best stories; but just as he arrived (on his own showing) at the most astonishing point, Napoleon patted him on the head with:

"Félix, you lie, my boy; there are no crocodiles in the place you speak of, nor ever were: but it is all one—proceed with your story."

This was more easily said than done. Félix was so thoroughly disconcerted by the First Consul's apostrophe, that it was impossible to recover the thread of his adventure.

"Well, it will do for another day," said Napoleon good-humouredly; "only remember that crocodiles do not devour those who bathe in the Bosphorus, otherwise it would have been much easier to kill Leander by that means than by drowning, as he had no boat, poor fellow!"

We promenaded for some time in these beautiful gardens and their fine greenhouses. They are greatly improved since; yet the Botanical Gardens were even then the most complete institution of the kind in Europe. Other museums were richer in particular articles, but ours alone possessed that superiority in all, which has since rendered it the universal rendezvous for the study of natural history. Napoleon observed that day, "It is my wish to render this the most attractive spot to all learned foreigners in Paris. I wish to draw them here to see and admire a people in their love of science and the arts. The museum of natural history shall be what those of sculpture and painting, and of ancient monuments, will be. Paris should be the first city of the world. If God grant me a life long enough, I would have her become the capital of the universe, in science as well as power. Our painters are already the first, the best in Europe. Excepting Canova and Appiani, Italy herself cannot boast talents equal to ours in painting and sculpture. Their poets also are inferior to ours. Cesarotti and Alfieri cannot dispute the palm with our young writers. In short," added he, "I am proud of my country, and I would have her always mindful of what she is and may be."

We visited the Cabinet of Natural History. The First Consul, remarking on the length of a serpent from the island of Java, was reminded of those of Egypt, and consequently was led to speak of the Psylli. He joked much about Denon, who was bent on knowing the flavour of these creatures (not the Psylli, but the serpents), and Junot declared that the first he ate, on his initiation, seized his chin, and would not let it go, twisting itself five or six times round his chin, which in truth was immoderately long. Speaking of serpents, the First Consul related to us a droll incident that had occurred in his own house at Cairo. Junot was there, and has since repeated it to me much more at length.

One morning, at breakfast, the Psylli and serpents came under discussion. The General-in-Chief said he believed only in the serpents. "I believe there are mountebanks in Egypt," added he, "as well as elsewhere. The Psylli exercise their juggling talents there, with even more facility than our men with a divining-rod seek for water; and when a Psylle announces that he is going to eat a serpent, I verily believe he meets with more gapers than another would on the Pont Neuf."

"I assure you, General," said Junot, "that I have seen these men perform inconceivable feats. I have seen the chief of those creatures do incomprehensible things."

"What! the chief of the serpents?" said the General-in-Chief.

"No, General, the chief of the Psylli. You may laugh at me, but, on my honour, it would astound you to see his performances."

"I tell you they are conjurers, and nothing else. Hold! you shall have proof. Go instantly to the Chief of the Psylli," said he to a domestic interpreter; "send him here, with two of his men."

The chief of the Psylli lost no time in obeying the summons. As soon as he arrived the General-in-Chief told him, through the medium of the interpreter: "There are two serpents in this house; find them, and thou shalt have two sequins (twelve francs) for thyself, and as much for thy followers."

The Psylle prostrated himself, and asked for two troughs filled with water. When they were brought he stripped himself, then filled his mouth with water, laid himself flat on his face, and began creeping, in imitation of the reptile he was in search of, and spouting the water through his closed teeth to mimic its hissing. When he had in this manner made the tour of the ground-floor, he said to the General-in-Chief, with a savage laugh: "*Mafiche, mafiche,*" which signifies "There are none." The General-in-Chief echoed his laugh, and said: "*Comment diable !* can this idiot really play the magician?" And he ordered the interpreter to give the Psylle to understand that the serpent had been seen. "Oh! I know that," said the Psylle. "I felt it on entering the house."

"There, now," said the General-in-Chief, "now the comedy is beginning. Well; seek thy serpent, and if thou findest it thou shalt have two additional sequins." The Psylle climbed with the same manœuvres a staircase which led to the upper story, where Bourrienne lodged, pursued by a troop of inquisitors with the General-in-Chief at their head. The corridor was lighted by a loophole overlooking the country, through which the unvarying azure of the beautiful Egyptian sky was distinguishable. The Psylle closed his eyes and shuddered. "There is your actor beginning his part," said the First Consul to Junot. The serpent-detector then said in a low voice: "There he is!" "I shall be delighted to pay him the honours of hospitality," said the General-in-Chief; "but, my friend, I think thou art mocking us. Dost know that this animal has completely mystified us with his hissing for the last hour, making us run about after his imaginary serpentship?"

The Psylle, nowise discouraged, still crept and hissed about, till presently an actual serpent was seen to interpose its long line across the loophole, and was heard answering with fraternal good-will the hissing of the Psylle; it was six feet in length, and Junot has assured me that its eyes sparkled through the dusky corridor like a bright fire. It approached the Psylle, and was no sooner within his reach than he caught it, with incredible address, in one hand, just below the jaw-bone, in such a manner as to oblige the mouth to open, when, spitting into it, the effect was like magic; the reptile appeared struck with instant death, and, during his lethargy, the enchanter extracted the venom from his poison-fangs.

"Well, my General, what say you to this adventure?" asked Junot of the General-in-Chief.

"What would you have me say to the result of chance? Your Psylle is a lucky impostor, that is all."

CHAPTER XII.

Study of New Men—My Dinners—Advice of the First Consul, and Changes in Society—The Days of the Consuls—The Household of Cambacérès—Messieurs d'Aigrefeuille and Monvel—A Dinner at the House of Cambacérès—The Solicitors at the House of the Second Consul—The Court of the Second Consul, and Promenade at the Palais Royal—Mademoiselle de Montferrier and Monsieur Bastarrêche—Beauty and the Beast—*Bon-mot* of Bonaparte—M. de Souza and his Wig—General Mortier and his Family—The Two Brothers of Berthier—Services of Mortier—His Retirement.

FOR some months after my marriage not a day passed that Junot did not introduce to me several of his friends, and a multitude of acquaintances. I was accustomed to see much company at my mother's. Her circle was a wide one, but it sank into insignificance compared with ours. This perpetual distraction was at first extremely fatiguing, and my mother, who came to install me in my new dignity of mistress of my house, giving me credit for the manner in which I acquitted myself of my arduous functions, added that, for her part, as a spectator only, one of these soirées more than satisfied her, and had its arrangement fallen on her it would have cost her a week's illness.

For some time I was of her opinion, but before a month had elapsed I was sensible of a growing inclination for company, and in a short time, aided by a disposition to view all things on the brightest side, and a lively interest in seeking out, and associating with a visible form, all circumstances relating to the life and character of men whose names had long struck my ears in society, and my eyes in the journals, I began to feel real pleasure in my new situation. Junot, to whom I imparted my change of sentiment, sincerely congratulated me upon it, and promised to assist me whenever my researches should require his aid.

There were at that time few open houses at Paris, the privilege being confined to the ministers and authorities; and even they received only large and formal parties. I was anxious to effect a reformation in this respect, and once expressed my wish to the First Consul, when he was mentioning his own desire to see a more free communication between the society of Paris and the members of the Government.

"Accomplish that, and you will be a charming little woman," said General Bonaparte. "If you make the attempt you will succeed, for you know what it is to hold a drawing-room. Let Citizen Cambacérès see that for this purpose it is not sufficient merely to give a dinner."

The Consul Cambacérès received company every Tuesday and Saturday, and for the first six months of the year ix. no other house could stand a comparison with the Hôtel Cambacérès;* it was soon, however, not only imitated, but excelled. The principal members of his household were Messieurs de Lavollée and Monvel, secretaries, and Messieurs de Chateauneuf and D'Aigrefeuille, who had no appointed functions, but voluntarily acted as chamberlains, and the moment a lady was announced one of these gentlemen went to the door to receive and conduct her to a chair.

* This splendid house was situated in the Rue de Provence, at the corner of the Rue Taitbout, and had a very fine garden.

I had a great friendship for Cambacérès, which neither absence nor distance ever impaired; yet I must acknowledge that, notwithstanding the host's peculiar elegance and superior powers of pleasing, and notwithstanding even that friendly welcome and perfect politeness which, under the influence of the master's example, extended itself to the very lowest domestic of the household, no sooner had you passed the gate of the Hôtel Cambacérès than the very air seemed impregnated with ennui, sleep took possession of the eyelids, and a sort of lethargy suspended every faculty as completely as in the temple of Morpheus.

The dinner-party never exceeded five-and-twenty, and of these the proportion of ladies was small; there were never, indeed, more than two of such consideration, from the offices of their husbands, as that their pretensions to precedence might have occasioned jealousies. There was an excellent cook; and the carving fell to the department of the *maître d'hôtel*, Cambacérès himself never doing the honours, except of a dish of rare game.

This was a great innovation in the etiquette of French society, but I found it agreeable; I cannot, however, say as much for his custom of entertaining the guests nearest to him with an enumeration of all his maladies of the day, assuring us he was too ill to eat, yet always concluding by making an excellent meal. He had great conversational powers, and his narratives acquired novelty and grace from the turn of his language. His evening drawing-room was crowded with judges, registrars, and other officers of all the courts in France, who seemed already to anticipate the future Arch-chancellor; he bore, indeed, even at that period, the character of the ablest civilian in the country.

The Third Consul, too, had already entered upon his future department, the Financial and Administrative; and he also had his two evenings appropriated weekly. How many original figures have passed before my eyes in these two houses! How often, when my eager scrutiny has been awakened by the announcement of a name which had figured conspicuously in the Revolution, have I been disappointed by an insignificant or repulsive exterior! how often, seated beside such a one the whole dinner-time, which with Cambacérès was never short, I have been stupefied by the utter nullity of his ideas! but on communicating my feelings to Cambacérès, he would answer, "This man's reputation was the result of chance; opportunity fell in his way, and instinctively he seized it by the forelock."

The conduct of Cambacérès during the Revolution has been much talked of, and I do not pretend to excuse it. I hate the sanguinary years with which his name is connected, and everything that recalls them; but, difficult as the task may be, I would fain see him exempted from the censures which attach to the men of that period. Napoleon did not approve of the events of 1793, but he excused the famous vote of Cambacérès by the reflection that the thing once done—that is to say, the King once condemned—the interests of France, and especially of Paris, demanded the immediate consummation of that terrible drama.

He disapproved of the sentence, which he characterized as a resolution unjustly adopted towards a man who was guilty only of the crimes of others; and I never heard him pronounce the name of Louis XVI. without the additional epithet of "*the unfortunate King.*" I record his opinion here, because I conceive that on a matter so momentous, and which so nearly concerns his own destiny—since it still influences that of France—it must be of the highest interest to us.

Cambacérès was originally Councillor in the Court of Finances of Languedoc. When the Comte de Perigord*

---

* The Comte de Perigord, Prince de Chalais, uncle of M. de Talleyrand, and brother of the Archbishop of Paris, of whom I have spoken

presided over the states of that province, of which he was commandant in 1786, Cambacérès was in misfortune. M. de Perigord, always benevolent and ready to assist the needy, asked and obtained for the almost indigent Councillor a pension of two hundred francs, and for his father one of two thousand francs, out of the royal lotteries.

The courtesy of Cambacérès was general, but his countrymen from Languedoc he welcomed with a peculiar urbanity, the more invaluable that it had none of the varnish of fashionable politeness. Many Languedocians went direct to the Hôtel de Cambacérès on alighting from the diligences; he received them with kindness, examined their petitions, and if he could not assist them, unhesitatingly told them the truth, pointing out at the same time how they might obtain other advantages, and never failed to forward their interests. I may be allowed to call Cambacérès an honest man; for, looking around on all his equals in power, I have never found one of such absolute good faith and probity, to which many others can testify.

His figure was extraordinarily ugly, as well as unique. The slow and regular step, the measured cadence of accent, the very look, which took three times as long as another's to arrive at its object—all was in admirable keeping with the long person, long nose, long chin, and the yellow skin, which betrayed not the smallest symptoms that any matter inclining to sanguine circulated beneath its cellular texture.

The same consistency, though probably unstudied, pervaded his dress; and when demurely promenading the galleries of the Palais Royal, then the Palais Egalité, the singular cut and colour of his embroidered coat; his ruffles, at that time so uncommon; his short breeches, silk stockings, shoes polished with English blacking, and fastened

---

in the first part of these Memoirs. He was an intimate friend of my mother.

with gold buckles; his old-fashioned wig and queue; and his well-appointed and well-placed three-cornered hat, produced altogether a most fantastic effect.

Even the members of his household, by their peculiarities of dress, served as accessories to the picture.

He went every evening to the theatre, and seldom failed to make his appearance afterwards with his suite, all in full costume, either in the gardens of the Tuileries or of the Palais Egalité, where everything around exhibited the most ludicrous disparity with this strange group, whose solemn deportment and deliberate and circumspect discourse might serve to personify the disciples of Plato following their master to Sunium.

The First Consul was sometimes annoyed that the ridicule attached to his colleague appeared to recoil upon him, and I remember once seeing him enraged as he listened to the translation of a passage from the English journals. The Second Consul was caricatured, and from the Second to the First the transition is so easy that the journalist made no scruple of it. The First Consul stamped his foot, and said to Josephine:

"You must interfere in this matter—do you hear? It is only a woman that can tell a man he is ridiculous; if I meddle I shall tell him he is mad."

I know not whether Madame Bonaparte achieved her commission to the Consul Cambacérès; but this I know, that although always highly distinguished for his knowledge, his politeness, and his dinners, he yet always remained that which had so highly discomposed the First Consul.

Cambacérès had a charming grand-niece, the daughter of his nephew, M. Duvidal de Montferrier. I have always wondered that he did not place her at the head of his establishment; but perhaps he was terrified by the aspect of her companion, whom it would have been difficult to exclude, for he was the husband, and the most jealous upon earth! Among the events of life, there are always some much more difficult to comprehend than others. Of this class was the marriage of Mademoiselle Rose de Montferrier with M. Bastarrêche, a banker of Bayonne, afterwards established at Paris in partnership with M. Jubié, the possessor of an immense fortune, but the most frightful of monsters.

It would be impossible faithfully to portray Mademoiselle Rose de Montferrier at the age of eighteen, because, with eyes and profile of corresponding beauty, her principal charms consisted of a nymph-like figure, and a complexion of which no comparison can give an idea. It was superior even to Madame Murat's; it breathed an animation, a warmth of colouring which, without metaphor, reminded one of the flower whose name she bore, and with the delicacy of its tints was combined the velvet of the peach.

Considering the high position of Cambacérès, it was naturally expected that Mademoiselle de Montferrier would make a brilliant match. But long afterwards, even after the death of M. de Bastarrêche, Napoleon could not forgive Cambacérès for consenting to it: "It is the Beauty and the Beast realized," said he. All Paris heard with surprise that the young lady showed no repugnance; and with this news circulated magnificent details of the splendid equipages and wedding-dresses; nothing was talked of but diamonds, pearls, and jewels innumerable given by *Azor*.*
"*Ah!*" said the First Consul, "*the present makes us forget the future.*"

Before quitting the Consul Cambacérès, I must relate an adventure which happened about this time. A Portuguese, named Don Alexander de Souza, had just arrived in Paris, on his road to (or from) an embassy at Rome.

* "*La Belle et la Bête, ou Azor et Zemire,*" an opera then in vogue.

M. de Souza was a very little man, about four feet ten or eleven inches high, and the whole of his delicate person cast in a most diminutive mould: he was not only thin, but absolutely shrivelled; yet he had the air of a gentleman, and his manners were those of a person of quality. The authorities received him with something more than the cordiality due to the friend of our enemies, and M. de Souza had nothing to complain of on his passage through Paris. The Second Consul would not let slip such an opportunity to give a sumptuous dinner. All the authorities were invited, and many of his friends; Junot and I were of the number, as were Duroc, Lannes, and Mortier, now Duke of Treviso, and then Commandant of the First Military Division.

I have not before mentioned this excellent man or his wife, all goodness, simplicity, and gentleness. He was Junot's superior as Commandant of the Division, while Junot was only Commandant of Paris; but we lived on the best and most friendly terms; for General Mortier was, and still is, the best and most worthy of men; but at this period he would laugh like a child, and his mirth sometimes compromised the dignity of the General Commandant's epaulettes.*

M. de Souza, on occasion of this dinner, wore a magnificent coat of Segovian cloth, embroidered in gold with a perfection we cannot attain in France. A frill of fine cambric rose almost imperceptibly at the top of his well-buttoned coat, in the English fashion, and his head displayed a peruke *à la Pitt*, more fully to exemplify that

---

* General, afterwards Marshal, Mortier was killed on the 28th of July, 1835, while riding by the side of Louis Philippe on the Boulevard du Temple opposite the Jardin Turc, by the explosion of the infernal machine invented and fired by Fieschi, with the intention of killing the King and his two sons.

Portugal was not only the very humble servant of England, but equally the submissive slave of her minister.

M. de Souza was seated at table between me and Madame Jolivet, wife of a Councillor of State. All the civilities lavished on the foreign traveller failed to banish the ennui with which this republican land seemed to inspire him. I was obliged to stifle my yawns in answering some trifling questions, and had little hope of a gayer termination of the repast, when an incident, certainly not included in the instructions of Cambacérès to his *maîtres d'hôtel*, gave a new turn to the aspect of affairs.

Cambacérès had for some time placed his household on a very respectable footing: his domestics had all the superb livery of the Consuls, and the *maîtres d'hôtel* had exchanged their black dresses for maroon cloth, with wrought gold buttons. There were always two courses at the Second Consul's, and as each course consisted of eighteen or twenty removes, it may be supposed the arm of the *maître d'hôtel* intruded pretty frequently between each of the guests; but poor little Souza's stature presented no obstacle; the dishes passed over his head; and on one of these occasions, one of the purveyor's gold buttons, being loose, hitched in the little gentleman's wig and carried it off.

The catastrophe was sudden, and no one knew how it had happened; even the *maître d'hôtel* himself had moved some distance before he discovered his involuntary theft; meanwhile the bewildered eyes of M. de Souza were seeking his wig in the direction of the ceiling, as if he imagined it had really taken wings, and those of the thirty persons around him, fixed on his startled figure, caused him an embarrassment which completed the burlesque of his appearance.

Yet we should all have behaved decently had he taken

the accident in good part; but, wishing to be dignified under his misfortune, he thought, perhaps, to impress us vastly by saying, with the utmost seriousness, to the *maître d'hôtel*, who came in all haste to apologize:

"Sir, will you restore me my wig?" And he set to work to replace it; but the discomposure which was evident through all his studied calmness prevented his accurately distinguishing the position of the tuft *à la Pitt*, and the wig, to my inexpressible satisfaction, was put on all askew, so that the tuft just surmounted the right ear, till Madame Jolivet, in a tone of more than usual acerbity (for she was offended at the incivility of her neighbour, who had not addressed a word to her since he had conducted her to her seat), said to him, "Sir, your wig is awry;" and as she spoke she obligingly raised her hand to the head of the little gentleman, who bounded away from her friendly assistance with a vivacity that had nearly dashed me to the ground.

I had avoided looking at either my husband or General Mortier, certain that my suppressed laughter must have burst forth; it became, however, at length uncontrollable, and appeared equally to master the whole company; for no sooner had mine exploded than a mad and inextinguishable peal resounded from every side; but General Mortier's was loudest, and so violent as to oblige him eventually to rise from table. The polite host, on whose imperfect vision this by-play was lost, no sooner understood the matter than he exhausted himself in apologies to M. de Souza, who, while panting with rage, replied, bowing, that it was of no consequence; and the unfortunate wig, in spite of Madame Jolivet's officious care, remained awry. General Mortier, I am sure, will to this day remember that dinner and the hearty laugh it afforded him.

Having mentioned Mortier, I must complete the portrait

of a friend. General Edward Mortier, at the time I knew him, in 1800, was of about the same age as most of the general officers of the army; and this similarity of years is not surprising, for the youth of France, inflamed with the love of their country and the desire of defending her, simultaneously deserted their firesides to enter the service.

These young men left their cherished families and brilliant fortunes, that offered them all the enjoyments of luxury, for hard couches and munition bread, which they were seen carrying on the bayonet, gaily singing the *Marseillaise*. But of all this bright and valorous troop not a single young man was seen running about Paris exciting the people to revolt, shouting at the Clubs, breaking the lamps, committing, in short, the acts of men at once divested of reason and disaffected to public order.

General Mortier lodged in a large Hôtel in the Rue des Capucines, with his wife, his sister-in-law, and a young family. In the same house were Madame César Berthier (whose husband was under the command of General Mortier), General Menard, and another. General Mortier had married a young and charming wife, who inspired me at first sight with friendship.

Without being extremely pretty, or in any other way personally remarkable, she pleased by an expression of mildness, and a general gracefulness which prepossessed at the first glance. A good mother, and fond of her home, from which it was difficult to entice her, her thoughts were chiefly devoted to the domestic happiness of her husband and family. She had an agreeable sister, perhaps even prettier than Madame Mortier, but less pleasing, as she had more formality and self-love.

In this house we seemed, from the moment of entering, to breathe peace and happiness. I felt myself cheerful as soon as I set my foot upon the staircase; but these sensations would all have vanished had I but mistaken the door and entered the ground-floor, where a clamour prevailed that might have typified the infernal regions.

General César Berthier, brother of the Minister of War, might be a very good soldier: I am no judge of such matters. All I can say is, that he had a very genteel and agreeable wife, whom he made miserable with so little reserve that I speak of it no more openly than he himself did in my presence, whom he scarcely knew. Madame César Berthier was sister of Madame Leopold Berthier; but the manners of the two brothers widely differed. Leopold, with more amenity of language and more disposition to please than César, does not appear to have had much power over the heart of his wife, for she divorced him to marry General Lasalle, the most amusing and bravest of profligate hussars. Leopold had wit, a qualification very scarce with César; and his stammer and bluntness of language spoiled the little he had. Both ladies were natives of Versailles; their maiden name was d'Aiguillon, but they were no way related to the ducal house of that name.

Madame César, when young, must have been very engaging, for she was well shaped, had a little turn-up nose, fair hair, and arms of remarkable beauty. At the time I knew her she was beginning to be marked with an eruption, but she was still young, and on the whole a pretty and elegant woman, fond of the toilet, and successful in its disposition. Her daughter, Madame Bruyère, is a charming woman.

My esteem for General Mortier was first inspired by my husband, who had much regard for him, and held both his civil character and military talents in high respect.*

---

* The military reputation of General Mortier has no need of my pen to illustrate it in its brilliancy; but I would fain instance his integrity in Hanover, which glorious era and many other achievements of his life are attested by the eloquent lines of M. Bignon.

Probity and honour were amongst his conspicuous virtues. Junot, who was restive under authority, and knew how to obey only one man, was sometimes at issue with his superior, which always grieved him. I have often seen him, after writing a letter, repent, and immediately disavow it; and constantly on such occasions have I been witness of General Mortier's kindness of character.

Though young, he had the advantage of Junot in years, and slight as was the difference, it justified him in offering some fraternal and jesting remonstrances to his junior, and sparing him many an unpleasant collision with the First Consul, provoked by his hot-headedness, which would certainly have been magnified by such men as Bourrienne, Fouché, and some others, who, by their situation about the First Consul, had access to his ear to prejudice those who enjoyed his favour. General Mortier's post gave him ample means of mischief, but he never injured a single individual.

Mortier was distinguished from the moment of his entrance into the service. He first joined the Army of the North, then that of the Rhine; and afterwards, in our day of misfortune, he valiantly seconded Masséna in the defeat of the Austro-Russian army. In the Moretta-Thal, near Schwitz, he had a remarkable engagement, in which he repulsed General Rosenberg, just arrived from Italy with Russian troops to fall upon us; an action which had a direct influence on our fate, and France ought to bear sincere gratitude towards all who belonged to this Army of the Danube.

His conquest of the Electorate of Hanover, with an army inferior in number by more than two-thirds to that of the enemy; in short, the convention of Sühlingen constitutes an honourable monument, which Marshal Mortier raised at once to the glory of his country and to his own. Again, he was in a most perilous situation at Diernstein,* on the banks

* In 1805.

of the Danube, with only five thousand men of the Gazan division. Encountered by the Russian vanguard under the command of Prince Bagration, twenty-five thousand strong, he not only resisted, but forced his passage, and rejoined the main army on the opposite side of the river.

At the head of the Eighth Corps in the next campaign, 1806, he attacked the Elector of Hesse Cassel, and in one day the whole of Westphalia fell into our hands, with the treasure, provisions, and military stores of the enemy. Mortier might have been enriched by more than glory in this action; but he left to his country the charge of providing him with a recompense. Some weeks afterwards he took possession in the name of France of the Electorate of Hanover, which his sword had conquered two years previously. Here, though as Marshal Commanding-in-Chief, and as it were thrice-puissant Pro-Consul, he might have exercised his power as he would—ask the inhabitants! They will tell you, even to this day, that Mortier's conduct was that of an honest soldier.

Next came the day of Friedland, to which he valiantly contributed. Then he went to take a command in the Peninsula. The victory of Ocaña, in destroying the strongest of the insurgent armies, composed of fifty thousand men, while the French were but twenty-five thousand, was of immense importance to the interest of France, for it decided the invasion of Andalusia. Having penetrated the Sierra Morena, he did not entangle himself in its defiles; but, leaving that task to Marshal Victor, he traversed Spanish Estremadura, laid siege to Badajos, carried it at the end of fifty-four days, and made seven thousand prisoners.

Returning from thence to Russia at the head of the Young Guard, he gave new proofs of devotion to his country and its Chief. Then came the campaign of 1813. Still in command of the Young Guard, Mortier's conduct was, like the past, faithful and brave. Lutzen, Kœnigswartha, Bautzen, Hochkirch, Wurtschen, and Reichenbach, saw his efforts, sometimes unsuccessful, but never useless.

In the battle of Dresden, again, he deserved praise. He defended, step by step, the soil of his country. Overcome by the Prince of Sweden and General Bulow, he fought not the less bravely at Craonne, La Fère, Provins, Nangis, Meaux, Lagny, Saint Mandé, and at length at Paris.

In retiring to his estate at Plessis Lalande, Marshal Mortier has had leisure to meditate on the progressive misfortunes of his country, that country which he had served so gloriously. I have experienced a moment's happiness in retracing so illustrious a life. It has not many parallels.

CHAPTER XIII.

The Quintidi and the Parade at the Tuileries—The Young Man with the Petition—The First Consul and the Young Man—The Governor of the Bastille and the Pension—M. De Latude, and Forty Years in a Dungeon—M. de Sartine and Recriminations—Vincennes, the Bastille, and Bicêtre—Santerre, Rossignol and Ronsin—The Dynamometer—The Revolutionary Army and the Infernal Legions—The Girl and the Burned Village—General Charbonnier and the Aide-de-camp—"Art thou a good Patriot?"—General Vandamme and his Sabre Exercise—The Village *Ultérieur*—The Scheldt a Fine Road.

ONE Quintidi,* at the moment that the First Consul was descending to hold the review in the court of the Tuileries, an event happened sufficiently singular to attract attention and interest. In the dense crowd that surrounded the line was a young man of about fifteen, dressed in a worn but neat black coat, which indicated that its master was above the hireling class. His figure was interesting; he was pale, and his neighbours observed that he trembled violently, often put his hand to his bosom, and appeared impatient to see the First Consul.

When the drums beat the young man's emotion became so powerful that his breast was seen to swell with the palpitation of his heart. The First Consul descended the stairs,

* One of the ten days of which the "week" consisted—in the Revolutionary Calendar.

and, as he reached the middle of the vestibule, the young man threw himself before him and presented a paper. The last few months had so teemed with plots and attempts against the life of the First Consul that twenty arms, all strangers to his suite, were instantly stretched forth to seize the boy, who, raising his hand and fixing an imploring look on the First Consul, still held forward his petition.

"Leave the young man—I am going to speak to him," said the First Consul; and advancing towards him: "What do you want, my boy?" demanded he.

The young man could not reply, but falling on his knees, presented his petition. The First Consul read it with an expression of countenance which struck all who surrounded him. His eyes then rested with a look of deep commiseration on the still kneeling young man, to whom he said:

"Rise, *mon enfant;* we kneel to God alone. Is your mother still in Paris?"

An almost stifled "Yes" escaped the lips of the young petitioner.

"Acquaint her that a pension of twelve hundred francs is awarded her, and will commence six months prior to the present date."

At the sound of these words the poor youth fell again on his knees, raising towards the First Consul his tearful eyes and trembling hands, which endeavoured to seize his; but his emotion was too violent. His extreme paleness increased on hearing the favour granted to his mother; but it speedily gave place to purple. The veins of his forehead swelled till they were ready to burst, his eyes closed, he fell insensible at the feet of the First Consul, and Nature bringing her own relief, a profuse hemorrhage ensued, and the First Consul was covered with the poor boy's blood.

"A surgeon," cried he instantly—"a surgeon!" But

joy, it is said, is never fatal; the young man recovered his senses, and bursting into tears, seized almost forcibly the hand of the First Consul, and kissed it with transport.

"You are a Providence to my family!" exclaimed the youth; "I will pray for you every day of my life."

The First Consul smiled as he pressed the young hand, and pursued his way to the review; but before he mounted his horse he recommended the boy to Junot, and to the Minister of War, and then gave him a friendly salute, saying:

"If you wish to enter the service, apply to the General Commanding the City of Paris; he will mention it to the Minister of War, and we will seek to do something for you."

The young man answered only with a low bow, and followed the First Consul to the steps of the portico. He saw the beautiful *Désiré* brought; the General, leaping lightly to his saddle, galloped off, and was soon amidst the thronged ranks of his soldiers, followed by a numerous and brilliant suite, who surrounded him as the satellites of a planet constantly revolve around their centre; he saw those grenadiers, still black with the powder of Marengo, with their high leather caps overshadowing their faces; that fine regiment of *chasseurs*, then commanded by Eugène Beauharnais; those gilded uniforms, those horses, that military music; and last of all the magician, who fascinated with his look of fire all who approached the sphere of his influence. . . . The young man cried: "Yes, I will serve! I will be a soldier, that a ray of that glory may fall on me."

This young man, so unfortunate and so grateful, was the son of Monsieur Delaunay, Governor of the Bastille, massacred the 14th of July, 1789.

Junot said to me one day: "I must bring you into conversation with a man of whom you have certainly heard, and whose Memoirs, you have, of course, read; M. de Latude—do you know him?" "Ah!" I exclaimed; "M. de Latude, and you ask whether I know him? I do not know him personally, but I am well acquainted with his misfortunes, which have so deeply interested me, that I should be delighted to see himself." Two days afterwards Junot told me: "This morning M. de Latude will breakfast with us; he will bring Madame Lemoine, for he no more moves without her than without his ladder."

It is well known that M. de Latude, when young, wanting to obtain a favour of Madame de Pompadour, thought to excite her gratitude by writing her a letter with his own signature, announcing that accident had just discovered to him a plot for poisoning the Marchioness by means of a box of confectionery, to be conveyed to her that very day, after which, mixing a harmless emetic with the sweetmeats, he despatched them anonymously. M. de Sartine, the Lieutenant-General of Police, was summoned in haste, and fell into great disgrace for having suffered so heinous a plot to be detected by a stranger. Returning enraged to his office, he accused his first commissary; he the second; and so on, till all their recriminations ended in a full disclosure of M. de Latude's artifice.

M. de Sartine's vengeance was proportioned, not to the offence, but to the apprehensions he had endured from the favourite's displeasure; and the unfortunate intriguer was thrown into a dungeon at Vincennes, without any judicial form. At the end of three years he escaped by means of a ladder manufactured from his own linen, was retaken and confined ten years in the Bastille, when he escaped a second time; was again overtaken by the terrible vengeance of the Director of the Police, and finding a new dungeon at Bicêtre, was there recommended to the extreme rigour of the governor: in short, his captivity for a harmless though unworthy trick lasted thirty-seven years. On his first release, Brunetière had been acquainted with him and had told me this story, but had afterwards lost sight of him, to my great regret, for I ardently desired to see M. de Latude.

I received him with a respect and tenderness truly sincere; but my enthusiasm was not proof against an old dotard repeating his oft-told tale with a soporific prolixity, which occasioned me in despair to address Madame Lemoine. She was a retired mercer, who one day picking up a packet in the Rue Saint Denis, found it to be a tablet made of the crumb of bread on which, with a large fish-bone for his pen, the poor sufferer had written in his own blood the history of his imprisonment.

Madame de Pompadour and M. de Sartine being both dead, Madame Lemoine, who lost no time in applying to the Superintendent of Police, had little difficulty in procuring his liberation in consideration of his long detention; she devoted herself wholly to her grateful *protégé*, who always called her his guardian angel; and uniting their scanty means (for De Latude enjoyed from funds at Junot's disposal a pension of two hundred francs), they lived together nearly on the terms of father and daughter.

His ladder was a real masterpiece of human patience; it contained a hundred pieces of wood, all cut with a penknife from the faggots which served him for fuel; and the cord, composed of single threads drawn from his linen, and twisted by himself, was nearly of the thickness of my thumb. On his first flight from Vincennes his ladder was not long enough by fifteen feet, and he was therefore obliged to drop down, and dislocated his wrist.

Madame Lemoine told us that the First Consul had desired to see M. de Latude, and I pictured to myself how completely he, who could not tolerate much talking from his most intimate friends, would be wearied by the puerile and tedious loquacity of this *affecting victim of despotism*, who had passed forty-one years of his life in various prisons. The visit of M. de Latude left a distressing impression on my mind, for it destroyed a pleasing illusion.

In the course of the same week I experienced a surprise of a different kind, also caused by a person I had never seen, and whose name sounded in my ears like a cry of carnage.

One morning, while we were at breakfast, a tall stout man presented himself, of an unobjectionable appearance and countenance. Junot saluted him; but I perceived that his salute was constrained. Our breakfast over, we passed into the drawing-room. The stranger walked forward with a firm and resolute step. "This is an odd person," thought I to myself. Junot offered him coffee, which he refused with, "No, thank you, General, I never take my cup in the morning; as for a small glass, if Mademoiselle will permit——'

"It is my wife," said Junot in a very serious tone.

"Ah! *c'est la citoyenne Junot!*" and the personage began to stare at me with an attention which excited rather merriment than anger; for it was evident that this man, though rude by nature, had no intention of being so. "Ah! it is the *citoyenne Junot! Diable*, colleague, you have not taken your soundings ill."

I whispered to Junot to tell me the name of this *General*, for it seemed that he had at least pretensions to that title. "No," replied Junot, "you must guess it; it is a name prodigiously well known."

Meanwhile the tall man was conversing with Junot's first aide-de-camp, M. Laborde; but I could gather nothing from the absurdities, solecisms, and ill-arranged sentences which were passing between them.

An instrument lay on the table, invented and constructed

by Reigner, the mechanical armourer, for measuring the human strength, by pressing with the two hands two bands of leather which confine a semicircular plate of brass, engraved with a scale, and furnished with a needle, which is made to move in proportion to the force of the pressure, and indicates by the number to which it points the strength of the individual.

Junot took it up, and pressing it, made the needle run so rapidly and forcibly, that it nearly struck the opposite extremity of the dynamometer, indicating a very unusual strength of wrist. The strange General then took up the instrument, but instead of using, examined it, and then said, laughing:

"Stay! that resembles those implements I took with me when I went down yonder to the west with Ronsin and Rossignol. I had also a learned aide-de-camp, a mathematician, with me.

"Well, when the Convention appointed me to command the republican army, I refused, because I know myself, and know that I am not strong in the article of manœuvres: I refused, but what of that? What the Convention chose, it chose. I was obliged to take the command of one of the invincible columns. Ronsin commanded another, and poor Rossignol, he had a third. Well, I told you just now I had a learned aide-de-camp. He declared to the Convention that all the instruments, of which he gave me a list, would be required for this campaign, and they gave me them all. Two little waggons were filled with them.

"Away I carried them; my aide-de-camp, Platière,* made use of them, and then I sold them;" and he ended with a loud laugh; but my laughter stopped short. This speech had made him known.

---

* Nephew of Roland the minister, whose name was Roland de la Platière.

It was Santerre! Santerre the brewer, of the Faubourg Saint Antoine, who was, on the 11th of August, 1792, appointed Commandant of the Parisian National Guard, who had the custody of the Royal Family in the Temple, and who commanded the troops on the 21st of January, 1793; he was first sent into La Vendée to command a corps with those two wretches whom he had named in my hearing. I had heard from inhabitants of Saumur, Montagne, and other neighbouring towns, frightful details of all that Santerre had done in La Vendée.

Though his name is known as associated with the great political tragedy, yet it figures in few lines of history, and on one or two pages so stained with blood as to destroy the possibility of distinguishing those actions in which he figures. I knew much of him, but was, I confess, far from imagining that this man would himself become the narrator, to afford me new light on the horrors committed in La Vendée by what were called the *Infernal Legions*, commanded by himself, Ronsin, and Rossignol. He required no hint to assure us, himself, that he had written to the Ministry of War, and at the same time to the authorities, advising them to send waggons loaded with combustibles into La Vendée to consume all the woods and coppices, and even all furze, heath, and broom, by fire, so as to cut off the retreat of the Vendeans.

"It is a terrible conception to be tolerated by reason," said Junot, when this man was gone; "and yet perhaps humanity itself would have followed that course, in order to put an end in six months to evils which lasted forty. It would at least have been more humane than letting loose upon them, like bloodhounds, the capitulated garrisons of Mayence and Valenciennes, and afterwards those *Infernal Legions*, led by the dregs of the most abject Jacobins."

I asked him why he would not tell me Santerre's name.

"Faith, because I did not care to introduce to you so creditable an acquaintance. I am not best pleased with his visits, and accordingly they are not very frequent. He is an odious creature; he is neither military, civil, citizen, nor artisan; he abandoned his own profession, and all the professions at whose doors he has knocked have refused him admission. Republican General as I am, it is not possible for me to give my hand in the middle of the Tuileries gardens to Santerre, *the Revolutionary General*, which means General commanding the Revolutionary army, where the guillotine marched always in readiness, like a piece of artillery with the match alight.[*] I do not like such characters," said Junot; "I am a Republican by taste and principle; but I have a horror of the blood, the massacres, the confiscations, which constituted that frightful system of horror under which France groaned for several years. Santerre is a wretch, and he is under a sort of surveillance from the Staff of Paris, which obliges him to present himself, I believe, once a fortnight. Well! this man, I am sure, says now that I am haughty, and have not fraternized with him; no, certainly I have not, because I cannot esteem him."

I inquired whether he was brave; several officers, who had arrived since his departure, answered no—that is, that his reputation was extremely doubtful.

Santerre once wrote to the Commune of Paris: "Learn that I have burned all the mills, with one single exception, and this narrowly escaped; I fortunately learned before setting it on fire that it belonged to a patriot."

In a hamlet near Savenay he met with a young girl, who pleased him, and he told her so. Her instant answer was, that she was a Vendean, and he not only a Blue, but a chief

---

[*] Lannes, Bessières, and several other Generals of Napoleon were known to entertain similar views.

of the Blues, and that, consequently, there existed between them obstacles which could never be removed. The girl had a grandfather, sixty-five years of age. The Chief of the Blues had the village again ransacked, and finally burned; he then carried off the young girl and her unhappy grandfather, who died in a state of idiocy from grief! Poor old man, and poor France!

At this period of my life, no day passed that I did not see Napoleon, at least, unless my mother was very ill. It was easy for me to seek a conversation with him upon what I had seen, nor was he backward in questioning me about all that interested me, so that he was not long in ignorance of Santerre's visit.

"How is that?" said Napoleon; "I thought he had been dead these four years. Well, what say you of him? Is he not handsome and engaging? These are the honest men who would fain see the happy days of 1793 restored. M. Santerre would find it delightful to obtain the epaulettes of Lieutenant-General, as he did those of Brigadier-General, by leading to the scaffold men less worthless than himself. Did you know Rossignol?" I had never seen him; but in the course of a quarter of an hour I was perfectly acquainted with him, for his own question brought to the First Consul's recollection accumulated details respecting this man, Ronsin, and Charpentier, which were really curious; and Junot afterwards filled up their outlines for me.

"He is one of the most remarkable evidences that we can oppose to all that the manifestoes have said against us," observed the First Consul, when the name of Charpentier was mentioned. "That man commanded an army—that of the Rhine, at a time when we had everything to fear; all our frontiers were exposed, like a dismantled town after an assault, yet perhaps no victories have been more splendid than those then gained by young soldiers, in absolute want of bread, shoes, money, and of clothing, and under Generals such as Charbonnier, Santerre, Ronsin, and Rossignol. Rossignol, speaking of *Les Echelles*, in Savoy, said one day in a Committee of Public Safety, with perfect seriousness:

"'I can easily understand that my infantry could pass, because my men, however loaded, can mount a *ladder;* but for my cavalry and artillery, though a thousand devils should interfere, they could not teach a horse to climb a *ladder.*'"

On the subject of General Charbonnier no one was more amusing than M. Dietrich, the lively young officer I met at the Opera the evening of the explosion of the infernal machine. He had served on the staff in Holland, when Vandamme, happily for the army, was also there. It was ascertained one morning that the English had landed. M. Dietrich was instantly sent to the headquarters of the General-in-Chief; this was General Charbonnier, who, though it was but little after nine, was found at table, and already half intoxicated.

"General," said he to the unprepared Commander, "the English have landed—your orders are urgently wanted; be pleased to honour me with them, and I will instantly set out again."

The booby of a pretended warrior looked at him with eyes somewhat unsteady, and inquired:

"Art thou a good patriot?"

"Yes, my General."

"Well! seat yourself there; breakfast, and send the English to the devil."

M. Dietrich was then but eighteen, full of gaiety and mirth; and certainly his mirth could not want a better occasion; but he feared General Vandamme, who, he very well knew, was capable of shortening him by the head had he failed in any part of his duty. Aware of the critical nature of his situation, he endeavoured, while the General-in-Chief employed himself in swallowing some dozens of Ostend oysters, to persuade him into giving orders for the regiments to march; but, finding all his efforts unavailing, he was at length resolving to return to the Chief of the Staff, when Charbonnier, who, like all drunkards, had one fixed notion, recalled him.

"Stay there," said he; "I am going to speak to you—take a glass."

"Thank you, General, but it is too early; I am neither hungry nor thirsty."

"What! too early! I am wrong, then, in drinking and getting my breakfast? Well, thou art but a silly prattler. Take a glass, I tell you."

M. Dietrich accordingly drank his health, in hopes of soothing him and being permitted to retire, but the latter was more easily proposed than executed.

"So," said the General, "you are a good patriot!"

"Yes, General, a very good patriot; but, unhappily, so insignificant a point is not the present question. A serious object has brought me here. General Vandamme is expecting me, and is, meanwhile, exposed to the enemy's fire."

There had been some fighting, and an hour's suspension of arms had been agreed on, to wait M. Dietrich's return. Vandamme was one of the bravest men in the world, but fiery and passionate, and quite capable of surprising and killing General Charbonnier. The young officer's head was filled with these reflections; he had no hope but in the General's speedily rising from table, and that a cup of coffee might sober him. Suddenly he heard the cannon, and a brisk fire of musketry; and, starting up, he exclaimed:

"Do you hear? do you hear? In the name of Heaven, General, call one of your officers, and send orders!"

"What is the matter now? Leave me alone, you and your —— Republic. Leave me alone to finish my breakfast as becomes a General-in-Chief."

"But, General——"

"Ah! this is too much; I repeat to you, once for all, leave me in peace."

"But, General, you are exposing the army to the greatest danger."

"Bhrrr!"—and he began to sing.

"General Vandamme's division cannot possibly hold out without support. It will be compelled to yield the ground! Where would you have it take refuge if obliged to fly?"

"Ah! they in flight!—they! No, no!—and if they should, leave them alone; the fools know the roads well enough."

At that moment the quick gallop of a horse was heard; in less than a minute General Vandamme was in the room, and his sabre whizzing round the ears of Charbonnier.

A nobler figure than that of General Vandamme at this period cannot well be imagined; his finely-formed head, his regular features, his beautiful curly hair, his glistening eyes, which, when angry, seemed to flash fire, his exquisitely-turned hand, altogether opposed a perfect contrast to the ignoble appearance of Charbonnier. Vandamme, justly incensed, stood before his brutalized chief, making his sword fly round his head, and recommending him to prepare for instant death.

"This is thy last hour, wretch! How! is thy soul base enough to deliver up thy comrades to be massacred by the enemy, and that enemy the English? Let everything be instantly in order; let the troops march; or rather stay here and sleep thyself sober; the army has no need of thee to conquer." And pushing Charbonnier from him with a violence that flung him to the farther end of the room, he went away with Dietrich, and both jumping on their horses, rushed into the midst of the fire just as the artillery opened.

Vandamme's valour in circumstances doubly critical from the stupidity or treason of Charbonnier was eminently conspicuous. The incapacity of one might have destroyed the army, but the courage and conduct of the other saved it. This was the first attempted descent of the English, before the arrival of Brune in Holland.

Charbonnier, after the departure of Vandamme, began to grow gradually sober. The cannonading was so incessant that he could not doubt the whole army was engaged. In the midst of his intemperance, and of that thick cloud which blocked up every avenue to his brain, he yet retained some portion of that bravery which made him originally remarkable, and had procured for him the appointment of a military Proconsul. He plunged his head into water, and mounting his horse, hastened to the battle; but all was already retrieved by General Vandamme.

Afterwards, when peace and order had revisited us, the First Consul awarded to each his due. Charbonnier returned to the rank of a Chief of Battalion, and had the command of a garrison. It was this same Charbonnier, who, receiving one day despatches from the Convention, which directed him to wait ulterior orders (*des ordres ultérieurs*), spent a whole week in seeking on the map the village *Ultérieur*.

Another time, when he was giving very particular orders for the passage of cavalry from Antwerp, the Commissary, who had attentively followed Charbonnier's finger on the map, ventured to ask him where the road was.

"What!" said the General; "do not you see this road?"

"I see nothing, General."

"How!" and he stamped, for he was passionate—"how! not see that road! It is large enough, however; it is superb! I am sure it is more than a hundred feet wide!"

I can well believe that, for it was the Scheldt!

CHAPTER XIV.

M. Charles—Unimpeachable Antecedents—Madame Bonaparte at the Serbelloni Palace—Espionage of Madame Leclerc—Bonaparte's Eyes, and the Police of the Hall of the Throne—Arrest of M. Charles at Milan—Conversation with Pauline Bonaparte—Reciprocal Affliction and Consolation—Madame Bonaparte's first Residence at Malmaison—Madame La Générale—Sister Rosalie and the Almoner of the Army of Egypt—The Master in the Master's absence—Madame Bonaparte's Divorce advised by Gohier—Return from the Army of Egypt, and Banishment of M. Charles—Bonaparte and Duroc on the Boulevards, and Unexpected Encounter—Junot's Friendship for M. Charles—The true Friends of Junot.

AMONGST the friends introduced to me by Junot were some whose names especially attracted my attention; for instance, Monsieur Charles, born at Romans, of an obscure family, who entered the army at the commencement of the Revolution, in a troop of cavalry formed at Besançon, and was a Lieutenant, when being ordered into Italy, he was attached as Assistant to the Adjutant-General Leclerc at Milan; and when the latter, on his marriage with Pauline Bonaparte, was made a Brigadier-General, Charles was also promoted to the rank of Captain, and appointed aide-de-camp to the General.

Just at this time Madame Bonaparte (Josephine) arrived at Milan, and lodged at the Serbelloni Palace, where she had an establishment as a Sovereign.

M. Charles was introduced to her in common with all the officers of the army, and as he belonged to the establishment of General Bonaparte's brother-in-law, he obtained more than common attention.

Napoleon, almost always absent from home, was either occupied in Milan itself, or in journeys in the neighbourhood; he therefore did not see anything that transpired there but what fell immediately beneath his own eye. His sister, Madame Leclerc, was not like him; she was unoccupied, but desired some sort of employment, and therefore commenced a strict watch over the conduct of a sister-in-law whom she hated, such an occupation being as good as any other; but I believe she deceived herself, for although she was not long in ascertaining that M. Charles and Madame Bonaparte were in close communication, and that this intimacy occupied much of their thoughts, she found that this attachment might be, but was not in fact, anything more than a tender friendship.

M. Charles was about twenty-seven or twenty-eight years of age; small, well-made, with good features, a dark clear complexion, and hair black as jet; he was altogether attractive, although a little deficient in the polish of elegant society. He wore a superb hussar's uniform covered with gold lace, and breakfasted at the Serbelloni Palace whenever Napoleon left it, and no one in the army or in Milan was a stranger to the interest Madame Bonaparte testified for him.

This fact reached at length the General-in-Chief. Through whom? Probably his own eyes! So it might certainly be presumed; for those penetrating eyes constituted the sole police of the Throne Room at the Tuileries: and such was their clearness and precision that the darkest corner of the Hall would scarcely avail to escape their keen inquisition. Be this as it may, at the headquarters of the Army of Italy it was suddenly rumoured that M. Charles had been arrested by order of the General-in-Chief, and would certainly be shot.

I do not answer for the cause of General Bonaparte's displeasure against M. Charles; I am narrating only, and though, like Werther, I should narrate the same thing for the tenth time, I could say no more than I do, that M. Charles was arrested against the will, and perhaps on account of *Madame la Générale-en-chef*, a proceeding grievous to both, at least so it may be presumed. Madame Leclerc, who was known to be *goodness itself*, said to me, " In short, conceive, Laurette, that my sister-in-law had nearly died of vexation; and we certainly do not die of vexation from merely parting with our friends. There must be more than friendship concerned in this matter. For my part, I have comforted my brother, who was very unhappy. He was aware of it all when he came to Paris, before he set out for Egypt. Poor brother !"

And the kind sister pitied him most liberally for the unhappiness which she herself had probably caused him. Madame Leclerc was a droll character to study. She has been well sketched and well painted; but so strange was her character, that no one has ever succeeded in making a finished picture of her.

M. Charles was obliged to quit the Army of Italy, and, returning to Paris, the interest of Madame Bonaparte procured him a partnership in the mercantile house of Louis Bodin; there he made a great fortune, which was afterwards impaired. He kept a good house, and associated with the bankers, the only class which held regular receptions at the time of Madame Bonaparte's return from Italy, and her husband's departure for Egypt. It was then she purchased Malmaison, and established herself there.

A friend of my mother, who was inhabiting Ruelle, used to tell us that she saw *Madame la Générale*, the name she was known by in the village, walking very late in the garden. " By moonlight," said Rosalie, " and when, leaning on the arm of her son, her white dress and flowing veil are contrasted with his dingy attire of black or blue, the effect is quite fantastic. They might be taken for phantoms. Poor woman ! she is then thinking, perhaps, of her first husband, who fell a victim to the Revolutionary executioners ! Thinking also of him by whom, through the mercy of Providence, her loss is repaired, and of whom a cannon-ball may in a moment deprive her. How does he manage, down yonder, to hear Mass amidst all those Turks, Mademoiselle Laure ?" asked the pious girl. " Why, I suppose he has a chaplain," answered I ; and at that time I really believed it.

Madame Bonaparte sometimes came to Paris to visit Barras, Madame Tallien, and Madame Gohier, to whom she was very partial ; sometimes she would also see her mother and brothers-in-law, but not often, for she did not like them ; the war, however, though certainly mutual, was not begun on their side. She was then in direct hostility with Joseph, the mildest and best of men, and at enmity with Madame Bonaparte the mother, and Madame Lucien, an angel of goodness. I know not what caused the animosity that had arisen between them, but I was sufficiently acquainted with Madame Lætitia and Madame Christine to answer for them.

Malmaison, at the time I am speaking of, was a pretty country house with agreeable environs, but very inconvenient and most unwholesome. Brunetière, who was somehow mixed up in the affair, told me that Madame Bonaparte had made this acquisition as a child buys a new toy that strikes her fancy, without considering whether it will long amuse her. The park was small, sloping on all sides, and resembled a pretty English garden.

It was enclosed, excepting the length of the lawn in front of the château, with a wall stretching along the road of St. Germain; the lawn was bordered with a ha-ha, on the brink of which stood a small flight of iron steps, affording a resting-place and a view over the road, which could also be seen from the park. The fine plantations that now surround the château, and all its out-offices, were not then in existence.

M. Charles inhabited Malmaison in the quality of master; friends, we know, have privileges. Gohier, who was always thrown into a brown study by the recollection of the 18th Brumaire, but was otherwise an honest and sensible man, strongly persuaded Josephine to a decided step.

"Divorce," said he, when all in tears she refused the advice he gave her to break off a connection which compromised her in the eyes of the world "divorce; you tell me it is only friendship that exists between M. Charles and yourself; but if that friendship is so strong that it impels you to violate the observances of the world, I shall say to you, as if it were love, divorce; because friendship so exclusive will stand in lieu of all other sentiments. Believe me, all this will cause you regret." Gohier was right; he saw the matter in its true light, but Josephine would not listen.

When, after his return from Egypt, Bonaparte was on the point of himself effecting what Gohier had some months previously advised should be done prudently and quietly, Josephine screamed, wept, and was in despair. She would not hear of a divorce when he was at a distance, much less could she endure it when the splendour of his glory enlightened all Europe with its rays; but in consenting to surrender his proposal, he exacted, as an absolute condition, the banishment of M. Charles, and her promise never to see him more.

Napoleon detested M. Charles; he never mentioned him, or suffered him to be named in his presence. But I know some incidents on this subject which have excessively surprised me, for I did not believe him susceptible of so much emotion.

One morning when Napoleon was walking out with Duroc to survey the works of the bridge of Austerlitz, which was then building, a cabriolet dashed at a rapid pace along the boulevard. Duroc felt the Emperor press his arm for support and rest heavily upon it, and saw him at the same time grow unusually pale. Duroc would have cried out for assistance, but the Emperor silenced him with, "It is nothing; be quiet!" The cabriolet contained M. Charles, whom Napoleon had not seen so close since he left Italy.

What could be the sentiment which agitated him? Was it still love for Josephine? He loved her no longer: he was then attached to an enchanting woman, the only one he ever really loved. Napoleon considered this man his enemy, and hated him.

Not so Junot; he had been intimately associated with M. Charles in Italy, and they entertained for each other a sincere friendship. Junot did not always bestow his regard so well; he was far more easily deceived by appearances than I was on his behalf, frequently granting his friendship where it was betrayed, while he denied it to his true friends. How long did he distress me respecting Duroc! but at length he came to his senses. Duroc was the best of friends.

M. Charles purchased, in the year 1803 or 1804, a property called Casan. His affairs being subsequently much embarrassed it was sold, and he returned to Romans, his native town, where he lived retired and respectably,

CHAPTER XV.

Superior men appreciators of Bonaparte—Rival Generals—Klèber's Feelings towards General Bonaparte—Klèber's Letters—Bonaparte's Eyes turned towards the East—Projects of a great Man—Desire of preserving Egypt—Explanation of Bonaparte's return from Egypt—The Army of Druses—The Successor of Klèber—General Menou—Junot, Lanusse, and the consequences of a Duel—Bonaparte's Enmity towards Tallien.

ALL the leaders of thought of the day have avoided either thinking or speaking ill of Napoleon. Châteaubriand, Lamartine, Victor Hugo, Casimir Delavigne, the Abbé de la Mennais, all these men have passed judgment on the Colossus; they have seen his faults, but have recognized his great qualities: these learned men have not spared their criticism, mingled with approbation. Klèber, though his enemy, yet profoundly admired him, because his fine genius was capable of appreciating greatness.

When Bonaparte was Commander-in-Chief in Italy, other Generals, jealous of that young head so useful to his country, could not assemble but they must discuss, with reflections not over-charitable, the military operations of the young General, who, as some said, after having announced his intention of conquering Italy, like another Hannibal, was now gone, like him, to take his rest at Capua. This was in allusion to his retiring on Piedmont after having threatened Lombardy.

Klèber, who had talent enough to understand this manœuvre, and who, being yet a stranger to Napoleon, was not then at variance with him (which, it may be observed, he uniformly was with the General commanding him), did full justice to Bonaparte's abilities, both military and civil; and on these occasions always defended him against the mediocrity which attacked him, with that vigour and generosity inspired by talent and courage.*

Bonaparte was haunted by visions of the East. He would sometimes dilate on this subject for three hours without intermission, and often uttered the greatest follies with inconceivable seriousness. He frequently conversed on the subject of the East with our friend Admiral Magon, questioning him upon India. Napoleon would listen with avidity, watching the Rear-Admiral's countenance, and seeming to snatch the words from his lips. Sometimes he would exclaim:

"It is there—it is in India we must attack the English power. It is there we must strike her! The Russians will not allow us a passage to Persia; well, then, we must get there by another road. I know that road, and I will take it!"

Originally, Turkey was the scene of his projects; but his ideas were afterwards very different, and more practicable. When the Egyptian expedition was at last decided on,

---

* Above four-and-twenty original letters of Klèber are in my possession. These letters are remarkable for their clearness and precision, and particularly for the admirable skill displayed by their writer at the very time when the English considered him ruined and without resource. Junot bore Klèber that animosity which he entertained towards all who disliked Napoleon; yet he appreciated him, for, having served under his orders in the Syrian expedition, he had had opportunities of observing his masculine and superior mind.—*Laure Junot.*

Napoleon said to Junot and to some others of his officers :

"I am going to repair, if possible, the misfortune of our ravaged or lost colonies. Egypt will be a magnificent compensation ; and the acquisition of that beautiful country for France shall be the object of this expedition."

Such were his predominant views during the passage, on his arrival, and while he resided there. How much did he suffer when he saw his fleet destroyed, and all the means of internal safety endangered by that loss!

Bonaparte's ardent passion for the retention of Egypt is so well known to all who were with him, that it appears to me impossible for the most perverted mind to see his return to Europe in any other light than as a struggle for the preservation of that colony, which in his very dreams formed a nucleus for the incessant discharge of shafts against England.

Was his project of forming a junction with an army of thirty thousand Druses near Mount Lebanon nothing? and that of conquering those parts of Egypt that were inhabited by tribes easily guided, uniting those tribes with the Druses, and attempting to penetrate into Persia, was this nothing?*

One day, speaking of Egypt, he made use of an expression which I then thought very extraordinary, and I jokingly reminded him of it three days before his coronation.

"It is vexatious," said he, "to have been prevented meeting my Druses ; *I missed my fortune.*'

* In the War Department were deposited some masks, made, it is said, in 1801. According to one version, they were designed to protect the soldier from excessive cold ; according to another, they were intended to preserve the men, their eyes especially, from the very fine sand with which the deserts between Russia and Persia are covered, as the Emperor proposed prosecuting his enterprise in that direction, after making peace with Alexander on the Neva, as he had already done on the Niemen.

General Menou had been long in the service before the breaking out of the Revolution; had served in India, and had acquired in his travels a love of the marvellous sufficiently amusing, but which prevented all reliance on his tales. It is a singular coincidence that this same General, the Marquis de Menou, who turned Turk in 1801, presided over the Constituent Assembly on the 19th of June, 1790, when those throngs were introduced, calling themselves Arabians, Chaldeans, Syrians, Americans, Poles, Prussians, etc., etc., and he very gravely replied to the oration of the Arabs: "Gentlemen, it was Arabia which gave the first lesson of philosophy to Europe: France now discharges the debt by giving you lessons of liberty." When commanding the Republican troops, he was defeated at Saumur by La Rochejaquelin and Lescure. On the 14th of October he commanded in Paris, but resigned.

Of an adventurous disposition, though no longer young, he joined the Egyptian expedition by his own desire. By the assassination of Kléber after the battle of Heliopolis, he, as senior, succeeded to the command. His administration was able, but, like that of the Generals of Madame de Pompadour and Madame du Barry, distinguished by the goodness of its suppers and the disgrace of its army.

Abercrombie, with 18,000 Englishmen, landed at this same strand of Aboukir, and Menou lost the battle of Canopus, and with it the possession of Egypt. Shut up in Alexandria, and cut off from all communication with the rest of his army, he had not even the consolation of effecting the reduction of Cairo, a charge which devolved upon Belliard: the definitive capitulation at length received his signature, and, returning to Europe, he was well received by Napoleon, who appointed him Administrator-General of Piedmont.

One day, soon after the arrival of General Vial, the

envoy of General *Abdalla* Menou, the First Consul being in his cabinet with Berthier, Junot, and Bourrienne, who were busily unsealing the numerous fumigated packets brought by General Vial, the First Consul hinted his intention of changing the command of the Eastern army; he spoke of Menou, lauded his pleasing manners in a drawing-room, his agreeable way of telling a story.

"But," added he, "all that is useless at the head of an army; and Kléber, with his cynical sayings and his rough exterior, is far better suited to the Army of Egypt in its present situation." The Generals then in Egypt came under consideration, and when Berthier named some of them he shook his head; at length he resumed the conversation after a long silence, and as if talking to himself:

"Regnier?—Damas?—Friant?—No, none of these.—Belliard?—He is a child, though a brave one.—Old Leclerc?—No.—Well! after all, Abdalla Joseph Menou serves our turn best yonder, Berthier; but we must give him an able chief of the staff, or rather second in command, and here we have a choice."

This suggested an idea to Junot. "General," said he, "you know best what you are about, but *I* know whom I should choose." The First Consul turned on him an interrogative look. "General Lanusse."

"Oh! oh! you do not bear malice?"

"Why should I, my General? I fought Lanusse for a foolish gaming quarrel, which, besides, was but a pretext. I thought he was not attached to you, that he partook the sentiments of General Damas."

"Oh! as to him, he does not like me, indeed! Well, I have a great mind to appoint him."

"General Damas, my General?"

"Yes. Lanusse has talent and courage, but Damas is not behind him in either, and as a general officer he is of quite a different calibre: besides, Lanusse has confounded democratical notions, and is in correspondence, as well as his brother, with a man so immoral as to compromise even his acquaintances; think of the effect M. Tallien's friendly support must produce. I do not like M. Tallien. I hate that man; he is wicked himself, and a corrupter of others. The two Lanusses are both gamesters, and they have learned it of him. But Damas, he is an Aristides."

This was true. Damas was one of those virtuous and extraordinary men whom nature but rarely moulds.

He died only two or three years ago, in the Rue du Saint Père, Faubourg Saint Germain, in the bosom of his numerous family; his funeral was simple (for his circumstances had been very limited), and borrowed all its solemnity from the presence of a group of Generals, his former brethren-in-arms. General Edward Colbert, his aide-de-camp in Egypt, pronounced his funeral oration, in which he professed his attachment to his former General.

CHAPTER XVI.

Lucien's Embassy to Madrid—Bonaparte's Orders relative to Egypt—Lucien's Letter to General Menou—A faithful Friend of the Republic—Reduction of Egypt, and Tardy Mission—Sicily—Naples and M. Alquier—The Sister of the Queen of the French—Mesdames de France at the Palace of Caserta—M. Goubaud, the Roman Painter—The Princesses and the Tricoloured Cravat—The Painter of the Emperor's and King of Rome's Cabinet.

AT this time, Lucien having accomplished the principal object of his embassy in Spain, turned his attention to his brother's orders respecting Egypt, and sent my brother-in-law, M. Geouffre, on a mission to General Menou; he had at first selected for that service M. Clement, first adjutant of the Consular Guard, and embarked him at Barcelona; but the secret had not been well kept; the English were apprized of the hour of sailing, and M. Clement, with his written instructions, fell into their hands.

Lucien was satisfied of my brother-in-law's entire devotion to him, and felt, moreover, assured that with his address, experience, and knowledge of the world, he would not suffer his mission to miscarry, even though he should be taken by the English, who lay in wait at the entrance of every port to take every vessel that ventured from shore.

The French ambassador obtained an order from the King of Spain for the arming of an American vessel; my brother-in-law embarked in the disguise of a sailor, and as far as Malta the voyage was favourable. There he was informed of Menou's capitulation; but not being able absolutely to rely on his authority, determined, as the safest course, to seek some Italian port, and attaching two of his comrades to his fortunes, they took flight in a small boat, and landed on the Sicilian coast, which they found entirely deserted, the inhabitants being frightened away by the frequent invasions of Algerine corsairs.

The sanitary laws of Sicily were that year excessively severe, under the apprehension not only of the plague, but also of the yellow fever, which was raging violently in Spain. As any quarantine would have subjected him to extreme inconvenience and delay, M. Geouffre took every possible precaution to avoid observation, and found an asylum for the night in an old chapel, whose ruins gave melancholy evidence of the devastation committed by the pirates. The next morning a priest who was passing the ruined chapel on his road to Palermo undertook at my brother-in-law's request the delivery of two letters from him; one to the Spanish Consul, who also fulfilled the functions of the French Consulate; and the other to the Governor of Palermo, in both of which, with a very slight and excusable departure from truth, he represented himself as attached to the Spanish embassy.

The next day the priest returned with favourable answers, and M. Geouffre, with his two sailors, whom he amply recompensed, and the priest who served him by the road both as interpreter and paymaster, arrived at Palermo, where he was most graciously received by the Spanish Consul, and procured through his means every facility for his progress to Naples. From that place he embarked in a small felucca, and landed at the foot of the mole, certain of finding at the house of the French Ambassador, Alquier, whom Lucien

Bonaparte had succeeded at Madrid, every accommodation he could desire. With Alquier no secrecy was necessary on the subject of his Egyptian mission, and they lamented together its ill success, and the important loss the nation had sustained.

The French Ambassador presented my brother-in-law at the Neapolitan court, then in all its brilliancy, and preparing for the double nuptials of the Prince of Asturias with a Neapolitan princess, sister of the present Queen of the French, and of the Infanta Donna Marianna with the Prince Royal of Naples. The Princess of Asturias I had the honour of being particularly acquainted with, and was much distinguished by her; her memory is very dear to me.

After a short stay in the beautiful and harmonious Parthenope, which still mourned the divine Cimarosa, my brother-in-law returned to Spain, having derived no other advantage from an expedition that endangered both his liberty and life than that of having seen Naples and its enchanting bay.

Parthenope has recalled to my mind a story that occurred in that same Italy, and very near Naples; it relates to Madame Adelaide and Madame Victoire, and happened at this period. Mesdames de France inhabited the Castle of Caserta, a royal country-house belonging to the Court of Naples.

Their Court was still tolerably numerous, and to divert the tedium its younger members must otherwise have contracted from their recluse mode of life, the Princesses frequently had little balls, composed only of their own suite. A single violin formed the orchestra, under the direction of M. Chazote, governor of the young Comte de Chastellux. It seems he was not very clever, and that Collinet would not have been likely to engage him as his second, for he inhumanly mangled the most common airs, such as the *monaco, les deux coqs,* and other new dances.

The dissonance was once so insupportable to the practised ear of Madame Adelaide, that, starting from her seat, she took the violin from M. Chazote's hands, and her Royal Highness played through the whole country-dance with a taste and precision which called forth the gratitude and amazement of the dancers, nearly all of whom were ignorant that she could handle the instrument. Madame Adelaide appeared as much amused with fingering her bow as the dancers in following it, for no sooner had she concluded the country-dance she had carried off from poor M. Chazote, whom she told to "Go and dance," than she tuned her instrument, and issued the word of command, "To your places."

But the Duchesse de Narbonne, who perhaps thought the Princess was forgetting her dignity, majestically crossed the room, and remonstrated with such firmness that the excellent Princess surrendered her own amusement and that which she was conferring. A spectator has assured me that nothing could be more picturesque and graceful than Madame Adelaide, in her stiff Gothic dress, playing so unusual an instrument; at a little distance, Madame Victoire, who could never laugh, even in the salons of Versailles, and was now cold, serious, and severely melancholy, appeared to look with a reproving eye on her sister, while the young Louise de Narbonne, the ornament of the Court, as she would have been of Versailles, and the two Comtesses de Chastellux, all three young, pretty, and dressed with the simplicity becoming their age, formed a striking contrast with the starched exiles of the old Court.

M. Goubaud, the young Roman painter of the household of the princesses, made an exquisite sketch of this little scene.

Youth loves smartness, and is coquettish in males as well as females. This young M. Goubaud, who was in high favour both with Mesdames de France and Madame de

Narbonne herself, who was never prodigal of her favour, was then a pretty boy of eighteen or twenty. One day he went out to attend a fair, or village *fête*.

Goubaud, while eyeing the pretty girls, paid no attention to the most coquettish, and running after the most timid, suddenly spied an immense silk handkerchief with a broad border of lively and glaring colours. The *fête*, the peasant-girls, all disappear before the flattering idea that that very night, or on the morrow at farthest, he shall outshine the whole household of Mesdames in this large and many-coloured cravat. He purchased it, and returned to Caserta as enraptured with his bargain as if he had bought the Pope's tiara, which, be it said *en passant*, was not then at Rome.

The next day was Sunday, and it was the custom of the house for the Princesses to pass to Mass through the ranks of their assembled household, inclining their heads, speaking to the women, and smiling at the men. Goubaud, decked like a bridegroom, and proud as a peacock, had placed himself opposite to an open window, where he might appear in all the plenitude of his beauty. The usher of the chambers, opening the folding-doors, announced Madame Victoire and Madame Adelaide.

Madame Victoire, whose habitually calm countenance seldom betrayed any feeling, on perceiving the young Roman appeared perfectly astonished. She paused a moment, seeming about to speak; then, apparently unwilling to compromise her dignity, she recovered her composure, and passed on without noticing the confident and smiling salute of the good youth. He now awaited Madame Adelaide, who was far more beloved than her sister; but she not only passed like Madame Victoire without speaking to the young painter, but darted on him an indignant glance which distressed him. The Duchesse de Narbonne, who followed, fixed on Goubaud a piercing look, which seemed to say, "What! have you such audacity?" The young artist mentally reviewed every act of his that could possibly have given offence, and finally comforted himself with the reflection that the displeasure of his patronesses was undeserved.

The return from Mass was equally solemn, and the whole establishment, modelling their conduct after that of the Princesses, seemed to shun Goubaud as if he had just imported the yellow fever from Cadiz.

The young artist, who had a grateful and susceptible heart, retired to his study and gave himself up to melancholy reflections; scarcely had he entered, when a messenger from Madame de Narbonne brought him a brief and precise order to quit Caserta that very day.

His patience now deserted him, and anger for a moment superseded grief; but his eyes falling on the magnificent view which unfolded before him all the magic images of beauty, surrounding a dwelling in which, welcomed as a friend, as a beloved child, he had passed the happiest days of his life, "I should be mad," thought he, "to retire without inquiring the cause of my disgrace;" and he immediately requested a parting audience of Madame de Narbonne, who granted it on the instant; but as he entered, panting for breath, "What!" cried she in a fury, and without giving him time to speak—"what! you have the boldness, the impudence, to present yourself before me in your odious cravat?"

Goubaud was confounded.

"My cravat, *Madame la Duchesse!*———"

"Yes, sir; your cravat. Is not exile a sufficient misfortune? Must Adelaide and Victoire of France, the daughters of Louis XV., be persecuted in that exile, insulted even with the sight of a tricoloured flag?"

"*Ah! mon Dieu!*" cried Goubaud, and the immense corners of his cravat striking his eyes, he snatched it from his neck and stood dismayed, as if really criminal; the cravat was as perfect a tricolour as the flag which now waves over the Château of the Tuileries. The poor youth held in his hands the accusing witness, and believed it had been placed there by some mischievous demon who had fascinated his eyes.

Born and bred in Italy, and in retirement, he had never seen the tricoloured flag, nor even thought of it but as associated with the misfortunes of those kind and benevolent Princesses for whom he would have laid down his life.

He had little difficulty in explaining the innocence of his intentions to the good-natured Duchess, who undertook to plead for him with his benefactresses. She soon returned from her compassionate mission with a free pardon, giving him at the same time, from the royal ladies, a packet containing a dozen superb white cravats, and ordering for the altar of the chapel a painting of the Assumption of the Virgin, which the grateful artist commenced without the loss of an hour, and in a few days his study was again visited by the Princesses, "to cement the pardon," as Mademoiselle Adelaide expressed herself.

Goubaud was afterwards miniature-painter to the Emperor Napoleon, and in 1813 was appointed painter to the King of Rome and the children of France; and he has recently finished a splendid picture of the captive Napoleon.

CHAPTER XVII.

Malmaison—Its Park—Bonaparte's Project—Mademoiselle Julien—The Consul's Tent, love of Air, and the Fire in Summer—Apartment of Mademoiselle Hortense—Manner of Life at Malmaison—Female Breakfasts—Facility of Madame Bonaparte in granting her Protection—Madame Savary and Madame Lannes—Madame d'Houdetot and M. de Céré—Unexpected Favour, Mission, Delay, and Disgrace—The Memorial and the Bill.

THE park of Malmaison was enchanting, notwithstanding its proximity to the barren mountain on one side. The river, though running far below, imparted strength and luxuriance to its vegetation; and nothing could be greener, more fresh, or umbrageous, than the field from which it was separated only by a ha-ha, and that part of the park itself which is bounded by the road. The extent of the park did not exceed a hundred acres; and Bonaparte, on his return from Egypt, endeavoured to persuade Mademoiselle Julien, a rich old maid of the village of Ruelle, as an act of good neighbourship, to sell him, at her own price, an adjoining garden, or small park, by which addition Malmaison would have been placed on so respectable a footing that he need no longer have blushed to compare it with the magnificent estate of his brother Joseph.*

* See page 155.

The First Consul had a small private garden, separated only by a bridge from his private cabinet. It was here that he took the air, when labour rendered moderate exercise necessary to him; for at that time, and for two years succeeding, he allowed himself no repose but what nature imperatively required. The bridge was covered in and arranged like a small tent; here his table was carried, and he would employ himself with State papers, saying that he felt his ideas become more elevated and expansive in the air than when seated beside a stove and shut out from communication with the sky.

Yet Bonaparte could not endure the smallest degree of cold; had fires lighted in July, and wondered that others did not suffer like himself from the first breath of a north wind.

Our life at Malmaison resembled that usually led when much company is assembled together at a château in the country. Our apartments consisted of a chamber, a boudoir, and a room for the chambermaid, all very simply furnished. That occupied by Mademoiselle Hortense differed from the others only by a folding-door; and this apartment was not assigned her till after her marriage. All opened on a long and narrow paved corridor, looking into the court.

We chose our own hour of rising, and until breakfast our time was at our own disposal. At eleven the ladies all met for breakfast in a small low salon of the right wing, opening to the court; but, as in Paris, gentlemen were never admitted to the party, unless, occasionally, Joseph, Louis, or one of the family. Breakfast was followed by conversation, or the reading of the journals, and someone always arrived from Paris to have *an audience*, for already Madame Bonaparte gave audiences, contrary to the express orders of the First Consul, and patronized petitions, though his anger at her interference had already caused her abundance of tears;

but when a beautiful pearl necklace or bracelet of rubies was offered, through the hands of Bourrienne, or of any other friend, the elegance of a present so wholly unconnected with the matters in hand suppressed all curious speculations into the nature of the mine which produced it.

The First Consul was never visible till dinner-time. At five or six in the morning he descended to his cabinet, and was there occupied with Bourrienne, or with the Ministers, Generals, and Councillors of State, till the dinner-hour of six, when the party was generally joined by some invited guests. All the suite of the First Consul were at this time enlarging his household by marriage; Colonel Savary had just married a relation of Madame Bonaparte (an unhoped-for happiness to a man whose life knew no other impulse than the desire of advancement); his wife was pretty, but had bad teeth.

Madame Lannes was really handsome, and in high favour at Malmaison, of which she was every way worthy; gentle, unconscious of envy, and never sacrificing to a jest the peace or reputation of another. In person she might have formed a model for the most beautiful Madonnas of Raphael or Coreggio; such was the symmetry of her features, the calmness of her countenance, the serenity of her smile. I first saw her at a ball, where she scarcely danced, although her figure was light and elegant. In the dignified station to which fate exalted her after the death of her husband, the Duchess de Montebello's conduct was perfectly irreproachable; and she was ever ready to oblige or serve others as far as was consistent with the severity of the Emperor, who would inevitably have discouraged and opposed any affair recommended by a woman, and with the apathy of the Empress, who, on quitting her early home, had not, as assuredly the Archduke Charles would have advised her, created for herself a new one.

But to return to Josephine and her morning audiences. This was the only time that the surveillance of the First Consul left her at liberty, and he then committed the duty to Bourrienne, who tells us "he would have deemed it disgraceful to act as a spy on the wife of his friend," and therefore contented himself with concealing from the First Consul such acquisitions of jewellery, etc., as made no claim on the public finances. I must, however, do Madame Bonaparte the justice to say that she saw nothing of all these intrigues, but confined herself to writing a few lines to Berthier, who had much more consideration for her than any of the other Ministers; so little interest, indeed, had she with them, that importunity alone could not give any weight to her requests; the influence of Mademoiselle Hortense, had she exerted it, would have been far more effective.

But if Madame Bonaparte's credit with the authorities was at a low ebb, her reputation for it was also injured by her own proceedings; for example, amongst her most attached friends was Madame Houdetot, and her interposition was for once successful in recommending that lady's brother, M. de Céré, to the First Consul's favour, in which sense, good manners, and a pleasing address rapidly advanced him. He was becoming a familiar on the establishment when he was sent on a mission, and a certain day fixed for his return, after which he was to receive the appointment of aide-de-camp. But, alas! youth is heedless, and M. de Céré exceeded his appointment by a whole fortnight.

Napoleon, doubly incensed by the neglect of his orders and by his own error of judgment, a circumstance not very common, would listen to no solicitations for pardon, and peremptorily prohibited the young man's reappearance before him; while Madame Bonaparte observed that "a volcanic head, leading into follies for want of reflection, should not be associated with the indolence of a creole."

After many months had elapsed, determined on a new effort to recover his lost ground, he solicited, through the medium of his sister and of Savary, who was also his friend, an audience of Madame Bonaparte, and to his great joy was desired to repair on the morrow to Malmaison, furnished with a very clear and explicit memorial, which Josephine promised to forward. Arriving at the château, he found Madame, as usual, gracious and enchanting; she told him that the First Consul, already predisposed by her, would easily overlook an irregularity which M. de Céré promised to obliterate by future good conduct, and concluded by receiving his memorial, and recommending him to come himself in a few days for the answer.

The poor young man, intoxicated with the success of his overtures, demanded by anticipation the congratulations of his friends; but he discovered, before retiring to rest, that the memorial was still in his pocket, and he had left as its substitute in the hands of his patroness a long bill from his tailor. In despair at an incident which threatened annihilation to all his new-raised hopes, he passed a sleepless night, and early in the morning was again on the road to Malmaison, determined, as his last chance, to explain the whole affair to Madame Bonaparte. His consternation may be imagined when, advancing with outstretched hand to meet him, she anticipated his explanation with:

"How happy I am! I have delivered your memorial to the First Consul, and we read it together; it was admirably drawn up," added she, with an approving smile, "and made a great impression upon him.* He told me Berthier should

---

* This story of an unread document recalls one of an English curate, who on one occasion preached a sermon to the orthodoxy of which considerable exception might be taken. Hearing that a representation was likely to be made to his archdeacon which would be likely to hinder his further preferment, he at once posted a copy of his sermon to the bishop

report it, and within a fortnight all will be settled. I assure you, *mon cher*, this success, for I consider the affair as concluded, made me the whole of yesterday the happiest woman in the world."

If the actual memorial had not been at that moment in his pocket he would have persuaded himself it was really in the hands of the First Consul, and that his unhappy carelessness was all a dream!

From this instance it may be inferred that Madame Bonaparte, though perfectly good-natured, and with the utmost disposition to oblige, could not be entirely depended upon in the management of any affair. She desired to confer favours, but this desire yielded to the smallest apprehension of the First Consul's displeasure.

Bonaparte was very partial to Malmaison, and insisted on all the visitors being entirely at their ease; it was always he who opposed the restraints of etiquette, which already Madame Bonaparte liked, and would fain have introduced, although as burdensome to herself as to others.

---

of the diocese for acceptance in the ordinary way, and that prelate, being very much occupied, sent him a letter of congratulation without reading the sermon. Fortified by this approval, he was able to speedily put his foes to the rout.

CHAPTER XVIII.

The Wednesdays at Malmaison—The Stage Company at Malmaison—Bonaparte treated like a Boy—Dinners in the Park—Party at Barriers, and the First Consul without his Coat—Fright of Madame Bonaparte—Rapp, Eugène, and the Veteran Soldier recognized by the First Consul—Voluntary Engagement—Curious and touching Scene—Panic Terror at Malmaison—The Inhabitants in Dishabille.

EVERY Wednesday there was a grand dinner at Malmaison. The Second Consul was always of the party, with the Ministers, the Counsellors of State, some particularly esteemed Generals, and a few ladies of unspotted reputation; for Napoleon was then rigorous in the choice of Madame Bonaparte's society. We acted plays in the evening, and the part of the abigails fell to my lot. Madame Savary was also of our company; Junot was our best actor, and Bourrienne, Eugène Beauharnais and Lauriston had talent. It was no trifle to play before, not only an audience of three hundred persons, but the First Consul in particular; for my part I should have preferred doubling the number, could he have been by that means excluded.

It was singular enough that I, certainly the most free with him of the whole establishment, and the most ready to answer his pleasantries—I, in short, who already gave indications of the woman who, according to his own confession of St. Helena, treated him as a boy (*en petit garçon*), the day that he addressed to my ears words to which it did not become me to listen—I could not endure his criticisms, just or unjust, on my performance, however convinced that he was mistaken, and that I best understood my own business with the assistance of Dugazon, my prompter.

The dinner-hour, as I have before said, was six; and when the weather was fine the First Consul ordered the table to be laid in the park on the left of the lawn; the dinner was soon despatched, and he found it wearisomely protracted if we sat more than half an hour.

When he was in good humour, the weather fine, and he had a few minutes' leisure from the labour which even at that time was killing him, he would play at barriers with us. He cheated us, as at *reversis*,* would throw us down, or come upon us without crying *barre!* but these tricks were only calculated to raise a laugh. His coat was on such occasions laid aside, and he ran like a hare, or rather like the gazelle, which he would feed with a boxful of tobacco, and tell her to run after us, and the tormenting animal tore our clothes, and sometimes our legs.

One fine day after dinner he exclaimed, "Let us play at barriers!" Off went his coat, and the next moment the conqueror of the world was racing like a schoolboy. The park at Malmaison was not then as complete as it now is, although the most shameful vandalism has spared no efforts to extinguish the remembrances attached even to a few plants. It was separated only by a ha-ha from an open field, afterwards purchased for a plantation, and the curious could observe from this field all that passed in the park.

Madame Bonaparte had been leaning with Madame

* A game of cards still in vogue with the dowagers of the Faubourg Saint Germain.

Lavalette on the iron railing which overlooked the ha-ha, when, advancing a few steps, they were alarmed by the sight of two men, of rough manners, shabby dress, and very suspicious appearance, who were eyeing the First Consul and whispering to one another. I had ceased playing, and at this moment approached Madame Bonaparte, who took my arm, and sent Lavalette to seek her husband or Eugène, but charged her to be careful that the First Consul did not discover her errand, for he detested any precautions.

She met Rapp, who required no stimulating whenever the shadow of danger threatened his General; in a few seconds he was beside the men, and, accosting them somewhat roughly, demanded their reason for standing there frightening ladies, and threatened them with arrest. They stoutly maintained their right to look at their General, who, they were certain, would not drive them away, and appealed to Eugène, who, coming up at that moment to see what was the matter, recognized one of the intruders for an old chasseur of his regiment. The veteran explained in humorous and military phrase that the loss of his arm having disabled him for further service, his brother wished to be accepted as his substitute; and to arrange this affair, they were come in search of their commander, when the sight of the First Consul at full play had arrested their steps; and, having finished this explanation, they turned away.

Bonaparte, with his eyes which saw without looking, and his ears which heard without listening, had from the first word been in possession of a key to the whole scene: he remembered the old quartermaster of his chasseurs, who at Montebello or Marengo had lost an arm while defending the life of a wounded officer. The First Consul had himself caused him to be carried off the field, and as the veteran had since been presented to him on parade, he recalled his features. "Oh! oh!" said he, "there are the *Invalides* in retreat. Good-day, my boy. Well, you are come to see me, then? Come! face about! march once more at the command of your general. Conduct him, Eugène."

And passing his arm around Josephine's waist, he led her to the entrance of the château, where we met the two brothers, Eugène, and Rapp. The old chasseur presented his brother to the First Consul, reminding him at the same time that no legal obligations demanded his services. "It is a voluntary engagement, General," said he, "and you are his Recruiting-Captain."

"Since I am the Recruiting-Captain," said the First Consul, "the recruit must drink my health and that of the Republic. Eugène, take charge of your soldier, my boy; you will pledge him in my name."

The old chasseur watched the departing steps of his General, and, when he disappeared from his sight, burst into tears.

"Come, come, my old comrade, a little more self-command," said Eugène; "why, the deuce, you are like a woman!"

"Ah! talking of women, a pretty mess I have made," said the maimed veteran; "why, I have spoken to the *Générale Consule* as if I were speaking to Nanny and Peggy. And yet she seems all goodness, yonder brave *Citoyenne.*"

Whenever the First Consul played at barriers we all walked, and both cards and chess were superseded. This evening, therefore, he retired to his cabinet, and we saw no more of him. Madame Bonaparte had been so frightened by the sight of the men that nothing could rally her spirits. Eugène, Bessières, and Junot were all returned to Paris, and, no one remaining to cheer her, we spent the evening in enumerating and recounting all the vain attempts made within the last year against the life of the First Consul.

His wife loved him; the influence of gratitude on a good heart had bound her to him. She cried, and embracing me, said, "The figure of this man has made such a terrible impression on me, that I am certain I shall not sleep to-night; and Bonaparte, if he hears me complain, he is angry. He never has anything to fear, according to his own account."

We all retired to our chambers with the nervousness that pervades a party of children who have been listening to ghost stories, and midnight had not struck before the whole château, buried in sleep, might have resembled that of Beauty in the Sleeping Wood, if the moonbeams had not been occasionally seen to glimmer on the arms of those faithful guards, those *chasseurs à cheval,* who silently paraded the park, watching over the safety of him who was the safety of all.

Suddenly a report of firearms was heard from the ditch of the château, and instantly, before we could recover our breath, suspended by fear, everyone was on foot. The First Consul was already in the corridor in his dressing-gown, holding a taper, and crying with his powerful and sonorous voice, "Do not be frightened; there is nothing the matter."

He was as calm as if his sleep had not been disturbed: this I can answer for, because my glance of inquiry was fixed upon his countenance; he was calm without indifference, but he was evidently a thousand cubits above the apprehension of danger. His destiny was not fulfilled, and he knew it!

The alarm arose from the carbine of one of the chasseurs having gone off in consequence of his horse stumbling on a mole-hill.

When the First Consul heard the report of his aide-de-camp he laughed, and called through a little door at the foot of the grand staircase :

"Josephine, dry your eyes ; a mole has done all the mischief ; no great wonder, for it is an ugly animal. As for the chasseur, two days' arrest, to teach him and his horse not to pass again over my lawn. As I suppose he has had a fine fright himself, his punishment shall not last longer. Good-night, ladies ; go to bed again, and sleep well." In passing by my door he added : " Felice notte, Signora Loulou, dolci riposo " " Felicissimo riposo, Signor Generale."

CHAPTER XIX.

Influence of the Weather on the First Consul—The Lord of the Château—Imperious Requisitions of the First Consul—The Ravine and the Calash—Useless Tears of Madame Bonaparte—Concession of the First Consul in my favour—Bonaparte's Ill-humour and Irascibility—Madame Bonaparte's Journey to Plombières—Madame Louis Bonaparte replacing her Mother at Malmaison—Madame Bessières— *Reversis* and the *Hearts*— *The Fish* — Little Bièvre—The Court and the Cage—The First Consul reading his Despatches in my Chamber—Five o'Clock in the Morning—Admirable Maxims on the Duties of a Chief Magistrate—Seeing Everything with one's own Eyes, and the Petition of a Widow—Pretty Writing and Declaration—Amorous Assignations turned over to the Minister of Police—Six in the Morning—Visit of the next Day—A Gazette—Mademoiselle Abel and the Prince of Wirtemberg—The Archduke Charles—A Compliment from Bonaparte—Breakfast at Butard—Night of Distress—Carrying off the Key and the Door Doublelocked—Fresh Visit of the First Consul—The Master-key—Embarrassing Situation and Cruel Perplexity—Arrival of Junot at Malmaison—Monge, and the First Consul's Gaiety—A Game of Chess with Bonaparte—Junot's mistaken Suspicion—Indescribable Situation—Junot Asleep, and the First Consul at my Door—Incredible Scene—Bonaparte and myself in a Calash—The Lie given in Form, and without any Consequences — Explanation — My Mother's Letter shown to the First Consul—End of a Painful Scene, and my Departure for Paris—Return of Madame Bonaparte, and Visit to Malmaison—The Anniversary and singular Memory of the First Consul.

AIR and exercise were necessary to Napoleon's existence, and the privation of them, from rain or any other cause, chafed his temper, and made him not only disagreeable, but really ill, so that his humour at dinner was a pretty good index to the state of the weather. Alas! I can but too easily perceive that he sank under the double misery of a scorching sun and a compulsory seclusion. The quintessence of barbarity was exhausted in the conduct of that monster in human shape delegated by England to St. Helena.*

The First Consul was soon tired of retracing his own steps through the park at Malmaison, which was not sufficiently extensive to admit of his riding as he might have done at Morfontaine; and he often regretted not having an equally fine estate.† Mademoiselle Julien decidedly refusing to sell, he sought elsewhere the means of enlarging his park, and entertained at one time the singular notion of purchasing the Île Channorrier, which is very considerable, well planted, containing fine lawns, and situated in the middle of the Seine. When Josephine pointed out the impracticability of his scheme, he replied:

"At Morfontaine the lakes are on the other side of the road; a subterranean passage may easily be made, and by buying all the tract between the road and the river, and planting it as an English garden, it seems to me that it might be done."

M. de Channorrier, however, refused to sell his island, and Napoleon purchased the woods of Butard, which made a delightful addition to his park; and so enchanted was he with his new acquisition that on the second or third day afterwards he insisted on taking us all there, that Madame Bonaparte might inspect the pavilion, which he was disposed to make a rendezvous for the chase. Josephine was

---

* See the narratives of the imprisonment at St. Helena furnished by O'Meara and Las Cases and others.

† See page 142.

suffering under one of those dreadful headaches which so often tortured her, poor woman! and for which there was no other remedy than sleep.

"Come, come! go with us," said the First Consul, "the air will do you good. It is the sovereign remedy for all pains."

Madame Bonaparte dared no longer refuse; she sent for a hat and shawl: and she, Madame Lavalette, and I mounted an open carriage. Napoleon preceded us, with Bourrienne; the aide-de-camp on duty had not been summoned for this excursion, with which the First Consul was as much delighted as a boy enjoying a holiday. He was on horseback, and sometimes galloped before us, then came back and took his wife's hand; as a child running before its mother returns to embrace her and then renews its race.

No words can describe the terrors of Madame Bonaparte in a carriage, and it is as difficult to express my own impatience, when I see a want of compassion for such weaknesses; they are troublesome, it is true, but are fruits of education, and no fault on the part of their victims, on whom they inflict a sort of martyrdom. Napoleon was not of my mind; he had no pity for his wife, and made no allowance for her.

As this was the first time of our going to Butard, the postilion did not know his way, and the road we followed brought us to a rivulet with banks sufficiently steep to render the passage somewhat difficult for a carriage. The moment Madame Bonaparte descried "this precipice," as she called it, she forbade him to proceed a step further. The pricker, knowing her nervousness, answered, when interrogated, that the passage might really be dangerous.

"See there!" cried she; "I will not go to Butard this way. Go and tell the First Consul that I am returning to the château, unless he knows some other road;" and ordering the postilion to turn his horses, we retraced our way, but had not driven many yards before the First Consul rejoined us.

"What is the matter?" said he, with that expression of countenance peculiar to himself when anything displeased him; "what is this new whim about? Return whence you came," added he, slightly touching the shoulders of the postilion with his hunting-whip; and, setting spurs to his horse, he galloped off again. We found him beside the fatal rivulet, examining its pretty high banks, but as he had just crossed it on horseback, everyone else must pass it too.

"Come," said Napoleon to the little lad who drove the carriage, "a good plunge, then draw in the reins, and you are over."

Madame Bonaparte uttered a piercing shriek, to which the forest re-echoed. "You shall never keep me in the carriage. Let me out!—Bonaparte!—I entreat you in mercy!—Let me out!" Weeping, and clasping her hands, she was truly an object of pity. Napoleon looked at her, but, far from relenting, he shrugged his shoulders and roughly commanded her to be silent. "It is absolute childishness; you *shall* pass, and in the carriage. Come, did you hear me?" said he, swearing, to the postilion.

I saw it was time to interfere for myself, not without hope that the diversion might convince him of his error.

"General!" said I to the Consul, beckoning the pricker to come and open the door for me; "I am responsible for another life; I cannot stay here. The jerk will be violent, and may not only injure but kill me in my present condition," said I, smiling; "and you do not wish that, do you, General?"

"I," cried he, "do you the smallest harm! You!

Alight; you are in the right: a jolt might do you much harm." And approaching the carriage, he himself assisted me to descend, for he had dismounted from his horse at the commencement of the scene. Encouraged by the kind expression of his countenance, I ventured, perhaps ridiculously enough, to say, as he supported me to alight:

"And a jolt may be very injurious to Madame Bonaparte, General, for if she were as I am——"

The First Consul looked at me with an air so amusingly stupefied, that, instead of jumping down, I stood on the step, laughing like a young fool as I was; and all at once he responded to my laugh in a tone so shrill and clear that it made us start. At length I jumped down, and Napoleon, who had instantly resumed his former gravity, reproved me for the imprudence of such an exertion. Then, as if fearful he had not been bitter enough in testifying his discontent towards his wife:

"Put up the step and let the carriage proceed," said he, with a tone which admitted of no reply. Madame Bonaparte was so pale, and suffered so acutely, that I could not avoid saying to Napoleon:

"General, you appear cruel, and yet you are not so. Madame Bonaparte is ill, she is in a fever: I conjure you, suffer her to alight!" He looked on me with an expression which made my blood curdle.

"Madame Junot, I never loved remonstrances even when a child; ask Signora Lætitia and Madame Permon, and consider whether I am likely to be tamed since." Then, perceiving that his words, and still more his look and tone, almost frightened me, he added, "Well, come, let me help you over *this formidable stream, this frightful precipice.*"

When we had crossed, Napoleon saw that the carriage did not stir, for Josephine, crying as if her execution was preparing, entreated the postilion to stay another minute, as a condemned criminal would beg a reprieve.

"Very well, sir," said the First Consul; "do you choose to obey my orders?"

And this time it was not lightly that he applied a stroke of his whip to the postilion's back, who instantly whipping both his horses, made them take the plunge, and the carriage crossed the brook, but with such difficulty that one of the springs was broken and a pin loosened.

Madame Bonaparte's whole frame was disordered with pain, fear, and rage, and conscious that such passions give an interesting expression only to young faces, she wrapped herself in a large muslin veil, and we were sensible only of her sobs till our arrival at Butard; when her husband, incensed at finding her still in tears, pulled her quite roughly out of the carriage, and dragging her to a short distance in the wood, we could hear him scolding the more angrily because he had set out prepared for a joyous excursion. It would appear that Josephine had other reproaches to make him than concerned the passage of the rivulet, for I heard Napoleon answer her:

"You are a simpleton, and if you repeat such a word I shall say a wicked simpleton, because you do not think what you are saying. And you know that I have a mortal antipathy to all these jealousies that have no foundation for them. You will end by putting it into my head. Come! embrace me and hold your tongue; you are ugly when you cry: I have told you so before."

Our return was melancholy, in spite of the reconciliation. Madame Bonaparte let fall a few spitefully honeyed words upon my special favour in being permitted to quit the carriage. This leads me naturally to a circumstance which occurred the following year, and the remembrance of which has served me as a clue to many mysteries.

Madame Bonaparte was gone to Plombières without her daughter, who remained behind to do the honours for the ladies at Malmaison. Plays were acted every Wednesday; we had hunting-parties, and the evenings were spent in laughing and chatting. Madame Louis Bonaparte, who was just married, was the most engaging of brides as she had been of girls, and Madame Bessières formed a very agreeable addition to our select society; she was gentle and witty, sensible and good. Never did I see the First Consul so agreeable as during that fortnight; he was amiable, constantly good-humoured and joyous, amused himself with making me recite Italian verses, and then we played at *reversis*, at which we laughed incessantly.

The First Consul was sure to have all the hearts in his tricks, and when anyone tried to force Quinola, not a single heart could be found in the other three hands, so that he carried off all the stakes, crying:

"I have all the fish!—all the fish! Who will buy all the fish in the house?"

At other times he played chess, and as he was not expert at the game, he had recourse to stratagem as at *reversis*. The game could never be finished because there were always found two bishops commanding either the white or the black squares. He was the first to laugh at these contrivances, but was annoyed if they were too seriously noticed; and as he never played for money they were a subject for joke rather than for resentment.

Thus we led a merry life, and the summer slipped pleasantly away; yet some of us wished to return home. I was particularly desirous to be mistress of my own house, though only seventeen, and to see my husband's recent gift to me, the produce of his wedding portion from the First Consul; this was the estate of Little Bièvre. I wished also to visit my mother and friends, whom I had not seen for some months; but we were obliged to abandon our projects; we could not even go to Ruelle, for our carriages and horses were at Paris; we saw our husbands, to be sure, every day, and might have returned with them, for it must not be supposed that we were prisoners; yet the Consular Court was already a cage, the bars of which were indeed veiled with flowers,—nevertheless, it was a cage. Eventually, the flowers became more scarce, but the bars were gilt.

One morning I was in a profound sleep, when suddenly I was awoke by a slight noise near me, and perceived the First Consul beside my bed. Thinking myself in a dream, I rubbed my eyes, which produced a laugh from him.

"It is really I," said he; "why so astonished?"

One minute had sufficed to wake me entirely, and by way of answer I extended my hand towards the open window, which the extreme heat had obliged me to leave open. The sky was still of that deep-blue which succeeds the first hour of dawn. The sombre green of the trees showed that the sun was scarcely risen. I looked at my watch, and found it was not yet five o'clock.

"Really!" said he, when I showed it to him; "no later than that? so much the better, we are going to chat," and taking an armchair, he placed it at the foot of my bed, seated himself, crossed his legs, and established himself there as he used to do, five years earlier, in my mother's easy-chair at the Hôtel de la Tranquillité. He held in his hand a thick packet of letters, on which was written in large characters, "For the First Consul, for himself; for him alone, personally:" in short, every form of secrecy and security was adopted, and successfully, for the First Consul reserved for himself alone the letters superscribed with those words; and when I told him that such an employment must be troublesome to him, and he should refer it to some confidential person, he answered me, "By-and-by, perhaps; at present it is impossible. I must answer all. At the commencement of the return of order I must not be ignorant of any want, any complaint."

"But," said I, pointing to a large letter, which by its bad writing, and the awkward position of the seal, showed that its author was not much accustomed to epistolary labours, "this letter probably contains only a request which might have been made through the intervention of a secretary." Napoleon opened the letter, and read from one end to the other, three long pages, filled with very indifferent writing. When he had finished he said to me, "Well, this letter itself proves that I do right in seeing with my own eyes. Here, read it."

It was from a woman whose son had been killed in Egypt. She was the widow of a soldier who died in the service, and having no means of subsistence she had written, she said, more than ten letters to the Minister of War, the First Consul and his secretary, and had received no answer.

"You see it is necessary I should myself see all that is especially recommended to my attention." And he rose to fetch a pen from a table, made a sort of mark, probably agreed upon between Bourrienne and himself, and again sat down as if in his cabinet. "Ah! here is a trap," said he, taking off one, two, three, four envelopes, each highly scented with essence of roses, and inscribed in a pretty handwriting, with the talismanic words, *for the First Consul only*. He came at length to the last envelope, and a laugh soon burst from him, of which I, who knew the rareness of such hilarity, expected no common explanation.

"It is a declaration," said he, "not of war, but of love. It is a beautiful lady, who has loved me, she says, from the day she beheld me present the treaty of Campo-Formio to the Directory. And if I wish to see her, I have only to give orders to the sentinel at the iron gate, on the side of Bougival, to let a woman pass dressed in white, and giving the word *Napoleon!* and that [looking at the date], faith! this very evening."

"*Mon Dieu!*" cried I; "you will not be so imprudent?" He looked attentively at me; then said, "What is it to you if I do? What harm can it do me?"

"What is it to me! What harm can it do you! Really, General, those are strange questions. May not this woman be bribed by your enemies? The snare, you will say, is too palpable. For all that it may be perilous; and you ask me what does your imprudence signify to me!"

Napoleon looked at me again, and then began to laugh. "I said it in joke; do you think me so simple, so stupid, as to nibble at such a bait? I am receiving such letters every day, with meetings appointed sometimes at the Tuileries, sometimes at the Luxembourg, but the only answer I make to such worthy missives is that which they deserve;" and stepping again towards the table, he wrote a few words, referring it to the Minister of Police.

"The deuce, there is six o'clock!" he exclaimed, hearing a timepiece strike, and approaching the bed he collected his papers, pinched my foot through the bedclothes, and smiling with the graciousness which sometimes brightened his countenance he went away singing, with that squalling voice, so strongly contrasted with the fine sonorous accent of his speech—

> "Non, non, *s'il* est impossible
> D'avoir un plus aimable enfant.
> Un plus aimable? Ah! si vraiment," etc.

It was his favourite air. Madame Dugazon, in the character of Camilla, must have made a great impression on him, for this was the only song he repeated; but, from the first day of singing it, he said *s'il est*, etc. Junot, who heard him say it at Toulon, could never cure him of the habit; he never sang this song, however, unless in excellent humour. I thought no more of this visit; and neither I nor my waiting-maid took any notice of the quantity of envelopes he had left on the ground.

About nine in the evening the First Consul drew near me, and whispered, "I am going to the Bougival Gate." "I do not believe a word of it," said I in the same tone. "You know too well the irreparable loss to France should any evil befall you. If you say another such word I will tell Madame Hortense, or Junot."

"You are a little simpleton," said he, pinching my ear; then threatening me with his finger: "If you think of telling one word of what I have said to you, I shall not only be displeased but pained." "The last consideration would suffice, General." He gazed at me: "The mother's head, the mother's head, absolutely!" I made no answer; and, perceiving that I kept silence, after waiting some minutes, he passed to the billiard-room.

The following morning I was again awakened in surprise by the same knock at my maid's chamber-door, and the First Consul entered, as before, with a packet of letters and papers in his hand. He again begged my pardon for waking me three hours too early, but added:

"Why do you sleep with your window open? It is fatal for women who, like you, have teeth of pearl. You must not risk the loss of your teeth; they resemble your mother's and are real little pearls." And he began to read the journals, making marks under several lines with his nails. He sometimes shrugged his shoulders, and muttered a few words, which I did not hear. He was reading, I think, a foreign gazette, written in French; from a question he put to me, I think his subject was the Prince of Wirtemberg, eldest son of the Duke, and now King of Wirtemberg.

This young Prince had been found in Paris, almost in disguise, with a young lady of good birth, whom he had not run away with, but seduced. The ear of the Duke, it appears, was not easily gained, and Mademoiselle Abel could not obtain the only reparation which can be offered to a credulous girl. Junot had been concerned in finding the young people. Having no interest in the story, I had but a confused knowledge of it, but what I heard was not to the credit of the young Prince. His countrymen, it appears, did not judge more favourably, for the article was vehement.

"Have you seen this young lady?" asked the First Consul. I replied in the negative. "Ah! I remember, when I wished Junot to take her home, that you might take charge of her, he leaped several feet high. And the young Duke?" said he. I had not seen him either, or did not remember to have met him, and was quite unacquainted with his person.

"He is one of those young fools who think themselves privileged in all things *because they are princes*," said the First Consul; "he has behaved ill in this affair, and the father of the girl, being known as a diplomatist, should have insisted more strongly on the reparation." Then striking the journal with the back of his hand: "Here is a man who will never incur a syllable of reproach! the Archduke Charles. That man has a soul, a golden heart. He is a virtuous man; and that word includes everything, when spoken of a prince."

After running through some journals and letters, the First Consul again pinched my foot through the bedclothes, and descended to his cabinet, uttering a few false notes. I called my waiting-woman, who had not been long in my service, and without explanation prohibited her ever opening the door to anyone who might knock so early in the morning. "But, Madame, if it be the First Consul?" "I will not be awakened so early by the First Consul or anyone else. Do as I bid you."

The day resembled others, except that in the evening we took an airing towards Butard. As we passed near the spot which had so alarmed Madame Bonaparte the First Consul praised my courage.

"Nay," said I; "I think I was rather cowardly to alight."

"That was a precaution for your situation, and does you credit; I saw, nevertheless, that you had no fear."

Perhaps it never happened to Napoleon to say so long a compliment twice in his life, and it so surprised me that I could not answer; but it reached other ears than mine, and the surprise was not for me alone. "I should like to give you a breakfast here the day after to-morrow," said the First Consul, when we were in the Pavilion; "we will have a little hunting before and after; it will do me good, and amuse us all. The day after to-morrow, Tuesday, I give you all the rendezvous here, at ten."

Entering my apartment, I gave orders to the waiting-maid, and went to bed much wearied, without knowing why. I was depressed; I wished to see my friends; that home so happy, so animated, the charm of my life, was not for me at Malmaison. I was treated with kindness, but I lived amongst strangers. Besides, I scarcely saw my husband, and I knew I was necessary to him, and was yet too young to guess that this necessity would not be eternal.

I spent the night in tears; I would have given years of my life — that life yet in its morning, and whose day promised such beauty and brilliancy — to the familiar spirit who would have transported me to the side of my mother and husband. At length I fell asleep, like children when their eyes are fatigued with weeping. But my sleep was agitated, and the first light of morning scarcely penetrated my venetian blinds before I awoke, fancying I had heard a noise near my door; but, on listening, I heard nothing. Suddenly it occurred to me that I ought to take the key, for my maid would certainly not dare to refuse the First Consul, and I was determined these morning visits should not be repeated. I saw no harm in them, but knew enough of the world to avoid the construction that might be put upon them. I rose, therefore, very gently, and crossing my maid's room, was not a little surprised to find the door as unsecured as when we went to bed; the key was outside, and the bolt unfastened.

For a moment I was enraged, but, restraining myself, gently opened the door, withdrew the key, double-turned the lock, and, carrying the key with me, returned to my bed, without the power of sleeping; my watch was at hand, and I followed the motion of the fingers until, as they pointed to six, I heard the First Consul's foot in the corridor. He stopped at the door and knocked, but much less loudly than the preceding days. After waiting a moment he knocked again, and this time awoke my maid, who told him I had taken the key. He made no answer, and went away.

When the sound of his steps died away on the stairs leading to his cabinet, I breathed freely, and burst into tears. I looked on the First Consul as a brother, or perhaps rather as a father, since my sentiments towards him were always founded on deep admiration. He was the protector and support of my husband; and Junot himself had the tenderest affection for him: in what light would he view this gross distrust which deprived him of a moment's distraction in conversing with a child he had known from her birth! But having taken my resolution, I became more tranquil; and desiring my maid to shut the door from her room, I was again in a sound sleep, when the door opened violently and I saw the First Consul.

"Are you afraid of being assassinated, then?" said he, with a sharpness that relieved me of all fear; for when any attempt is made to curb me I grow restive, and he might read in my countenance that I was more offended than repentant. I told him, that having risen very early, I had taken the key out of my maid's room, choosing my chamber to be entered only by my own door. Napoleon fixed on me his eyes of the falcon and eagle together, and made no reply: a foolish timidity prevented my telling him my resolution; and I bitterly repented it.

"To-morrow is the hunting-party at Butard," said he; "you have not forgotten it since last night, have you? We set out early, and, that you may be ready, I shall come myself to wake you, and, as you are not amongst a horde of Tartars, do not barricade yourself again as you have done. You see that your precaution against an old friend has not prevented his reaching you. Adieu!" and away he went, but this time without singing. I looked at my watch, and found it nine o'clock, which distracted me, for at that hour all the chambermaids were about in the house, and it was impossible but some of them must have seen him go in or out. "But how did he get in?" I asked myself.

I called my maid Caroline, and asked her why she had departed from my orders. She told me that the First Consul had opened the door with a master-key, and that she dared not hinder his entering my room.

Hereupon I reflected on the course I should pursue. My first suggestion was to demand a carriage of Madame Louis Bonaparte, but what reason could I assign? Ten years later I should have gone to the stables and ordered a carriage, but at seventeen, a timidity, not of character, but of manners, deterred me. I dressed myself, therefore, and went to breakfast with a determined purpose, but great irresolution as to the manner of executing it. Duroc, who would have been my adviser, my friend, and, above all, my means of acting, was absent in Lorraine, and never was I in so much need of his friendship. There was not an individual in the château whom I deemed capable of comprehending my situation.

Madame Louis Bonaparte was kind, sensible, and sufficiently acquainted with the world to know what was due to its observances, but an all-powerful consideration arrested me as I was rising to consult her. I fell back almost stunned, and uncertain what course to adopt. I was determined to return to Paris, and knew that by writing at once to Junot that I was ill and wished to return home, my carriage would arrive in the course of the next day; but it was the same day, Monday, that I resolved to go, not Tuesday, and still less Wednesday. Then again, I was unwilling to appear uncivil to Madame Louis Bonaparte, or to wound the First Consul's feelings.

"*Mon Dieu!*" I exclaimed, dropping my head on my hands; "what can I do?" At the same moment I felt myself pressed in a gentle embrace, and a well-known voice inquired: "What is the matter, then, my Laura?" It was my husband; I threw myself into his arms, folded my own around him, embraced him, kissed his hair and his hands, and so eagerly caressed him that my cheek was scratched by one of his epaulettes, and the blood flowed.

"What is the matter, then?" repeated Junot, stanching the blood and drying my tears. "What is the matter, my poor little one? Look at me, then: do not you know four days have elapsed since I saw you?" "My love, I want to go away—to return to Paris." "Oh, you may be assured that as soon as Madame Bonaparte returns I will take you with me." "And why not now?" "Now! before her return? nay, you do not think of it, my darling?"

I insisted no further, for my plan was now arranged. Junot, though, with all the other acting authorities, prohibited from sleeping out of Paris, frequently visited Malmaison, sometimes after dinner, sometimes in the morning, but, in either case, departed not till we had retired for the night.

This day Junot arrived and stayed to dinner by the First Consul's desire, communicated through the aide-de-camp on duty. When we assembled in the dining-room the First Consul was in high spirits, joked all dinner-time with M. Monge, and made him explain more than ten times over the nature of trade-winds, with which he was himself perfectly well acquainted, but the worthy man had so singular a mode of arranging his hands when speaking, and of running post in his narrative, that he was very amusing, and would have been ridiculous had he not combined the most excellent heart with his great knowledge.

After dinner billiards were introduced as usual; I played a game of chess with the First Consul; and at the usual hour we all separated—some to their rest, and others to return to Paris. I prevented Junot's accompanying Bessières by telling him I had a commission to give him for my mother; and, as I must write, it would be necessary to return to my chamber.

When there, my earnest and persevering supplications that Junot would carry me home with him inspired him at last with the idea that some one had offended me, and his unbounded rage and resentment against the supposed defaulter absolutely terrified me; but, reassured on this head, no arguments, no entreaties could prevail with him "to carry me off," as he said, "in the night, like a heroine of romance." I am now sensible that he could not sanction so ridiculous an act, but I was then very young.

Our discussion had been very long, and at half after twelve, finding Junot resolute, there remained no other expedient than that of persuading him to stay. Here I was much more strongly armed, and after some resistance he said with a smile: "Happily, there are no longer arrests to fear, but you will procure me a scolding;" and he remained.

I double-locked my maid's door, carefully drew the bolts, and took away the key; my own door I left simply shut, with the key outside, and all thus disposed I went to bed, very foolishly convinced that I had adopted the best means of making the First Consul understand that since he was pleased to honour me with his visits, I should prefer any other hour for receiving them to that which he had chosen.

As the village clock was striking five, I awoke; all was quiet in the château, as in the middle of the night. The weather was beautifully serene, and the fine foliage of the park plantations gently undulated in the wind, while a golden ray already tinted the upper branches. All this silence and repose formed so striking a contrast with my own mental uneasiness that I could not avoid starting when my eye fell on Junot sleeping by my side. His sleep was tranquil; yet was there something at once imposing and picturesque in that fine and manly figure, that countenance embrowned by the suns of Africa, that youthful forehead already ploughed with scars, those marked features, and that fair head encircled with a Turkish turban of red and brown, which had accidentally fallen in his way overnight, and been adopted as a nightcap. He was not strikingly handsome, but it could not be denied that he was good-looking.

The half-hour had just struck when I heard the First

Consul's steps resound in our corridor. My heart beat violently; I could have wished Junot at Paris, or concealed; but at that moment a sleeping movement partly opened his shirt, and displayed two wounds received at the battle of Castiglione; a little further, just below the heart, was that given him by Lanusse, when in defence of his beloved General he drew his sword against a brave brother-in-arms. "Ah!" thought I; "I fear nothing: there is an impenetrable buckler," and resting my head on my pillow, I awaited the event.

The door opened noisily. "What! still asleep, Madame Junot, on a hunting-day! I told you that——" The First Consul as he spoke advanced, and now stood at the foot of the bed, where, drawing aside the curtain, he stood motionless at the sight of his faithful and devoted friend. I am almost sure he at first believed it a vision. Junot, on the other hand, scarcely awake, leaning on one elbow, looked at the First Consul with an air of astonishment that would have diverted a less interested spectator; but his countenance expressed no symptoms of displeasure.

"Why, General! what are you doing in a lady's chamber at this hour?" He uttered these words in a tone of perfect good-humour. "I came to awake Madame Junot for the chase," replied the First Consul in the same tone; "but," after a prolonged glance at me, which is still present to my memory, notwithstanding the thirty years that have since intervened,—"but I find her provided with an alarum still earlier than myself. I might scold, for you are contraband here, M. Junot."—"General," said Junot, "if ever a fault deserved pardon, it is mine. Had you seen that little siren last night exercising all her magic for more than an hour to seduce me, I think you would pardon me."

The First Consul smiled, but his smile was evidently forced. "I absolve you, then, entirely. It is Madame

Junot who shall be punished," and he laughed that laugh *which laughs not*. "'To prove that I am not angry, I permit you to accompany us to the chase. Have you a horse?"—"No, General, I came in a carriage."—"Well! Jardin shall find you one, and I allow you to lecture me at your leisure" (because he was a bad huntsman). "Adieu, Madame Junot; come, get up and be diligent," and he left us.

"Faith!" said Junot, jumping up in his bed, "*that is an admirable man!* What goodness! Instead of scolding, instead of sending me sneaking back to my duty in Paris! Confess, my Laura, that he is not only an astonishing being, but above the sphere of human nature."

When we were all ready and assembled on the stone bridge in the garden, several carriages and saddle-horses were brought. A small phaeton led the way; the First Consul seated himself in it, and beckoning to me, said: "Madame Junot, will you honour me with your company?"

These words were accompanied with a smile whose expression did not please me; I got in without reply; the door was shut, and the little light carriage, inclining to the right, followed an alley that led to one of the iron gates of the park. I knew the First Consul would only remain in the carriage from the château to the rendezvous, where he was to mount his horse; but the drive appeared to me very long, and I would have given anything to escape.

When we were at some distance from the château, the First Consul, who till then had been watching the horsemen as they passed us to go to the rendezvous, turned towards me, and crossing his arms, said: "You think yourself very clever." I made no reply, and he repeated: "You think yourself very clever; do you not?"

As his tone was now positively interrogative, I answered with firmness, "I do not give myself credit for extraordinary sense, but I think I am not a simpleton."—"A simpleton, no; but a fool." I was silent. "Can you explain the reason why you made your husband stay?"—"The explanation is clear and brief, General. I love Junot; we are married, and I thought there was no scandal in a husband remaining with his wife."—"You knew I had prohibited it, and you knew, too, that my orders ought to be obeyed."

"They do not concern me. When the Consuls signify their will as to the degree of intimacy that shall subsist between a married couple, and the number of days and hours that should be allotted to their interviews, then I shall think of submitting; till then, I confess, General, my good pleasure shall be my only law."

Here I was growing uncivil, for I was angry, and probably my manner put him out of humour too, for he resumed with asperity, and a sort of irony: "You had no other reason, then, but love for your husband in making him stay?"—"No, General."—"You have told a lie there."— "General——"—"Yes, you have told a lie," repeated he in an irritated tone; "I understand the motive of your proceeding. You have a distrust of me, which you ought not to have. Ah! you have no answer," said he, in a tone of triumph.

"And if I have been impelled by a different motive from the distrust you speak of, General—if I have perceived that your visit at such an hour in the chamber of a young woman of my age might compromise me strangely in the eyes of the other inhabitants of this house?" I shall never forget Napoleon's expression of countenance at this moment; it displayed a rapid succession of sentiments, none of them evil.

"If that be true," said he at last, "why did you not tell me your uneasiness? Have I not shown you friendship enough, naughty child, within the last week to obtain your confidence?"

"There I was perhaps in fault. I should have considered that you had known me a child, General; that my relations love you; that you were once tenderly attached to my mother" (he looked on the other side of the road); "and, above all, that there was another and a stronger reason which should have encouraged me to tell you what I thought of this visit on the second or the third day; this is that I am the wife of Junot—of the man who loves you best in the world. This morning when I heard your step when you were about to enter my chamber, I confess I had some fear of your resentment: but looking at the scars upon his bosom, received partly for your glory, I assured myself that you would never be the cause of suffering to the noble and excellent heart which beats perhaps more strongly for you than for me, in the scarred bosom of Junot."

"You are reading me almost a homily. Who talks of afflicting Junot? Why not have spoken to me?"

"And how was I to do so? When yesterday morning you employed a method that might be called unworthy, to enter my apartment, after my conduct should have shown you, General, that the morning visit which you had the goodness to make me was viewed by me in its true light, as unbecoming; you entered only for a minute, and in a humour certainly not inviting confidence. I was left then to my own resources, and my judgment has perhaps erred."

"Is there none of your mother's advice in all this?"

"My mother, General! how could my mother direct me? My poor mother! I have not seen her this month." "You can write;" and Napoleon's searching glance seemed to pierce me with its scrutiny. "General, I have not written to my mother that I was not in safety under your roof; it would have given her too much pain."

"Madame Junot, you have known me long enough to be assured that you will not obtain the continuance of my friendship by speaking in the manner you are now doing; there is nothing wanting to your proceedings but that you should have communicated to Junot the device you have so happily imagined." And again I met the same investigating look.

"I shall not reply to that challenge, General," replied I, with impatience I could not disguise; "if you grant me neither sense nor judgment, allow me at least a heart that would not wantonly wound one whom I know, and whom you know also." "Again!" and he struck the frame of the carriage with his clenched fist; "again! hold your tongue!"

"No, General, I cannot; I shall continue what I would have the honour of saying to you. I entreat you to believe that neither my mother, my husband, nor any one of my friends, has been informed of what has passed within the last week. I must add that, imputing no ill intentions to you, it would have been absurd on my part to complain of a mark of friendship, because it might compromise me; but I thought proper to put a stop to it at whatever price; and, in so doing, my youth has no doubt led me into error, since I have displeased you. I am sorry for it; but that is all I can say."

We had nearly arrived; the dogs, the horns, all the clamour of the chase were audible. The First Consul's countenance assumed a less sombre hue than it had worn during my long speech. "And you give me your word of honour that Junot knows nothing of all this foolish affair?" "Good Heaven! General, how can you conceive such an idea, knowing Junot as you do? He is an Othello in the violence of his passions; an African in heat of blood; his feeble French reason would not have had strength enough to judge sanely of all this: and——." I stopped. "Well! what then? Come, do not make these pauses in speaking; nothing is more silly." "Well, General, if I had told Junot what has passed this week, neither he nor I would have been here this morning; you know Junot well enough for that, do you not?"

Napoleon, in his turn, made no answer, but played with his fingers on the frame of the carriage. At last, turning towards me: "You will not believe, then, that I meant you no harm?" "On the contrary, General, I am so convinced that you had no ill intention towards me, that I can assure you neither my attachment for you, an attachment dating from infancy, nor the admiration which I feel even more strongly than others, is at all lessened by it; and there is my hand as the pledge of my words."

I cannot express or explain the movement of his forehead, his look, and half-smile, as, gently shaking his head, he refused my hand. I was hurt at the refusal.

"We are at variance, then," said I, "because it has pleased you to follow a course in which all the blame is on your side, and you will *let the beard grow, and wear the dagger*,* because you have given me pain."

For a minute his eyes were fixed on the road; then turning suddenly to me, he extended his little hand, after having ungloved it: "Be assured of my friendship, Madame Junot; you might, had you chosen, have strengthened it; but early education is not easily eradicated. It inculcates sentiments, and those with which you have been inspired for me are not friendly; you do not like me, and I am sure——"

"I take the liberty of interrupting you, General, to request that you will not talk thus. You pain me; and so much the more as your arguments and inferences are both false. Tell me that you do not believe them; it would be too painful to me to leave you in such a persuasion."

The First Consul was looking at the dogs which the

* These are the customs of Corsica, when anyone is offended, or fancies himself offended, who thereby announces himself as an avenger.

pricker was leading in couples, and he turned so suddenly round as to derange the motion of the carriage. "You are going?" "On our return from the hunt, General, I have induced Junot to take me home, and here is a letter that, as you will perceive, would have determined me, independently of the incidents of the last few days" (I said this with a smile), "to go to my mother."

It was from my mother, urging my return to her, and I had received it while dressing that morning. "If the First Consul, or Madame Louis Bonaparte, should raise difficulties," added she, "show them my letter, and beg they will not detain a daughter from the bedside of her sick mother."

The First Consul, casting his eyes over it, shrugged his shoulders, and smiled with a sort of disdain which pained me. "And when do you return?" asked he with a tone of derision that might have offended a person better disposed than I was, and accordingly I answered with asperity: "Whenever I am wanted, for my part, General; but you may dispose of my apartment, I shall never again occupy it."

"As you will. For the rest, you are right to go this morning; after all this foolish affair, you and I should not meet with much satisfaction at present. You are quite right. Jardin! my horse." And opening the door himself, he jumped out of the carriage, mounted his horse, and galloped off.

On our return to the château, I told Madame Louis that my mother's health imperatively demanded my presence in Paris, and that I intended to return with Junot. She understood me, and I even believe she entirely understood my motives. She wished to detain me to dinner, but Junot's absence the preceding night required an earlier return, and, declining the invitation, we dined at Paris with my mother.

I visited Malmaison some time after Madame Bonaparte's

return from Plombières, where she had passed the season; that is to say, six weeks. The First Consul was tolerably cordial, but I could perceive that he still cherished the notion, equally eccentric and injurious, that I had been prompted in all that had passed during the last week of my stay. It gave me pain; but knowing no human means of defeating this prepossession, I left the task to time,* without changing the line of conduct I had marked out for myself.

A year afterwards I dined one day at Malmaison, while residing at Bièvre; satisfied with my charming home, I left it as little as possible, and always returned the same evening. That day I ordered my carriage at ten, but, as I was preparing for departure, a sudden storm came on, of such terrific violence as to injure the trees in the park. Madame Bonaparte protested against allowing me to go through such a tempest, and said that *my chamber* should be prepared. In answer to my persevering excuses, she promised me both linen and a waiting-maid, and urged the danger of crossing the woods at so late an hour. "I fear nothing, madame," I answered, "I have four men with me. Permit me, then, to take leave of you."

The First Consul was occupied, meanwhile, in pulling the fire about with the tongs, and apparently paying no attention to the conversation, though I could perceive a smile on his countenance. At last, as Madame Bonaparte insisted still more strongly on my staying, he said from his place, without resigning the tongs or turning his head: "Torment her no more, Josephine; I know her; she will not stay."

* I know to a certainty that, at this time, *false reports* envenomed all the words of my mother to the First Consul's ears, and I am nearly sure that this story came to the knowledge of persons who would make a pernicious use of it towards us both. The First Consul long retained a rancour, which he certainly would not have felt had it not been both instilled and carefully nourished.

CHAPTER XX.

The Theatres—My Boxes—The First Representation of *Pinto*—M. Carion de Nisas and *The Death of Montmorency*—Vanhove and Louis XIII.'s Snuff-box—Tortures of the Inquisition—Partiality for the *Théâtre Feydeau*, and the Performances of Elleviou—The Italian Opera—The Duke de Mouchy's Duets with Junot—Cimarosa—The *Théâtre de Montansier*—The Masquerade, a Comic Scene.

ONE of the advantages attached to Junot's position as Commandant of Paris was a box at each of the theatres. I confess I was truly grateful for the amusement I thus enjoyed. It afforded me also the means of bestowing pleasure, which was always to me one of the greatest I could enjoy, and in good truth it was not sparingly accorded to me. Tickets for morning and evening representations were eagerly asked, and I received, at a much later period, no less than eleven requests for the loan of my box at the *Comédie Française* for the second representation of *The Templars*. I had opportunities of being generous seven or eight times a day : I accorded them in the belief that by so doing I should secure, if not real friends, at least a sort of amicable relation with my numerous acquaintances which might survive the obligation. I was young when these ideas occupied my mind.

I went frequently to the theatre—a pleasure with which

I had hitherto been so little acquainted that I had visited the Opera but once and the French comedy three times: at the first representation of *Pinto*, the most glorious of disturbances past, present, or to come; that of *Montmorency* by Carion de Nisas; and the *début* of Lafont, which was so stormy that I verily thought the *Théâtre Française* must have been built with unusual strength to resist such attacks.

Pinto, fine as is the subject of the Braganza conspiracy, of which Lemercier was fully capable of taking the utmost advantage, did not suit the taste of that era of clipping scissors and decisive words, which demanded: "Take away that phrase." "Why?" "Because I do not choose that it should stand there." "What is the objection to it?" "I will not allow it." "But surely there is some reason against it—is it unsuitable?" "Not at all; but no matter, it must be removed."

In speaking of my mother's acquaintances, I was in error in omitting the most witty, perhaps, of the circle, M. Carion de Nisas. I know few minds of more various powers, more agreeable, gay, and inoffensive, and withal more *piquant;* but notwithstanding his great dramatic talent he was unfortunate in his theatrical productions. I shall never forget the state of mind he was in at the first representation of *The Death of Montmorency*, which I believe killed him more effectually than the *Connétable* was killed, and that owing to circumstances altogether foreign to his work.

The tragedy contained some fine verses and interesting situations; the Cardinal's political views, and the entire scene in which he develops his plans for the aggrandizement of France, are strikingly beautiful, and the inconsistencies of the piece might have passed unperceived if it had been better performed; but Talma, who played Montmorency, was the only one of the *corps dramatique* that seemed to possess common-sense. Baptiste the elder, Madame Petit-Vanhove, and more especially Vanhove the father, were all out of their element. But Vanhove was admirably placed for producing laughter, which completed the despair of M. de Nisas.

Vanhove the elder had the trifling fault of getting tipsy, not to say actually drunk, on the night of a first representation especially. As he was a wretched performer habitually, it might be hoped that wine would produce a happy effect upon him; but not at all, he was so much the worse. The day of the first representation of *The Death of Montmorency*, notwithstanding the most careful supervision from his daughter, and Talma, who was his son-in-law *in petto*, he drank a little to give him courage, as he said; but by the evening, when it was necessary to assume something of a royal air, his spirit was found mounted a little degree beyond courage.

Although Louis XIII., the great personage he was destined to represent, is not suspected of having been a snuff-taker, there was no such thing as persuading him to give up a round case containing a pound of snuff, which he called his snuff-box. His daughter, already dressed for the part of Anne of Austria, used every possible argument to prevent his appearing upon the stage with this piece of contraband goods. He was thoroughly tipsy, and had taken up a phrase from which there was no driving him.

"Prove to me that Louis XIII. did not take snuff, and I will lay down my arms: prove it to me." "But, my father——" said Madame Petit-Vanhove. "Prove to me that Louis XIII. did not take snuff."

And he so stuffed his unfortunate nose that it was scarcely possible to hear his voice, while the fumes of the snuff further increased his drunkenness; and so completely did he parody some of his part that laughter prevailed over both hisses and applause. M. de Nisas came occasionally to our box, which enabled me to observe a torment of which I should otherwise have had no conception. At one period he was ready to expire; pale, with suspended respiration, and his forehead steeped in perspiration; in fact, it was impossible to laugh—that would have killed him outright. He looked without seeing, and seemed to have but one sense in which all the others were absorbed. What a terrible punishment! I cannot imagine how anyone can voluntarily submit to such torture! I think I should be more at my ease in the water-trench of the holy tribunal.*

Setting aside the partiality of friendship, the play contained some fine passages; amongst others, I remember the following, which was given with much effect: Montmorency, condemned to death, is about to be rescued by the soldiers and the people; his sister, his wife, and the Queen who loves him, are listening with the utmost anxiety to the issue of the attempt; the Cardinal is relating it, and concludes with these words: "In reply to the mutineers, I threw them his head."

The situation at this instant is admirable, and reminds one of Iphigenia. The piece, however, failed, and failed utterly, which proves that a man of genius may write a bad tragedy; and I fear this happens not unfrequently.

The *Feydeau* was one of the theatres at which I passed my evenings with the greatest pleasure; it boasted at that

---

* In the prisons of the Inquisition in Spain three kinds of torture were in use, of which that by water was the most agonizing. The patient lay extended in a kind of trench or coffin open at the feet and at the head; his face was covered with a wet cloth, on which water was thrown, intended to filter drop by drop into the throat, and as the nose and mouth could not breathe through this cloth, which intercepted at once the air and water, the result was that on removing it the cloth and throat were found full of blood from the small vessels which had burst.

time a degree of perfection which it has never recovered. It possessed several admirable performers, and the chief among them was Elleviou—a treasure, not only for his own excellence, but because the other actors in performing with him were emulous of rising to his height; its orchestra was complete, and its charming pieces were played with perfection.

The charm which our native music—gay, brilliant, and expressive—has for our French ears did not prevent our enjoying the Italian Opera, which was established at Paris in the year 1801. The company occupied at first a small theatre, called the Olympic Salon, in the Rue Chantereine. This theatre, not much larger than a salon for private representations, drew together the best society of Paris. Its open boxes, between high pillars, required full dress, an obligation sufficiently agreeable to ladies; and I remember to have seen the first tier of boxes entirely occupied by very elegantly-dressed women, almost all young; and, what was still more remarkable, all of my acquaintance, except the inmates of two boxes.

My mother, who found a sovereign panacea for all her sufferings in good Italian music, never failed to take her place in my box on the night of the Opera Bouffe. The Duc de Mouchy frequently accompanied her. He was then, and has ever since been, an excellent *dilettante*. He was passionately fond of Italian music, and sang charmingly in the bouffe style. I have often accompanied him and my husband in that duo from *The Clandestine Marriage*— " Se fiato," etc. Neither of them ever failed in note or time; and the harmony of intonation and expression was perfect. The Duke had a superb voice, a full and sonorous baritone, which it was delightful to hear; Junot was far behind him, and had no other merit than correctness and time. His voice was harsh, because *to the right about face,* and *by fours to the left,* will not form a supple voice, even if it has the good fortune to remain correct; and my lessons were not sufficiently vigorous to make him an accomplished musician.

The Italian Opera naturally leads to some mention of Cimarosa, who was scarcely fifty years old at his death. He was born at Naples, and educated at the Conservatory of Loretto, where the works of the incomparable Durante formed his chief study. He left the Conservatoire young, and, according to the then prevailing fashion amongst struggling composers, had to make choice of a patron. He was acquainted with Madame Ballante, whose immense fortune gave her the means of patronizing the arts. She received the young musician, and soon found how honourable to herself would prove the protection she extended to him.

Madame Ballante had a daughter who did not listen with impunity to his ravishing notes; she loved him passionately, and the mother permitted his addresses; they were married, but after a brief but happy union she died, leaving a son. He was in despair; his mother-in-law, Madame Ballante, had educated and adopted a young orphan, whom she bestowed on Cimarosa, saying: "My friend, she is my second daughter!" Alas! his tender heart was not destined for happiness: his second wife also died young, leaving him a son and a daughter.

Cimarosa, besides extreme goodness of heart, possessed much talent and considerable information. He sang to perfection, and accompanied his voice with brilliant execution. My brother, who was enchanted with his compositions, as those who have a soul for music must always be, once spent a whole morning with him trying music, Cimarosa at the piano, my brother accompanying with his harp. Cimarosa gave a theme, which Albert took up and varied; the author then sang it in various keys and movements, as a barcarole, canzonet, polacca, romance, etc., and this delightful contest lasted three hours. "The most agreeable hours," my brother has often observed, "which in my life I have ever passed in this manner."

Cimarosa was a charming companion, gay, fond of a laugh, and possessing in the highest degree that generosity which is always inherent in an artist of true talent. How many unfortunate emigrants has he not relieved! When at Paris, his beautiful *Finale del Matrimonio, Pria che spunti*, or *Quelle pupille tenere*, were applauded with rapture approaching to frenzy; it was not known that the profits of these immortal productions were devoted to the comfort of our happy countrymen. But he lived under a Government incapable of appreciating him, and, instead of a wreath in the name of the country, persecutions and chains were the reward of his humanity—persecutions which, it is well known, hastened his end. He attempted, but in vain, to struggle against Royal terrorism; more skilful than the Republican, its cruelty was even more active and permanent. This, it is true, could not easily be, but the horrors committed at Naples are not known to the public, and the eye which could penetrate that multitude of assassinations, legal robberies, and religious persecutions to which Naples was at this time a prey, would turn aside in disgust.

Madame Ballante was also a victim to the trouble which distracted that beautiful country; she lost all her fortune, and Cimarosa had the consolation of receiving her at his home. "You are the mistress of my house," said he; "is not everything I possess your property? Are you not my mother?" Cimarosa died on the 10th of January, 1801; his name will be as immortal as his works.

But to return to Paris. The Opera was always the admiration of Europe, but has greatly improved since the period of which I am now writing. Another theatre was at that time much frequented—the *Théâtre de Montansier;* Tiercelin, Vertepré, Brunet, and Bosquier-Gavaudan attracted thither all the lovers of frank and hearty gaiety; its receipts exceeded those of the Opera by fourteen or fifteen thousand francs per annum.

For some weeks I had experienced so ardent a desire to see a masquerade that I began to feel absolutely unhappy in finding the carnival drawing to a close without having joined in this amusement, just then reintroduced by the First Consul, who had himself attended them. I determined to ask my mother to take me to one; but my first word brought an answer that put a stop to all my hopes in that quarter. " In the first place," said she, " it wearies me beyond everything; in the next, I do not choose that you should go to gape for four hours in a room full of dust and the odour of rancid oil." "I gape!" cried I, "gape at a masked ball, which everyone asserts to be the most diverting of all amusements!" " You do not know what you are talking of," replied my mother; "but, if you are obstinate, go with your husband; your marriage is still sufficiently recent to permit you to be seen together, even if you should be recognized."

At this moment my aunt Comnéna came in. She had been some time at Paris, and, while waiting the arrival of the rest of her family, lived with my mother. She was still a young woman, gay, because she was happy, and taking pleasure in everything.

As soon as she heard of my want of a chaperon, she offered to accompany me to the ball at the Opera, and so enchantingly that I could not refrain from jumping up to embrace her, while I returned a thousand thanks. " It is understood, then," said she. " I shall dine with you; we will mask to the teeth, and give ample provocation to many people who will never suspect us of being at the ball to-night."

Now, it is necessary to explain the cause of the extreme avidity with which the masked ball was attended. This innocent pastime had been suppressed from the commencement of the Revolution, because it was unknown to the Romans and Athenians. Here, however, was a slight mistake, for at Rome tradition shows that if masquerades did not actually exist, there was, at least, a sufficient approach to them to authorize ours. At length the generation which was passing away wished to divert itself once more under a mask; and the generation which was looking up demanded cheerfulness; with one voice, then, the masquerade was called for. Two only had yet been given.

Junot laughed at my desire to go to this ball, and said the same thing as my mother: "Ah, my poor Laurette, how you will be overpowered with *ennui!*" "Ah!" exclaimed I, scarce able to restrain my tears, "you are all leagued against my pleasure; why should I be wearied where everyone else is amused?"

"Let them say on, niece, we will be amused too; and at two o'clock in the morning your husband shall see whether you are wearied, and repent of his impertinence." "Agreed," cried Junot, "I wish for nothing better; we shall see."

We dined very gaily, and passed a delightful evening; my aunt was always communicative, open, sincere, and possessed excellent spirits. My delight, however, was great when midnight arrived; I summoned my maid, and my aunt and I were ready in an instant. While I was looking in the glass to see how my domino became me, I started and gave a piercing cry on perceiving behind me a great black phantom, with large brilliant eyes and a negro face.

"Oh, heavens, how you frightened me!" I exclaimed, while Junot embraced me, laughing heartily. "Oh! oh! is this your courage? how will you bear, then, to find yourself amongst two thousand such masks?" I looked at him, and was still frightened; his great black figure was anything but agreeable. "But why have you made yourself such an object?" "Why? was it not agreed that I should give an arm to you and my aunt?" "What of that?" "What of that? Would you have me promenade the salon of the Opera with my face uncovered? A pretty concern we should make of this masked ball! No, I sacrifice myself for your pleasure to-night; let us take our masks and be gone."

I did not wait a second order, but the horses went too slowly to please me; I thought we should never reach this much-desired Opera-house. At length we entered as the clock struck one, Junot giving us each an arm. On first stepping into the room and casting my eyes round me, the effect of the novel and strange scene upon me was like that of walking the deck of a ship. My head was giddy; I grasped Junot's arm with all my strength; my aunt made me sit down; this indisposition was the effect of the sudden light and excessive heat.

When I had recovered myself, "Now," said Junot, "how do you propose to proceed? You are to amuse yourself according to your taste, and you are to be very much amused, you know; you should speak to some of your acquaintances." "I see none," said I. My aunt laughed, for some persons that she recognized were passing every minute, and she began to predict that I should speak to no one all night. "Come," said Junot, "take courage."

My heart beat and my cheeks burned, as though I was about to commit some bad action, but, summoning resolution, I addressed myself to M. Victor de Laigle, whom I was in the habit of meeting at my mother's, and, indeed, at the entertainments of all my friends. I approached him, and in an accent which I intended to be witty, said to him, "Good-evening, how do you do?"

He took my hand, eyed my figure, examined my feet, and

then muttered : " Hem—hem—not much amiss. Well ! but have you nothing to say to a man beyond inquiries after his health ?" He retained my hand a moment longer, then, dropping it, turned on his heel, saying, " What a stupid mask !"

What I felt at this moment it would be impossible to describe ; to hear myself called stupid by an acquaintance ! It confused me beyond all conception, and I stood rooted to the spot and actually stupefied. M. Victor de Laigle was by this time at the opposite end of the room, laughing and jesting with other masks, and no doubt saying, " I have just escaped from the stupidest little mask, yonder, that I ever encountered."

It was in vain that Junot and my aunt reasoned with me ; nothing could console me for having been called stupid in conversation. " But you must agree," said Junot, " that you deserved it ; was ever such a thing heard of as asking a man how he is, in company, by way of conversation ?" " What would you have had me say ?"

" Faith ! I can't tell : anything but that." And in truth he was in the right ; it was scarcely possible to be more foolish than I was this night. I never mentioned this little scene to M. Victor de Laigle, and he is still ignorant of it, unless Junot charitably informed him who it was who was so anxious about his health at the masquerade. The result of this wearisome night, from which I expected so much pleasure, was to give me a disgust for masked balls, which for years I could not get over ; nor, indeed, have I ever again taken pleasure in them.

CHAPTER XXI.

The Private Theatre of Malmaison—*Esther* at Madame Campan's—Eugène Beauharnais and M. Didelot—M. de Bourrienne an Excellent Actor—Representation of *The Barber of Seville*—Madame Louis Bonaparte as Rosina—Madame Murat—Rivalry between the Companies of Neuilly and Malmaison—Lucien Zamora and Eliza Alzira—*Lovers' Follies*—My Despair and the Tight Boots—The Officer in White Satin Slippers—The Theatrical Sabre and a Real Wound—Comic Acting of Cambacérès—The First Consul Director of the Stage—Mr. Fox and Bonaparte's Three Countenances—Isabey and the First Consul—General Lallemand—Michau's Tragi-comic Adventure during the Revolution.

Everyone who has trodden the boards of a private theatre will agree with me that no circumstances of their lives afford reminiscences more abounding in pleasure and gaiety than the rehearsals, and everything, in short, that is merely preparatory. But in candour they must equally admit that the actual scenic representation is absolute torture. I have experienced both, and can speak from practical knowledge.

Mademoiselle de Beauharnais's success at Madame Campan's in the representations of *Esther* and other pieces, in which Mesdemoiselles Auguier and Mademoiselle Pannelier, as well as herself, gave proofs of remarkable talent, naturally induced her to bring the theatre of Malmaison into use. Eugène Beauharnais was a perfect actor. I may, without partiality, say that Junot had superior talent; M.

Didelot was an admirable Crispin; I acquitted myself tolerably in my parts; and General Lauriston was a noble Almaviva, or any other lover in Court dress.

But the cleverest of our company was M. de Bourrienne; he played the more dignified characters in real perfection; and his talent was the more pleasing as it was not the result of study, but of a perfect comprehension of his part. Grandménil and Caumont, at that time the supporters of such characters at the *Comédie Française*, could have discovered no flaw in M. de Bourrienne's performance of Bartholo, of Albert in *Lovers' Follies*, of the Miser, or of Harpagène; in *The Florentine* he might, perhaps, even furnish them occasionally with a turn of expression worth seizing and copying.

The First Consul himself was almost the sole manager of our dramatic repertory. It was at first but limited, for we dared not venture on first-rate plays, or undertake parts beyond our capacity. We played *The Heir*, *The Thoughtless Ones*, *The Rivals*, *Defiance and Malice*, and a number of charming little witty pieces, which certainly have not been equalled since either in good sense or good style. Afterwards we grew bolder; the First Consul himself demanded longer plays. The repertory was all at once increased by fifty pieces, which were put into our hands with a careful distribution of the several parts in conformity with our individual talents. The theatre of Malmaison had at that time an excellent company; latterly it was open to everyone, and was no longer endurable.

The first play acted at Malmaison was *The Barber of Seville*, and in saying that this representation was perfect I do not hazard a word that memory can call in question. We have still many survivors of that merry and delightful period, and I fear no contradiction in asserting again that *The Barber of Seville* was acted at the theatre of Malmaison better than it could now be performed in *any theatre in Paris*.

Mademoiselle Hortense de Beauharnais took the part of Rosina; M. de Bourrienne that of Bartholo; M. Didelot, Figaro; General Lauriston, Almaviva; Eugène, Basile; and General Savary sneezed in perfection in the part of the Sleeper Awakened.

I have just observed that Bourrienne played well because he understood and felt his part. The same may be said of Mademoiselle Hortense. Gaiety, wit, sensibility, delicacy, all that the author Beaumarchais meant to infuse into his Rosina, she caught instinctively; she entered into the character of the young and fair Andalusian with all her native grace and elegance. To her fine acting she united a charming figure and an exquisite carriage, especially on the stage. Many years have elapsed since those joyous evenings, but my memory still forcibly recalls the graceful and pleasing image of Mademoiselle Beauharnais,* with her profusion of fair ringlets beneath a black velvet hat, ornamented with long pink feathers, and the black dress so admirably fitted to her small and symmetrical shape. I seem yet to see and hear her.

Her brother Eugène was equally perfect as Basile, and M. de Bourrienne in the part of Bartholo. General Lauriston succeeded well in the various situations of Almaviva, though some fault was found with those of the soldier and the bachelor. He was not altogether perfect till the grandee of Spain reappeared under the mantle of the student. M. Didelot was excellent in Figaro.

But our success was most remarkable in that point which generally reduces the managers of private theatres to despair; that is to say, the perfect correspondence of the

---

* Hortense Beauharnais, wife of Louis Bonaparte.

whole piece: the parts were thoroughly learned, and everything went off well.

Madame Murat sometimes acted at Malmaison. She was very pretty. Her hands and arms were beautiful, and her fair bosom acquired new brilliancy beneath a black velvet bodice, with a gold stomacher; but she had an unfortunate accent, which was particularly fatal to the parts she selected. Her sisterly relation to the First Consul, however, screened this defect from observation, whereas Madame Louis Bonaparte, had she been but the wife of an aide-de-camp, must have been applauded for the excellence of her acting.

This reminds me of an incident which befell me, partly through the instrumentality of Madame Murat, or, at least, through her want of acquaintance with the stage. There was a sort of rivalry between Malmaison and Neuilly. Lucien frequently acted both in tragedy and comedy with his eldest sister, Madame Bacciochi. Lucien acquitted himself admirably, and declaimed to perfection. His only failing, and that not altogether dependent on himself, was the modulation of his voice, which was too shrill and in too elevated a key for a tragic tone. But this inconvenience was slight, and Lucien gave great satisfaction as Zamora. I have heard his performance criticized; in my own judgment I did not perceive the defects attributed to him, and I was delighted with him almost throughout the part.

Not so with Madame Bacciochi. Her acting was irresistibly laughable. The First Consul found it so, and, far from flying into a rage, as M. de Bourrienne represents, he did nothing but laugh during the whole play whenever his sister appeared on the stage, and when we returned to the drawing-room, he exclaimed: "I think we have seen Alzira beautifully parodied." He repeated the same thing

ELIZA MARIE ANNE BONAPARTE,

GRAND DUCHESS OF TUSCANY, PRINCESS OF LUCCA AND PIOMBINO
(COUNTESS OF CAMPIGNANO).

1777—1820.

to Madame Bacciochi herself, who was not the best pleased with it.

Plays of all kinds, of three and afterwards of five acts, were performed at Neuilly—we had no fear of tragedy, still less of comedy. Regnard's *Lovers' Follies*, not too perfectly represented, spurred us to emulation. It was got up at Malmaison. Madame Louis was to undertake Agatha, Lisette was assigned to me, Albert to M. de Bourrienne, Erasto to Eugène, and Crispin to M. Didelot.

By this arrangement the piece would have been well managed, but the spirit of mischief intervened. Madame Louis, always good-natured and yielding at the first request, reversed the whole order of things. Madame Murat performed Lisette. Agatha, a part which I did not like, and which was not suited to me, fell to my lot, and as the climax of misfortune, for some reason I do not remember, Eugène could not play Erasto; this was known only two days before the representation, and Junot was obliged in that time to learn the whole part, and to act it with only a single rehearsal; but all this was nothing compared to what followed.

This unfortunate part of Agatha is very difficult; it requires much judgment. A ray of reason must be always perceptible to the lover, while the guardian, though an acute and sensible man, must believe his young ward a confirmed idiot; then a degree of sentiment must pervade all that chaos of singing, dancing, accident, and battle; in short, it is extremely difficult to play the part well, and Dugazon, who was my instructor and set his heart on my success, had nearly overset my courage by saying to me one day:

"You must not play this part; you will fail as completely as they do at Neuilly." "Oh, don't say so!" I exclaimed, terrified at the idea. "I have not a doubt of it," he proceeded; "and the more certainly as you are horribly supported. The General, too, has a part that does not suit him. The play will be a total failure."

And thereupon Dugazon began to mimic everyone who was to support the dialogue with me, and with such buffoonery that it was impossible to avoid laughing till the tears came. My self-love, however, would not permit me to laugh at his prophecy that the play would prove a failure, and I did all in my power to prevent it; but there was no remedy, and the hour of the tragi-comedy arrived at length.

To form a just conception of the nervousness (that is the proper word) felt by us *Comedians in Ordinary* of Malmaison, it should be premised that on the day of our representation, which was generally Wednesday, it was the First Consul's habit to invite forty persons to dinner, and a hundred and fifty for the evening, and consequently to hear, criticize, and banter us without mercy. The Consuls, the Ministers, the Diplomatic Corps, Councillors of State, Senators, their wives, and all the members of the then Military Household of the First Consul, formed our audience. But the most terrible was the First Consul himself. There he sat in his box, close beside us, his eyes following us and accompanying their glances with a smile more or less arch at the slightest departure from the piece.

The morning of the representation of *Lovers' Follies*, Dugazon said to me, after hearing Bourrienne rehearse Albert admirably: "Well, take courage, my pupil, you will save the State. You two may do wonders. Crispin is good, too. As for the General, his part is nothing. Come, carry this off successfully, and you will deserve well of the country by foiling a conspiracy."

In the part of Agatha the dress is changed five or six times. I had requested Madame Murat, and Dugazon also had charged her, not to enter the stage to commence the third act without first ascertaining that I had completed my officer's dress under my black domino as the old grandmother. The two first acts had passed off tolerably, with the exception of a few errors of memory and some little deficiency of spirit; but the piece still marched—it was soon destined to *limp*.

Whether from misunderstanding or forgetfulness, Lisette appeared upon the scene without troubling herself about me. The question whether or not I was ready was, however, deserving of attention, for but a very short scene intervenes between that in which I receive the money from Albert and my return as an officer. It was therefore imperatively necessary that I should be in full costume underneath my great black cloak, and I was accordingly putting on my boots when I heard the first lines of the act; I cried out directly, but in vain; I had not yet come to the end of my troubles. The day was suffocatingly hot: agitation and fear threw me almost into a fever, which did not accelerate matters; the boots would not come on, and while my waiting-maid pulled till she almost broke my leg, my ankle began to swell. At length I heard the speech preceding my own, and throwing the boot ten feet off, I hastily assumed my black domino, and entered upon the scene; but my poor head was wandering. I mechanically repeated the words assigned me, but my feet at the moment occupied my whole attention.

In an interval between the couplets I whispered to Junot: "What can I do? I cannot get my boots on!"

"Hey! What?" said he, for he could not hear. I repeated the same thing to Bourrienne, but as I spoke very low and quickly neither of them understood; this little by-play, however, so puzzling to them, began to excite more notice than I wished in other quarters. At last I made my exit, ran to my boots, and endeavoured to draw them on— impossible; the foot was still more swelled, and I might as easily have shod the Colossus of Rhodes as have driven my feet into either of them.

At this moment Dugazon, who was roaming about behind the scenes, arrived to witness my despair. He ran up to me, and, embracing me, said : All goes on well, but what the deuce were you looking for under your feet just now ?" As my brain at the moment retained but one fixed idea, I answered, staring at him in utter consternation : " I cannot get my boots on !" " You have not your boots on ?" said he, swearing—"you have not your boots on ?"

At that moment my husband's valet, who was to bring me a very small sabre that I had ordered, tapped at my room door, and presenting a sword as large as Mahomet's Damascus blade, told me in his German jargon that my sabre was not ready, but that he had brought me the smallest of the *Cheneral's*, and it was necessary to be cautious in using it, for it would cut like a razor.

" Here is a new trouble !" I exclaimed.

" Eh ! do not be uneasy," said Dugazon, capering ; " it is all very well. You have a greatcoat ; never mind black shoes, keep on your white ones. Agatha is mad : it is no disguise. All those about her know that an access of her malady has just seized her, and that she has assumed a military dress because her head is unsteady. Well, she has forgotten her white shoes ! Really, upon my honour, this is not amiss."

Saying this, he pushed me on the stage, and it was fortunate that he did so, for my turn was come, and I should never have had the courage to appear thus as an officer of dragoons in white satin slippers. I took good care not to look towards the First Consul's box ; to have seen his smile or frown would have struck me mute.

The result of this fine story is that I played the last scene like a true maniac. But, owing to those unlucky boots, I forgot the Turkish sabre and its sharpness, and when at the conclusion Agatha flourishes it about the ears of Albert, and then suddenly falls into a swoon, the point of the unfortunate Damascus penetrated my white slipper and made a deep cut in my foot, of which I still bear the scar.

But let me ask, Was anyone ever seen to enter a theatre in the dress of a dragoon officer and in white satin slippers?

The First Consul was for six months unmerciful upon those unlucky white slippers. I verily think he would have dragged them into a discussion even upon the bull *Unigenitus*.

I now remember it was the same day that, the conversation turning at table on the pleasure of acting in the country, the First Consul said to Cambacérès, who expressed his participation in it: "That this pleasure could consist only in hearsay, for he surely had never taken part in a comedy." Cambacérès seemed piqued, and replied in an accent really amusing when contrasted with his melancholy and severe countenance:

"And why, Citizen First Consul, do you think that I have not gaiety enough to act in comedy?" "Really, Citizen Cambacérès," replied Napoleon, "I think you have no gaiety at all."

"Well, I have very often acted in comedy, nevertheless, not only at Montpellier, but at Béziers, at the house of an old family friend, where for six months in the year the theatre was in activity, and one of the parts in which I was eminently successful was that of Renaud d'Aste."

"And did you sing?" cried Madame Bonaparte, and all the party laughed, but Cambacérès, no way disconcerted by our hilarity, continued: "And as all characters suited me alike, I played equally well Le Montauciel in *The Deserter*." This time the laugh was universal. But Cambacérès was not easily turned from an agreeable subject, and having once entered on the history of his scenic adventure, the petty jealousies and intrigues of his company, there was no stopping him under half an hour; the rather, as Napoleon, his elbow on the table, listened with an attention which did not surprise me, because I had observed the interest with which he would attend to our reports of the thousand little incidents that arise during the rehearsal of a play.

The First Consul should have been seen in his functions of stage manager to be known under an aspect entirely different from all his portraits. "The First Consul at Malmaison, the First Consul at St. Cloud, and the First Consul at the Tuileries," said Mr. Fox to me, "are three men forming together the *beau idéal* of human greatness; but I could wish to be a painter," added he, "to take his portrait under these different characters, because I should have three resemblances of the same face with three different aspects."

The statesman was right; I had remarked it before him, and was pleased at hearing my own idea so strikingly expressed by the man whom, of all Englishmen, I at that time most highly appreciated. It was perfectly true, and Bonaparte at Malmaison was admirable in extreme simplicity.

One of our best actors was Isabey, perhaps the very best, Queen Hortense excepted. He, however, ceased to form often a member of our *corps comique* rather than *dramatique*, for reasons which were but imperfectly explained.

One day the First Consul, on dismounting from his horse, and traversing the gallery adjoining the centre salon at Malmaison, stopped to examine a portfolio of engravings which had been placed upon a table at the park end of the gallery. Isabey is said to have entered a moment after him from the theatre, and by the opposite door at the end next the Court. The First Consul was then slim, and wore the uniform of the *guides* or *horse chasseurs* of the Guard—that beloved uniform, the very sight of which makes the heart beat. Eugène Beauharnais, as I have before observed, was Colonel of that fine regiment.

Isabey, who had not heard the First Consul return from his ride, seeing a small slender figure at the end of the gallery, dressed in the uniform of the *chasseurs*, and observing the two epaulettes, supposed it to be Eugène, with whom he was extremely intimate, and determined to take him by surprise. Dexterous, light, active, and supple as a cat in his movements, he advanced softly, without the slightest sound, to within a short distance, then, taking a spring, leaped at one bound upon the First Consul and alighted on his neck. Napoleon imagined the house was falling, or that the *old gentleman* was come to strangle him. Rising up, he disengaged himself by main force from his new-fashioned collar, and threw poor Isabey in his turn upon the ground, and, presenting to his dismayed view a countenance for which he was certainly little prepared, demanded in a severe tone:

"What is the meaning of this buffoonery?"

"I thought it was Eugène," stammered out the luckless youth.

"And suppose it was Eugène," replied the First Consul, "must you needs break his shoulder-blades?" And he walked out of the gallery.

This story was soon bruited about. The First Consul had too much tact not to perceive that his was the ridiculous share of the adventure; Isabey understood it to the full as well, and both would willingly have kept the secret. But whether the one in the first moment of his panic related the whole to Eugène himself, or the other in his resentment could not withhold it from Madame Bonaparte, the affair got wind. I know that a short time afterwards its truth was denied. At all events, if it caused the departure of Isabey and his loss to our company, I must call it an act of useless injustice.

General Lallemand, at that time aide-de-camp to my husband, was also one of our best actors. I have seen but few good comedians, and of those very few indeed were his equals. His talent was natural, but had been improved by the instructions of Michau, from whom he imbibed a portion of that ease and humour which was the principal charm of Michau's own acting.

This excellent man once said to me, "It is always useful to make people laugh," and in illustration of this truth related an anecdote of himself. Passing once quietly along the streets, he encountered one of those disorderly mobs that were in the habit of parading Paris in those happy days when the lamp-posts served for hanging up our gallant citizens: they would have made him join their march, but he resisted, and demanded in the name of that liberty, whose scarlet ensign was as usual conspicuous in the foremost group, that he should be suffered to continue his route in pursuance of his own affairs. The discussion was brief, the lamp was shattered, and poor Michau, already stripped of his coat, was on the point of being hoisted in its place, when a fat fellow, with his plump arms bare, and a red and jolly face, rushed into the midst of the banditti and snatched Michau from their grasp, exclaiming:

"What are you about, simpletons? don't you know 'Punch of the *République*'?" The *Comédie Française* was at that time called the *Théâtre de la République*.

And thanks to his title of "Punch," with which his deliverer, the butcher's boy, had invested him, Michau found himself at liberty, and accepted the apologies which two hundred rascals offered for their design of hanging him, as coolly as if they had simply trodden on his toes!

CHAPTER XXII.

The Fruit of our Triumphs, and the Peace with Austria—Brilliant Festivities at Paris—Revival of Trade—The Balls of Malmaison—Luxury and Elegance—Negotiations at Luneville—General Brune's Victories—The Archduke Charles and Marshal Bellegarde—Early History of General Brune—His Exploits in Holland and Italy—The Convention of Montfaucon—The Battle of Pozzolo—Brune appointed a Marshal of France—His Interview with Gustavus IV.—His Disgrace—His Command in Provence—His Tragical Death and Prophetical Verses—Madame de Montesson and the Lieutenant of Hussars—Bonaparte chooses to be informed of everything—Junot's Supposed Police.

A SERIES of victories of the French arms had at length determined Austria to conclude a treaty of peace; it was signed at Luneville by Count Louis von Cobentzel for the Emperor and Germanic Confederation on the one part, and by Joseph Bonaparte in the name of the French Republic, which might still call itself One, and more than ever Indivisible.

All who had been concerned in the Congress came to Paris to share in the magnificent *fêtes* which the First Consul commanded, that the people might have an opportunity of testifying their joy; and that a free circulation of money might revive commerce, and give work to that multitude of individuals who, to the number of a hundred thousand, exist in Paris by the labour of their hands—a labour which, though chiefly devoted to objects of luxury, produces those commodities which the higher classes, especially in seasons of festivity, can no more do without than the lower can subsist without bread. The *fêtes* given by the Government were a signal not only to Paris, but to the whole of France, for balls, dinners, and social assemblages of every kind. Hence commenced in Paris, at this period, life and gaiety, which ceased not to animate it till the change introduced in 1814. Each succeeding day brought ten invitations for the evening.

The almost Oriental luxury which the Emperor afterwards introduced into his Court was not then known. Madame Bonaparte, who possessed in the highest perfection the art of dressing, set the example of extreme elegance. No sight could be more charming than a ball at Malmaison, composed of the numerous ladies connected with the Military Household which the First Consul had just formed, and who constituted, without having yet received the name, the Court of Madame Bonaparte.

All were young, many were pretty, and I know but one ugly enough to merit the epithet. When this beautiful group was attired in robes of white crape trimmed with flowers, and their hair ornamented with garlands as fresh as the complexion of their merry faces, smiling with happiness and good-humour, it was a charming and striking spectacle to see the animated dance which derived its zest from their gaiety in the same room in which the First Consul and the most eminent persons in Europe were promenading. These assemblies required a continual renewal of dress, and the first year of the Consulate saw the revival of that trade in the manufacturing towns of France, which again became an honour to the country. The Government officers, no doubt, made smaller accumulations, or laid out less money on estates; but shopkeepers sold their goods, domestics procured places, and workmen got into employment through the medium of from eight to ten thousand balls and five or six thousand dinners, which were given in the course of the winter at Paris. It followed that the silk mercers sold a million yards of satin or velvet, crape and tulle in proportion, the shoemakers manufactured their shoes, the artificial florist was called to assist at the toilet with his flowers, the hairdresser and dressmaker with their industry, and the perfumer with his gloves, fans, and essences.

The higher classes of trade were equally indispensable; the jeweller, the goldsmith, the glass and porcelain manufacturer, the upholsterer, the cabinet-maker, all flourished; the money passed through their hands into those of their workpeople, and the immense population of this great town were all employed and all happy, because the superior classes received company, and expended their incomes in an honourable manner.

I have known the people of the Faubourgs at this period, when to be peaceful they asked only to be employed, and work was furnished to them in abundance. More virtues or more noble sentiments will nowhere be found than among the working classes of Paris. Never did they rise into tumult through the whole course of the Revolution except when driven into violence by misery and hunger. Hunger! the most imperious of wants! that which blinds the eye and deafens the ear to all other considerations, and ripens the fruits sown by an improvident Government— despair and revolt.

But at the epoch* of which I am writing things were not so; all prospered. The Peace of Luneville, which secured to France the Rhine as the limit, had been signed. The concessions stipulated at Campo-Formio between General

---

* The 9th of February, 1801.

Bonaparte and Count Louis von Cobentzel were confirmed; these concessions were the Duchies of Milan, of Mantua and Modena, together with the Ionian Islands, to be added to the Cisalpine Republic. All was glory shed upon France by the First Consul, and sensibly felt by a grateful nation.

All this was not, however, conceded without much hesitation on the part of the Austrians; it was the necessity of retreating on all sides before our cannon which first induced Austria to treat without the consent of England, notwithstanding her recent engagement to the contrary. This was a great victory gained over English gold. But Joseph Bonaparte, after having given some grand dinners at Paris to the Count von Cobentzel, in which department we had given him all the assistance in our power, was obliged to maintain against him at Luneville many long and warm discussions upon every point to be surrendered, for, alas! we were unreasonable, and asked, the plenipotentiary thought, too much. Happily for the success of Joseph's negotiations, he received, just at the critical moment, a courier from General Brune, bringing a copy of a despatch to the First Consul, announcing a victory in the true Republican style of conciseness:

"Citizen First Consul,

"I have the honour to inform you that I crossed the Adige yesterday, 1st of January, immediately above Verona; which puts me into a position to announce to you very shortly the occupation of that town.

"I salute you with respect,
"Brune."

Accordingly, on the 3rd of January Verona was occupied by our troops, as well as Vicenza some days afterwards, and the Brenta was then crossed. In fact, the army was now on the march, and with sufficient rapidity to form a junction with Moreau, who, on his part, encamped at the distance of twenty-five leagues from Vienna, had concluded an armistice with the Archduke Charles, a good prince, an honest man, and a great captain,* but often unfortunate. M. de Bellegarde, who was so too (that is, unfortunate; for the rest I am not competent to speak), took the same method to obtain some quiet sleep.

An armistice was concluded between him and General Brune, and three weeks after the glorious Treaty of Luneville was signed, which wholly restored Marshal Bellegarde's repose, and I may add *en passant* that of some other Austrian Generals-in-Chief, who had had enough of this war. The Prince Charles was the only one of them whose noble conduct, even under every reverse, was worthy of his exalted birth and great soul. I more than esteem the character of this Prince, and believe I know it as well as a personage of his rank can be known without the advantage of personal access.

Brune, who gave so fortunate an impetus to the diplomacy of Luneville, was born at Brives, and, like all natives of the South, was ardent, active, fond of literature, poetry, and the fine arts; he possessed a large share of information, betook himself to composition, and, to facilitate the publication of his works, became a printer. When the Revolution opened Brune was young; his head and heart confessed but one idea—glory and his country. He soon cast away his pen, ink, and paper, and took up sword and gun to enter one of those battalions of heroes which France produced by thousands in those radiant days of glory and liberty, and which were formed without the necessity of beating to arms. His battalion of the Seine and Oise was commanded by General Lapoype.

None of our Marshals have been so misrepresented as

* Who defeated Napoleon at the Battle of Aspern.

Brune. He was not one of Moreau's Generals, as it was the fashion to denominate those who had served in the Army of the Rhine. Had the restored Princes believed him so, they would surely have protected him from the popular fury, as senseless as all the accusations which have been advanced against him; but Brune did not belong to the Army of the Rhine, neither was he in Paris in the autumn of 1792.

Those, therefore, who accuse him of participating in the horrible saturnalia of the Septembrisers, to which, had he been at Paris, he would neither in heart, word, nor jest have assented, should, before staining his life with a falsehood, in order to palliate the horror of his death, have ascertained whether in physical possibility he could have committed the atrocious crime with which he is charged, and of which an alibi of several hundred leagues is, I apprehend, a sufficient refutation. Brune was not at Paris in September, 1792, but at Radmack.

Brune advanced rapidly to an elevated rank in the army; he had courage and agreeable address, a union always tending to success, but at this period insuring it. The cannon made gaps in the ranks with a frightful rapidity, and so caused rapid promotion for those who obtained the notice of their chiefs, though it might be only to advance them more certainly to the honours of a soldier's grave. The cradle of Brune's glory was the Army of Italy, then under the command of Kellerman and Brunet.

It is remarkable that, notwithstanding the activity of Brune's military life and a renown well earned before General Bonaparte's accession to the command of the Army of Italy in 1795, he is scarcely mentioned in the journals of the time; the *Moniteur*, for example, notices him only in 1797. Brune, however, largely contributed his portion of the glory to the three brilliant days preceding and following the battle of Rivoli, which decided the fate of Italy. He was soon after made Commander-in-Chief of the army in Helvetia; laid siege to Berne, and by its surrender compelled the submission of all Switzerland. From thence he was transferred to the Texel, to oppose the landing of the Anglo-Russian army under the command of the Duke of York, which might have been a fatal event for France, while at the same moment Masséna was sinking in Switzerland under the superior force of the enemy.

The road to Paris was open to the enemy, and Brune, with 20,000 men, whom the Directory kept in a state of inefficient provision, was to check the advance of an Anglo-Russian army which had been disembarked at Alkmaar, and was joined by a Dutch force of 18,000 men. The Duke of York was entirely beaten at Bergen-op-Zoom, which led to the capitulation of his whole army at Alkmaar; and Masséna at the same time gained the battle of Zurich—two victories which saved France, as Marshal Villars had saved her at Denain.

Peace now gave a momentary security to our frontier, and the overthrow of the Directory opened a prospect of good government for France: the First Consul's anxious care was directed to the re-establishment of order in those fine provinces so long desolated by internal conflicts, and he sent Brune into the West, where General Hedouville had already prepared a convention, which was signed almost immediately after, and secured the submission and tranquillity of both sides of the Loire. At this period the First Consul appointed Brune to the command of the Army of Italy, which brings us to the point whence we set out.

It was in the month of November, 1800, that Macdonald, at the head of the Army of the Grisons, comprehending the importance of his junction with Brune, penetrated into the Valteline by the passage of the Splugen, one of the most elevated summits of the Alps, and, braving tempests and avalanches, succeeded in his prodigious efforts by the most unprecedented display of courage and industry. But to the Chief of the Staff of this army, General Mathieu Dumas, is to be attributed, perhaps almost even more than to Macdonald himself, this triumph over the elements and Nature: all the resources which patience, vigilance, activity, and philanthropy could supply to the warrior, he provided, in forestalling his wants and protecting him from other dangers than those of the sword and the cannon.*

Brune, meanwhile, was attempting the passage of the Mincio, in face of the fine army of Marshal Bellegarde; the Battle of Pozzolo, in which Suchet, unsupported, sustained for many hours the whole weight of the enemy's forces, and which was finally decided by an admirable charge of cavalry, under Davoût, enabled him, on the 25th, 26th, and 27th of December, 1800, to effect his purpose, and nearly destroy the Austrian army. Its ultimate important influence upon the conditions of the Peace of Luneville has been already detailed.

Brune now returned to France, retired to his estate of Saint Just, in Champagne, did good in his neighbourhood, and amused himself with literature. In 1804 he was one of the sixteen Marshals whom Bonaparte appointed on the establishment of the Empire. In 1807 Brune was ordered with a *corps d'armée* into Swedish Pomerania; he took Stralsund and the Isle of Rugen, and forced the Swedish army to retire. His interview with the King of Sweden during the siege of Stralsund, the particulars of which, as published by Gustavus, Brune denied to be correct, caused Napoleon's high displeasure; he continued for many years in disgrace, and the name of the conqueror of Bergen and

---

* See Memoirs of General Count Mathieu Dumas (English edition), vol. ii., p. 162. (London: Bentley, 1839.)

the pacificator of the East was, during this period, never pronounced.

On Napoleon's return, however, in March, 1815, Marshal Brune was drawn from his retirement and accepted a post of great confidence and delicacy—the command of the Eighth Military Division, which committed the peace of the South to his keeping. The restoration of Louis XVIII. and his re-entry into Paris found Brune at his post; he went to Toulon himself to restore the white flag there, lest its reappearance should be the signal for popular tumult, and was afterwards summoned to Paris. It was on his way thither, at Avignon, that he met with the dreadful death which has stained the era to which it belongs with indelible infamy. Many particulars of it I received from an eyewitness.

Marshal Brune on reaching Avignon was warned that much agitation prevailed in the town, and that it was particularly directed against him; he was strongly recommended to avoid passing through; but turning a deaf ear to all advice, he commanded his postilions to drive to the post-house; here an armed mob of 800 men, calling themselves Royalists, besieged him in a room to which they had driven him for refuge; the Mayor, the Prefect, and a few *gens-d'armes* succeeded in protecting him during four hours from their infuriated attacks, while 3,000 citizens looked with apathy upon the atrocious scene, without affording the smallest assistance. The gallant resistance of the police was at length overpowered, and under the stupid pretence that the Marshal had been the murderer of the Princesse de Lamballe—a vile slander generally circulated, and which I have already refuted,* in proving that he was not at Paris when that tragedy was performed—he was put to death by the mob in the most

* Page 208.

barbarous manner; his lacerated corpse, after being dragged through the mud, was thrown into the Rhone; and the river refusing to contain it, it lay two days unburied upon the strand, whither the waves had cast it.*

Junot was necessarily acquainted with many facts and events, because the military Commandant of a great city receives a daily report as to its order or condition, and this opened to him an infinity of doors of observation, into which sometimes he would not even look. Frequently, indeed, have I seen reports given in by the old Adjutant Laborde, which Junot has made him transcribe in order to omit certain names, or some words which might compromise the parties concerned in them, and were of no importance to the safety of the First Consul. On this subject I will cite an anecdote.

---

* A curious incident, which occurred eighteen years previously, closely connected with the tragical event, took place in Italy in the year 1797. General Masséna was called to Milan by General Bonaparte, then commanding in chief, to assist at some national festival. The command of Masséna's division then devolved on Brune, who celebrated the same *fête* at Padua. A banquet was given at which much patriotic poetry was read and sung. General Brune, who was wedded to literature, and fond of poetry, heard some stanzas of a song, the sentiment of which pleased him, and he composed impromptu the following couplets, which he sang in conclusion:

> " Against one, two hundred rise,
> Assail and smite him till he dies;
> Yet blood, say they, we spare to spill;
> And patriots we account them still!

> " Urged by martial ardour on,
> *In the wave their victim's thrown*,
> Their fanatic joy to fill!
> Yet these men are patriots still!"

Little did he suppose himself prophesying, and yet with what strange accuracy are the details of his horrible death here related in anticipation!

A lady of some importance in good society was involved in the reports concerning some conspiracy under the Consulate (I do not remember whether it was the infernal machine or that of Chevalier), but the fact was that this lady, perfectly innocent, had been induced by the giddiness of a young fool to give him an asylum against the political proscription he had incurred, while he represented the cause of his danger to her as totally different from the fact. The *gendarmerie* traced him, and took him from under the wing of Madame de Montesson. The lady no sooner discovered the real state of the case than in great alarm she hastened to visit Junot. She was held in much consideration by the First Consul: Madame Bonaparte was attached to her; she felt herself deserving of their good-will, and the bare idea of figuring in an affair which must come under the cognizance of the tribunals distressed her exceedingly.

Junot immediately perceived that she had committed no intentional error, and the report was altered; the name of Madame de Montesson did not appear in it—there was no occasion that it should; the young man was arrested, which was the required point. Some time afterwards the First Consul asked Junot: "In what house was the young Lieutenant of the 12th arrested?" For a moment Junot was embarrassed, but he remembered that it had been stated in the report that he had been taken when walking in the Champs-Elysées, and he answered accordingly. The First Consul answered Junot, pulling him by the ear:

"You have a bad memory, Junot; he was arrested at Madame de Montesson's house." He then added more seriously: "You were right, my dear Junot, in listening to Madame de Montesson's request; I have a respect for her, and I am glad you did not insert her name in the report, but you should have mentioned it verbally to me, and not have entirely overlooked the circumstance."

In this little trait the character of Napoleon is very conspicuous. He would always know everything, and was offended by the smallest concealment. Junot discovered Fouché to have been the channel by which the First Consul became acquainted with this affair.

I have reported this little story to prove that Junot suppressed whatever tended to scandal, if it had no immediate reference to the Emperor's safety. Many of these reports are to this day among his papers; they are purely military, but in these times of trouble were the depositories of many names connected with affairs into which the police were prying, but which, fortunately for their proprietors, fell into the hands of a man of honour. With respect to the large sums which Junot received for the secret police of the capital, and of which he remitted an annuity of 3,000 francs to a reporter,* I know nothing of them.

I suppose, however, that the First Consul, unwilling to charge all the appointments of the Commandant of Paris upon the military funds, gave Junot a pension upon the extraordinary revenue raised by the Minister of Police, and which was solely at his own disposal; the daily reports were drawn up at the office of the Military Staff of Paris, or the Quai de Voltaire, and were brought to Junot by the Chief of the Staff, the Adjutant-General Doucet, under whose orders several district adjutants exercised a close *surveillance* over the peace and good order of Paris; these were Junot's agents and bulletinists, but they were not police spies. I may add that never did Junot, nor Marshal Mortier, who, in his quality of General Commanding the First Military Division, was his chief, in the performance of their duty compromise one innocent person. But I can easily conceive

---

* The exact expression in the original is not altogether complimentary, "*à un mauvais bulletiniste.*"

that there are men whose crooked policy, wishing always to remain in shadow, would endeavour to the utmost to frustrate the object of all these cares, and, failing to do so, would spare no slander which might bring those cares into disrepute. Hence I apprehend the origin of the animosity with which the Military Staff of Paris has been pursued.

CHAPTER XXIII.

Count Louis von Cobentzel—His taste for *Fêtes* and Frivolities—Anecdote of his Embassy to the Court of Catherine—The Theatre at the Hermitage—The Ambassador as Comtesse d'Escarbagnas—The New Courier and his Despatches—Change of Costume—Victories of Bonaparte and Diplomacy in Masquerade — Lord Whitworth—Talents and Manners of Count von Cobentzel—Count Philip von Cobentzel, his Successor.

COUNT LOUIS VON COBENTZEL, who had just signed, at Luneville, the treaty of peace between Austria and France, was the greatest lover of spectacles, *fêtes*, and all kinds of merry diversion, that I have ever met with in my life. The Emperor, his master, had made a judicious selection in appointing him envoy for signing a treaty of peace. He interested himself in the programmes of all the intended *fêtes;* enjoyed them by anticipation, and gave his opinion on the preparations.

I frequently saw him, for, as he was passionately fond of plays, and I had a box at all the theatres, he preferred going privately with Junot and me to appearing in the official box of the Minister for Foreign Affairs.

Count Louis was middle-aged, very ugly, and is truly reported to have resembled Mirabeau. He had the same sallow face, and his eyes, which, however, bore no other resemblance to those of Mirabeau, were equally small. He had also the same enormous head of hair, which gave so singular an effect to Mirabeau's countenance. Count Louis was lively and sensible, but withal had plenty of follies— follies which he is said to have only adopted in imitation of Prince Kaunitz. He had been for a long time Austrian Ambassador at the Court of the great Catherine, and retained a profound and enthusiastic admiration for that Sovereign, who kept a theatre, played herself, and carried the condescension so far as to write comedies for the amusement of her Court. When Count von Cobentzel was once launched on this favourite topic it was a vain hope to extract a word from him that did not bear reference to the theatre at the Hermitage, in which his frightful person would certainly not set off his dramatic talents to the best advantage.

The First Consul related to us one evening that M. de Cobentzel had had a temporary stage constructed in the palace of the Austrian Ambassador at St. Petersburg, principally with the object, as you may suppose, of acting himself. One day the Ambassador was to assume the character of the Comtesse d'Escarbagnas. The Empress had promised to be present, and the *Count-Countess* was dressed early to be in readiness for appearing on the stage the moment the Czarina had taken her seat. She arrived, and the Ambassador was sought for, but neither *he nor the Countess* could be found.

At length, after a tiresome search, he was discovered in his cabinet, in male attire indeed, but with his hair puffed, in high-heeled shoes, and so suffocated with passion that he could scarcely articulate the words, "Hang that villain for me!" pointing to a man who was praying all the saints in heaven to defend him from the supposed madman.

This was a special courier from Vienna arrived in haste, with very important despatches, and specially ordered to deliver them into the Ambassador's own hands; for Catherine II. made no scruple of violating the seals, not only of her own subjects, but of foreigners, and even Ambassadors, whose diplomatic character is sacred amongst the most savage nations. M. de Beausset, when Ambassador from France, made serious complaints of this gross breach of international law. The courier was a young man, recently attached to the Foreign Office, and had never even seen the Count von Cobentzel. He arrived at seven in the evening, just as the Count, having finished his toilet as Comtesse d'Escarbagnas, was complacently contemplating the reflection in a large looking-glass of a figure which has perhaps never since been paralleled; smiling at his whimsical visage, adding a patch, flirting his fan, enlarging his hoop, and repeating the most striking passages of his part. At this moment the courier from Vienna was announced. The Count replied that he would see him the next morning, but at present he was otherwise occupied; recommending that he should repose himself for the night, and leave business till the morning.

But the young man was a novice in diplomacy, and scrupulously conscientious in discharging his commission. His orders were to use all diligence and at whatever cost to reach St. Petersburg before midnight on this very day. He had arrived, and loudly and pertinaciously insisted on seeing the Ambassador. One of the secretaries informed M. de Cobentzel of the courier's orders. "Why, what does the obstinate fellow want? Is he possessed? Well, send him in!"

The secretary, accustomed to the fooleries of his master, without an instant's reflection on the necessity of preparing a stranger for the interview, introduced him into the cabinet, saying, "There is the Ambassador." And the courier found himself in the presence of a woman dressed in the fashion of his grandmother's days, who advanced affectedly to meet him, and while putting with one hand an extra patch on a round cheek, already concealed behind a thick coat of rouge, stretched out the other to receive the packet, saying: "Well, sir, let us see these important despatches." The courier turned round instead of answering, to request an explanation of the strange spectacle that thus presented itself. But the secretary had vanished, the door was shut, and he found himself alone with the burlesque vision.

"I wished to speak to the Ambassador," cried the young man, whose brain, somewhat heated by the fatigue of several days' rapid travelling, was nearly overset upon seeing a feminine figure seize the Ministerial packet and endeavour to snatch it from him, saying all the while, "Here is the Ambassador! I am the Ambassador!"

The young Austrian was strong, and retained a firm hold of the despatches confided to him; but, beginning to be frightened, he called for help, insisting on seeing the Ambassador, and refusing to recognize him under this disguise. In vain Count von Cobentzel ran after him round the cabinet, explaining why on this particular occasion he was dressed in his fine brocaded gown and velvet petticoat. Greek would have been more intelligible to his companion. At length the Count exclaimed in despair:

"Well, blockhead, you shall see him, you shall see your Ambassador," and, entering his bedchamber, he threw off his gown and petticoat, and returned to the obstinate courier in white silk stockings, high-heeled shoes, black breeches, and puffed hair—another edition of my dragoon's dress and white satin shoes.

Accordingly, the young courier, more than ever persuaded of his insanity, persisted in refusing to surrender the Imperial packet, until the Ambassador was growing seriously angry, when, to complete his fury, the Empress's arrival was announced to him. The secretary of the embassy explained this strange scene to the diplomatic messenger, and persuaded him at length to give his despatches into the hands of Count Louis von Cobentzel. The Count read them, and found them indeed a singular prologue to the comedy he was about to perform.

They announced to him that Beaulieu and Wurmser had no better fortune in Italy than the Archduke Charles upon the Rhine. That General Bonaparte, then twenty-six years of age, was taking possession of Italy at the head of 36,000 Frenchmen, and was beating General Beaulieu, notwithstanding (and very probably on account of) his seventy-six years, though he had 50,000 men under his orders. They also warned the Ambassador that it was of the utmost importance to induce the Czarina to give effect to her promises, so long since made, of placing an armament by sea and land at the disposal of the Allies, and pressed him not to lose a moment in communicating this intelligence to the Empress, and in entering upon the question of the armament.

This order admitted of no delay in its execution; Count von Cobentzel felt it, and I may say painfully. England was at this moment about to sign a treaty of subsidy and alliance with Russia; Austria was deeply interested in avoiding the smallest offence to England, and the Count felt that it would be an agreeable compliment to the British Ambassador to consult him on this important occasion. Lord Whitworth was sent for and came. To form a just conception of this interview the two personages should be known.

Lord Whitworth (who was educated at Tonbridge School) was tall, perfectly well made, and handsome, with a countenance and manner of the highest distinction. I have never known a man better calculated to represent a nation, great, prosperous, and haughty; always magnificently dressed, even at the Consular Court, it may be imagined how particular he would be at that of Catherine II., where Eastern luxury prevailed to a magical extent. Imagine, then, the contrast he would present to the countenance, figure, and manners of M. de Cobentzel, always a little burlesque, and decorated on this occasion, for the amusement of the persons who witnessed the conversation, in the absurd accoutrements of the Comtesse d'Escarbagnas.

The English peer received the Count's communication with the cold politeness habitual to him, and, recommending him not to keep the Empress waiting, went to apologize for a delay which admitted of no apology but the truth. I believe, though I am not quite sure of it, that the Empress, in her impatience to be informed more at length of the details of events of which the English Ambassador could only give the outline, required the immediate presence of the Count von Cobentzel, who came in his gown, hoop, and puffs to the audience.

Count Louis von Cobentzel, though really agreeable, was much less so than he would have been had he permitted his own good sense and information to direct his manners, instead of servilely copying those of Prince Kaunitz and Prince Potemkin, to both of whom he affected to bear a personal resemblance, and whose frivolity and morality, both of the school of Louis XV., he assumed together with an exclusive predilection for the great world. This world was the Court, beyond the luminous circle of which all to him was chaos.

His good sense made him understand that a generation had sprung up in which were to be found names bearing a lustre of renown fully equal to that of heraldic blazonry. He knew this, but to his aristocratic ears the sound of the word "citizen," applied to the Head of the Government, produced discord in all social harmony; and he could not reconcile himself to the necessity of addressing Madame Lannes without the title of Princess. He had talent, however, and was, as I have said, agreeable; he related multitudes of anecdotes about the Court of Russia, all very amusing; that of the Comtesse d'Escarbagnas did *not* come from himself, but was told me at a later period by the Count's cousin, Count Philip von Cobentzel, who very soon succeeded him as Ambassador at Paris, and remained here till our rupture with the Austrians in 1804.

In 1801 also a treaty of peace was signed at Florence between France and Naples. It is worthy of remark that in this treaty the Isle of Elba was made over to France, although not as an object of much consideration, for it was always regarded as a barren and savage rock; thirteen years later it became the only asylum of the monarch to whom it belonged.

CHAPTER XXIV.

The Ambassador at the Theatres—The Vaudeville—The *Comédie Française*—Fleury—All Superiority Dangerous—The Duc d'Orleans and the Blacksmith—Fleury, "King of Prussia" and the Comte de Perigord in Prison—Paul I. and General Sprengporten—Portrait of Madame Recamier—Gradual Change in the State of Society—The Bankers' *Fêtes*—Foreigners in Paris—Death of the Emperor Paul and Accession of Alexander—The Russians at Paris—The Chevalier Kalitscheff and the Count Markoff.

LOUIS VON COBENTZEL was fond of joking, especially when he was, as he called it, incognito; that is to say, when he left two dozen ribands and medals in his carriage, and retained but two or three; which, with his black coat, almost French, his silk stockings, diamond shoe-buckles and full-dressed head, made him a personage not very likely to diminish the merriment of such of the frequenters of the Montansier and the Vaudeville as should chance to meet him in the corridors. Our box at the Vaudeville having a private entrance and staircase from the Rue de Chartres, made it particularly agreeable to the Ambassador, and his frequent presence there was an additional attraction and amusement to us.

In the seasons of 1800, 1801, and 1802, the Vaudevilles resumed the gaiety which the stern events of the preceding years had greatly diminished; song was resumed, and farce did not seek its subjects in Plutarch, Livy, or the State

Trials. Pero and his friends, Scarron's marriage, and a thousand other such subjects, were more suitable to this temple of gaiety than ambitious names, the very sound of which is sufficient to chase away mirth. At this moment the companies of the Vaudeville and the Théâtre de Montansier were particularly well chosen.

The *Comédie Française* was also in its glory. Talma, Lafont, St. Prix, Monvel—what an admirable constellation of talent! Then Mademoiselle Raucourt, Madame Vestris, Monsieur Fleury, Mademoiselle Georges, Mademoiselle Duchesnois, Mademoiselle Volnais, and Mademoiselle Bourgoin; the recent *débuts* of the four last still divided the society of Paris into rival factions; but greater than all these was Mademoiselle Mars, already the queen of comedy.

Fleury was one of the performers at this theatre who pleased me best; I never heard him assume any character without giving it full effect, by his excellent judgment and good sense. His manners were those of a perfect gentleman, fully imbued with the *ton* of good company, with none of the affectation of the present day.

I must especially speak of the triumph of his art in the character of Frederick in *The Two Pages*. Many persons can yet remember the astonishment of Prince Henry when he saw his brother upon the stage, speaking, walking. blowing his nose—in all points Frederick himself. And that mask, as it may be called, with which, at his pleasure, he assumed another face, was wholly furnished by a play of the muscles altogether his own, and for which he was in no degree indebted to any theatrical contrivance. This was proved to me in a singular manner by the Comte de Périgord.

This nobleman was thrown into prison during the Reign of Terror, when not ostracism only, but imprisonment and death were frequently the reward of genius, as well as of aristocracy of whatever kind; even success in the lowest grades of life was not exempt. For example, the Duc d'Orléans had for a companion in death a blacksmith, who had been denounced and condemned because the president of his Section was also a blacksmith and had hung fewer bells than his neighbour.*

The entire company of the *Comédie Française* were for similar reasons under lock and key, and M. de Périgord was painfully surprised at meeting in prison so many persons who had contributed to his enjoyment in the days of happiness. But a Frenchman, it is well known, can be gay even in the presence of death, and the friend and companion of Marshal Saxe was not very likely to be otherwise. Every time, therefore, that the old Count met Fleury in the gloomy galleries of their prison he stopped, made a low obeisance, and said, "How does your Majesty do?"

"At the instant," continued M. de Périgord, "the King of Prussia stood before me, such as we have seen him in *The Two Pages*, such as he was at Potsdam two years before his death: his back bowed, but his carriage imposing nevertheless, the same air, and the same play of countenance. And this total change effected in a few seconds, in a damp dungeon, by the light of a grated casement, and when a turnkey might interrupt this dramatic entertainment by marching us before the revolutionary tribunal, that is to say, to death!"

There is great talent, no doubt, in this active and ever ready play of the features and alteration of the whole person; but I think the mental firmness of the man, which will permit him to exercise these faculties in the midst of the most imminent danger, is still more worthy of admiration than the powers of the actor.

* Referring to the bells then used on the peaked collars of the horses?

The Austrian Embassy was not the only one which at this period enlivened Paris; the Emperor of Russia, if he had not an actual representative at the Consular Court, had at least a medium of communication with the First Consul in the person of General Sprengporten. Charmed with the generosity with which Napoleon had treated Russia, in sending home without ransom or exchange, well clothed and provided for, the eight thousand prisoners taken at Alkmaar on the surrender of the Anglo-Russian Army, Paul had charged General Sprengporten with a letter of thanks to the First Consul, but without giving him any diplomatic status.*

This General gave charming *fêtes;* and though himself of a disposition habitually melancholy, arising from his exile from his native country, to which his engagements in the Russian service were a bar to his ever returning, he so frankly testified his desire to see his guests well amused that it was impossible to avoid being so. He was, moreover, a bachelor; and this circumstance contributed to the freedom of intercourse and mirth which his house offered.

It was here that I first saw Madame Recamier; I had heard her much spoken of, and I acknowledge that my mother had prejudiced my judgment concerning her, in persuading herself, and consequently me, that Madame Recamier's reputation was exaggerated, and that she must necessarily be a person of overbearing pretensions.

Great, then, was my surprise when I beheld that lovely face, so blooming, so childish, and yet so beautiful! and

---

* General Sprengporten was not a Russian, but born in Finland of an ancient family. At the period of the famous revolution in Sweden in 1776, he was much attached to the cause of Gustavus III., but he arrived at Stockholm too late to assist the young King; the *chapeaux* had beaten the *bonnets*, and Gustavus was the conqueror. Sprengporten afterwards passed into the Russian service, and although not formally Ambassador at Paris he was treated and listened to as such.

still greater when I observed the timid uneasiness she experienced in her triumph. No doubt it was pleasing to be proclaimed the unrivalled beauty of the *fête;* but it was evident that she was pained by the envious glances of the females, who could not wholly suppress the ill-will with which they witnessed her monopoly of adoration.

Madame Recamier truly deserved that homage ; she was really a pretty woman ! The expression of her eyes was mild and intellectual, her smile was gracious, her language interesting ; her whole person possessed the charm of native grace, goodness, and intelligence. She reminded me at first sight of the Madonnas of the Italian painters ; but the resemblance consisted wholly in expression— not in regularity of features.

It was the mind which animated her eyes and blushed in her cheek ; the smile which so frequently played upon her rosy lips expressed the unaffected joy of a young heart, happy in pleasing and in being beloved. When Madame Recamier was in England she excited the same enthusiasm in the multitudes who thronged to see her, because there is in grace and goodness a charm which exercises its power, without appeal, over the people of every country.

At the time when I first met Madame Recamier she was in the prime of her beauty and of her brilliant existence. M. Recamier was at the head of one of the first banking-houses of Paris ; his misfortunes were not then foreseen. He had, therefore, the means of giving to his charming consort all the enjoyments of wealth and luxury, as a poor return for her tender attentions and the happiness which she shed over his home and his life. M. Recamier's house was a delightful residence ; nothing was comparable to the *fêtes* he gave to foreigners recommended to him, and whose choice of M. Recamier for their banker was no doubt fixed by the desire of an introduction to his wife. Curiosity attracted them to his house; they were retained there by a charm which acted equally upon old and young, male and female.

Madame Recamier is an indispensable figure in contemporary Memoirs. Not that she either reflected or impressed her era, but because she could have belonged to that era alone. One cannot expect to find, in future times, a woman like her—a woman whose friendship has been courted by the most remarkable persons of the age; a woman whose beauty has thrown at her feet all the men whose eyes have once been set upon her; whose love has been the object of universal desire, yet whose virtue has remained pure; whose unsullied reputation never suffered from the attacks of jealousy or envy; a woman who lost none of the affections which had been pledged to her, because in her days of gaiety and splendour she had the merit of being always ready to sacrifice her own enjoyments to afford consolation—which no one could do more sweetly and effectually—to any friend in affliction. To the world Madame Recamier is a celebrated woman; to those who had the happiness to know and to appreciate her she was a peculiar and gifted being, formed by Nature as a perfect model in one of her most beneficent moods.

Since the 18th Brumaire society had been reuniting and grouping round a Government which offered it at length not only security but prosperity. The peace with Germany, that which was in progress with Russia, and a preliminary treaty already far advanced with Great Britain, afforded a bright horizon to replace those thick clouds which weighed upon the bosoms even of individuals, oppressing all with fears, not only for their possessions but their lives.

Paris once more became the abode of joy and pleasure. In the two first years of the Consulate the finest *fêtes*, except those of the Government, the Ministers, and other authorities, were given by the richest bankers, such as M. Recamier, M. Perregaux, and two or three others; then followed MM. Seguin, Hainguerlot, and other opulent persons, who returned to France in pleasures the wealth she had bestowed upon them.

These *fêtes* were soon rendered more brilliant by the presence of numerous foreigners of distinction, who crowded into France as soon as they were permitted to travel. Italy, England, Switzerland, sent their contributions of visitors who, in exchange for the gold with which they enriched us, were taught the arts of refined entertainments.

The Russians followed the Germans as soon as their new sovereign gave them permission to quit their frozen regions. The Emperor Paul was just dead; and Alexander, the eldest of his sons, had mounted the throne at twenty-three years of age. The despotic domination of the Czars immediately gave place to a paternal government, as much wiser as it was more gentle. I remember that at this period the Russians who came to Paris cherished for their young sovereign a sentiment bordering upon idolatry. Many kept his portrait in their inmost apartment, beside that of the favourite saint, surrounded like it with lights and gems, and as much venerated as St. Alexander Newsky or St. Nicholas.

Our definitive arrangements with the Court of St. Petersburg, however, did not proceed very rapidly. M. Sprengporten was recalled and replaced by the Chevalier Kalitscheff, who also had no diplomatic rank, but was simply the bearer of a letter from the Emperor of Russia to the First Consul. One remarkable circumstance attached to his mission was that, though sent by the Emperor Paul, before he could deliver his letter the throne was already filled by Alexander. He was soon succeeded by the Count Markoff, in quality of Minister Plenipotentiary, which, however, he did not assume till two months after his arrival here. General Hédouville was appointed by the First Consul to reside at St. Petersburg in the same capacity: all appointments of this nature were made with extreme caution; the Foreign Powers feared even to form alliances with France, for the Directory had rendered them suspicious of our good intentions.

CHAPTER XXV.

A Visit from Rapp—An Invitation to Malmaison—Conversation on the Road—Rapp's Attachment to the First Consul—Chagrin and Melancholy of Bonaparte—Uneasiness of his Two Aides-de-Camp—Bonaparte refuses his Breakfast—A Ride on Horseback and fear of Assassins—The Horses at Full Gallop—Deep Affliction of the First Consul and his Conversation with Junot—A Dinner at Malmaison—The Loss of Egypt—Great Projects overthrown—The intended Pillar—The Action of Nazareth—An Order of the Day the Proudest Title of Nobility—The Picture and the Portrait.

ONE fine morning in the summer of 1801 Rapp joined our breakfast-table, bringing an order to Junot to attend the First Consul at Malmaison, and an invitation to me to spend the day there. We set out immediately after breakfast, and as Rapp was returning to Malmaison we gave him a place in our carriage.

I have already spoken of Rapp as a brave and frank soldier, but the quality which marked his character most strongly at this moment was his ardent attachment to the First Consul. Rapp, Duroc, Lannes, Bessières, Lemarrois, and two or three others of the Army of Italy and Egypt sympathized perfectly with Junot in this respect, and uttered precisely the same language. The First Consul was to them (as an adored mistress would be to most young men) the thought which predominated over every other.

On this occasion we remarked that Rapp was thoughtful,

and that a strong feeling seemed to oppress him. We had scarcely reached the Barrière de l'Etoile when Junot, who had been contemplating Rapp's countenance, caught the reflection of its melancholy, and before we arrived at Nanterre he said to his brave brother-in-arms, taking his hand :

"Rapp, there is something the matter yonder . . . the General———" And his eye, fixed upon the excellent young man, seemed to fear a confirmation of his apprehensions.

Rapp at first bowed his head without answering ; then pressing Junot's hand, " I know nothing," he said ; " but the General has certainly received some painful news. I know him as if I had spent my whole life by his side, and when his forehead wrinkles and his eyelids fall. . . ." Here he knit his eyebrows as Napoleon was accustomed to do when deep in thought. "Then when retaining this melancholy air he pushes away his plate at dinner, throws up his napkin, removes his chair, walks to and fro, and orders three cups of coffee an hour hence, I say to myself that he has met with some cause of distress. This is the life he led all day yesterday, and this morning the same course has recommenced. This is why I am returning to Malmaison, though my attendance ended at noon. But I should be miserable in Paris."

Junot pressed Rapp's hand : the brave fellow had so entirely expressed his own feelings ! I looked at both of them ; Junot's eyes were wet, and Rapp was looking out of the coach window ashamed of his emotion.

" But," said I to them, " permit me to tell you that you are behaving like children. What ! because the First Consul is perhaps out of humour, or, at the most, because you believe him to be vexed, you are so unhappy as to be absolutely ashamed of your feelings ! I repeat it, you are as unreasonable as two babies."

Their two faces turned towards each other to take a mutual survey; and I burst into a laugh. Rapp was offended. "I may be ridiculous in expressing over-anxiety," said he; "but I who have seen the General's altered physiognomy . . . you know, Junot, I who have seen him know that it is not ill-humour; it is grief. Yesterday morning, after rising from breakfast, which he had not eaten, he ordered the horses, and we rode out to the park of Bougival. We were alone with Jardin; so long as we were within sight of the house the General walked his horse; but we had no sooner passed the paling than he spurred it, and the poor beast galloped up the stony road of Bougival, where he might have been killed ten times over; for if the horse had stumbled upon one of the round and polished stones the hill is strewn with he might have rolled to the bottom without the possibility of being saved. When we reached the summit, there, under the fine trees at the entrance of the wood, he stopped short. The horse was blown and could not advance a step.

"I rode up to the General : he was alone : Jardin was still a long way behind. I then thought no more of the horse falling ; but I pictured to myself in the dark and desert wood assassins in waiting to dog my General's steps. I saw that the most devoted guardianship cannot be so active but that danger may outstrip it ; he had been there two minutes, and alone ! The misfortunes which might have been accomplished in this short time presented themselves so forcibly to me that for a moment I forgot myself. I took the liberty to tell the First Consul that he rode like a madman, and did not know what he was about. "Why the devil, General," said I, "do you alarm those who are devoted to you in this way?"

"What! you spoke to him in that manner!" said Junot, with a look of astonishment.

"Certainly," replied Rapp, "and why not? You all try to frighten me out of speaking frankly to the First Consul; but I cannot believe it would displease him: he knows when the heart speaks." Rapp accompanied this speech with a collection of energetic words which may be dispensed with here. His language had nothing coarse in it, but he often introduced into it interjections and exclamations to which it would be difficult to do justice in writing. "But to return to what I was saying just now about the General; when I pointed out to him the solitude which surrounded us, he smiled, so. . . ." And Rapp smiled with an expression of disdain and bitterness, at the same time inclining his head in a manner altogether peculiar to Napoleon, and which those only who have known him well can figure to themselves or understand.

"'Then he said to me: 'Danger has no terrors for me, Colonel Rapp; there are even moments when I court it, for some days of my life are heavy to bear.' And thereupon he recommenced his furious gallop, but this time, if we were not in a level country, at least the road was such that it was practicable to follow him. Jardin and I did not let him outride us, but kept our horses close on the heels of his. We rode in this manner six leagues, I think; however, on our return, the First Consul seemed much more calm than when we set out."

Junot was thoughtful. All that Rapp had said did indeed indicate that some great trouble affected the First Consul. Junot questioned his comrade; but Rapp, who could easily remark the emotion which the countenance of Napoleon exhibited, was wholly deficient in that fine discrimination which could trace such emotion to its cause. I was perfectly astonished at the style, almost of eloquence, in which he had just related the particulars of his preceding day's ride, and I recognized in it a new proof that the eloquence of the heart is the most poetic; that of genius, when compared with it, appears cold and formal.

When we arrived at Malmaison, the First Consul was in his cabinet. He immediately sent for Junot, who, for above an hour, was closeted with him. Some time before dinner we saw them walking in the alley which leads towards Jonchére* and Bougival. Junot was serious, and seemed to listen with great attention to the First Consul. Sometimes the countenance of Napoleon became animated; once he stopped opposite the house, and, as if he would explain demonstratively to Junot what he was saying, he traced some figures with his feet upon the sand, and probably finding this mode insufficient to his purpose, asked Junot for his sword, and, without drawing it from the scabbard, used it to trace his explanatory figures with more ease.

When we entered the dining-room the First Consul was already at table; he placed me by his side, and talked of things so entirely indifferent that it was manifest he was supporting a conversation to which he gave no attention at all, only to avoid the awkwardness of total silence. I examined him narrowly, and was convinced that he was under the influence of a strong impression. Alas! the subject was but too serious; we had lost Egypt!

In returning to Paris, Junot was strongly affected. He told me all he had learned from the First Consul, and how much he was himself distressed in seeing the affliction which weighed upon a great mind whose every sentiment was powerful and ardent.

"It is so long," said Junot, "since I have known his projects with respect to Egypt! When we walked upon the Boulevards Neufs on one of those fine summer evenings which then afforded us all the pleasure we enjoyed; when

---

* A country house, which afterwards belonged to Eugène.

we were at Paris, unhappy and unemployed, then it was that the First Consul spoke to me of the East, of Egypt, of Syria, and the Druses; and when these brilliant dreams subsequently became glorious realities, when General Bonaparte saw in his own hands the power of executing such important projects, I know that he considered it the finest moment of his life. I know not what Heaven may have in store for him; but I may affirm that to constitute Egypt the station from whence, at some future day, the blow should be struck which should annihilate the prosperity of England was his most cherished purpose, and was about to receive its accomplishment. When, then, he said to me to-day, 'Junot, we have lost Egypt!'* I felt all the pain with which he would receive the intelligence that Egypt was actually lost: and my heart throbbed with anguish. Rapp was right! the General suffered cruelly yesterday!"

Junot repeated to me all that had passed during the two hours he had been alone with the First Consul. Not only had Napoleon, during this conference, spoken like a patriot, and wept over the irreparable loss which the commerce and prosperity of France had sustained, but he had felt as the chief of the army and the friend of his soldiers. He regretted the land which the blood of thousands of Frenchmen had enriched! those burning sands where their bones must wither! "He had intended," said Junot, "to raise a monument to Sulkowsky, to Julien.... 'I would have erected at the foot of Mount Tabor a pillar on which the names of the three hundred brave men whom you com-

* It is necessary, in order to understand the ulterior objects of Napoleon with respect to India after he should have conquered Egypt, to read the instructions given by him to M. de Lascaris [which are to be found in M. de Lamartine's *Pilgrimage to the Holy Land*, vol. iii., p. 145]. This account, taken from the papers of M. de Lascaris, furnishes proofs of the gigantic conception of Napoleon, and is highly interesting.

manded at Nazareth should be inscribed. We also should have braved ages, and posterity would have found our glory in the deserts of Syria'—but as the Consul said," continued Junot, "'My projects, and my dreams, England has destroyed them all.'"

Junot then described to me a plan which had hitherto only been sketched out, but which was about to receive its completion. At the time of the famous action of Nazareth, where Junot, cut off from the corps to which he belonged, found himself at the head of a few hundred men opposed to the Grand Vizier's advanced guard of three thousand, commanded by Ayoub-Bey, and obtained a complete victory, one of the finest achievements in our wars, the General-in-Chief immediately ordered that this victory should be consecrated in the most glorious manner.* The Order of the Day, then issued, had not yet been executed, but the First Consul, in the most affectionate terms, assured Junot that it should be forthwith. I here insert that Order of the Day; it is a noble trophy to preserve; my children are entitled to be proud of it. They have no cause to fear that their hereditary nobility should be contested, for they will always be the sons of the conqueror of Nazareth.

HEADQUARTERS BEFORE ACRE,
2 Floréal, Year vii.

ORDER OF THE DAY.

The General-in-Chief, desirous of giving a mark of his particular satisfaction to the three hundred brave soldiers, commanded by General Junot, who in the action of Nazareth repulsed a Turkish corps of cavalry of three thousand men, took five standards, and covered the field of battle with the dead bodies of the enemy, Orders:—

Art. 1. That a medal of 12,000 francs shall be given as a prize to the best picture representing the action of Nazareth.

---

* Two dukedoms, it is said, were on the point of creation by Napoleon had it not been for disasters in the Peninsula: Junot, as Duke of Nazareth, and Jourdan, as Duke of Fleurus.

Art. 2. The costume of the French in the picture shall be the uniform of the 2nd light infantry and the 14th dragoons. General Junot and the Chiefs of the Brigade Duvivier, and of the 14th dragoons, shall be represented in it.

Art. 3. The General Staff shall cause our artists in Egypt to draw the costumes of the Mamelukes, the Janissaries of Damascus and Aleppo, the Maugrebins and the Arabs,* and shall send them to the Minister of the Interior, inviting him to cause copies of them to be executed and transmitted to the principal painters of Paris, Milan, Florence, Rome, and Naples, and to name the judges who shall award the prize and the period when it shall be announced.

Art. 4. The present Order of the Day shall be sent to the municipality of the commune of all the soldiers who shared in the action of Nazareth.

The General-in-Chief,
BONAPARTE.

ALEXANDER BERTHIER,
 General-of-Division, Chief of the Staff.

I believe that this Order of the Day is unique in our wars. The Directory, which was not fond of acknowledging the glory of our arms, was obliged to publish it, and directions were given that General Bonaparte's orders should be executed. The competition took place after the return both of General Bonaparte and Junot, and the prize was adjudged to M. le Gros, who received orders for the picture, but never completed it. The magnificent portrait of the Duke of Abrantès, the immortal work I may call it of M. le Gros, was destined for this picture of the action of Nazareth. The portrait, of which the head, or rather the face, only is complete, is a *chef d'œuvre*, not only for the painting but the resemblance. How often has my heart thanked M. le Gros!

---

* These troops composed the Turkish corps opposed to Junot and his brave division.

CHAPTER XXVI.

Mystification—The First Consul represses it—The Princess Dolgorouky—Mystification of the Institute at her House—Robert—The Catacombs—The Plank at St. Peter's.

At this period, when strangers abounded in Paris, a fashion existed which, in its various ramifications, served for the daily amusement of society. This was the art of mystification, *anglice* hoaxing, which had just sprung up amongst us. To make game of one's friends was an amusement of old standing; but now, for the first time, men made the art of mystification, as it was called, a profession, a regular means of livelihood: for example, an entertainment was to be provided in the best manner for a party of friends; M. or Madame N. must be mystified: but how? Send for Musson, Thiémé, or Legras; it was done with the same ease that you would send to Corcelet,* the Chevet of that day, for a truffled turkey.

But there existed a more general species of mystification in which a whole party were made actors, and that without the help of the inimitable Musson; I am about to give a special instance of this kind presently. The First Consul, who detested this diversion, was the cause of its falling into disuse, by the expression of his displeasure. Junot and I

* Corcelet was still well known at Paris in 1836, but the shop of Chevet was more visited by the epicureans.

were once warmly reprimanded by him for having caused the mystification of a man by the whole audience of a theatre, without any intention on the part of the spectator-actors. But the scene which I am now about to relate especially concerns the Russian Princess Dolgorouky, who arrived in Paris at the time when these follies were still rife, though fear of the First Consul had rendered them less frequent than they had once been.

This lady was by far the most distinguished amongst the Russians at Paris, for her qualifications of person, mind, and manners. She was called impertinent, but as I never found her so I can say nothing upon that subject; she was certainly stiff, with some bombast and more affectation; but her manners were nevertheless those of the best society. She was polite, but distant; she never conferred an obligation without hesitating; at a first introduction she curtseyed even without smiling, nor was it till she was certain of finding the person that pleased her that she advanced graciously to offer her hand.

She was thought handsome by some, because she was tall and finely formed; but this striking figure was surmounted by a countenance of harshness and severity almost repulsive. La Harpe, the Abbé Delille, and others of our literati, held her in high respect, and the superiority of her intellectual acquirements could not be denied; from all this resulted the reputation not only of a witty but of a learned lady—the character in the world the most alarming. Some young people, or perhaps some ladies, wearied and annoyed by the ceremonious airs of the noble stranger, whose haughtiness was ill-placed in a country where liberty, and especially equality, were at that moment in their verdure and activity, determined to make her the subject of a mystification. Her pretensions as a *bel-esprit* were well known, and were made the text of the drama.

The Princess* occupied a very small house in the Faubourg Saint Honoré, where she could not dine more than eight or ten persons; if she wished to entertain twenty she was obliged to invite them to tea. The Princess returned home one afternoon about five o'clock, much fatigued by a traveller's visits to the curiosities of Paris, and had just taken up a reclining position upon a sofa when the folding-doors of her drawing-room opened, and her groom of the chambers announced M. de Lacépède.

M. de Lacépède would have been heartily welcome to me or to any of my friends, because we were personally acquainted with him; but the Princess had never seen him, and notwithstanding her learned reputation it is by no means sure that she had read any of his works. Be this as it may, there he was; and as he was the politest of men the compliments of the *entrée* went off very well. The gentleman was not under the smallest embarrassment, but the lady thought the hour he had chosen for his visit a somewhat strange one. A few minutes, however, only elapsed before the door was opened again to admit M. de Lalande. He was presently followed by M. Suard. At length, in about a quarter of an hour, the most important Members of the Institute, the greatest strangers to the world of fashion, from the solitude to which their scientific studies confined them, were all assembled in the Princess Dolgorouky's little drawing-room, except, indeed, those who happened to be acquainted with the hostess, whose situation was every moment becoming more uneasy from the increasing number of her singular visitors.

This was, however, neither the place nor the occasion for the exhibition of those stately airs which disconcert inferiors. The Princess had sense, and though incapable of understanding the extraordinary situation in which she found

---

* She was a daughter of the Princess of Nassau-Usingen.

herself, she perfectly understood that she was at home, and whatever might be the cause of this truly eccentric meeting, it was for her to prove that her humour was not always so disagreeable as was reported. The conversation, nevertheless, became more and more difficult to sustain. One of the learned visitors had raised a discussion respecting some ivory fossils which had been found, I know not where, and referred continually to the Princess, who was equally at a loss how to answer or where to hide her head. At length a familiar face presented itself to her notice; her friend Millin was announced.

"So," said he to the Princess, kissing her hand with as much respect as if she had been the favourite sultana—"so it is by a singular accident only that I have heard of the scientific treasures and rare curiosities you have received from your northern estates! I, the most faithful, the most devoted of your servants! Oh, Princess, Princess!"

She looked at him with amazement; but at length obtained from him, rapidly and in an undertone, an explanation of the whole mystery, and learned that, two days before, the most distinguished Members of the Institute—the elect, in fact, from every section of the most learned—had each received an invitation in his own proper name to dine with her. A note appended to the invitation informed him, moreover, that some most curious objects of natural history had been sent to her from her estates in Siberia, which she not only desired to submit to the examination of the most scientific men in France, but proposed to offer to their acceptance.

Not another word was wanting to attract the attention of the whole learned body. The division of one of M. Demidoff's mines would not have tempted these minds devoted to science and learning; but the possibility of possessing a true moon-stone, the carcass, or even a rib of a fossil elephant, had drawn these talented men from their retreat. M. de Lacépède had missed the single hour's sleep he allowed himself each day while engaged on one of his great works, in the hope of seeing some skin, or some delicate bone which he might recognize as the spoil of one of those superb serpents a hundred and eighty feet in length which overran the world some twenty-five thousand years ago.

Millin had not seen these invitations, for the authors of the hoax had taken good care not to send them to the acquaintances of the Princess, but he, having met M. de Lalande at the Tuileries, had learned from him that there was to be a scientific meeting at the Princess Dolgorouky's, together with its cause; he wondered much that he had been forgotten, but fortunately determined, nevertheless, to make one of the party.

The result of this explanation by M. Millin was the discovery that the Princess had been hoaxed, a matter of serious concern to one who thought so much of the observations which might be made upon her, but she parried it with all the show of indifference she could assume, and followed the excellent advice of Millin, to retire for a week or two into the country. Her friends had more wit than to undertake the refutation of the story, one of the most ill-judged proceedings imaginable, unless supported by incontestable proofs.

The learned men implicated in the transaction, when the true state of the case came to be whispered among them, sneaked one by one out of the house, and *restaurateurs* being by no means so numerous as at present, they found some difficulty in procuring a dinner at six o'clock in the evening. Aware of the ridicule to which they were exposed (and who so sensible to ridicule as such men?), they took care to be silent, and thus the matter dropped, forgotten in ten days, as everything is at Paris unless supported by a prolonged discussion; and this adventure, which never gained much credence, was nearly unknown, and entirely failed to effect the purpose of its contrivers. After awhile it was formally denied, but was perfectly true nevertheless.

"The dignity of science was somewhat compromised," said old Robert, who was as ready in conversation as at his easel; "this affair would have made a good subject for the pencil," and, in fact, the interior of the drawing-room, with the perplexity of the hostess, and the dismayed countenances of her guests when they found that neither serpents, elephants, nor dinner were forthcoming, would have made an amusing scene.

This Robert was an excellent old man; he had an affectionate friendship for me, which I cordially returned. He was a man of intelligence, had seen much, and retained much, and his judgment being good, his conversation was extremely attractive. It was he who was the hero of that adventure so famous in the annals of the French Academy at Rome, and which has furnished the text to M. Delille's fine poetical episode of the Catacombs.*

But how cold and colourless, how devoid of interest, are those verses in comparison with the rapid and animated narration I received from Robert's own lips, when, at seventy-nine years of age, sitting by my fireside, he related the peril he had run in studying the frescoes in the Catacombs of St. Sebastian at Rome from having lost the threads which guided him through the intricacies of these prodigious vaults.† With what simple, yet glowing, because heartfelt, eloquence did this old man portray the horrors of

---

* In his poem entitled *L'Imagination*.

† Robert is well known as a painter of ruins; he found his ball of twine only on the second day, which enabled him to trace his way out of the Catacombs.

the youth of twenty creeping for two days in living agony, among the stones from which he had been copying, in search of a ball of thread! His remembrance of the mother he was to see no more, of his country, and of that glorious futurity of which the imagination of a youthful artist had dreamt, and before which a leaden curtain was falling. Then comes physical suffering, with its overwhelming force; he is hungry, he is in pain, in torture. But what words can paint the delirium of his joy, when, by accidentally dropping his hand upon a heap of bones, it feels his guardian ball!

Soon after this adventure of the Catacombs he fell again, and by his own fault, into a danger equally imminent, but less known. He was one day in St. Peter's, after the hour of prayer, alone, contemplating in the calmness of solitude the thousand wonders of the Christian giant. Suddenly he saw a cord descend from an opening in the cupola: a workman approached it, fastened to it a bucket full of water, and the cord was drawn up again. He perceived that they were mending the roof, and was seized with a desire to mount the cupola.

"I was curious," said he, "to see what harm had befallen this Colossus of modern architecture, which, rearing its head into the air, seems to deride the ruined monuments which surround it, saying to them: '*I am eternal!*' Its pride seemed to me to be greatly abated, for this cord, this bucket, this solitary workman, appeared so insignificant; I was no longer afraid, but determined to go up to discover what was the matter."

He mounted accordingly, and, having reached the summit, was at first seized with admiration at sight of the prospect which lay extended before him—a magnificent, but living, panorama, illuminated by that sun to which no other can compare, enveloping all Nature with that veil of golden hue which floats only on the buildings, the trees, the fields of

Italy. Then, looking round nearer to him, he saw some masons and tilers repairing, as they sang in their monotonous and nasal tones, some damage the roof had sustained. For the greater facility of bringing up the water, they had tied two long planks together, fixed them across the opening in the dome, and from them, by means of a cord and bucket, drew up the water; the two planks might be about two feet and a half in width, and the whole apparatus being intended only to support the bucket of water, no one concerned himself about its strength.

Eyes of twenty years see danger only to laugh at and brave it; it came into Robert's head that the appearance of St. Peter's, looking down upon it from above, must be very extraordinary, and the fancy soon became an ardent desire that Robert felt compelled to satisfy, without considering that the plank which he proposed to use as a bridge crossed an aperture three hundred feet from the ground. He set first one foot upon it, then the other, and presently behold him on this frail pathway without the possibility of turning back.

When Robert related this history to me, at the moment of his launching upon this plank, where my imagination represented him suspended between the sky and that marble which seemed destined to break his head, I was seized with the same vertigo that threatened him in his insane course; we gathered round him, listening eagerly to his words, and following him step by step on his aerial bridge.

"Having reached about a third part across I became desirous," said he, "of enjoying the spectacle I had set my mind upon, and cast my eyes downwards. Instantly a singing whizzed in my ears, a cloud first of blackness, then of fire, spread itself before my eyes. Fortunately I had the presence of mind to stop. I cannot describe what I felt at this moment in hearing close to me the most execrable imprecations murmured in an undertone by the workmen. I reopened my eyes and determined to walk on, for I was convinced that if I remained another moment in my present situation I should die even without falling. I felt that my rescue depended upon myself, that my strength of mind alone could save me."

He advanced with a firm step along this narrow plank, at the extremity of which he might recover a life at present so uncertain, when he felt it crack under his feet! he was now in the middle of the plank, and the weight of his body so much exceeding that of the small bucket of water, seemed necessarily about to break it down and precipitate him to the marble floor. A young man, looking on with affright, heard the crash, and exclaimed: "The plank is split; the poor fellow must——" He did not finish the sentence, for the master mason laid his hand upon his mouth and pressed it violently. Meanwhile Robert proceeded, and at length stepped upon a solid footing. He looked behind him, saw the plank, the gulf, the death he had escaped, and, throwing himself upon his knees, returned thanks to God.

"Oh, my friends," said he to the workmen, "how fortunate I have been!" But, instead of sympathizing in his joy, the workmen laid hold of him and beat him so violently that he cried out for help. "You provoking Frenchman, rascal, torment!" bawled out the masons in chorus, "you have frightened us out of our senses," and the blows continuing to pour upon his back, Robert thought he should go mad. "Will you leave me alone?" cried he, half laughing and half angry. "Ouf," said the master mason, "I can scarcely breathe yet!" "And why," said Robert, "did you shut that poor boy's mouth?" "By St. Peter! would you have had me let him cry on till he had made you lose what little reason you had left?"

Robert took the mason's hand and pressed it with real

and cordial friendship; this rough frankness, expressing such strong interest, however strange the mode of testifying it, went straight to the heart, and affected it perhaps more deeply than the most ceremonious expressions of interest uttered by a man of the world. Robert saw this man frequently during his stay at Rome, and painted two pictures for him, one of which was a sketch of this event, which I believe has been engraved, but I am not sure.

CHAPTER XXVII.

Lessons in Elocution—Mysterious Visit—Ride to Issy—Mademoiselle Clairon's House — A Waiting-maid's Costume — Mademoiselle Clairon at Eighty Years of Age—Extraordinary Dress—The Bust of Voltaire—The Monologue of Electra—Mademoiselle Clairon and Talma—The Queen of Babylon without Bread—M. de Staël—Mademoiselle Clairon relieved by the Government — She does Justice to Mademoiselle Mars—Nightly Sound of a Pistol-shot.

I HAD received lessons in elocution from M. Laurent, and had even had some lessons from Larive, when we occasionally met him at Saint Mandé, at the house of a friend to whom he was related. But I had also had a very different mistress, if I may apply the term to the advice given on the subject of declamation to a young girl not destined for the theatre.

M. Brunetière, who was my guardian, and fulfilled to the utmost of his power the duties of the office, frequently took me into the country in his cabriolet when my fatiguing watchings in 1798 and 1799 were visibly injuring my health. We were not absent on these occasions more than an hour or two, yet even this my mother thought long; and so did I, because I could not be easy unless I was beside her to see that the thousand-and-one fancies, which as soon as formed became necessary to her comfort, were complied with.

M. Brunetière one day said to me: "I am going to take you to visit a very celebrated person; but I shall not tell you her name, you must guess it." Then, inclining towards my mother, he said some words to her in a whisper, adding aloud: "Will you give me leave to take her?" "Most certainly I will, and gladly," she replied, and added: "Loulou, look at her; examine her closely, and tell me what impression the person you are going to see makes upon you."

We set off about noon, on a lovely day of spring, to take, as M. Brunetière called it, "A bath of air, to refresh," said he, "that face of fifteen which is as pale as the one I am going to show you." And in truth I felt, as we passed through the Bois de Boulogne and a part of the Park of Saint Cloud, that joy which the breezes of spring never fail to inspire after a tedious confinement in close air. We entered the village of Sèvres, and turning to the left reached Issy, which was to be the turning-point of our drive.

We stopped before what had been a handsome house, but the dilapidated and neglected appearance of which surprised me. I could not conceive how an aged woman could take up her lodging in a house which looked so desolate. The servant rang a long time without receiving any answer, except from seven or eight dogs, who performed counter-tenor, bass, and baritone, in chorus, under the leadership of a great mastiff in the courtyard, who acquitted himself admirably in his office, barking according to order.

An old woman at length appeared to let us in. The extraordinary style of her dress arrested my whole attention; it was so strange a mixture of old-fashioned French with the Greek and Roman costume, that all the laws of politeness could scarcely restrain me from laughing at the old *femme-de-chambre.* Her apron trimmed with festooned muslin, and ornamented with ribbon at the pockets, announced her quality of waiting-maid. On recognizing M. de Brunetière she uttered an exclamation of joy: "You are come at last! Oh, how pleased Mademoiselle will be! And Mademoiselle Alexandrina, too, I suppose? How much she is like you! Dear young lady, you have a worthy papa. And to think that we have no fruit to offer the dear child!"

During this monologue M. Brunetière assisted me to alight from the cabriolet, and we crossed a small court amid the clamorous yelpings of the dogs, whom the old woman beat with a switch, and M. de Brunetière wished heartily at the devil.

At length we reached the apartment of the mistress, who proved to be a very old lady, notwithstanding the title of Mademoiselle given her by her servant. She had been a fine figure in her youth, and age had not yet robbed her of a particle of height; her hair, white, but unpowdered, was drawn up behind in the Grecian style, and formed in front a *toupet*, which showed a still noble forehead, and a brow corresponding to all the expressions of an eye calm but animated. The costume of this lady, whose air imposed respect at first sight, was as extraordinary as that of her *femme-de-chambre*. She wore a sort of muslin mantle, which did not hang as mantles usually do, from the shoulders, but was folded round her in the form of antique drapery. A robe below it was shorter than the mantle; both were white, and bordered with garlands of laurels.*

This lady, at once singular and attractive, was seated in a large arm-chair well lined with pillows, with a bearskin under her feet, and a table covered with books before her. A bust of Voltaire of great beauty stood upon it, as did a portrait of Lekain; many other busts and portraits were

---

* These dresses were much in fashion about 1795, and were printed at M. Oberkampf's manufactory at Joüy.

hung round the room, or attached by brackets to the walls, which were barely covered by paper, dropping to pieces from the effect of damp. The desolation of the house seemed even more striking in this room, surrounding with its misery an aged lady who had evidently been accustomed to the indulgences of affluence.

On seeing M. Brunetière, far from expressing the joy her maid had promised, she bent her brow, compressed her lips in a manner I have never seen in any other person, and exclaimed: "Ah! ah! Monsieur, here you are, then, at last! and where is your ambassador that he is not come also? He would have judged for himself of the condition of the asylum which is left to Electra and to Semiramis." So saying, she raised her arm in a theatrical manner, pointing towards a part of the ceiling through which the water was falling into the parlour, though it was on the ground-floor. "So!" she continued with an accent impossible to describe, "M. le Baron de Staël still fails in his word, his plighted oath! And why, sir, why do not you, who know what his engagements to me are, oblige him to fulfil them? for in fact, sir, it even rains in my room."

I looked at and listened attentively to this woman, as singular in her speech as in her costume, yet experienced no inclination to laugh, nor the smallest idea of ridiculing her. I even felt pain at hearing her complaints of ill-usage. M. Brunetière, who was no way responsible for the condition of things, approached her, kissed her hand with an air of deference which seemed to soften her, and presenting me to her by name, said: "Her mother is a Comnena." The old lady endeavoured to stand up, but could not.

"Mademoiselle," said she, "I knew your father and your uncle well; they both did me the honour of visiting me. I am rejoiced to see you. Permit me——" And taking my hand, she kissed my forehead with a solemnity which made M. de Brunetière smile. I was dying with impatience to know the name of this remarkable person who, surrounded by evidences of poverty, and herself giving the idea of the ruin of a superior nature, inspired me with an indefinable species of respect. My guardian at length took pity upon me.

"You see that Mademoiselle Clairon is surrounded by objects worthy of herself and her glorious recollections," said he, pointing to the busts of Voltaire and Lekain.

But my eye did not follow the direction of his hand; it fixed immediately upon the person whose name I had just learned. Mademoiselle Clairon! so famous, so admirable in the parts of Electra, Aménaïde, Idamé, Semiramis! the woman sung by Voltaire, praised by all Europe! there I saw her, almost eighty years of age, in a state bordering on destitution, and apparently accusing as the author of her misfortunes a man whose name should have been a guarantee that talent in distress would have found protection from him.

I looked at her, and my eye probably expressed a part of my thoughts; for taking my hand with that of hers which she was able to use (the other was paralytic), she said to me, "Yes, my dear young lady, it is Clairon that you see. I am the woman whom Voltaire thanked for the success of his pieces; I am the woman whom all Europe came to hear pronounce the fine verses of that immortal genius." And she bowed to the bust of Voltaire. "My country," she added with a bitter smile, "has been grateful and liberal in praises, and has given me many laurels."

Again she pointed to the bust of Voltaire, and I observed that it was surrounded by emblematic crowns, numerous papers, and a thousand other trifles, all of which Mademoiselle Clairon had probably received during her long theatrical career. "I have offered to him," said the actress, "all the fruits of my success; it is to the master that the pupil owes all her credit." And raising herself in her chair, with theatrical dignity she recited an ode addressed by Voltaire to herself, in which, reversing Mademoiselle Clairon's observations, he thanked her for the success of his works. "But he did not believe a word of all that," she said, with a smile of intelligence; "and he was right." She possessed, nevertheless, a degree of vanity of which it is difficult to form an idea.

My guardian, seeing how much Mademoiselle Clairon interested me, begged her to recite some passages from one of her favourite parts; she considered for a moment, and then commenced the fine monologue of Electra, which she went through with admirable talent. I know not whether at this day we should consider her performance so perfect, but I was delighted, and promised myself many visits to Issy with my guardian. She was fond of conversation, and supported it with grace; her language was correct, and she professed a profound contempt for all innovations upon the ancient manners. She told us that there was a worthy little man named Talma who had the audacity to give himself out as her pupil. "I know not how he performs," said she, "but that is of no consequence to me. I have sent a message to that miserable successor of Fréron, who leaves neither the living nor the dead in peace, desiring him to put into his papers that I never gave lessons to M. Talma." —"But he has great talent," said I timidly, for I was overpowered by her royal air. "Oh, I do not contest that," said she politely, but in that tone of voice which seems to say, "I pay no attention to your opinion." I know that she afterwards heard Talma, and was enraptured with his performance; also that she gave him some advice which he profited by.

In taking leave of Mademoiselle Clairon I begged permission to visit her again, which she granted with the utmost graciousness, adding: "Make my most profound respects to your mother. I had the honour of seeing her when she first came to Paris in her Greek dress; she was a star of beauty!"

M. Brunetière at parting approached Mademoiselle Clairon and put into her hands a rouleau, at the same time saying something to her very low, to which she answered aloud: "This comes in good time, for the baker would no longer furnish bread to the Queen of Babylon. But you are a worthy man. Mademoiselle"—and she addressed herself to me, showing the rouleau M. Brunetière had just given her—"do you see this money? your guardian gives it out of his own purse that poor Clairon may not die of hunger. He gives it for that man who is without principle, that ambassador, that husband of a celebrated woman, in short, for the Baron de Staël, who suffers the rain of heaven to find its way into my poor abode."

M. de Staël had purchased an estate of Mademoiselle Clairon; the deeds stipulated that the house in which she resided at Issy should be kept in repair at his expense. Not one of the clauses were ever fulfilled. M. Brunetière, though an excellent man of business, could not draw blood from a stone. Madame de Staël, his wife, who had but little regard for him, could not pay his debts, however just; and in the midst of these claims and refusals Mademoiselle Clairon was dying with hunger. On our way home my guardian, who was M. de Staël's counsellor and friend, related to me this transaction between him and the great actress, but added: "I beg you, my child, not to repeat what you have heard to-day; Mademoiselle Clairon is unhappy, and as poverty sours the disposition she is unjust towards M. de Staël." "But he does not pay her," said I, "since you are the guardian angel who saves her from perishing with hunger. How is it that your friend Gohier does not rescue her from this state of distress?"

"The Government is too poor. But do you speak to Lucien upon the subject; young lips may with much grace beg bread for such a woman as Mademoiselle Clairon; M. de Staël cannot pay her, and I have heavy charges upon me."

I spoke to my brother-in-law upon the subject. Mademoiselle Clairon received material assistance from Lucien, but it was not till the Ministry of Chaptal that she was effectually relieved from want. In a collection of autographs of celebrated persons, two curious papers on this subject are preserved; the one, in some very energetic words of Mademoiselle Clairon, requests bread from the Minister of the Interior; the other has the two equally expressive lines which follow:

"*Good for two thousand francs, payable at sight to Mademoiselle Clairon.*—CHAPTAL."

I saw her occasionally. She was fond of me, but Talma and Mademoiselle Mars caused perpetual disputes between us. I was angry, because, as she did not see their performance, she could not appreciate all the talent of these two beings endowed with dramatic genius. Talma might be criticized, but Mademoiselle Mars was even then a diamond of the first water, without spot or defect. At length I was one day much surprised to find my old friend quite softened towards my favourite actress, and never could attribute the sudden change to any other cause than her having seen Mademoiselle Mars in one of her characters; she did not admit it, but I am almost certain of the fact. I had spoken so much of her that it was scarcely possible she should not wish to see her to judge for herself.

In *The Pupil*, Mademoiselle Mars, in the simple action

of letting fall a nosegay, unveils at once the secret of a young heart. This expressive touch is one which could not be described, and yet Mademoiselle Clairon spoke to me as if she had seen it; nor do I think that she would have imbibed from any other source opinions sufficiently strong to overcome her prejudices, though I know that an old M. Antoine, a friend of Lekain, gave her frequent accounts of all that passed at the *Comédie Française*. I have, however, no doubt that she had been carried thither herself in a sedan-chair, and had seen and admired our charming actress. I have often seen Mademoiselle Mars off the stage since that time, but I do not remember to have ever mentioned the circumstance to her—she could not but have been flattered by it.

It is well known that Mademoiselle Clairon was the cause, the innocent cause it is said, of the suicide of a man, who killed himself by a pistol-shot. Ever afterwards she heard that shot every night at one o'clock, whether asleep or at a ball, on a journey or at an inn—it was the same thing; it penetrated the music of a *fête*, it awoke her from repose, and it resounded equally in the court of a posthouse or of a palace. I cannot answer for it that there was no exaggeration in all this; but she who usually spoke in an exaggerated strain here laid aside all that could give any suspicion of seeking after effect. Albert, who believed in magnetism, wished after hearing Mademoiselle Clairon's relation to demonstrate to me that the thing was possible.*
I laughed then. . . . Alas! since that time I have myself had a terrible lesson to cure me of incredulity.

* A part only of her Memoirs, written by herself, has been printed.

CHAPTER XXVIII.

Napoleon's Smile—His Account of the Action at Algeciras and Admiral Linois—His Joy at the Success of the French Fleet—The Humiliation of England his most Anxious Desire—Activity in the Ports of the Channel—The Flotilla of Boulogne—Brunet's Jest upon the *Péniches* — He learns Discretion — Inundation of Pamphlets — Frequent Disputes between Fouché and the First Consul—M. de Lucchesini—A Dinner and Diplomatic Imprudence—Madame de Lucchesini— Probable Authors of the Pamphlets—The Public Baths of Paris—The Mysterious Packet—"A Fortnight of the Great Alcander"—Bonaparte and Bussy de Rabutin—Relation of my Adventure to Junot—False Conjectures and my Mother suspected— Pamphlets burnt by her—Letters and more Pamphlets from my Brother—My Brother's Letter presented to Napoleon—Dramatic Scene in the First Consul's Cabinet—Remembrance of a Wound— Bonaparte reckons up his True Friends—His Lively Interest in my Mother's Illness—Anecdote of the Army in Italy.

THOSE who were much about the person of Napoleon can never forget the winning expression of his features when he smiled; his eyes then became truly eloquent, their expression softened; and if the sentiment which produced the smile had anything truly noble in it, its effect was infinitely heightened; it was then that his countenance became almost more than that of man.

Well do I remember one of those fleeting but sublime moments when the combat of Algeciras roused the emotion of his soul; his countenance, as he recounted the circumstances of this action, and dwelt complacently upon his words, became truly interesting. The valour of Rear-Admiral Linois excited the sympathetic love of glory in Napoleon, and more especially when it caused the triumph of our flag over that of the Three Leopards.

Admiral Linois, with two ships of the line—one of eighty guns, one of sixty-four—and a frigate of forty, fought Sir James Saumarez, who commanded two ships of eighty guns, four of sixty-four, two frigates of thirty-six guns, and a lugger, in the Bay of Gibraltar, before Algeciras, and took one of his sixty-fours, called the *Hannibal*.* All the glory of this action belonged to Admiral Linois, for he received very slight assistance from the Spanish land batteries. This success was followed by another equally brilliant; Captain Troude, who commanded the *Formidable*, one of Admiral Linois's two eighty-gun ships, was separated from the squadron a few days afterwards, and fell in with Sir James Saumarez and his three sixty-fours, to which he gave battle, and compelled Sir James to abandon one of them.

* [The errors in the narrative above are so numerous that it is impossible to correct them *seriatim*. For instance, this sentence should read in reality—"*Admiral Linois, with THREE ships of the line, TWO of eighty guns, one of SEVENTY-four, a frigate of THIRTY-EIGHT guns, and SEVERAL SPANISH GUNBOATS, fought Sir James Saumarez, who commanded ONE ship of eighty-guns, FIVE of SEVENTY-four, and a lugger, etc.*" No English frigates were present on this occasion. The *Hannibal*, an English *seventy*-four, was captured through grounding under the guns of the Spanish batteries.

Sir James Saumarez's force was undeniably repulsed on this occasion (July 6, 1801), but his ill success was more than retrieved a few days later in the open ocean in an engagement with the same ships, reinforced by the *Hannibal* (which had been got afloat by great exertions) and several line of battle-ships from Cadiz, three of the latter being three-deckers. Vide James's *Naval History* (crown 8vo. edition), vol. iii., pp. 96-118, for further details.

The gallantry of Captain Troude is probably based upon the partially mythical account which appeared in *Victoires et Conquêtes* (tom. xiv., p. 168).]

These facts Napoleon related; but it is impossible to describe the expression of his countenance while he invoked blessings on Rear-Admiral Linois for having attached a gleam of glory to our fleet. Naval victories were rare at that time, and the First Consul took the most lively interest in this; I can affirm it, because I saw it. I saw it when he was only Chief of the Government, not yet even Consul for life—much less Emperor! But he was General Bonaparte, the conqueror of Arcola, of Lodi, of Marengo, the true patriot. He loved his country then, and he always loved it! But at that time, happy in being the first of men, he wished for no other title.

The Rear-Admiral received the only recompense which then made the heart of a Frenchman beat—a sword of honour. But his grateful country multiplied that recompense a thousandfold in the praises she still bestows on him who gained a triumph for our flag.

Since the Treaty of Luneville, Napoleon had resumed in all their activity his views of an invasion of England. He had laid them aside to give his whole attention to more important affairs; but since the pacification of nearly the whole continent had become certain, and England appeared to be the sole impediment to a universal peace, the First Consul openly stated that he would stake everything to compel her to treat with the French Republic. All who had an opportunity of closely studying the character of Napoleon knew that the predominating desire of his mind was the humiliation of England. It was his constant object, and during the fourteen years of his power, when I was always able to observe his actions and their motives, I knew his determination to be firmly fixed upon giving to France the glory of conquering a rival who never engaged upon equal terms; and all his measures had reference to the same end.

Boulogne was selected in the year 1801 as the chief station of the enterprise against England. The greatest activity suddenly prevailed in all the ports of the Channel; camps were formed on the coast, divisions of light vessels were organized, and multitudes were built. The flotilla, as it was called, created apparently with the greatest exertion, and all the apparatus of preparation, spread, as was intended, alarm on the opposite shore. The Boulogne flotilla was composed of extremely light boats, so small that at Paris, where everything forms the subject of a jest, they were called walnut-shells.

Brunet, who at this time was a truly comic actor, performing in some piece which I do not remember, was eating walnuts, the shells of which, after a little preparation, he launched upon some water in a tub by his side. "What are you doing?" said his fellow-actor. "Making *péniches*," replied Brunet. [This was the name by which the flat-bottomed boats of the flotilla were known at Paris.] But poor Brunet had to atone by twenty-four hours' imprisonment for his unseasonable joke on the Government; and the day after his release the same piece was performed. When Brunet should have made the interdicted reply he was silent. The other actor repeated the inquiry as to what he was doing. Still Brunet made no answer, and the other with an air of impatience proceeded: "Perhaps you do not know what you are about?" "Oh yes!" said Brunet, "I know very well what I am about, but I know better than to tell." The laugh was general, and so was the applause; and, in truth, nothing could be more droll than the manner in which this was uttered; Brunet's countenance was of itself sufficient to provoke universal hilarity.

A very curious incident occurred to me about this time, which is connected with other circumstances that give a striking colour to the character of the period. This was the immense number of libellous pamphlets current in the second year of the Consulate, directed especially against the First Consul and his family. Bonaparte at last became violently provoked with Fouché upon the subject; and his displeasure burst out in several curious scenes, the more annoying to the Minister because they did not occur privately between himself and the First Consul, but before fifteen or twenty persons; I was myself present at two of them, one at Malmaison and the other at the Tuileries.

These pamphlets Bonaparte greatly suspected to proceed from the foreigners in Paris, and even from the Diplomatic Corps, that of Prussia especially, for the obsequious bows and language of the Marquis de Lucchesini, whose character was calculated to displease the head of the Government, were very much at variance with the opinions he used to inculcate.

The Revolution with him was inseparable from the horrors of 1793; he would admit none of the benefits which these misfortunes had procured for us, and held liberal principles of all kinds in the most supreme contempt. He had much sense and wit, and could be agreeable when he pleased, notwithstanding a very ugly face. I never liked, however, his measured phrases, his cold politeness, and his eternal ironical smile; and I always thought his excess of cunning anything but sagacious.

We met him one day at dinner at the house of Madame Divoff, a Russian lady, established at Paris, and wholly French in her feelings. He was in one of those moods of frankness which, unless intended to serve a particular purpose, are not, I think, quite advisable in a diplomatist. Junot, who was always open and unsuspecting in his conversation, entered into much disputation with him upon some very singular questions; the Concordat, for example, in which, strangely enough, M. de Lucchesini defended the First

Consul's proceedings against the objections of Junot; and the nomination of the King of Etruria, of which also the Ambassador approved, and which the republican principles of Junot looked upon as the first blow to our liberties.

Though very moderate in his language, M. de Lucchesini certainly in this debate exceeded the limits of his instructions; and Junot said much which would have been more suitably confined to his own closet than uttered at the table of a stranger amongst a mixed company. It was, however, a singular spectacle to see the dispute between these two parties so oddly supported: the one the adorer of Bonaparte, blaming his wish to reign; the other his enemy, rejoicing to see him take up sceptres and crowns as playthings, perhaps already foreseeing the embarrassments they would occasion, and hoping they might ultimately prove the rock on which his power would be wrecked.

The First Consul heard the particulars of this conversation the following day; but it was not until some months after that Junot learned that his General had been dissatisfied with the dinner and the discussion; Napoleon did not like to be blamed by a friend, any more than by other people, and this dinner was not without consequences.

These pamphlets which inundated us with their venom were supposed to be chiefly concocted by persons attached to the Northern Embassies, and Madame de Lucchesini was even said to be active in superintending them. She was not present at the dinner I have spoken of above, or her husband would have received a hint to be more prudent, for she had quite sense enough to understand that his ambassadorial functions were not in keeping with such unreserved discourse. She was, however, very ridiculous, affecting at forty-five the airs of a coy maiden of sixteen; speaking like a child, and professing incapacity to pronounce the letter *r*, unless, indeed, when she forgot herself.

I think myself that the First Consul was rather unjust in laying the dissemination of these pamphlets so much to the account of the recognized representatives of the Northern Courts. The two Counts von Cobentzel were incapable of such treachery, and if M. de Lucchesini and M. Markoff could have sanctioned it, it must have been unknown to their Governments. The Emperor Alexander, whose young heart beat with the chivalrous honour peculiar to the morning of life, did not, it is true, love Napoleon in 1802, but he already began to feel, notwithstanding the storm which rose soon after, a portion of that admiration on which the friendship of the Niemen was founded, and the soul which admires greatness is incapable of a base action.

I am disposed to believe that those scandalous libels and personal invectives were the productions of many unaccredited agents, who came amongst us for the double purpose of sowing discord and seeking pleasure. The First Consul was never able to unravel the whole mystery of this iniquitous manœuvre. Two hundred specimens of these atrocious writings were seized in the boudoir of a young and pretty woman; in a perfumed and ornamented retreat, which should have harboured only romances, flowers, and billets-doux. The First Consul laughed when this fact was reported to him, but it was with a laugh of bitterness.

In relating the occurrence which connected me with these detestable pamphlets, I must observe that comfort had not then reached its present pitch amongst us, especially in the interior arrangement of our houses. A private bathroom was a luxury which appertained to very few; but the deficiency in this respect was in a great degree remedied by the convenience offered to the public by the baths of Tivoli, of Albert, and of Vigier, which were frequented by ladies of distinction. I was in the habit of using Albert's; and was one day in the bath when the young woman who usually attended me gave to my maid a large packet directed to Madame Junot the Younger. It was brought, she said, by a respectable man dressed in black and advanced in years, but of whom I knew no more by her description than of a Chinese mandarin.

On opening it a multitude of little sheets of note-paper flew about, which on inspection proved to be covered over the four sides with very small and fine writing in a perfectly legible hand—the whole of them copies of three different pamphlets, and a few of one number of a Royalist journal, which, Fouché's active police having suppressed it in print, was now disseminated in written copies to the amount of several hundred. One of the pamphlets was particularly scandalous, and was entitled *A Fortnight of the Great Alcander*. It appeared every fortnight, professing to give a journal of the First Consul's proceedings, and was filled with such stupid absurdities that it was a subject for neither laughter nor anger, but very fit to excite disgust. The First Consul was preposterously accused of lavishing extravagant sums on his mistresses; and poor Bellilotte was attacked with a rancour which she certainly did not deserve.

The first time Napoleon heard of this scandalous journal he paid little attention to it, except to inquire what was meant by the Great Alcander. When he was informed that it was Louis XIV. he became seriously angry. "To Louis XIV.!" he exclaimed. "Ah! those people know very little of me to compare me to him—to Louis XIV.!" Then, taking up the libel again, he continued reading, occasionally striking the floor with his foot, and exclaiming, "Louis XIV.!" He would have an explanation of how and when the Great King, who was not great, obtained the title of the Great Alcander. He had never read the works of Bussy de Rabutin; he asked for them, looked them through in one night, and they offended him. "Your Comte de Bussy-Rabutin," said he to Junot the next morning at breakfast, "was a bad man." The speciality of the pronoun referred to the circumstance of Junot's having been born in the village of which Bussy-Rabutin had been Sieur, and where his mansion stood in very good condition in the year 1802.*

But to return to my packet; I examined all these innumerable little sheets to find some note or notice by which I might imagine to whom I was indebted for so singular a present, but in vain; they were but endless reduplications of the same three pamphlets and the *Royalist Journal*. One only clue could I gather, and that so very slight that I dared not affix much importance to it, or even speak of it; it was a very peculiar perfume.

Before I left the bath I closely questioned the girl who had taken in the packet, but with no effect; she evidently knew nothing of the person who delivered it; and I was obliged to return, wondering who could be so absurd as to place in the hands of a young woman so giddy as I was a collection of papers which might compromise so many people.

Who could have so strange an idea of my situation as to choose me, the wife of General Junot, the most devoted of

---

* In a tower attached to this mansion there was a collection of ill-painted portraits, but curious on account of the persons they represented. They were executed by Bussy-Rabutin during the periods of his various exiles, and were likenesses of most of the ladies of the Court of Louis XIV. In each picture was an emblem of the character of the woman, intended to express his own opinion of them. Madame de la Vallière had a violet; Madame de Montespan was represented as one of the seven capital sins. Madame de Sévigné, cousin of Rabutin, and whom he never forgave because she would not yield to his wishes, was placed in a scale; in the other was a chubby-cheeked zephyr, blowing with all his strength against her; beneath these scales was written, " Lighter than air."

the First Consul's friends, to be the depositary of libels against him, and against his sisters, one of whom was my particular and beloved friend! For a moment I thought of going to my mother for advice, but my good angel made me prefer applying to Junot, which I did without loss of time.

I found him on the point of setting out for the Tuileries to receive the order of the day, as he regularly did at twelve o'clock, whenever the First Consul was at Paris. I related my adventure to him, and he seemed surprised like myself; but he had much more experience of the world than I had, and immediately imbibed suspicions which directed his researches, and led him to the belief, afterwards confirmed, that this singular expedient was adopted to injure him.

"But why," said I, "did they take this packet to the baths? you see it must be a mistake." "That is precisely the circumstance which convinces me that there is no mistake in the case. The man, the gentleman as you call him, who delivered this packet, had no inclination to meet a face which would not have been so forgetful as the servant of the baths. There he has left no trace; here it would have been quite another thing; he might have fallen in with me at the door; for the same reason he did not go to your mother's house."

"Then it is really true that these venomous papers were intended for me," said I, weeping. "But why was I chosen? I could but do two things with them: either throw them into the fire or distribute them. The writers could hardly be so absurd as to intend the one or expect the other. All this puzzles me. The First Consul pretends that my drawing-room and my mother's are full of his enemies: a fine disturbance it would create if he should learn that I have here a whole edition of libels against him. I can hear him now! He would say directly that the authors knew very well whom they were applying to; or else, 'They certainly came from your mother.'"

Alas! my poor mother was then very ill, and was thinking upon very different and much higher subjects. Junot, however, did not hear me lightly; he was struck by the words, "They came from your mother." He embraced me, took up all the papers in the envelope and set out for the Tuileries. As soon as the order of the day was given he requested an audience of the First Consul, and, presenting the papers, related their history with perfect simplicity. As I had foreseen, Napoleon's first words were an accusation against my mother and myself.

"It is impossible," said he to Junot, "that these papers should have been sent to your wife without the knowledge that they would be well received—if only for the sake of amusing her mother." Junot made no answer; he knew the First Consul's prejudice, or rather mistake, respecting my mother, and he wished to convince him that neither she nor I could be in any way interested in the disagreeable affair; but he could not without proofs. He hoped to obtain some clue to the affair by means of one Fouillon, who was known to him as the editor of these pamphlets; he also had cognisance of several other persons who were concerned in this base proceeding; and he set to work in earnest to find out the motive which led them to choose for their agent a young woman much more disposed to laugh and dance than to read newspapers, still less libels.

Junot had good sense, a rapid and acute judgment; his *coup d'œil* was prompt, and his reasoning almost always right, notwithstanding his hastiness and vehemence. The maid of the bath was sent for, but her renewed examination threw no light on the subject; she knew only that the packet was directed to me, and, further, that the old gentleman had desired her to deliver it to Madame Junot.

"Perhaps my sister-in-law," said I. Junot shrugged his shoulders; in fact, that could not be; but the choice they had made of me for a political agent appeared so eccentric that I imagined everything rather than the possibility that I was upon the scene in my own individual capacity. Junot, seeing me affected to melancholy, if not indisposition, resolved to consult my mother that she might scold me. But what was his astonishment when she immediately said, "I have received just such another packet, my dear son."

"Let me see it, then," cried Junot; "let me compare the envelope with ours." "The packet!" answered my mother. "Do you really believe, then, that I should keep such low trash, conceptions fit only for the perusal of chambermaids? Truly not I!" "Then what have you done with them?" "Burned them all. When M. de Bois-Cressy, after unsealing the packet, had read some of the horrors it contained, I did not choose that my table should any longer be stained with such vile productions. I told him to put them all into the fire; at first he was not disposed to do so, because he preferred reading them. A hundred newspapers a day, as you know, would not satisfy his ravenous appetite for politics; but this abominable packet contained no newspapers, and the whole was committed to the flames."

Junot kissed my mother's hands, saying, "How I admire you for being so sensible!" My mother looked at him with a sweet smile. "It is not on your own account that you thank me, my son," said she, "but on Bonaparte's. Why should you be surprised that I could destroy attacks upon his reputation, and especially such as are absolutely false?—the little I saw of those libels certainly was so. If you think I cherish an unjust aversion to General Bonaparte you are very much mistaken. I do not entertain for him that admiration which transports into regions where no one can follow; but I consider him great, and even good, only his own interests lead him to forget or neglect those of others. Why should I not excuse that? It is the common failing of mankind. Well, he is as good as other men, but do not tell me that he is more than man."

This had always been my mother's manner of speaking of General Bonaparte since my marriage. Junot returned home thoughtful, but rejoiced to be able to relate to the First Consul my mother's war against the pamphlets. He wished to see me before going to the Tuileries, where he expected to find the First Consul in Madame Bonaparte's apartments, as he spent every evening there when they did not go into public. He repeated the anecdote to me, and I shared his surprise. I thought the affair more and more strange; but we had not yet come to the end of it. While we continued discussing the evening slipped away, so that Junot could not go to the Tuileries. The next day was devoted to a parade, so that he was again obliged to postpone his interview with the First Consul.

The evening of this day a courier arrived from Marseilles, where my brother was stationed as one of the three Commissaries-General of the Police of the Republic. The courier brought us a letter from my brother, with another packet of the same pamphlets and journals, the whole written by the hand, but by way of variety some of these were in the *Provençal* dialect, worthy of the days of the good King Réné. It was added that the pamphlets were sent by my mother, but through my agency; only they had the prudence to make me say: "You will easily understand why I do not write to you myself."

My brother, on whose good-nature they had relied rather too much, at first took this present for a hoax, as he could not for a moment believe it came from me. Albert had never participated in my mother's resentment, which he thought unjust, but was devotedly attached to the First Consul. I thought as he did; and without blaming my mother, whom we adored and respected, we did not exactly think with her respecting Napoleon. But Albert knew my mother's noble heart, and was perfectly sure that she would not join in such a tissue of vile abuse; and my name introduced into the affair was sufficient to convince him that it was all a deception.

He accordingly sent for one of the police officers whom he could trust, and charged him to make all possible research at Marseilles to discover who had transcribed the pamphlets and who had delivered them. And judging that my mother and myself might be compromised in this mysterious business, his affection induced him, without loss of time, to send a courier to Junot with the whole atrocious baggage of pamphlets, journals, and letters, several from me, but not written by me. Junot read Albert's letter, and leapt for joy at the thought of his triumph.

"I should not sleep to-night," said he, "if I did not see the First Consul; and it is not yet too late to ask for a moment's audience; besides, the affair is not a little complicated, and the First Consul must read Albert's letter."

I approved of his intention, and though it was nearly eleven o'clock he proceeded to the Tuileries. The First Consul, fatigued with the review of the morning, was just going to bed, but Junot was admitted at once. Napoleon made a remark upon the air of hilarity which his countenance exhibited; and Junot, without answering, put my brother's letter before him. He read it rapidly, and seemed struck by it, for he directly read it again, laid it upon the table, walked about the room, then took the letter up, and ran through it again, rubbing his forehead; at last he suddenly stopped before Junot, and said, "Can you give me your word of honour that your mother-in-law is not concerned in all this?"

"My mother-in-law!" exclaimed Junot, and he related to the First Consul the history of the burnt papers. As he spoke, Napoleon became by degrees more attentive; then began to walk rapidly up and down the room, and at last assumed an angry frown. Junot could not understand it. "If Madame Permon's opinion was not so well known," said he with bitterness, "she would not have such presents made her. See if such have been sent to Madame Gheneuc, or to the mother-in-law of any of my other Generals. Madame Permon dislikes me—this is known, and is the groundwork of the whole proceeding. People who detest me meet in her drawing-room; people who, before my return from Egypt, were prisoners in the Temple for their opinions—these are her friends. And you, great blockhead! you make them your friends also . . . you make friends of my enemies!"

Junot looked stupefied, staring at the First Consul. He make friends of his General's enemies! He thought it all a dream. "Of whom are you speaking, General?" said he at length. "Of M. d'Orsay, to be sure—he whom they call the handsome D'Orsay. Was he not on the point of being shot for a conspirator, and was he not sent to the Temple? Fouché told me the other day that he was a dangerous man."

Junot smiled bitterly. "General, you have given me to understand in two syllables to whom I am indebted for all this, and I shall know how to thank him. I shall begin by saying that Citizen Fouché has told you a falsehood in asserting that Albert d'Orsay was a dangerous man and a conspirator. He is the most loyal and honest man living, of the highest honour; and if, in returning to France, he has given his word to be faithful to the established Government, he will keep it. I should have thought, General, that as Fouché gave him the title of my friend you would have held him worthy of your esteem as a man of honour; for I could not give my friendship to anyone who was not. But, General, you should never have believed that an enemy of yours could be my friend." Junot passed his hand over his forehead, which was dripping. Napoleon knew him too well not to be conscious how much he suffered. He approached him, and pressed his hand affectionately. Junot was suffocating.

"Come! don't be childish. I tell you I am not speaking of you, my faithful friend. Have you not proved your attachment when I was in fetters? would you not have followed me to prison?" "I should have followed you to the scaffold!" cried Junot, striking his fist upon the table. Napoleon laughed. "Well, don't you see, then, that it is impossible for me to say anything that should go to your heart and hurt you, Monsieur Junot?" And he pulled his ears, his nose, and his hair. Junot drew back.

"Ah! I have hurt you," said Napoleon, approaching him, and resting his little white hand upon Junot's light hair, caressing him, as if he meant to pacify a child. "Junot," he continued, "do you remember being at the Serbelloni Palace at Milan, when you had just received a wound—just here—at this place?" And the small white hand gently touched the large cicatrice. "I pulled away your hair, and my hand was full of your blood. . . ." The First Consul turned pale at the recollection. And it is a remarkable circumstance that Napoleon spoke to me not less than ten times, in the course of his reign, of this incident at Milan, and never without starting and turning pale at the recollection of his blood-stained hand.

"Yes," he continued, with a movement as if to repress a shudder—"yes, I confess at that moment I felt that there is a weakness inherent in human nature which is only more exquisitely developed in the female constitution. I then understood that it was *possible* to faint. I have not forgotten that moment, my friend; and the name of Junot can never be mingled in my mind with even the appearance of perfidy. Your head is too hot, too heedless, but you are a loyal and brave fellow. You, Lannes, Marmont, Duroc, Berthier, Bessières." At each name Napoleon took a pinch of snuff and a turn in the room, sometimes making a pause and smiling as the name recalled any proof of attachment. "My son, Eugène—yes, those are hearts which love me, which I can depend upon. Lemarrois, too, is another faithful friend. And that poor Rapp, he has been but a short time with me, yet he pushes his affection even to an extent that might give offence; do you know he even scolds me sometimes?"

The First Consul, who had taken Junot's arm while speaking, was leaning upon him as he walked; then, standing near the window, he disengaged his arm, and, resting it on my husband's shoulder, compelled him almost to stoop as he leant upon him.

"How many of the persons now passing below this window," said Junot, smiling, "would give years of their existence to be where I am now, close to you, General, supporting that arm which can raise the world! Yes, I believe there are many who would make great sacrifices only to be able to say they had been so fortunate; but in all Paris there is not a heart as happy as mine is at this moment."

Napoleon disengaged his arm, looking at Junot with that ineffable smile to which he owed his power of conquering with a single word, and said, "Well, my old friend, we will say no more of this foolish affair of the pamphlets—but attend : what am I to think when I know that you receive so many of my enemies ? That your wife and your mother-in-law are intimately acquainted with numerous persons who are my enemies, who hate me and desire my fall ? nay, more, my death—as they have proved."

"But, General, give me leave to answer that among all the persons you speak of there is not one who, even before my wife's marriage, would have dared in her presence to use an expression disrespectful to you. With respect to my mother-in-law, I have frequently heard her speak of you, General, but never in terms which could give me pain. Madame Permon is too much attached to Madame Bonaparte, to your mother, and to all your brothers." "Oh yes, Lucien especially," interrupted the First Consul, with a bitter smile. "Lucien is her favourite. She thinks him a prodigy; nevertheless, Madame Permon is no Republican ! How do they contrive to agree on that point ?"

"I have not twice heard my mother-in-law talk politics since I have belonged to her family," replied Junot. "The subjects of conversation in her drawing-room are literature and music, a thousand important nothings, the affairs of society and fashion; and it must be confessed that the society of the old school understood the management of such conversation better than we do ; besides, General, if you were aware of the present state of Madame de Permon's health you would not suspect a person preparing for the grave to be amusing herself with such miserable trifles."

Here I ought to do full justice to Napoleon. When Junot was speaking thus of my mother he was some paces distant from him ; he stepped hastily to him and pressed his arm forcibly, saying: "Ah! what do you say? Is Madame Permon very ill?" "Dying, General; all the physicians we have called in agree upon her danger." "Corvisart must see her." He rang the bell. "Send someone immediately to tell Citizen Corvisart that I wish to see him. Is it possible!" said he, as he walked with an agitated step—"is it possible that a woman so fresh and beautiful only fifteen months ago can be so seriously ill? Poor Madame Permon! Poor Madame Permon!"

He sank into his arm-chair, put his two hands before his eyes, and sat some time without speaking; then, rising, he recommenced that rapid promenade which was his usual habit when strongly affected. "Desgenettes and Ivan must also be sent to her; it is impossible that the faculty should be unable to save a person so lately as healthy and fresh as a rose." "General," replied Junot, "Madame Permon's malady is of a deplorable nature in the history of the healing art; she will sink in defiance of medical aid." And hereupon he repeated Baudelocque's answer to him, when Junot, fearing for my mother's life, asked his opinion: "General, he who could cure such a complaint as Madame Permon's might boast of performing as great a miracle as if he had restored a decapitated man to life."

Napoleon seemed quite overwhelmed in listening to this sentence; but impressions, however strong, were only transiently marked upon his countenance; he soon recovered himself, and was apparently quite calm when Junot took leave of him.

My recent mention of my husband's wound recalls to my memory a trivial circumstance connected with it, which happened in Italy. This terrible wound, which had nearly cost him an arm, kept him confined six weeks; notwithstanding M. Ivan's fraternal care of his patient he was very long in recovering from its effects.

During the tedious hours that he lay upon a sofa, dressed in a white wrapping-gown, he played the agreable, being really a handsome youth ; and, as his greatest defect at that time was too high a colour, his complexion was improved by his loss of blood. Madame Bonaparte and Madame Leclerc were among the ladies who assisted in dissipating, by their presence, the tedium of confinement. One day, when they were making this visit of charity, Junot was very much enfeebled, not only by the effects of his wound, but of an abundant bleeding he had undergone that morning ; however, he collected all his strength to receive his charming visitors, happy in having beside his couch of suffering two of the most lovely women in Milan. For if Madame Bonaparte could not be compared in beauty to Madame Leclerc, she was very handsome at that period, and the extreme elegance of her manners and really fascinating gracefulness might well be taken as a substitute for more regular beauty. Indeed, if her teeth had been good I should have preferred her face to that of the most celebrated beauty of her Court.

The pleasing conversation of two such women was no doubt the best panacea for pain, and at first produced its full effect. Junot was the happiest of men to be attended by two such *sœurs de la charité*. Time, however, rolled softly on, and with its lapse matters changed. Junot's heart began to sink, his sight to fail ; he became paler, and at length his eyes closed. Madame Leclerc first perceived his condition, and, standing up, cried out : " Good heavens, Junot ! what is the matter ?"

Junot had still strength enough left to extend towards her the hand which lay upon his bosom, and instantly Pauline's white gown was covered with blood. The bandage round his arm had unfastened, and the blood, confined within the thick sleeve of his wrapper, had flowed gently and unperceived till his strength was nearly exhausted ; but the effort of moving his arm in a moment of surprise had caused it to spring forth in abundance, and Junot fainted completely. On recovering he found himself the object of the most anxious cares, tendered by the prettiest hands in the world. Heldt, his Alsacian valet, had replaced the bandage, and the ladies, after a few moments, left the patient to repose, and the accident had no other consequence than retarding his convalescence.

"But," said I, when he related this little adventure to me, "how was it that you did not feel that your arm was bathed in blood?" "I was aware of it," he replied ; "but could I desire these ladies to leave me?" "No, but you could have had the bandage replaced." "That could only be done in their presence when I was insensible; in any other case the thing was impossible."

I looked at Junot with amazement, asking myself if he had been educated by Yseulte with the white hands, or the fair Guinevere, for none but a Tristan or a Launcelot could have had such ideas ; when suddenly the remembrance of a certain promenade on the Boulevards in the year of grace 1795, when Junot was madly in love with Paulette Bonaparte,* crossed my mind, and the whole was explained.

* Pauline.

CHAPTER XXIX.

A Word about the Libels—Strange Ideas of Foreigners respecting the First Consul—Scene between Lannes and Napoleon—Errors respecting *Tutoying*—Traits of Napoleon—The Polytechnic School—The Aide-de-camp Lacuée and the Young Enthusiast at Malmaison—The Father's Pupil—Severity of the Abbé Bossu—The First Consul an Examiner—Scene in his Cabinet—The Order of Admission.

I HAVE dwelt at some length upon the libellous pamphlets, because it furnishes a good ground for the extremely false ideas which existed in foreign countries of the interior condition of France, and especially of the intercourse which General Bonaparte had with those who surrounded him. It is an important circumstance of his life, and the cause of the judgments passed upon him in many countries where they did not take the trouble of investigating the truth of what was advanced concerning him. I believe the prejudices of distrust exaggerated the good as much as the bad, for, amongst the strangers who just now abounded in France, many entertained the most ridiculous notions, both for and against Napoleon.

One believed that he drank a cup of coffee every hour; another, that he passed entire days in the bath; a third, that he took his dinner standing, and a thousand absurdities each one more ridiculous than the other. It is remarkable that the most extraordinary versions of these absurdities came from England, and that the emigrants who returned from thence had formed opinions totally different from the reality. One whom I knew was perfectly astonished at seeing him, so entirely false was the impression he had imbibed.

One of these pamphlets, badly composed, and in manuscript, contained a most ridiculous scene, said to have passed between Napoleon and General Lannes, of which Madame Bonaparte was the subject. The whole is absolutely false, but it is a curious fact that at a later period a dispute really took place between Lannes and Napoleon, in which Madame Bonaparte was concerned. At the time of the affair of the military chest of the guards, General Lannes, who really was not so much to blame as was represented, learned that Madame Bonaparte had been attempting to screen the guilty parties at his expense, and gave vent to his wrath against her in the cabinet of the First Consul with a freedom which, perhaps, a friend should not have indulged in. He told Napoleon that instead of listening to the gossiping of an *old* woman he had much better take a young one. The discussion was warm; keen, and even abusive, words were not spared; General Lannes forgot himself so far as to speak in injurious terms of Madame Bonaparte, and was really in a passion on that occasion. But he had never before disputed with the First Consul; nor was the thing easy.

It is the same with the familiarity with which Lannes and others are said to have been in the habit of addressing him. I do not deny that some of these Generals used the pronoun *thou* in speaking to him, though fully persuaded of the contrary; but for this I can answer, that if such a habit ever existed it was disused after his return from Egypt. I never heard anyone *tutoyer* the First Consul. He did so by many of them, by Junot to the last;* it was only on ascending the throne that he ceased to address them in this familiar style in public, and in the cordial intercourse of private friendship which always subsisted between him and Lannes, Junot, Berthier, and two or three others, he continued to use the pronoun *thou*. But to say *toi* to General Bonaparte was quite another thing, and I do not believe Lannes ever did so.

Already in Italy we find Bourrienne did so no longer; Junot never did, nor did Berthier, who, with the army in Italy, was surely sufficiently intimate with him—if anyone could be. But after the campaigns of Italy and Egypt Napoleon felt too strongly the necessity of being obeyed, and of establishing around him that barrier of respect which familiarity destroys, to permit such a fashion of addressing him. In some Memoirs you might imagine General Lannes extending his hand to Napoleon, and accosting him with "*Bon jour, comment te portes-tu?*" But certainly, if in his sleep or in a fit of absence he had been guilty of such irregularity, the First Consul would have known how to repress it by some such reply as M. de Narbonne gave to the friend whom he had never seen: "Very well, friend, but what is thy name?" At least, I can affirm that during the long period in which I was witness of the intercourse of Napoleon with General Lannes I never either heard or saw anything of the kind.

In the time of the Consulate there was at Paris an Abbé Bossu, who received the candidates for the Polytechnic School. He was not the only examiner, but his veto was

* [Accordingly, in all the conversations between Napoleon and Junot in the French work, Napoleon always uses the pronoun *thou*, and Junot *you*; but as the French familiar style of *tutoying* would sound oddly to an English ear, the difference could not be marked in the translation. It is, in fact, using the language of the Quakers.—EDITOR.]

strict; he was a man of great learning and very severe. The Polytechnic School, created at first under the name of the Central School of Public Works, by virtue of a decree of the Convention in Germinal of the year iii. (21st March, 1795), after being disorganized by the destructive system which ruined us, had been reconstructed and put into activity by the First Consul in Frimaire of the year viii., immediately after his accession to power.* The analysis of the mathematical sciences, with their application to mechanism, geometry, etc.; the physical sciences, including chemistry and general physics, formed the course of study pursued in the Polytechnic School from its foundation. The most illustrious names in knowledge and science were then at the head of that battalion of young men whose youthful minds were eager to become participators in the sublime acquirements of their masters.†

The aide-de-camp on duty, one day crossing the court of the mansion at Malmaison, found there a young man of a pleasing countenance and good figure, well dressed, and bearing the stamp of good birth and good education. He was leaning against one of the (two) great sentry-boxes which stood on the east side of the inner gate, looking towards the house with an uneasy and melancholy air, and apparently seeking someone whom he might address. The

---

* The First Consul did not found the Polytechnic School, as is stated by many writers; he re-established it the 16th December, 1799, which may have given rise to the error. It was the Convention that organized most of the fine institutions of this nature in France.

† France owes much to such men as Monge, Berthollet, Vauquelin, Fourcroy, Chaptal, and Lagrange, so famous in literary and scientific acquirements; they are highly to be esteemed on account of their great services to the country, and were foremost in their arduous endeavours to organize this celebrated school on the best footing. It is, indeed, unrivalled in Europe; and almost every Frenchman of celebrity or of deep erudition has been bred up within its walls.

aide-de-camp, M. de Lacuée, approached him, and with his habitual politeness inquired if he wanted anything there. The young man, starting from his profound reverie, answered:

"Ah, sir! I want what everyone tells me is impossible, and yet I shall die if I cannot obtain it: I want to see the First Consul. At the door of the house I was repulsed—I was asked if I had an appointment. Oh that I could have one! I believe an appointment to meet the most adorable mistress could not make my heart beat so violently as would an appointment with General Bonaparte. I must speak to him."

And the young man again cast his large black eyes, moistened with tears, upon the mansion. M. de Lacuée was always attracted towards anything that presented itself to him out of the ordinary routine. He saw a romantic adventure in the rencontre; he advanced towards the young man, who was standing in an attitude of natural grace leaning against the sentry-box, and looking with longing eyes to the house, and said, "Well, sir! what do you want with the First Consul? I am the aide-de-camp on duty, and will undertake to present your request if it is a reasonable one." "You, sir!" exclaimed the young man, springing towards M. de Lacuée, seizing and pressing the hand he offered him; "are you the First Consul's aide-de-camp? Oh, if you knew what a service you could do me! I must be conducted to him." "What do you want with him?" "I must speak to him." Then he added in a low tone: "It is a secret."

Lacuée looked at his youthful petitioner, who stood before him, his bosom palpitating, his respiration hurried; but with purity and innocence in the expression of his countenance. "This young man cannot be dangerous," said Lacuée to himself; and taking him by the arm, he led him into the Inner Court. As they passed the gate, Duroc and Junot entered on horseback, coming from Paris; they stopped, and alighted to salute their comrade, who related his little adventure. "What!" said both of them at once, "you are going to introduce him without even knowing his name?"

Lacuée acknowledged that he had not asked it. Junot then approached the young man and told him that the First Consul was certainly very accessible, but, still, that it was necessary to know the motive which urged anyone to request an audience, and that it was impossible to announce an anonymous solicitor.

The young man blushed like a girl; but he gave his name, adding with a respectful bow: "It is true, General. My father lives in the country, and his knowledge is sufficiently extensive to enable him to instruct me in all branches of elementary education, directing my studies with a view to my admission into the Polytechnic School. Judge, then, of my distress, and his also, when on our presenting ourselves to the Abbé Bossu, who it appears is the person who must decide whether or no I can be entered, he absolutely refused to examine me as soon as he was informed that my father only had been my instructor, and that I had not been taught by any professor. 'Of what consequence is that,' I asked, 'if I know what is required?' But he was inflexible, and could not be induced to put a single question to me."

"But," said Duroc, with his natural mildness, "it is a rule, and whether a good one or otherwise is alike to all comers. What do you wish the First Consul to do in the case?" "To examine me," answered the young man with the most engaging simplicity; "I am sure that when he has put any questions to me that he may judge proper, he will pronounce me worthy of sharing the studies of those young persons of whom he proposes to form officers capable of executing his great designs."

The three comrades looked at each other and smiled; Duroc and Junot thought as Lacuée had done, that this young man with his ardent speech and look of fire could not but be agreeable to Napoleon, and Duroc went to broach the matter to him.

"So the young enthusiast would have me examine him?" said he, with one of his most gracious smiles; then rubbing his chin, he continued: "How could such an idea have entered his head? It is a very singular thing." He walked about for some time in silence, then added: "How old may he be?" "I cannot tell, General, but should guess about seventeen or eighteen."

"Let him come in." The young petitioner was introduced. His brilliant countenance expressed his happiness as he cast his eye upon the First Consul. He looked as if his existence depended upon the first word of Napoleon, who advanced towards him with that smile which cast over his countenance a charm entirely different, at these moments when he intended to be gracious, from his usual expression. "Well, young man," said he, "so you wish me to examine you?"

The youth trembled with joy, and could make no answer; he stood silent, with his eyes fixed on the First Consul. Napoleon did not like either the boldness of presumption or the bashfulness of fear; but that which he now saw was silence, because the heart spoke too loudly—and he understood it.

"Compose yourself, my boy; you are not at this moment sufficiently calm to answer me; I am going to employ myself in other affairs; by-and-by we will resume yours." "Do you see that young man," said the First Consul, leading Junot to the recess of a window; "if I had a thousand such as he the conquest of the world would be but a promenade." He turned his head aside to contemplate the youth, who, plunged in meditation, was probably revolving in his mind what questions were likely to be put to him. In about half an hour Napoleon commenced the examination, in which the young candidate acquitted himself admirably. "And have you really had no other instructor than your father?" asked the First Consul with surprise. "No, General; but he was a good master, because he knew how to bring up a citizen to be useful to his country, and especially to follow the great destinies which you promised to it."

Junot observed that they were all astonished at the almost prophetic expression with which the youth pronounced the last words. "I am about to give you a line which will open the sanctuary to you, my child," said the First Consul; and he wrote a few words upon a paper, which he presented to the young man.

On arriving at Paris he hastened to the Abbé Bossu, who, on seeing him, exclaimed: "What do you come again for? There is nothing here for you."

But the youth held a talisman which was equal to a magic ring, and which the Abbé Bossu having read could not refuse to obey; it was as follows:

"*M. Bossu will receive M. Eugène de Kervalègne. I have examined him myself, and find him worthy of admission.*
"BONAPARTE."

The young man accordingly became a distinguished pupil of the Polytechnic School. His advancement in life was rapid at first; my brother knew him at Toulon, where he had an appointment in the Department of Bridges and Roads. His attachment for Napoleon amounted to idolatry.

The First Consul long remembered this adventure, and one day related it to Cardinal Maury at a dinner at Saint Cloud; the Cardinal, it happened, knew the young man's family, and confirmed him in the good opinion he had formed of his character, disposition, and adventurous spirit.

CHAPTER XXX.

Illness of my Mother—My First Pregnancy—The Pineapple—Madame Bonaparte's Goodness—Predictions with Cards—Wager between the First Consul and Madame Bonaparte on the Sex of my Child—New Year's Day—Celebration of Twelfth Day—Junot's Distraction and his Visit to the Tuileries—Kindness of the First Consul—His Message—The News of my Accouchement carried to the Tuileries—The First Consul's Compliments and his Lost Wager—Extraordinary Conduct of my Father-in-law—The Barcelonnette—St. Helena Memorial refuted.

My poor mother was now suffering under a state of severe illness which neither our cares nor our affection could alleviate, but which she endured with admirable fortitude. Her distressing state added to my indisposition. The final stroke which was to inflict on me this heart-breaking grief was not yet given, but it was threatened, and contributed to my present suffering.

I was at this time far advanced in my first pregnancy, and had suffered much; surrounded by the tenderest attentions, spoiled, as I may say, by my own family, and bearing about me the child who was to make me proud of the name of mother, I ought not, perhaps, to have been sensible of suffering.

At that period the culture of the pineapple was not so well understood as it is at present, and it was consequently a great rarity. In my peculiar situation I became possessed of a longing for this fruit that produced a degree of intense suffering; and in order to gratify my whim Junot, with the affectionate gallantry of a man whose wife is about for the first time to make him a father, ran all over Paris, offering twenty louis for the object I so much coveted. Disappointed in his endeavours, he informed Madame Bonaparte of the circumstance, and she, with her characteristic kindness of heart, sent me the only one that was procurable from the hothouse at Malmaison. From a singular revulsion of feeling this delicious fruit, so eagerly desired by me, and obtained with so much difficulty, became, when actually in my possession, positively distasteful.

No one could be more kind than Madame Bonaparte always was to young women in my situation; she entered into our feelings and interested herself in everything that could be agreeable to us; in these circumstances she was truly amiable. On hearing of the pineapple she prophesied that I should have a daughter, and in support of her opinion proposed a game of patience. I knew by experience all the ennui which this unfortunate game promised; but there was no refusing, and in spite of my incredulity I was compelled to sit down and see my destiny settled by the caprice of the cards. It is known that the Empress Josephine was superstitiously credulous in these matters; and, in fact, I was witness, in the years 1808 and 1809, to two events of this kind not a little extraordinary. This time she kept me above an hour, cutting with the right hand and the left, naming days, hours, and months, and ended at length by confirming her prediction of a girl.

"Or a boy," said the First Consul, who came in at that moment, and who always made game of Josephine's cards; "Madame Junot will have either the one or the other, and if I were you, Josephine, I would not risk my reputation for sorcery by a too confident prediction." "She will have a girl, I tell you, Bonaparte; what wager will you lay me of it?" "I never bet," said the First Consul; "if you are sure of the fact, it is dishonest; if not, it is as foolish as losing money at play." "Well, bet sweetmeats, then." "And what will you lay me?" "I will work a carpet to put under your feet at your desk." "Well, now, that is something useful. On such terms I will bet you that Madame Junot has a boy. Now, mind," said he, turning to me, "that you do not make me lose;" and laughing as he looked at me, he added: "But what will become of the wager if you should have both a boy and a girl?" "I will tell you, General, you must give me both wagers."

And there was something so ridiculous in this idea of boy and girl coming at once that even I could not refrain from joining in the laugh, while my look of consternation increased the mirth of the First Consul, my husband, and everyone else who was present.

We were now at the period of New Year's gifts and visits, and I was admiring like a child, as I then was, all those brilliant and useless trifles which custom demands should be offered by the gentlemen to a lady whose house they frequent, when two friends came to increase their number and add their good wishes, which were not merely the tribute of etiquette. They were General Suchet and his brother. After the conversation which the occasion demanded, we fell into a discussion upon the merits of those family meetings which this season brought with it; and it was agreed that the celebration of Christmas, of New Year's and Twelfth Days, the birthday and saint's day of the head of the family, and other festivals, were favourable to the maintenance of domestic harmony, and were therefore worthy of being preserved.

If the family is numerous, occasion is thus furnished for ten or twelve convivial meetings in the course of the year;

and, if the members have conceived any mutual offence, the embarrassment of meeting otherwise than cordially, on the birthday of the grandmother or aunt, will often cause the coolness which had begun to take place to disappear, and slight disputes will thus be prevented from becoming serious quarrels. The two brothers were fully capable of appreciating such feelings; they were perfectly united; the General always displayed the tenderest friendship for his brother Gabriel, which the latter returned with the sincerest affection and respect; his love for his brother was that we feel for the object of our pride. In furtherance of these observations the General proposed that we should meet on Twelfth Day, to which I assented with great satisfaction.

"Yes," said my good mother-in-law, who was never silent when a project of pleasure was on foot, "we will by all means draw king and queen." "Yes, let us draw," said Junot; "I engage you to sup here the evening after to-morrow upon a truffled turkey." "Agreed," said General Suchet; "we will come here the evening after to-morrow, and then for the turkey, and truffles, the cake, the drawing, and plenty of laughter."

I was now in momentary expectation of my confinement, and, notwithstanding the efforts of my mother-in-law to support and comfort me, looked forward to the moment with dread. In the night of the 4th of January we had an alarm, which called up my mother-in-law, who had not undressed for a week past. Marchais was summoned, and pronounced that twenty-four or forty-eight hours would settle the business, and left me, recommending composure and sleep.

I was out of spirits during a part of the succeeding day; I performed my religious duties and wrote to my mother, because she had forbidden me to leave the house; I then arranged my baby-linen and basket, and in this occupation I found the entire dissipation of my fears and melancholy. In the little cap with its blue ribbons, and in the shirt, the sleeves of which I drew through those of the flannel waistcoat, I thought I could see the soft and fair head and fat little mottled arms; in my joy I imagined the pretty clothes already adorning my promised treasure, and pressed them to my bosom, longing to clasp and to see my child, to feel its breath, while I said to myself: "And this little being which I expect will be all my own!" Oh, what days of joy were before me! Junot found me leaning over the cradle in a sort of ecstasy, and when I explained to him the cause of an emotion which his heart was well formed to understand, he embraced me with a tenderness of which I felt prouder than I should have done six months earlier.

My thoughts now took quite a different direction; I not only did not fear, but I desired the decisive moment; and when my friends met in the drawing-room they found me as gay and as happy as any young wife or young girl could be. Madame Hamelin formed one of our party. She was then young, gay, lively, and a most ready assistant in promoting that easy confidence which forms the great charm of intimate association. She had an original and striking wit, bordering a little on the maliciousness of the cat, and sometimes showing that she had tolerably long claws; but I believe that, like puss also, she did not put them out unless attacked.

The evening passed off cheerfully; my mother-in-law was delighted to see me in perfect oblivion of the critical moment, which, however, she knew could not be far distant. We sat down to table, and the turkey, the cake, the madeira and champagne redoubled our gaiety. In half an hour we laughed so heartily that even to this day I think of it with pleasure. At length came the moment of drawing; General Suchet sat beside me; I do not exactly recollect whether the prize of royalty fell to him or to me; since that time so many sovereignties, which seemed vastly more solid, have sunk into visionary crowns that my memory may well be excused its want of accuracy on this point.

But whether the General had received his crown from me or whether he had made me his queen, he addressed me in a compliment so absurd that it provoked a violent fit of laughter, with which the room resounded, and which was echoed with equal noise by seventeen or eighteen persons who surrounded the supper-table. I stood up to answer, with my glass of water, for I never in my life could drink wine, to the numerous glasses filled with sparkling champagne which were extended towards me, when I fell backwards into my chair, a cry escaped me, and my glass dropped from my hand. But the sudden attack which had caused this commotion was over in an instant, my cheeks recovered their colour, and I looked up. Junot, still paler than I had been, holding his glass of champagne, was looking at me with an air of consternation.

The rest of the company seemed nearly equally alarmed, and the grotesque expression of so many countenances hardly recovered from a fit of hilarity, while, as in duty bound, they were assuming on the other side of their faces the solemnity which the circumstances appeared to require, resembling at once *Jean qui pleure* and *Jean qui rit*, produced so risible an effect that I relapsed into a fit of uncontrollable laughter. My mother-in-law now came behind my chair, and whispered: "Take my arm, my dear daughter, and come to your room." "No, no!" said Gabriel Suchet, "we cannot spare our queen!"

Hereupon he began to relate a story so absurd that I laughed again as immoderately as before, and was again interrupted in the same manner: my mother-in-law told her son that I must be removed and a carriage sent for Marchais. Junot came to me, took me in his arms, and almost lifted me from my chair. This time the General interposed, offered to bet upon the sex of my child, and would with difficulty permit my husband to carry me away. He led me, however, to my room, obeying his mother's behests with as much simplicity as any honest bourgeois, any M. Guillaume or M. Denis, of the Rue de la Perle or Rue Saint Jacques. He busied himself in regulating the temperature of my room, in calling my nurses together, giving them fifty orders at once, which neither they nor he understood, ordered the horses, and returned to my side already expecting to hear the cries of his child; but I was in no such hurry.

During this tedious season of watching and anxiety Junot was almost distracted; he threw himself at intervals on the mattress which had been laid for him in the parlour, then got up, walked the room with hasty steps, crept to my bedroom door and tried to get in, which I had positively prohibited, and returned to his apartment, where his aide-de-camp, General Lallemand, sat up with him all night, endeavouring with arguments and consolations of friendship to calm a little the violence of his agitation and to restore something like composure to his mind.

Junot on leaving me by no means recovered his self-possession; he wandered through the rooms all opening into each other, which at both extremities brought him to one of the doors of my chamber, found repose in none of them, and at length, unable longer to endure his confinement, snatched up a round hat which happened to meet his eye and sallied forth into the street. Without once considering which way he was going, habit or instinct led him to the Tuileries, and he found himself in the Grand Court without knowing how he had got there. Before ascending, however, the staircase leading to the First Consul's apartments the consideration of his dishabille crossed his mind; "But no matter," said he, as he looked down upon his brown coat, "I am sure of finding here a heart which will understand my feelings."

All his comrades in the antechamber were astonished at the expression of his countenance and the disorder of his dress; but none of them felt any disposition to ridicule; and the First Consul, as soon as he heard that Junot wished to see him, sent for him into his cabinet. "Good God! what is the matter, Junot?" he exclaimed with surprise on seeing him. "General, my wife is in labour and I cannot stay at home," was the answer, but in a voice almost choked with tears. "And you are come to me to seek courage; you are right, my friend. Poor Junot! how you are upset! Oh woman, woman!"

He required a relation of all that had happened from my first seizure, and though Junot dared not give utterance to his apprehensions, yet Napoleon gathered from all the facts he described that my life was actually in danger, and his conduct in this moment of anxiety, when his discernment penetrated into a mysterious horror, was that of the tenderest and best of brothers. "My old friend," said he to his faithful and devoted servant, pressing his hand—a very rare caress—"you have done right in coming to me at this moment, as I hope to prove."

So saying, he left his cabinet, and, leaning upon Junot's arm, stepped into the salon where the statue of the great Condé stands, and walked up and down, talking of the only subject which interested his companion, for he was too well versed in the management of the human heart to interrogate chords which would certainly have been mute at such a moment. Amongst other things, he asked my husband how he came to the Tuileries. "On foot," was the answer; "a species of desperation drove me from home, though my heart is still there, and I wandered hither without knowing which way I came." "And may I ask you, then," said Napoleon, "why you look out of that window ten times in a minute to see if anyone passes the gate? How should they come here to seek you if your servants do not know where you are? if your officers saw you come out in plain clothes? It seems to me that they are more likely to suspect you of throwing yourself into the river than of coming here." He called and gave his orders. "Send a footman immediately to Madame Junot's to learn whether she is yet put to bed, and if not, let the family be informed that General Junot is here."

He again took my husband's arm, and continued to converse with him with such affecting kindness that Junot could not repress his tears. He was attached to his General, to that vision of glory which commanded admiration; but in such moments as the present Napoleon's conduct could not fail to subject to him the whole heart and affections of the individual whose sufferings he thus alleviated, even if he had not been already devoted to him body and soul. This day riveted, if I may say so, the chains which bound Junot to Napoleon.

Seeing him leave the house in a state bordering on distraction, Heldt, his German *valet-de-chambre*, followed him into the Tuileries, and on his return home informed the aide-de-camp Laborde where the General was to be found.

Junot had been three-quarters of an hour with the First Consul, whose arm rested on his, obliging him to remain a prisoner when he would rather have been at large and have had the power to come and learn the result of all his uneasiness. The footman could not yet be returned when Junot, emboldened by the First Consul's goodness, begged to be allowed to inquire for him. "I should have been told," answered the First Consul, "if he was returned. Remain quiet." Then dragging him still farther on, they were presently in the gallery of Diana. There Junot's uneasiness became so violent that Napoleon several times looked at him with astonishment, and with an accent to which it is impossible to do justice, repeated: "Oh woman, woman!"

At length, at the moment that Junot was about to escape without listening to anything further, M. de Laborde appeared at the farther end of the gallery; he had run with such haste that he could scarcely speak, but his countenance was full of joy.

"My General," he said, as soon as he had recovered his breath, "Madame Junot is safe in bed, and is as well as possible." "Go, then, and embrace your *daughter*," said the First Consul, laying a stress on the word "daughter"; "if your wife had given you a boy they would have told you at once; but first of all embrace me": and he pressed him affectionately in his arms. Junot laughed and cried, and, thoughtless of everything but the event which had just occurred, was running away, when Napoleon said to him: "Stay, giddy-pate, are you going through the streets without your hat?"

He returned to the First Consul's cabinet, where he had left his hat; the time was not yet come when the Prince of Neufchatel would not have presumed to enter the Emperor's presence, even at three o'clock in the morning, without his coat buttoned, his ruffles, dress boots, and his plumed hat under his arm. "Give my love* to your wife, Junot, and tell her that I have a twofold quarrel against her: first, because she has not given the Republic a soldier; and secondly, because she has made me lose my wager with

---

* The words *tu feras mes amitiés* was a form of speech very often used by Napoleon to those he loved.

Josephine. But I shall not be the less her friend and yours." And again he pressed Junot's hand and let him go.

It would be impossible to describe the delirium of joy which was painted on Junot's countenance and actuated his manners when he returned to me. He bathed his daughter's little face with tears of delight so soft, so pure, that it was easy to see his happiness without his uttering a word. Then throwing himself on his knees beside my bed, he took my hands, kissed them, and thanked me for his child, his daughter, his little Josephine.

But notwithstanding his joy, Junot perceived that something weighed upon my heart which was not connected with my past sufferings.

"What is the matter?" said he, embracing me again. "Nothing, but a great deal of happiness." "I know you, Laurette; I see the tears in your eyes; your heart is not at ease. What is the matter?"

I looked at him without answering; the tears rolled down my cheeks, but I would not speak. At this moment M. Marchais came in. "What! again?" he said to me. "My dear General, you should scold your wife, and the way I see you employed gives you additional right to do so!" Junot at this moment had his child in his arms and was embracing it. "You shall hear all, then. Oh, Madame Junot, make no signs to me; I shall not heed them! You must know, then, General, that this young mother, who is a little heroine for courage, as soon as she was safely put to bed, and had learned that you were not at home, sent for your father that he might give his blessing to your child. I went myself to seek M. Junot, but he refused to come as soon as he learned that the infant was a girl. At length he was persuaded; but when Madame Junot, notwithstanding her weakness, took the babe in her arms to present it to him, saying: 'My father, bless your grand-daughter, it is another heart that will love you,' instead of embracing the child, he replied in a tone of vexation :

"'It was not worth while to make all this noise about a wretched girl. What is your husband to do with this little crying thing? He will give it a pretty reception . . . and the First Consul too! do you think he does not wish his Generals to have boys?' If I had any authority over your father other than that of a physician in his patient's chamber, I confess I should have used it with some severity. I have frankly told you all this because it is a part of my duty, and because to-morrow, or the day after, a similar scene might have a fatal effect upon Madame Junot. It has affected her seriously, because she believes that the birth of a daughter is a great grievance to you, and it is in vain that I have represented to her that a mother of seventeen and a father of twenty-nine years of age will have time enough to pray for boys without being in despair at a first disappointment, and meanwhile the grandfather may fret as much as he pleases."

Scarcely had M. Marchais' first words struck Junot's ears than he understood the cause of my distress; and he seated himself upon my bed and wept with me, while he dried my eyes with his handkerchief and kisses.

Then taking up his daughter out of a little basket* of fine embroidered muslin, made on purpose that she might lie in it upon my bed, he placed her in my arms, and embraced us both with an air of such joyful delight as left no doubt of the sentiments of his heart, which, however,

---

* This barcelonnette was the tasteful production of Mademoiselle Olive — in form of a swan, the feathers of which were embroidered in relief with white cotton ; the wings, a little spread, made a sort of handle to lift it by ; the back was open, forming the cradle, and from its neck and reverted head fell a veil of white Indian muslin for the curtain, which was gathered up in the beak of the swan.

never could be doubtful to me. But the first moment of my father-in-law's denunciation was terrible ; no doubt he had no intention to injure me, but he might have killed me. " Mamma," said I to my mother-in-law, who just then came in, " you were right, you see ; he loves it as well as if it had been a boy."

" Did not I tell you so ?" replied this excellent woman. " My son's heart is too good and too noble to entertain the ideas his father would have given him credit for."

I have been led into some minute particulars connected with my first accouchement in order to expose the falsehoods which the Memorial of St. Helena has propagated. I am confident that the Emperor was wholly incapable of saying what is there attributed to him in the chapter entitled " Junot and his Wife."

CHAPTER XXXI.

The Society of Artists and Literary Men—Talma's Gaiety—The Poet D'Offreville and his Conceit—The Tragedy of *Statira*—The Hoax projected—Talma's Part in it, and the Intended Reading—The Dinner-party—An Improvisation—Visit to the Theatre—Tiercelin and *The Farce and No Farce*—D'Offreville an Unintentional Performer—The Lost Manuscript—The Poet's Despair and Good Appetite—The Poet in the Cabriolet, and the Vicious Mare—His Lamentations—The Hackney Coachman.

I HAVE always been fond of the society of artists and literary men, and in whatever situation fortune has placed me I have made it my principal study to assemble around me the chief talents of the day. Amongst a crowd of distinguished men I had the happiness of receiving Nadermann, Garat, Denon, Girodet, Lefebvre, Robert the Elder, Lemercier, Millin, Delille, Talma, and many others.

The last name upon this list reminds me of an adventure in which Talma played a part, certainly not that of Cinna or Orestes. To what perfection he acted those dignified parts with which French tragedy abounds is well known, but at the time I am speaking of he was immersed in the gloom of those English tragedies which he rendered so terrible, and the contrast made his gaiety in society, which provoked the cheerfulness of all around, peculiarly striking.

My readers may remember a certain M. d'Offreville, who

lived like a salamander in a perpetual fire at Lucien Bonaparte's mansion of Plessis, and continued to fatigue everyone with his vanity and absurdity. On my marriage he presented himself to me with an epithalamium in each pocket, and an acrostic upon every one of Junot's names and mine; there was no resisting his folly.

His conceit made him ridiculous, and restrained every sentiment of commiseration which otherwise his age would have demanded. He was the butt of all his acquaintances.

After pronouncing a fine eulogium on himself, he would walk up and down the room majestically, with one hand in his waistcoat pocket and the other playing with his laced shirt-frill, which was in keeping with the other ornaments of his dress—his plaited ruffles, silk stockings, and buckled shoes.

He had composed a tragedy, on which he had bestowed ten years' labour to very little purpose; but he would rather have renounced his hopes of salvation in another life than have believed that any production in the world could be equal to his *Statira*. " Faith !" said Junot one day, " this man must be hoaxed; his incorrigible vanity deserves punishment."

He furnished us with the opportunity in a very few days. He came one morning to request I would perform a promise which, in a moment of gaiety, I had thoughtlessly made him, of procuring Talma's permission to have *Statira* read before the Committee of French Comedy.

I was much embarrassed, for I would not for the world have spoken of this production to Talma, Dugazon, or Fleury. I answered that I should shortly see one of these gentlemen, and would report the answer; but the good poet was not so easily satisfied, and he so strongly insisted on my giving him a letter of introduction to one or the other of the committee that I was really puzzled in what manner to put him off, when, fortunately, Junot came in and at once extricated me from my difficulties.

"Your work shall be read next week, M. d'Offreville," said he in a solemn tone ; "it shall be read at my house by Talma himself."

"Oh, General, you are too good! Oh, heavens! my work read at Madame Junot's; at your house, my dear General, and by Talma himself! it is too much!" Here was the poet in a delirium of joy at the idea of his tragedy being read by Talma. I could not understand Junot, but in two words he let me into the secret. The day was fixed, Junot arranged the whole affair, and communicated his project to Talma, who willingly undertook to second it. Our party consisted of the two Baptistes of the French comedy, Talma and his wife, Fleury, Dugazon, and Dazincourt. It was agreed that Talma, as soon as he saw D'Offreville, should speak to him of his tragedy, of the part he wished to take in it, and of the pleasure he should have in reading it after dinner.

I never saw such an expression of extraordinary joy as that which was portrayed on D'Offreville's burlesque physiognomy, when on my introducing him to Talma the latter addressed him with the most hyperbolical praises of his work, with an air of seriousness which was enough to make those acquainted with D'Offreville die of laughing. He bowed, thanked him in broken words, and in the most rapturous terms concluded by pronouncing Talma divine.

I think I never was present at a more amusing dinner-party in my life. The champagne and madeira soon put D'Offreville into excellent spirits, and he proposed favouring us with an improvisation, which he had been preparing from the day he had been assured that Talma would read his tragedy; but as it was to pass for an impromptu he had taken good care not to bring his written paper with him, never suspecting his memory of treachery. But the wine he had drunk, and the noisy mirth which surrounded him, had so confused his ideas that, after giving the two first lines their highest effect, after shading his eyes, and enacting all the monkey tricks necessary to produce a belief in an actual improvisation, he stopped short, wholly unable to recollect another word.

The total silence in which the whole party were listening to his recitation and awaiting its continuation added to his embarrassment, and made him look absolutely stupefied. After an interval of becoming solemnity General Lallemand interrupted the silence. " Indeed, M. d'Offreville," said he, " it is a sad thing that you cannot *recollect* any more of your *improvisation*." " I beg your pardon," said he, " I shall continue immediately," and he again repeated the two unfortunate lines :

"Say, Muse-loved Talma ; does thy voice divine
Deign with immortal fame my verse to crown——"

" My verse to crown—my verse to crown," and he would have harped upon the same unharmonious string for an hour if Talma had not cried out in his inimitable accent :

" ' While Tyre's proud walls re-echo my renown.' "

Now, this happened to be a line in the famous tragedy of *Statira ;* Junot had whispered it to Talma, who pronounced it instantly, to the admiration of the company. But D'Offreville saw nothing ludicrous in it ; on the contrary, he was ready to worship the man who was already master of the finest passage of his tragedy. " Is not that inspired poetry?" said he to Talma ; " how your talent will shine in performing so brilliant a character as that of my hero ! You are supremely fortunate, my dear sir ! But let me beg you to give me the unutterable pleasure of hearing these fine lines read with such judgment as yours; here is the piece." And he drew from his pocket the much-honoured *Statira*, wrapped in vellum, and tied with fresh bows of rose-coloured ribbon.

This last folly was almost too much for the gravity of the company. Talma was still holding his cup of coffee in his hand, when the simpleton gravely proposed to him to read five acts of pathos consecutively. Talma, in reply, took him by the arm, and leading him and me to the recess of a window a little out of the noise, said to him: "My dear sir, I understand from Madame Junot and the General that your work is full of beauties; now I should wish to read this *chef-d'œuvre* with all the attention it merits, and to be listened to with the respect I should demand for it. At present this is impossible; do you see those wild fellows, Baptiste the younger and Dugazon——"

The latter was at this moment relating to his auditors that he had once been aide-de-camp to the Commune of Paris, and describing his adventures in this capacity in the most laughable manner. "I therefore recommend," continued Talma, "that Madame Junot should indulge us with a promenade in the Bois de Boulogne or elsewhere; we shall converse while we are out upon literary and theatrical subjects, and when we return in the cool of the evening our minds will be composed and prepared to enjoy the delightful impressions which the reading of *Statira* promises, and which I engage to assist with my best abilities."

I seconded the motion, and Madame Talma supported us, so that D'Offreville, however anxious for the commencement of the reading, had no alternative, and as it was only a pleasure deferred, it was tolerably well received. I rang and ordered the horses, which were already harnessed to three carriages.

On my return to the salon equipped for the ride, Junot

approached me and said, in a perfectly natural tone: "I understand, my dear, that you intend to take a drive; in my opinion you had better pass an hour or two at the Théâtre Montansier, where they are performing a new piece, which I am told is charming. My box is not lent, and I will borrow that of the manager and M. D——." The name was an invention intended only to deceive D'Offreville, who would have supposed a scheme laid against himself if he had found several boxes hired beforehand; he was foolish, but not stupid.

Junot's proposition carried the day by acclamation, and we set out for the Théâtre Montansier, then at the Palais Royal. D'Offreville was put under the care of M. Charles, M. Lallemand, and M. de Laborde, first aide-de-camp to Junot. On reaching the theatre he proposed to join me in my box for the pleasure of conversing with Talma, but this was not exactly the intended plan. "No, no," said these gentlemen; "Madame Junot's box is full; you are going with us into one where you will see excellently."

Hereupon they made a preconcerted signal to the door-keeper, who opened the stage-box to the right of the audience; General Lallemand and M. de Laborde pushed D'Offreville into the box and shut the door, leaving him *tête-à-tête* with a man whom he did not know, and whose appearance was almost as singular as his own. This man was dressed in a scarlet cloth with copper buttons, yellow breeches, striped stockings, an immense cravat, a powdered wig with a great queue, and a three-cornered hat badly cocked, which he took off and put on again ten times in a minute.

D'Offreville, to whom his conductors had said, "We shall return presently," awaited patiently the commencement of the piece. The curtain drew up; but an actor in his stage dress came forward to announce that the principal actress being extremely ill, the performance could not take place. "What!" cried D'Offreville's neighbour in the red coat, with a hoarse voice, "what do you mean by that? I have paid three francs and a half to see the show, and I will see it, or— —" And here he stood up, leaning over the front of the box, and vociferating in a great rage. "Sir," said D'Offreville to him, pulling one of his red skirts, "it is not usual to talk in this manner here; they will turn you out, sir." "Hem! what is this fellow saying?" And, turning towards D'Offreville, the man in the red coat burst out laughing. "Ah, I know you very well! You come from the Estrapade;* you compose tragedies to make people laugh." "Sir, sir," said D'Offreville, "pray speak lower!" And he attempted to effect a retreat, but in vain : the door would not open; for General Lallemand, M. de Laborde, and M. Charles were behind, holding it fast.

At this moment a voice from the gallery shouted out: "James! James!" and James, who was the man in the red coat, looked up and answered: "Ah! ah! is it you, John? come here, my lad; here is plenty of room, come here."

And the accent and attitude of the watermen of the fens was perfect; for by this time my readers may have guessed that the man in the scarlet coat was Tiercelin the actor, and that the farce they were performing was *The Farce and No Farce*, represented for the second time only. Tiercelin, who was in the secret, played his part excellently, and what made the joke perfect, from my box, where we could see the whole, was that the audience in the pit took the introduction of D'Offreville for a new scene, and every time he leaned forward to Tiercelin to give his advice, several voices cried out "Louder!"

The poor author of *Statira* stood as much in dread of these cries as of his terrible neighbour, who, seeing the im-

---

* The Rue de l'Estrapade in Paris.

pression he made upon him, gave him from time to time a most menacing glance. "Oh!" said he, "I have told you I know you; you come from the Estrapade. You should cry out, like John and me, upon those thieves who take our money and give us nothing for it."

The piece proceeded. Tiercelin, or James as he is called, was furnished with a gourd, out of which he drank five or six times during the act. Generally he had nothing in his gourd, but it happened that evening, having a bad cold, that the gourd contained barley-water. When he saw the apprehension with which he inspired D'Offreville, it came into his head, to our great gratification, to offer him his gourd, recommending him to drink to recover himself, and to our still greater delight the other took it, so much was he afraid of his companion, and tasting, notwithstanding his expectation of having his throat burned with peppered brandy, was not a little surprised at swallowing nothing but warm water fit to make him sick. He drank, however, what was in the gourd, amidst the encouragements of Tiercelin, and the reiterated applause of the pit, which would have been delighted with this unexpected scene if the new actor could have been persuaded to speak louder.

But D'Offreville at length discovered the joke, and immediately precipitated himself, head foremost, like a ram in a rage, against the box door, and so furious was he that when the gentlemen outside opened it, he pushed through without seeing them. But he was not to escape thus, and all the young men of the conspiracy surrounding him, he found himself, without the power of retaliation, once more in my drawing-room in the presence of Talma. When he commenced his complaints we all told him he did not know what he was talking about; that the box he had been put into was the manager's, who had given an order to one of the common people, a waterman, who, it would seem, lived in the Rue de l'Estrapade and knew him, which he had given him to understand by his manner, rather vulgarly, to be sure.

"But," said Junot, "if I were you I should be very proud of being recognized thus, and for an author, even by people the most remote from your ordinary associates! D'Offreville, I should look upon the meeting with this waterman as the greatest homage to your great talents."

It would be absurd to make such speeches to a man who understood irony; but D'Offreville was persuaded to see in this adventure a circumstance of which he had a right to be proud; whether it were Tiercelin, or plain James of the Estrapade, on this point he could not divest himself of some doubt, but the actor or the waterman had said: "You compose tragedies!" This was enough to make him forget the warm water and the suspicious character which had been forced upon him.

"And when you are called for on the day of the first representation of *Statira*," said Madame Talma; "when, having made a sufficient resistance to the demands of an impatient audience, my husband and I will lead you between us upon the stage, that the whole house may be able to see you—a different homage will then be rendered to your talents!" D'Offreville listened eagerly, and seemed to enjoy in anticipation the ecstasy of his triumph. "But where are M. Talma and our *Statira* ?" said he, casting a glance of intelligence on M. Talma.

"Here am I," said Talma; "but where is the manuscript? Come, prepare the table, two wax lights and a glass of sugared water. But, M. d'Offreville, be so good as to give me your manuscript; for though I have retained many beautiful lines of this immortal work I have not learned it by heart." But D'Offreville was more ridiculous at this moment than he had been at any preceding part of the entertainment. His cherished manuscript was lost; nor could he recover it. The truth was that I had stolen it from the spot where he had concealed it, as the only means of avoiding the infliction. "My *Statira!*" he exclaimed in a kind of frenzy, as if he was calling his mistress; "my *Statira!*"

At length supper was announced. D'Offreville, at first in despair, found comfort in making a capital meal, a power which seldom failed him. They afterwards made him recite some madrigals, and two or three acrostics upon Laura and Andoche; then he repeated, as a child does his lesson, the letter he had received from Voltaire; and before rising from table he had become quite as vainglorious and as complete a braggart as ever. But when after supper his dear *Statira* was restored to him, when he had found upon examination that not a single absurdity was wanting to it, he proceeded to utter such a tissue of nonsense that Junot cried out in great wrath:

"'This man is absolutely incorrigible." "I have seen many such characters," said Talma, "but never one so thoroughly ridiculous."

Did he not wish to have his precious production read after supper! "We shall see about that some day next week," said Talma; "for to-night, or rather this morning, I entreat you to excuse me." It was already two o'clock. "And how am I to return home?" said the little man. "You know that Madame d'Offreville would die of grief if any harm should happen to me." This apostrophe was addressed to me in a somewhat petulant tone; for he could not forgive me for the occurrences of the day, though I was no otherwise concerned in them than as having shared the general mirth. "You know," he continued, "all the tenderness of that incomparable woman!"

The fact was that the wife was quite as ridiculous as her

husband; I dare say they were attached to each other, but to make a parade of love, when their joint ages amounted to a hundred and fifty years, was of itself absurdity enough. "Well," said M. Charles, "I am going to drive you home in my cabriolet." "No, no, I shall," said General Lallemand. M. de Laborde interfered with, "I propose myself that honour." "If M. d'Offreville will trust himself with me?" chimed in M. Bardin.

M. d'Offreville looked at them all in turn; the remembrance of the misadventures of the evening made him tremble; but he found M. Charles's countenance the most inviting. He determined to confide himself to his care; and making low bows to M. Talma, who bent still more profoundly in return, he ascended the slight cabriolet of M. Charles, to which was harnessed a little mare, known as the most vicious brute in Paris. To his other defects D'Offreville added that of being timid in a carriage, and his apprehension was converted into absolute terror when the cabriolet took, with the speed of an arrow, the road to the Pont Royal.

"Good God!" cried M. Charles, "what will become of us? the horse is running away; I have no power over it." "Sir, I conjure you—I entreat you; a wife who adores me, sir, is waiting for me . . . I beseech you, sir!" "What would you have me do?" said M. Charles, slightly touching the flanks of the mare with the whip—"what would you have me do? you see I have no command of the mare . . . she is running away . . . that's certain . . . God grant that she may not drag us to the river!" "M. Charles, let me alight. . . . You are a worthy man; you would not kill me. . . . Good heavens! here we are upon the bridge!"

"Well, so much the better; it proves that we shall not go under it; you see there is nothing to fear now. Will you be quiet? By Jove, you will put me in a passion presently!" exclaimed M. Charles, half angry and half laughing, for the old poet was trying to get hold of the reins.

"Oh, what will become of me!" muttered D'Offreville, almost crying, "and my wife, my poor wife!" "Ah! you shall see your wife again by-and-by," said M. Charles; "only let me get home, then I will put you into a hackney coach, and you shall return home to console your wife, who is no doubt fast asleep without thinking of you." "And do you live far off, my worthy friend? Heavens! how the cabriolet sways! Do you live far off?"

"In the Rue des Maturins." "The Rue des Maturins! then I shall not get home before five o'clock in the morning!" "Be quiet, will you! and let me drive the mare without meddling with the reins; and we shall arrive all the sooner."

At last they reached the Rue Neuve des Maturins. But not the least amusing part of the adventure to M. Charles was the anger of the hackney coachman to whose care he now confided D'Offreville, as they both stood and looked at his whimsical and disordered dress, besmeared with powder that had fallen from his hair. The coachman said he would not take charge of a masked and disguised person at a time when there was no carnival. D'Offreville, amongst whose delusions was that of being very eloquent, undertook to persuade the man to drive him home by speaking of his wife and her love, himself and his talent; and afterwards boasted of his success as a triumph of his oratorical powers. "The Muses," said he, "touched my lips, like Pindar's, with milk and honey."

[The truth was that M. Charles, unknown to his companion, had put a crown-piece into the coachman's hand.]

CHAPTER XXXII.

Creation of the Kingdom of Etruria—The King and Queen of Etruria in Paris—Their Son—*Fêtes* and Balls given to them at Paris—*Fêtes* of Messieurs Talleyrand, Chaptal, and Berthier—Napoleon accompanies the King to see a Representation of *Œdipus*—The First Consul's Opinion of the New King—Aristocratic Measure respecting Lists of Eligible Persons opposed by Napoleon—Institution of the Legion of Honour—Difficulties encountered by the First Consul—Regnault de Saint Jean d'Angely—My Mother's Conversation on the Projected Institution with Junot—The Concordat—Cardinals Consalvi and Spina—M. de Talleyrand authorized by the Pope to leave the Church and return to the Lay Community—Ratification of the Concordat—Creation of Bishops by Napoleon—Religious Ceremony in Honour of the Concordat—Display of Female Beauty—Offensive Remark of General Delmas upon the Ceremony—My Uncle Bien-Aymé consecrated Bishop of Metz—His Conversation with Napoleon.

WE have now attained a new and memorable epoch in our history, that of the re-establishment of thrones and of religion. The foundation of several republics was the work of General Bonaparte; when at the head of an army, not yet his subjects, his moderation procured him even more renown than his victories. Now that his powerful hand directed the destinies of France, he attempted to set up a petty crown, to place a baby sceptre in the hands of a man incapable of reigning, as if he would say to France, already grown unaccustomed to sovereignty: "See what a king is! Be not afraid of the phantom!"

This monarch, whose new dignity procured for him more ridicule than respect, was the King of Etruria, Don Louis, Infant of Parma, nephew of Queen Marie Antoinette,* and husband of the Infanta Maria Louisa Josephine, daughter of Charles IV. They came to Paris in the month of May, 1801, to thank the First Consul for their nomination to the Crown of Etruria, which was a stipulation of the treaty between France and Spain concluded on the 21st of March, at Madrid. By this treaty France acquired the Duchy of Parma, and ceded Tuscany to the Prince, giving him as an indemnity for his paternal inheritance the territory we had conquered from his uncle. But the King, Louis I., was very possibly ignorant who was the Sovereign of Tuscany before it fell to his share; though had he known it, I am by no means certain that he would on that account have refused the crown.

I never beheld two more extraordinary persons than these new Sovereigns. They assumed the incognito of Count and Countess of Livorno (Leghorn), and brought with them a *Countling*, who, though not quite three years old, was made of more importance than both his illustrious parents put together. Those who have not seen this royal personage at five years of age, in full Court dress, a hat and feathers under his arm; a sword at his side, decorated with a huge bunch of ribands; his poor little locks powdered and frizzed, confined in a bag wig, driven through the streets of Florence on the front seat of a state carriage, and, though fastened to his cushion, rolling from right to left like a little ball; the Queen Dowager, his mother, riding backwards in the most respectful attitude—whoever has not beheld this spectacle has missed one of those exquisitely ridiculous scenes which prolong laughter till it becomes painful.

* Maria Theresa had four surviving daughters, married to the King of Naples, the King of France, the Duke of Parma, and to the Duke of Saxe-Teschen respectively.

At the time I am speaking of, as the King his father was still living, the Prince Royal of Etruria was content to give his little hand to be kissed, whether asked for or not. As for his parents, all who remember their arrival and sojourn in Paris in 1801 will agree with me how totally dissimilar they were from all other human beings, especially if Her Majesty the Queen is to be compared with a woman of even moderate beauty, or the King with a man possessed of a single idea.

Fêtes were given to the King of Etruria, not from any regard to the new-fangled monarch, but from a spontaneous desire to meet the wishes of the First Consul, who well knew how to appreciate the sentiments which dictated the attention. The reception given to his tributary King, who was come to tender to the Republic homage for his Crown, was at once magnificent and in good taste. He was, in the first instance, cordially entertained at Malmaison.

The First Consul wished to become acquainted with the character of the man on whom he had bestowed a kingdom, enriched by the noblest monuments of art and science; a very few interviews, however, sufficed to prove that he was nullity personified. Not so the Queen. Her appearance was at first repulsive; but on further acquaintance, when she had thrown aside a timidity partaking in some degree of stateliness, which threw a restraint over her words and actions, she proved to be very agreeable.

M. de Talleyrand was the first of the Ministers who gave a *fête* to the new Sovereigns. The entertainment was given at Neuilly, in the month of June, when the country was in its highest beauty. Taste and ingenuity were displayed in all the arrangements, but both were lost upon him for whose enjoyment the whole was chiefly intended. The *fête* was Florentine, and its illusion complete. The beautiful square of the Pitti Palace was admirably represented, and when their Majesties descended to the garden they were surrounded by crowds of pretty Tuscan peasant girls, offering them flowers, singing couplets, and enticing the royal pair into their groups to hear verses in their own praise. This was followed by the famous improvisatore Gianni prophesying for them, in fine Italian verse, a long and prosperous reign. All this made no impression on King Louis. The Queen, who alone understood it, made acknowledgments for both.

The finest of these *fêtes* was that given by the Minister of the Interior. He had not, like M. de Talleyrand, the advantage of a villa in the country, but his garden was skilfully laid out to bear the appearance of a park, and the whole scene reminded one of fairyland. Three hundred and fifty ladies found seats in that fine gallery where Lucien in the preceding year had given such agreeable balls, which, pleasant as they were, certainly afforded no presage of M. Chaptal's evening of enchantment. The First Consul was enraptured; and though seldom known to take notice of such matters, not only expressed his satisfaction at the time, but long afterwards reverted to the invisible singers and the ravishing harmony of M. Chaptal's gardens.

Yet here, as at Neuilly, all the delicate courtesies shown in honour of the Sovereigns were appreciated by the Queen alone; the poor King could not find a word of thanks for so much pains expended on *fêting* and pleasing him; even when, in the midst of a Tuscan village, where Tuscan peasants were singing in chorus the beautiful lines of Tasso and Petrarch, which he could scarcely fail of understanding, a crown of flowers was offered him, accompanied by flattering verses, still not a syllable could he say—the same eternal and unmeaning smile, which seemed to express that he could not comprehend even the language and scenery of Italy, still sat upon his lips.

In the dance his Tuscan Majesty was really amusing. I had the honour of figuring near him at the ball given by the Minister of War on the anniversary of the Battle of Marengo, and congratulate myself on my wonderful self-control in preserving my gravity through the whole country dance. The King, dancing with Queen Hortense, skipped and jumped about in a manner by no means beseeming the royal dignity. In one of his capers a buckle from his shoe suddenly flew into the air, and alighted in my head-dress; and so highly was the King's mirth excited by its course and final resting-place, that he was nearly choked with laughter. We were little less diverted when, on examining the buckle to ascertain how it had found its way from the royal foot to my head, it was discovered that it had been only glued to the shoe.*

* This unfortunate Prince was very ill-calculated to recommend, by his personal character, the institutions to which the nobility clung with so much fondness. Nature had endowed him with an excellent heart, but with very limited talents; and his mind had imbibed the false impress consequent upon his monastic education. He resided at Malmaison nearly the whole time of his visit to Paris. Madame Bonaparte used to lead the Queen to her own apartments; and as the First Consul never left his closet except to sit down to meals, the aides-de-camp were under the necessity of keeping the King company, and of endeavouring to entertain him, so wholly was he devoid of intellectual resources. It required, indeed, a great share of patience to listen to the frivolities which engrossed his attention. His turn of mind being thus laid open to view, care was taken to supply him with the playthings usually placed in the hands of children; he was, therefore, never at a loss for occupation. His nonenity was a source of regret to us: we lamented to see a tall handsome youth, destined to rule over his fellow-men, trembling at the sight of a horse, and wasting his time in the game of hide-and-seek, or at leap-frog, and whose whole information consisted in knowing his prayers, and in saying grace before and after meals. Such, nevertheless, was the man to whom the destinies of a nation were about to be committed! When he left France to repair to his kingdom, "Rome need not be uneasy," said the First Consul to us after the farewell audience, "there is no danger of *his* crossing the Rubicon" (*Memoirs of the Duke of Rovigo*, vol. i., p. 363).

This *fête* of the Minister of War acquired a peculiar character from the supper being served in the garden, under tents, with all the military appendages of a bivouac, and from the charm imparted by the glorious day which this *fête* was intended to recall. The fireworks were so designed as to show to the First Consul that the army which surrounded him could honour him alone. A balloon was sent up in the course of the evening, which, against the dark azure of a clear sky, luminously traced as it rose the word " Marengo."

One evening during the King of Etruria's stay in Paris, the First Consul accompanied him to the *Comédie Française* to see *Œdipus*. The house was crowded to excess. All Paris was desirous to see, side by side, General Bonaparte, who as a private individual had created republics, and the King he was crowning, now that he was himself Chief of the most powerful Republic in the world. The manners of

---

I once heard the First Consul, in a conversation with his colleague, Cambacérès, treat his royal *protégé*, the King of Etruria, very severely. Of course his Majesty was not present. "This good King," said he, "evinces no great concern for his dear and well-beloved subjects. He spends his time in gossiping with old women, to whom he is very lavish of his praise to me, though in secret he murmurs bitterly at the thought of owing his elevation to the hateful French Republic." "It is alleged," observed M. Cambacéres, "that you wished to disgust the French people with kings by showing them this fine specimen of royalty, as the Spartans used to disgust their children with intoxication by showing them a drunken slave." "Not at all, not at all," resumed the First Consul, "I have no wish to excite a distaste for royalty: but the presence of his Majesty, the King of Etruria, will vex a good many worthy folks who are striving hard to revive a taste for the Bourbons " (*Mémoires de Constant*).

The King, though well received and well entertained, was in all respects a very ordinary man, not that I had an opportunity of judging of his character myself, but the First Consul told me that his capabilities were extremely limited; that he even felt repugnance to take a pen in his hand; that he never cast a thought on anything but his pleasures: in a word, that he was a fool (*Bourrienne's Memoirs of Napoleon*, vol. i., p. 447).

the new King were especially amusing when contrasted with those of the First Consul, who was always calm, serious, and well calculated to stand the gaze of millions.

When Philoctetes repeated the line, "I have made Sovereigns, but have refused to be one," the noise of the acclamations with which the theatre resounded was almost alarming. The whole house was shaken by applauding feet, while the audience in the boxes, who seldom take part in such scenes, unanimously joined in the cheers of the pit. It was the universal nation expressing to Napoleon the sentiment which filled all hearts.

As for the King, he started at first in his arm-chair, then laughed most complacently on observing all hands and eyes directed towards the box where he sat with the First Consul. But the mirth of those who knew him was complete when, finding the applause prolonged, he thought politeness required some mark of attention in return for such unequivocal proofs of an interest he was quite proud, as he said, of inspiring in so great a people, and he rose to make his best obeisance.

"Poor King!" said the First Consul, shrugging his shoulders. These words, "Poor King!" appear the more contemptuous from his mouth, covered as he was with laurels, and radiant with the glory of his great deeds. But on all occasions a word either of praise or contempt has appeared to me more impressive from him than from other men.

After a visit of some weeks the King and Queen of Etruria quitted Paris and proceeded to their own kingdom of perfumes, where they were received and installed in their throne by Murat. "The rising generation," said the First Consul one day, laughing, "were unacquainted with the face of a King; well, we have shown them one." But his countenance instantly recovered its seriousness, and he added: "Poor Tuscany! poor Tuscany!"

Shortly before the arrival of the King of Etruria in Paris, an aristocratic measure was under discussion—that of the lists of eligibility relative to elections, the object of which was to fill all official posts with select persons.

Cambacérès, strange as it may seem, pronounced strongly in favour of the lists, and the First Consul held a long discussion with him. Napoleon said that the lists were founded on a bad system, and on false and erroneous principles. "France," said he, "is a great Power, but it is the people who compose that power. This law, although a part of the constitution, is not therefore the less bad and absurd. It is not fifty, sixty, or even a hundred men, assembling together in a moment of tumult and excitement, who have a right to make a constitution and to alienate the rights of the people. The sovereignty of the people is inalienable." These are the very words of Napoleon; they were written in pencil by him who gave them to me, and he wrote them as they fell from the First Consul. Did they truly interpret his sentiments?

It was some weeks previous to this incident that the establishment of the Legion of Honour, one of the most remarkable events of the whole rule of Napoleon, was first talked of. This affair doubtless made an impression, but less than proportionate to the difficulty with which it had been effected. It would not, perhaps, have been possible to have achieved the victory so early had not the First Consul been powerfully seconded by Regnault de Saint Jean-d'Angely, a man of great ability, whose portrait is necessary here, as his name will be found in every page of Napoleon's history. Regnault, having, like nearly all the members of the Constituent Assembly and of the Convention, taken a denomination from the place of his residence, was, as his name indicates, from Saint Jean-d'Angely, where, however, his parents, who belonged to that class known before the

Revolution as the *bonne bourgeoisie*, had but recently established themselves. They intended their son for a merchant, but the young man determined otherwise for himself, and, finding his parents inexorable, quitted the paternal mansion, where no better prospect than an insufferable slavery awaited him, to wander he knew not whither. Happily he met a family friend, who, entering into his character and feelings, and being desirous to save both him and his parents from eternal regret, brought him back to his home, and induced them to educate him for the Bar. Thus was laid the foundation of Regnault's success. He studied, and very soon displayed a brilliant and original eloquence, combined with a force of reasoning, which placed him at once on a level with the most distinguished orators.

Napoleon, who knew how to discriminate between talent and mediocrity, designed Regnault, from the moment he heard him speak, for one of the speakers in his Council of State. Regnault, on his part, also judged the Colossus; and, strange to say, in many instances fathomed his real thoughts through the veil with which, though Napoleon was not deceitful, his simple and vigorous ideas were frequently covered. Regnault, in listening to discussions introduced by the First Consul, seldom coincided in the opinion first mooted by him; he opposed it, and, curiously enough, generally found himself maintaining the side of the argument which Napoleon really intended to preponderate. If this was the effect of address it was excusable.

The creation of the Legion of Honour, when it was first mooted, excited feelings and discussions of which, in the present day, it is impossible to convey an idea. The creation of an order of knighthood in a country filled with republican institutions, and resolved on equality, appeared at first, even to those who, from their reputation in arms, were entitled to be chiefs of the order, a sort of monstrosity. None of them had even imagined that the First Consul would one day assume the sovereignty of the State. I do not think that the Consulate for life had yet been talked of; Napoleon now held the office for ten years only.

"Well, after all," said my mother to Junot, "I assure you, my dear son, a green, red, or blue ribbon is a very pretty thing over a black coat or a white waistcoat. I am fond of these talismans of ambition. The Consular Court is now rising with an *éclat* far surpassing its predecessors. You will agree with me that, unless power possesses both the will and the means to make itself respected, it is indispensable to surround it with a sort of theatrical splendour to prevent its becoming an object of mockery. Bonaparte is a man of sense and tact; he understands all this, and reduces it to practice. You will see where all this will end——" And my mother gently nodded her head, as she changed her position on the sofa; for at that time, in compliance with the decree of her physicians, she scarcely ever rose from it.

Junot's demeanour as he listened to her harangue was droll; he saw plainly that she was jesting, but as he did not himself entirely approve this measure at the outset, he was at a loss for an answer. He was much perplexed also to guess how my mother had penetrated the secrets of the Council of State, in which the First Consul had spoken at great length, and with an eloquence the more extraordinary as oratory was by no means his forte; he possessed to an almost irresistible extent the art of compelling his auditors to adopt his views; but that he should speak for an hour together, and with real eloquence, was truly astonishing.

This was not the first time that my mother had surprised

us by talking politics, in which formerly she never interfered; but a heart like hers must follow the interests of those she loved. Until my marriage no warmer sentiment than a sincere friendship for a few individuals had caused her to look upon public affairs either with pleasure or uneasiness. But in fifteen months her attitude was changed. Her daughter was the wife of a man so intimately attached to the established order of things that the future welfare of that daughter depended on its preservation; her son had a lucrative office in the administration of the Republic; and the personal opinions of my mother were silenced by these strong ties which bound her to the existing Government.

She who had never busied herself with any political gossip now grew desirous of sounding public opinion; she had two or three journals read to her daily, and such of her friends as were in a situation to give her information were laid under contribution. My good and affectionate mother! all these habits so foreign to her former life were not agreeable to her. But it would have distressed her to be ignorant of anything in which we were interested; and through the elder M. Portalis she frequently learned rumours which did not reach Junot till he heard them from her two or three days later; not through any breach of confidence on the part of the Councillor, but merely because Junot did not attend the sittings of the Council, and their proceedings were not reported in the journals. It happened so in the case of the Concordat, one of those landmarks which denote a great epoch in the history of our Revolution.

Cardinal Consalvi, Signor Spina (since Cardinal Archbishop of Genoa), and Father Corselli, also a Cardinal later on, came to Paris to conclude the negotiation for the Concordat. I shall speak hereafter of Cardinal Consalvi;

I was at this time too young to know and appreciate him. The First Consul himself was much deceived respecting him, and there is every reason to believe that he was prejudiced against him by the Minister of Foreign Affairs.

A person every way worthy of credit says, in his excellent work upon the Consulate, that in a conversation he held with him at Malmaison, the First Consul mentioned that the Cardinal jested as freely as a young musketeer, and had told M. de Talleyrand *that he was as fond of pleasure as anyone, and that he had obtained a reputation for devotion which he did not possess.*

I repeat, the person who reports this conversation with the First Consul is a man of honour, and worthy of credence. What he reports the First Consul had undoubtedly said to him. I can equally answer for Napoleon. He could dissemble and give a false colouring to a story, but was never guilty of direct falsehood to the extent here imputed to him. The Minister must himself have been deceived, for had Cardinal Consalvi been as profligate as a Borgia, and as impious as the fifth Sixtus, it is impossible that he could so stupidly proclaim it.

All who have been honoured with his acquaintance know that, whatever political license he might allow himself in conversation, he never, in the man of the world or even in the man of gallantry, forgot the dignity of the Cardinal. I have held frequent and intimate intercourse with him, and have in my possession more than thirty of his letters; and I can affirm that I never heard him utter an unbecoming word, or received from him a single line that passed the bounds of decorum.

About this time M. Portalis the elder presented to the Council of State a brief of Pope Pius VII., authorizing M. de Talleyrand to return to a secular life. Regnault de Saint Jean-d'Angely asked : " What the Council could possibly have to do with the conscience of a man: we are called upon to admit or reject a brief that grants to a person all indulgence and enjoyment of those civil rights of which he himself is in possession. I contend that the Council cannot have anything to do with it."

Cambacérès, the President, put the question to the vote, and argued that the First Consul would be much displeased if the registry of the brief were refused. The permission of the Pope was finally admitted; M. de Talleyrand was restored to the lay community, and can now be buried without wrangle or strife whenever he shall quit his busy path of life.

It was the First Consul's desire that the promulgation of the Concordat, which had received his definitive ratification, should be attended with a religious ceremony, in all the pomp and circumstance of Roman worship. The Concordat concerning religious affairs, after being signed at Paris on the 15th July, 1801, by the Consuls, was sent to Rome, where it underwent a critical examination in the Conclave, and was then signed and ratified in all its integrity by the Pontiff, which, considering the Pope's Infallibility, methinks ought to suffice to quiet the consciences of those who should be content with being as good Christians as their Holy Father.

Fourteen prelates, more attached to remembrance of the past than to hope of the future, refused to recognise the Concordat. These fourteen bishops were then in London, where at least they lived in peace and without care; they were right not to change their lot: they would not have been so well treated in France; for the First Consul allowed the bishops only a sufficient revenue for maintaining a creditable establishment.* "'They should not have reason

---

* According to a statement made by the committee for regulating the allowances made by Parliament to be granted to the emigrants in Eng-

to blush," said the First Consul, "in fulfilling the highest ecclesiastical functions; they should also have the means of succouring the unfortunate within their dioceses; but archbishops and bishops must not absorb the revenue of a province, excite scandal, and, as in former days, bring religion into disgrace." Forty bishops and nine archbishops were instituted by the First Consul, who imposed the formula of oath to be taken by them on entering upon their dioceses.

From sixty to eighty ladies were invited to accompany Madame Bonaparte to Notre Dame. She had then no ladies of honour; but four companion ladies had voluntarily taken upon them the duties of that office. We assembled at the Tuileries at half after ten in the morning of Easter Day, in the year 1802. The Consuls occupied but one carriage. The First Consul had issued no orders, but it was intimated to the principal public functionaries that he would be pleased to see their servants in livery on the day of the ceremony. He put his own household into livery on the occasion: it was certainly showy, but, as yet, by no means well appointed. Madame Bonaparte was accompanied by her daughter and her sister-in-law: the rest of the procession followed promiscuously.

Madame Bonaparte and all the ladies were conducted to the gallery to hear the Te Deum, and the gallery of Notre Dame on that day presented an enchanting spectacle: it formed a magnificent conservatory filled with the choicest flowers.

Madame Murat's fair, fresh, and spring-like face, comparable only to a June rose, was surmounted by a pink satin hat and plume of feathers. She wore a gown of fine

---

land, there were but twelve bishops, who received each £250 annually from the money voted. This was in 1793.

MARIE CAROLINE LOUISE ANNONCIADE BONAPARTE

GRAND DUCHESS OF BERG AND CLEVES,

AFTERWARDS

QUEEN OF NAPLES

(COUNTESS OF LIPONA, DUCHESS OF TARENTUM).

1782—1839.

Indian tambour muslin, lined with pink satin and trimmed with Brussels point, and over her shoulders was thrown a scarf of the same lace. I have seen her more richly dressed, but never saw her look more beautiful.

How many young women, hitherto unknown, on this day took their degree in the realm of beauty, beneath the brilliant beams of a mid-day sun, rendered more glowing in their passage through the stained windows of the cathedral! The First Consul himself, the same evening, remarked upon the galaxy of beauty which shone in the gallery.

The ceremony was long. Cardinal Caprara, who officiated, was tedious in the extreme; and M. de Boisgelin was equally prolix in his sermon. At near three o'clock we returned to the Tuileries completely tired. One of the most striking circumstances of the day was the military display. The firing of musketry, the troops lining the streets, the salvoes of artillery, which, from the earliest dawn, had shaken every window of Paris, mingling the sounds of the camp with religious chants, and with that ecclesiastical pomp so justly in accordance with the solemnity, formed a combination truly imposing.

The First Consul was vehemently irritated by the answer of General Delmas to his question, How he liked the ceremony? "It was a very showy harlequinade," said the General, "and, to render it complete, wanted only the presence of the million of men who have shed their blood for the destruction of that which you have re-erected."

My uncle, Bien-Aymé, was Bishop of Metz; this reminds me of a conversation he had with the First Consul soon after his admission to the College of Episcopal Prelates. When first Canon of the Cathedral of Évreux he had been for many years the intimate friend of M. de Buffon. The First Consul, whom Junot had informed of this circumstance, wished to converse with the Bishop of Metz about this extraordinary man; and my uncle's astonishment at finding him intimately acquainted with the private life of M. de Buffon, who lived at a distance from him, and was precluded by all his habits from intercourse with Bonaparte, was particularly diverting.

CHAPTER XXXIII.

Death of my Mother—Junot's Kindness—Napoleon's Condolence in my Loss—Delicacy of Lucien Bonaparte—Misunderstanding between the Two Brothers—Lucien's Conduct in Spain—Madame Leclerc—Ridiculous Scene with her—Creole Costume—Her Mad Project—Failure of the Expedition to Saint Domingo—Death of Leclerc, and Return of Pauline—The Offering of the Widow's Hair.

A GREAT misfortune had befallen our family; my mother had ceased to exist. Her sufferings were over, but we had lost our friend, our delight. She had occupied all my time and thoughts, and the void produced by the removal of this adored object occasioned an anguish to which I know of nothing comparable. The affectionate and considerate conduct of Junot on this sad occasion sweetened the bitterness of my grief.

A proof that Junot well understood the heart of her he honoured, was his liberality to three hundred of the most distressed amongst the poor of Paris. They were relieved and clothed in the name of her whose funeral car they surrounded, and for whom they were mourning and offered prayers of gratitude. How much did this delicacy in giving and administering the consolation of which I should be most sensible endear my husband to me!

The First Consul was very kind at the time of my affliction. He appeared to bury in oblivion his former disagreements with my mother. Junot brought me messages of the most friendly consolation from him, and Madame Bonaparte did me the honour of a visit, with Lucien, who had just arrived from Spain. The sight of Lucien deeply affected me. I knew how dear he was to my mother. She loved him almost equally with my brother Albert: she rejoiced in his success and suffered in his disasters. His departure for Spain had much distressed her, and in her greatest agonies she made Junot repeat to her all the honourable traits of his mission to Madrid. Junot felt a degree of partiality for Lucien, as did all who were attached to the First Consul.

I have always been at a loss to account for the schism between the brothers, and I must in justice declare that I never heard from Lucien an unkind word against his brother, although the First Consul frequently made use of expressions which must have been wounding to him even in his absence. But Lucien's conduct in Spain, the treaty of Badajos, that of Madrid, the secret treaty of St. Ildefonso, by which Louisiana, surrendered to Spain by the shameful treaty of 1793, was re-ceded to us—all this made one esteem the man who, at a distance from France as well as in the chamber of her representatives, invariably defended the interests of his country and raised his voice in vindication of her glory and her prosperity.

Meanwhile we had lost Madame Leclerc; she had been strongly urged by her brother to follow her husband to Saint Domingo. I believe General Leclerc would willingly have dispensed with this addition to his baggage, for it was a positive calamity, after the first quarter of an hour's interview had exhausted the pleasure of surveying her really beautiful person, to have the burden of amusing, occupying, and taking care of Madame Leclerc. In public she professed herself delighted to accompany *her little Leclerc*, as she

LUCIEN BONAPARTE,
DUKE OF MUSIGNANO AND PRINCE OF CANINO.
1775   1840.

called him; but she was in reality disconsolate, and I one day found her in a paroxysm of despair and tears, quite distressing to anyone who had not known her as well as myself.

"Ah, Laurette," said she, throwing herself into my arms, "how fortunate you are! You stay at Paris. Good heavens, how melancholy I shall be! How can my brother be so hard-hearted, so wicked, as to send me into exile amongst savages and serpents! Besides, I am ill. Oh! I shall die before I get there." Here her speech was interrupted, for she sobbed with such violence that for a moment I was fearful she would have fainted. I approached her sofa, and, taking her hand, endeavoured to encourage her, as one would a child, by talking of its playthings or new shoes: telling her she would be queen of the island; would ride in a palanquin; that slaves would watch her looks to execute her wishes; that she would walk in groves of orange-trees; that she need have no dread of serpents, as there were none in the Antilles; and that savages were equally harmless.

Finally, I summed up my consolatory harangue by telling her she would look very pretty in the Creole costume. As I advanced in my arguments, Madame Leclerc's sobs became less and less hysterical. She still wept, but her tears were not unbecoming. "You really think, Laurette," said she, "that I shall look pretty, *prettier than usual*, in a Creole turban, a short waist, and a petticoat of striped muslin?"

Description can give but a faint idea of Madame Leclerc at the moment when her delight at being presented with a new hint for the toilet chased away the remembrance that she was on the eve of departure for a country where she expected to be devoured. She rang for her waiting-maid. "Bring me all the bandanas in the house." She had some remarkably fine ones which my mother had given her from a bale of Indian silks and muslins brought over by Vice-Admiral Magon. We chose the prettiest amongst them, and as my mother had always worn silk handkerchiefs for nightcaps, I was accustomed from my infancy to the arrangement of the corners in the most becoming manner; Madame Leclerc, therefore, when she examined herself in the glass, was enraptured with my skill.

"Laurette," said she, replacing herself on the sofa, "you know, my dear, how I love you! You preferred Caroline, but we shall see if you won't repent yet. Listen! I am going to show you the sincerity of my affection. You must come to Saint Domingo—you will be next to myself in rank. I shall be queen, as you told me just now, and you shall be vice-queen. I will go and talk to my brother about it." "*I* go to Saint Domingo, madame!" I exclaimed. "What in the name of madness are you thinking of?" "Oh, I know there are difficulties in the way of such an arrangement, but I will talk to Bonaparte about it; and as he is partial to Junot he will let you go to Saint Domingo."

While I looked at her in perfect amazement she proceeded, arranging all the while the folds of her gown and the fashion of her turban: "We will give balls and form parties of pleasure amongst those beautiful mountains" (the serpents and savages were already forgotten); " Junot shall be the commander of the capital. What is its name? I will tell Leclerc I expect him to give a *fête* every day. We will take Madame Permon too." And as she said this she pinched my nose and pulled my ears, for she liked to ape her brother, and thought such easy manners had an air of royalty.

But both the ludicrous effect of this scene and the weariness I was beginning to feel from it fled at once before the sound of her last words. My mother, who loved her with a tenderness equal to that of Madame Lætitia—my poor mother, who already lay on a bed of suffering from which she was never more to rise! I felt it possible that I might make an answer harsh enough to awaken the beautiful dreamer from her reverie; therefore, putting on my gloves, I was about to take leave, when Junot was announced; he had seen my carriage at the door, and, stopping his cabriolet, came to my rescue.

"You are just arrived in time," cried Madame Leclerc; "sit down there, my dear General, and let us settle everything; for it is high time," said she, turning to me; "you will have no more than enough for preparing Mademoiselle Despaux, Madame Germon, Le Roi, Copp,* Madame Roux—no, Nattier will do better, Mademoiselle L'Olive, Lenormand, Le Vacher, Foncier, Biennais" (and at each name of these celebrated contributors to the toilet, as she counted them on her fingers, she cast a glance of triumph towards us, that seemed to say, "See what an excellent memory I have, and how admirably I can choose my ministers!"). "As for myself," she added, "my preparations are made, I am quite ready; but as we set out very shortly you had better make haste."

Junot's countenance would certainly have diverted any fourth person who might have been a spectator of the scene; his eyes wandered from me to Madame Leclerc, who, perceiving his perplexity, said: "I am going to take you both to Saint Domingo, Madame Permon too, and Albert; oh, how happy we shall all be together!" Junot was for a moment motionless, till a tremendous burst of

---

* Copp was a famous shoemaker, the same who, after a most attentive examination of a shoe which one of his customers showed him, complaining that it split before she had worn it an hour, detected at length the cause of such a misfortune befalling a specimen of his workmanship:

"Ah," said he, with the air of making a discovery, "I see how it is, madame: you have been walking!"

laughter interrupted the silence—not very politely, it must be confessed; but I afterwards learned that the explosion was provoked by a wink of peculiar intelligence.

Madame Leclerc was astonished at such a mode of testifying his gratitude, expecting to see him throw himself at her feet, but she reckoned without her host. "Very pretty," said she, pouting; "will you please to explain the meaning of this gaiety? Methinks it is not exactly the way to thank an old friend who intends you a kindness." "Have you had the goodness to mention your intentions to the First Consul, madame?" said Junot, who, though growing more decorous, could not yet entirely overcome his risible propensities. "No, certainly not, for your wife has but just suggested the idea."

Junot turned to me with an astonishment that nearly set me laughing in my turn. "What! my wife go to Saint Domingo?" said he. "And why not? She will be the first person there next to myself; she is used to the world; she dresses well; she is elegant. I will give her some slaves, and Leclerc will make you commandant of that town—the —the——" "The Cape," said Junot. "Exactly, the Cape—the Cape." And she repeated like a parrot the word which in five minutes she would altogether have forgotten.

"I am infinitely obliged to you, madame," said Junot, with comic seriousness; "but really, with your permission, I should prefer remaining Commandant of Paris. Besides, there is a slight obstacle which you do not appear to have taken into contemplation." And, throwing his arms round me, he drew me towards him, embraced me, and hinted at my being in the family way.

Madame Leclerc opened her eyes even wider than was usual with her when surprised, and that was not unfrequently —a little mannerism that was not unbecoming, and said: "I did not think of that. But what of that," said she the next moment; "what does it signify whether your infant utters his first cry on the waves or on *terra firma?* I will give Laurette a vessel to herself. Ah! what say you to that, M. Junot? Am not I a capital manager? I will write immediately to Brest, where we are to embark, and order a vessel to be expressly prepared. Villaret-Joyeuse is a good-natured man; he will do anything that I desire. Come, let me embrace you both."

"As for embracing you, madame," said Junot, laughing himself almost out of breath, "I am assuredly too happy in the permission not to take advantage of it, but for our voyage we will, if you please, drop that project, which Laura's friendship for you no doubt inspired. Besides," added he, "I do not think the First Consul would consent to it. You know he likes to nominate his Generals spontaneously, and without reference to private feelings, such as would influence this affair." And he laughed anew. "But," he continued, "I am not the less grateful for your intentions, madame, and be assured I am fully sensible of them, only"— and again the unfortunate laugh redoubled— "another time be kind enough to prove them otherwise than by putting my little Laura to bed on the wide ocean, and giving me the command of the Cape instead of Paris, and all this for old friendship's sake."

Junot, kneeling on a footstool beside Madame Leclerc's settee, was kissing her hands all the while that he said this, in a tone which, though certainly of derision, and perhaps of a little innocent impertinence, could not be offensive. Madame Leclerc was not competent to understand the raillery of his expressions, but, by a sort of instinctive cunning, she perceived that he was making fun of her, and, whether really distressed at so peremptory a negative to her project, or at being laughed at in my presence by Junot, of whose former attachment for her she had a thousand times boasted to me, the fact is she repulsed him with such violence as to throw him from the footstool on the carpet, and said, in a voice choked with sobs:

"This it is to attach one's self to the ungrateful—I, who love Laura like a sister!" (and, in truth, that was not saying much). "And you too, Junot, who refuse to accompany and defend me in a country where I am to be deserted!" And her tears rolled in floods.

"I will never refuse to assist a woman in peril," said Junot, rising, and with an expression half in jest and half earnest; "but permit me to say that is not your situation." "Ah!" continued she, still weeping, and without listening to him, "you would not have made all those reflections when we were at Marseilles! . . . You would not so tranquilly have seen me set out to be devoured, perhaps. . . . How can I tell? In short, to face all the dangers of a land filled with savages and wild beasts. I, who have said so much to Laurette of your attachment to me."

This time it was impossible to restrain my laughter. Such an appeal to a husband in the very presence of his wife threw me into such a paroxysm of mirth that Junot, though beginning to be weary of the scene, could not forbear joining. "Come, be reasonable," said he to the beautiful Niobe with the freedom of an old friend; "do not weep; it destroys the lustre of the eyes, the bloom of the cheek, and renders the prettiest woman almost ugly—beautiful as you are!" After our departure we indulged for several minutes in a most immoderate fit of laughter.

"Is it possible," said Junot at length, "that you can have said anything tending to inspire her with the barbarous notion of your inclination to visit the country of the blacks?" I told him the whole story, and he in return explained to me why he had been so excessively amused by the capricious beauty's sudden proposal to carry me off eighteen hundred leagues from Paris, made with as much ease as one invites a friend to a week's visit at a country seat. "She still loves you, then?" said I.

"She!—in the first place, she never loved me, and in the next, supposing her to have returned in the slightest measure a love as passionate as beauty can engender in an ardent mind and volcanic head at the age of twenty-four, she has long ago lost all remembrance of it. No; you visited Madame Leclerc at a moment when she was under the dominion of one of those nervous affections to which women, and especially such women, are frequently subject. The sight of you instinctively redoubled her emotion, simply because it recalled happy days; then you talked to her of dressing à la Virginia, and she immediately recollected that at Marseilles, when I was madly in love, when the excellent Madame Bonaparte, the mother, was willing to accept me as a son-in-law, and the First Consul, ever prudent and wary, observed, 'You have neither of you the means of living,' I, in my delirium, answered: 'But, my General, think of Paul and Virginia—their friends preferred fortune to happiness, and what was the consequence?' The First Consul, who was never romantic, did but shrug his shoulders and repeat his usual phrase: 'You have neither of you the means of living.'"

"But," said I, "it could not be the bandana and the fashion in which I turned up its red and green corners that produced this jargon of unconnected folly." "You need seek no deeper for it. Madame Leclerc's imagination is perfectly stagnant on many points, and compensates itself by an incredibly creative faculty in others. Her ignorance is unbounded, and equalled only by her vanity. Well, these two properties, which make up her whole composition, easily open themselves a way which the most sprightly imagination, united with a few grains more of sense, would find it difficult to trace. I know her well; her vanity made her veritably believe that I should be but too happy to join this expedition to Saint Domingo." "And you think she would really have spoken to the First Consul if you had not arrived?" "Beyond all doubt, for she is perfectly sincere. She was convinced that all she was arranging, or rather deranging, in her pretty little head was entirely for our interests, and would have requested her brother's permission for my joining her husband's army as a special favour towards me."

I do not know whether it was a suggestion of the female imagination, ever restless, or perhaps more properly jealous, that made me observe on the possibility that Madame Leclerc, tenacious of her project of roaming with me amongst the blacks in a gown of striped muslin and a bandana jacket and turban, might yet mention it to her brother.

"Faith! you are very right," said Junot. "Beautiful creature as she is (and good and excellent, moreover, for her heart is free from malevolence), this affair might prove a rehearsal of the story of the bear knocking his friend on the head. We must forestall such favours."

The event proved my sagacity. The same day Junot related to the First Consul all that had passed between his sister and me, taking care, as may be supposed, not to throw in too strong a colouring. As for the picture itself, with all its subordinate attributes, the First Consul knew his sister too well to suppose the relative situation of the parties exaggerated. Three days afterwards he said to Junot with a smile: "You are bent, then, on going to Saint Domingo?" Junot replied only by a bow and a corresponding smile. "I am sorry, but you cannot go at present. I want you here, as I have given General Leclerc to understand, who wanted to persuade me that you would be more useful to me at the Cape than in Paris." Junot assured me that it was amusing to observe the countenance of the First Consul as he spoke this; it exhibited a rapid succession of novel impressions, recalling images of the past.

Yet the whole affair passed over Madame Leclerc's mind without penetrating beyond its surface, for she possessed no solidity, and all her conceptions were as uncertain and fugitive as her head was incapable of methodizing any plan. The next time I saw her she had forgotten everything but the bandana. She had been that very morning to my poor mother's to have her turban arranged by her hands, and my mother, though in extreme pain, had taken a sort of pride in setting it off to the best advantage round a head which in this dress was one of the prettiest imaginable.

The squadron at length set sail in the month of December, 1801. The dresses, hats, caps, and other frivolities which Madame Leclerc took out with her were innumerable. Thirty-five ships of the line, twenty-two frigates, and an immense number of gunboats followed the vessel which bore the lovely Cleopatra, and which had been furnished with every appurtenance of luxury, elegance, and utility, that the fair voyager might have no desire ungratified. The General was disposed to refuse admission to so many useless indispensables; but Madame Leclerc, at the first sound of objection, assumed a tone that instantly reduced her spouse to silence for the sake of peace during the exile to which he was condemned. This was a singular match — I could never comprehend its inducements — for the reason ascribed by report was absurd. Madame Leclerc treated her husband pretty despotically, and yet was afraid of him, not, indeed, properly of him, but of the First Consul. She required from him observances that would be very amusing in the relation.

The expedition to Saint Domingo encountered in its day plenty of approbation and plenty of censure. The censures alleged that it was folly to oppose the entire population of a distant colony, whose savage disposition refused all quarter to their adversaries, thus exposing our troops to the double perils of a murderous warfare and no less murderous climate. They were grieved to see so fine an army despatched to America before the remnant of that which the deserts of Africa had nearly engulfed was restored to us. They contended that, in spite of his profound ambition, in spite even of his cruelty, it was necessary to guarantee to Toussaint-L'Ouverture the government for life which had been conferred upon him by the colonists. He had very considerable military talents, a political address, or rather an ingenious cunning, which had saved Saint Domingo from the English yoke, and, above all, from its own passions. They were therefore of opinion that the First Consul should leave Toussaint-L'Ouverture at liberty still to call himself, if he so pleased, *the first of the blacks,** and that he should be acknowledged Governor of Saint Domingo, subject to the dominion of France—terms to which he would most willingly have agreed. But the First Consul justly observed that Toussaint was a hypocrite, who, while protesting his devotion to the Consular Government, was meditating the liberation of the French Antilles from the authority of the Republic. "I am the Bonaparte of Saint Domingo," said he; "the colony cannot exist without me. I must be preserved to her."

Such language on the part of such a man must have excited alarm for the future fate of the island and its dependencies, especially considering the character of his two Lieutenants, Christophe and Dessalines. A cousin of

---

* When acknowledged by the Consular Government Commandant of Saint Domingo, he had written a letter to the First Consul with this superscription: "Toussaint, the first of the blacks, to Bonaparte, the first of the whites."

mine in the marines, who, having arrived at Saint Domingo, served as a volunteer in the army, and was prisoner to Dessalines, has told me anecdotes of this *monster*—for he does not deserve the name of man—which surpass in sanguinary horror all the most tragical conceptions of the most gloomy and terrific imagination. Bonaparte knew the character of these men of blood, but he was desirous of restoring peace and abundance to that fine colony, and it could only be accomplished by maintaining the blacks. In the short interval between the submission and the second insurrection of the island (that is to say of the blacks) for which the re-establishment of slavery at Guadeloupe was the pretext, Saint Domingo recovered its prosperity; the lands were cultivated, and commerce revived. But Toussaint, who, on the submission of the colony, had ostensibly retired to live peaceably on one of his estates, soon began to contrive and organize another massacre of the whites.

England was no stranger to these new projects of Toussaint; she excited them, and, more than once, English gold paid the price of our blood. Toussaint-L'Ouverture was carried off in the middle of the night, transported on board a vessel, and brought to France. He was consigned to the Castle of Joux, and thence removed to the citadel of Besançon, where he died suddenly, which gave rise to an absurd rumour; for if the death of Toussaint was violent, as some voices have proclaimed, there should have been some actuating motive for the deed; but where can such motive be found?

Although General Rochambeau has been much censured, because none could venture openly to blame the First Consul's brother-in-law, it cannot be denied that one principal cause of the loss of Saint Domingo, and the destruction of that immense expedition which had sailed from Brest, L'Orient, and Toulon, was the unskilful and imprudent administration of General Leclerc.

Before we hastily decide on Rochambeau's errors, we should take all the circumstances into account, and, judging candidly of his situation, consider what he could have done without resorting to arbitrary measures, which the unhappy state of affairs drove him to the hard necessity of employing. Pressed on one side by the blacks, who thus irritated by the faults of his predecessor had raised the standard of revolt with more frantic fury and sanguinary rage than ever, he was hemmed in on the other by an English fleet, to whom he surrendered with the six thousand men that remained to him. Death seemed to have brandished his sickle with ambitious eagerness through the ranks of that army but two years ago in so flourishing a condition. Sickness, assassination, battle, had afforded him an ample harvest; the means of destruction multiplied around this devoted army, and only a very small remnant ever set foot again on their native soil.

Madame Leclerc returned to Europe bearing the corpse of her husband, which she had enclosed in a coffin of cedar, and then, cutting off her beautiful hair, affected the Artemisia. Her parade, however, of immoderate grief and ostentatious despair made but little impression; the First Consul himself, when told that his sister had sacrificed her hair to the manes of her husband without preserving a single lock, answered with a significant smile: "Oh, she knows full well it will only grow the more luxuriantly for its cropping."

CHAPTER XXXIV.

Peace with England—Remarkable Speech of Bonaparte to the Belgian Deputies—Glory of France under the Consulate—Concourse of Foreigners at Paris—English and Russian Visitors—Characteristic Anecdote of Mr. Fox—Lord and Lady Cholmondeley—The Duchess of Gordon and her Daughter Lady Georgiana—Public Magnificence and Private Economy of Napoleon—Bonaparte's Fine Coat—Story told by the First Consul to Josephine—The Power of Masses—Characteristic of Napoleon's Policy.

PEACE with England was definitely signed. The Treaty of Amiens had confirmed the preliminaries of reconciliation with our great rival on the 25th of March, 1802. On this occasion, which terminated all the differences of Europe, Joseph Bonaparte was again our messenger of peace. The temple of Janus was at length closed, and France exalted to a higher pinnacle of glory and real power than she has ever since attained, for she had emerged from a struggle with united Europe victorious, aggrandized, and respected. The colonies captured by England were restored to us. The course of the Scheldt was left in our hands, as well as the Austrian Netherlands, part of Brabant, Dutch Flanders, and a number of cities, as Maestricht, Venloo, etc.

A noble speech of the First Consul to the Belgian deputies is connected with this point of our history. On the opening of the conferences of Luneville they waited on the chief of the Republic to offer him their thanks for having supported the rights of a people who would accept no other protection than that of France. "It was in justice to ourselves," replied the First Consul to the deputation;* "the treaty of Campo-Formio had already recognized the position of Belgium. During the years which have elapsed since that treaty our arms have suffered reverses, and it was supposed that the Republic, less favoured by fortune, would weakly yield; but this was a serious mistake. Belgium, like all other territories acquired by treaties solemnly guaranteed, forms as integral a part of France as the most ancient of her provinces, as Brittany or Burgundy, and were the FAUBOURG SAINT ANTOINE IN THE OCCUPATION OF AN ENEMY, FRANCE COULD NEVER ABANDON HER RIGHTS." Such were the words of Napoleon, addressed to the Belgian deputies.

Yes; France was then resplendent in glory. Independently of the northern possessions, forming that national boundary for which it is the duty of every Frenchman to contend with his life, she was mistress of the German territory on the left of the Rhine, as well as of Avignon and the Venaissin, Geneva, and almost the whole bishopric of Basle, Savoy, and Nice. The Republic founded and protected States; she erected the Grand Duchy of Tuscany into a kingdom; Austrian Lombardy was transformed under her auspices into an Italian Republic; Genoa rose into a sovereignty under the name of the Ligurian Republic; and all these States sheltered themselves beneath the spacious folds of the tricoloured banner, relying on the vigour and vigilance of the Gallic cock. The Republic extended her protection to aquatic Batavia. By her recent treaties with Spain and Portugal she had recovered colonies capable of reviving her preponderance in another hemisphere. By the

* See the *Moniteur* of the month of October, 1800.

secret treaty of Saint Ildefonso, and the care of Lucien Bonaparte, her flag waved once more over Louisiana, that fine and fertile province, surrendered to Spain by the disgraceful and humiliating peace of 1793, but the possession of which now placed us in an imposing attitude in the Gulf of Mexico, and would prove a formidable point of attack against the American Union in case of a rupture. She had wrested from the Portuguese sceptre territories which, with their broad deserts, formed an impenetrable barrier for French Guiana. In short, the Republic, at this period of the Consular Government, was greater even than the Empire ever was. Napoleon's orb of glory was then, indeed, immensurable.

Paris now realized the vision of the First Consul for his great city; it had become the capital of the civilized world. Such was the concourse of foreigners that exorbitant prices were charged for the most inferior lodgings, and paid without hesitation. My situation as wife of the Commandant of Paris introduced me to all strangers of any celebrity, and I confess my most interesting recollections belong to this portion of my life. Russians and English were the principal actors on this scene. The English, greedy of travelling, and so long shut out from their European tour—for Italy, Switzerland, and part of Germany had, since 1795, been as inaccessible to them as France—gave loose to their joy with all the frankness and sincerity of their national character, which is so totally in opposition to the sophistry and artifice of their Cabinet. They flocked in crowds to Paris, and entered with ardour into the pleasures which France offered them in abundance, which they felt too happy in repaying with their gold. Society, too—the best society—then beginning to reorganize itself, presented attractions which their acute and judicious perceptions were equally capable of appreciating.

Among the English arrivals of that day were some names whose undying reputation fills the memory nearly to the exclusion of all others. Mr. Fox, for example, was one of those beings whom it is impossible to see, though but once, without remembering for ever, as a happy epoch in one's life, the day of introduction. His fine talents and noble character were the adoration of a majority of our countrymen. I shared with others in admiring the high feeling of Mr. Fox, when, seconded by Grey, and I believe by Sheridan, he summoned Mr. Pitt, the Minister of the day, to adopt a course not menacing, but conciliatory; in short, to make an attempt, by entreaties addressed to the Convention, to save the life of Louis XVI. "In the name of English honour," said this great man, "however vain your efforts, however useless your endeavours, try them at least, and show the world that kings do not stand by unmoved to see a brother sovereign murdered. Why do you talk of armaments?" he added with warmth, in reply to Mr. Pitt. "By what right would you immolate a thousand heads to revenge the fall of one, when a few decisive words might prevent the sacrifice?" What a contrast do these admirable arguments offer to the proceedings of the inflexible Minister, who by arming England, exciting Spain, and making a clamorous display of hostility, did but too probably accelerate the fate of the unfortunate Louis!

Mr. Fox's aspect did not at the first glance seem to justify his prodigious fame—his demeanour was even ordinary—and the first time that I saw him, dressed in a dark gray coat, and with his head somewhat inclined, he gave me the idea of a good Devonshire farmer—a man incapable of any pretension. But how rapidly were these opinions put to flight when the course of conversation brought the energies of his mind into view. His countenance became animated with the first sentence of interest that passed his lips, and gradually brightened with increasing intelligence till it was absolutely fiery and sparkling. His voice, subdued at first, rose in modulation till it burst upon the ear like thunder; and the same man, who but a few minutes before had appeared the most commonplace of mortals, was now an object of intense admiration.

I first saw him at a distance; he was next introduced to me at the Tuileries, where, in the midst of a multitudinous and noisy throng, it was impossible to put in operation any of the plans I had concerted for drawing forth the sentiments of one of the most distinguished and most justly celebrated men of the eighteenth century. At length he dined at my house, and the conversation, having first been of a general kind, turned afterwards on such topics as were more especially adapted to the illustrious stranger. The entire concurrence of opinion between Mr. Fox, Junot, and some of his other guests, precluded debate, but the affairs of England and the Ministry which had replaced Mr. Pitt were long under discussion, and the conversation, though tranquil, was of a remarkable character; when one of the company, who had been of the Egyptian expedition, and had returned with his mind violently exasperated, brought forward the awkward subject of the events in that quarter, freely indulging his rancour against England. Mr. Fox's countenance changed with a rapidity it is impossible to describe; we no longer beheld the leader of the English Opposition, but the advocate of Mr. Pitt, defending him with his eloquence amidst a circle of enemies. The conversation grew warm, and Junot soon took an unfortunate part in it. He had been made prisoner on his return from Egypt by a Captain Styles, conducted to Jaffa, and introduced to Sir Sydney Smith, who was negotiating there with the Grand Vizier the Treaty of El-Arich for the evacuation of Egypt; thence he accompanied Sir Sydney on board the *Tiger* to Larnaka, in Cyprus; here Junot, as I have before observed, contracted for Smith one of those chivalrous friendships which he was very capable of feeling and the brave English Commodore well calculated to inspire. He had more than once laid lance in rest as the champion of his friendly foe; and now, believing him compromised in something that was said respecting the infamous infraction of the treaty which he had guaranteed, and satisfied in his own mind that his gallant friend was the most honourable of men, "It was not his doing!" cried Junot, animated by a sentiment of truth and justice; "he would never have said, with Mr. Pitt, 'The destruction of that perfidious army is a matter of rejoicing; the interests of human nature require its total annihilation.' No. Sir Sydney Smith would be incapable of uttering such a libel on his profession and on human nature." Mr. Fox turned crimson, then pale as death; passed his hand over his eyes, and made no immediate answer; at the end of a minute that striking voice, which, with its sonorous tone, could overpower all others, murmured rather than articulated: "I beg your pardon; Mr. Pitt never used such words. No," answered the statesman, to whose upright and patriotic soul the imputation was truly painful; "those terrible words never fell from the lips of Mr. Pitt; they are Mr. Dundas's."*

* The following anecdote illustrative of Fox's character was communicated to me by an Englishman: At a time when he was much embarrassed in his pecuniary circumstances, a note of hand of his for three hundred guineas was presented for payment. There were no funds to meet this, and the unlucky creditor made repeated but useless application to get the bill cashed. By a stratagem he succeeded at last in seeing Mr. Fox, who was actually employed at the time in counting out several hundred guineas. The creditor's hopes of a satisfactory settlement of his claim were now very sanguine, especially as Mr. Fox showed no signs of embarrassment at being discovered in the employment he was engaged in. His dismay may therefore easily be imagined

Paris was also at this time the rendezvous of a multitude of English, who, though less celebrated than Mr. Fox or his brother, proved very agreeable acquaintances. Those whom I chiefly preferred were Lord and Lady Cholmondeley, Mrs. Harrison, a young widow from India of most simple, unaffected, and fascinating manners, the Duchess of Gordon and her daughter Lady Georgiana, Colonel James Green, and Lady E. Foster, afterwards Duchess of Devonshire. Lady Cholmondeley had considerably the advantage of me in years, but her manners and those of her lord were courteously polished. She talked to me of the glory of the First Consul and his companions in arms in a tone of perfect sincerity and goodwill—she blended so amiably with unqualified respect for the dignity of her own nation a just appreciation of the qualities of those I loved—that I was almost attached to her. The

---

when he was calmly told that, in spite of the display of wealth before him, Mr. Fox had not ten guineas at his own disposal. In fact, that the whole of the money on the table—about eight hundred guineas—was destined to discharge a *debt of honour*—a gaming transaction of the previous evening. When the creditor remonstrated upon the injustice of passing by his own legitimate debt in favour of one so much less pressing, Fox appeared astonished, and endeavoured to show that the *debt of honour* had a much higher claim upon his immediate attention, in so far as there existed no other security for its liquidation than his verbal assurance; whereas the holder of the bill possessed his signature, which would be ultimately honoured. "If this be a just mode of discrimination," dryly remarked the creditor, "I will instantly convert my claim into a debt of honour," at the same time tearing the bill into pieces; "and you will allow that as my demand now stands upon an equal footing with your last night's loss, as being simply a debt of honour, I have the advantage of priority, at all events." He well judged his man. Fox was too generous and right-minded to hesitate; he accordingly took the necessary sum from the heap before him, and satisfied the creditor whose debt, in justice, required immediate payment; and cheerfully resigned himself to fortune, in the hope of discharging the mere debt of honour.

First Consul, who received every morning circumstantial intelligence respecting the English in Paris, had a high esteem for the Earl and Countess Cholmondeley. The Duchess of Gordon is assuredly not forgotten by those who had the supreme happiness of seeing her in Paris in 1802. When I wish to divert my thoughts I call to mind her burlesque appearance and manners, which, as is well known, were, notwithstanding her duchess mania, very far from ducal.

The general aspect of society in Paris at that time deserves a place in contemporary memoirs. The First Consul required all the principal authorities to maintain not only a creditable, but a splendid, establishment. Nothing could exceed (and this fact will be attested by all living persons who knew Napoleon as I did) his extreme and rigid economy in all his private concerns, though when circumstances required it he could equal in magnificence the most sumptuous sovereign of the East; the liberality of Aboul-Cazem then presided over every arrangement. I remember his once admonishing Duroc for neglecting to transmit an order regulating the private breakfasts at the Palace which he had given him the evening before; the order, therefore, had been delayed but a few hours. "But an additional day's expense," said the First Consul, "is too much."

A few minutes afterwards one of the Ministers arrived. The First Consul immediately entered into consultation upon a *fête* that was to be given the following week on the 14th July, the anniversary of the destruction of the Bastille, which was observed till the re-establishment of royalty; the Tuileries were illuminated, and, as far as I can remember, the theatres were opened gratis. "Josephine," said he, with the tone of kindness he generally adopted towards her, for he was tenderly attached to her, "I am going to impose upon you a command you will have much pleasure in obeying. I desire you will be dazzling; make your preparations accordingly. For my part, I shall wear my fine suit of crimson silk embroidered with gold, presented to me by the city of Lyons; I shall then be superb!" This dress was, as he said, presented to him by the city of Lyons on the occasion of the *Helvetic Consulta* in the month of January preceding; and, to say the truth, he had already worn it and made a most singular appearance in it, which instantly occurred to my recollection when he talked of his *fine suit*, and I could not suppress a laugh. He perceived it, for nothing escaped his observation, and, coming up to me, said as he surveyed me with a half-angry and half-smiling air: "What do you mean by that sarcastic smile, Madame Junot? You think, I suppose, that I shall not be as smart as all those handsome Englishmen and Russians who look so sweet upon you and turn all your young heads. I am sure I am at least as agreeable as that English Colonel— that dandy who is said to be the handsomest man in England, and whom I can compare to nothing but the Prince of Coxcombs."

This expression, a dandy,* was a favourite word with Napoleon for designating men who displeased him. In the present instance he alluded to a tall Englishman called Colonel or Captain Matthews, and who passed for a devourer of hearts—English ones, be it observed. I could not avoid laughing still more heartily at this idea of the First Consul and his pretensions to elegance and fashion; whereas he had at that time an utter antipathy to everything that is called fashionable, and showed it in the most unqualified dislike of such young men as had the misfortune to pass in the world for agreeable and elegant. Soft speeches, graceful attitudes, and all other qualifications of

* *Godelureau.*

a beau, he treated with even more bitterness and contempt than he generally bestowed on the persons he most disliked. Madame Bonaparte presently afterwards made an observation in praise of M. de Flahaut, who, she said, possessed a variety of talents. "What are they? Sense? Bah! who has not as much as he? He sings well—a noble talent for a soldier, who must be always hoarse by profession. Ah, he is a beau! that is what pleases you women. I see nothing so extraordinary in him; he is just like a spider with his eternal legs. His shape is quite unnatural; to be well shaped——" Here his speech was broken in upon, for being at that time much given to laughing, I could not restrain a second fit on seeing the First Consul look with complacency at his own small legs (which, like his whole person, were then very shapely), covered with silk stockings, and a shoe sharp-pointed enough to have pierced the eye of a needle. He did not finish his sentence, but I am certain he meant—"to be well shaped his leg should be like that."

And yet no being could have less vanity than Napoleon; he was neatness itself, and extremely particular in his dress, but made not the slightest claim to elegance. For this reason the movement which approached his hand to his leg as he mentioned the spider legs of M. de Flahaut[*] set me laughing by its *naïveté*. He both saw and heard the laugh, and, what is more, he understood it, and coming towards me again said: "Well, you little pest! What do you find to laugh at? So you must make game, in your turn, of my legs. They do not figure as well to your fancy in a country dance as those of your elegant friends. But a man may both sing and dance without being a dandy. Let me ask yourself, Madame Junot, if Talleyrand's nephew

[*] This gentleman was subsequently one of the aides-de-camp of the Emperor.

is not a pleasing young man?" My answer was ready. The person he alluded to was Louis de Perigord, who, as we as his brother and his sister, now Madame Justus de Noailles, had a large fortune; he was then nineteen years of age, and already united to the acuteness of his uncle a sound judgment, sprightly wit, polished manners, and a vivid resemblance to his father's person. The last is a eulogium in itself.

Napoleon, then addressing Josephine, said: "I desire you will be dazzling in jewellery and richly dressed; do you hear?" "Yes," replied Madame Bonaparte; "and then you find fault, perhaps fall into a passion, or you erase my warrants of payment from the margin of my bills."* And she pouted like a little girl, but with the most perfect good-humour. Madame Bonaparte's manners possessed, when she chose it, a seducing charm. Her graciousness might be too general, but undeniably she could be, when she chose, perfectly attractive and lovable. When the First Consul announced his wish regarding her toilet she looked at him so prettily, walked towards him with such graceful sweetness, her whole manner breathing so evident a desire to please, that he must have had a heart of stone who could resist her. Napoleon loved her, drew her close to him, and embraced her. "Certainly, my dear love; I sometimes cancel your warrants of payment because you are occasionally so imposed upon that I cannot take it upon my conscience to sanction such abuses; but it is not, therefore, inconsistent to recommend you to be magnificent on state occasions. One interest must be weighed against another,

* This circumstance happened many times. I have myself seen two bills erased with the Emperor's own hand; one was for linen, the other for essences and perfumery. "You have your own linendraper, Mademoiselle L'Olive," said the Emperor, "why try an unknown warehouse? You must pay these new fancies out of your allowance."

and I hold the balance equitably though strictly. Here, I will tell you a story, which will do wonders as a lesson if you will but remember it. Listen, too "—beckoning us to draw near—" listen, too, you young giddy-pates, and profit by it.

"There lived at Marseilles a rich merchant who received one morning, through the hands of a young man of good family and fortune, a letter strongly recommending the bearer to his notice: the merchant, after having read the letter, instead of either throwing it aside as waste-paper, when he found that it covered one only of the four sides of the sheet, tore it in two, placed the written half in a leaf of his portfolio, and the other half that would serve for writing a note upon into another portfolio, which already contained a number of similar half-sheets.* Having attended to this act of economy, he turned towards the young man, and invited him to dinner for that very day. The youth, accustomed to a life of luxury, felt but little inclination to dine with a man apparently so mean. He accepted the invitation, however, and promised to return at four o'clock. But as he descended the narrow counting-house staircase, his mind rapidly reverted to the observations he had made upon that small gloomy room, with the two long offices which led to it, encumbered with dusty ledgers, and where a dozen young men were working in melancholy silence; he then repented of his folly in accepting the invitation. The duties of the toilet were discharged more for his own satisfaction than in compliment to the host who expected him; and that done, he proceeded to the banker's house. On arriving there he desired to be conducted to the

---

* Paper was far more costly at the beginning of the century than it is now. Anyone who has much correspondence also knows that the space taken up by it would be half as much again if every blank sheet were also filed.

merchant's lady. A number of valets in rich liveries led him across a small garden, filled with rare plants, and after conducting him through several apartments sumptuously furnished, introduced him to a handsome drawing-room, where he found the banker, who presented him to his wife, who was young and pretty, and elegantly attired: he himself was no longer the unattractive-looking personage his guest had seen in the morning, while the manners and conversation of fifteen or twenty visitors, who were assembled in the drawing-room, led to the inference that this house was one of the most refined in the city. The viands were excellent, the wines exquisite, the table covered with an abundance of massive silver-plate; in short, the young traveller was obliged mentally to admit that he had never partaken of more delicate fare or seen a greater display of magnificence; and he was more than ever confounded upon ascertaining from one of the persons near him that the banker gave a similar entertainment twice a week. While coffee was serving he ruminated on all that he had witnessed. The banker, observing his fit of abstraction, succeeded, by drawing him into conversation, in finding out the cause of his perplexity, and observed emphatically: 'You are too young to understand how masses are formed, the true and only power; whether composed of money, water, or men, it is all alike. A mass is an immense centre of motion, but it must be begun—it must be kept up. Young man, the half-sheets of paper which excited your derision this morning are one among the many means I employ for attaining it.'"

I was much struck afterwards by this idea of masses as the foundation of power, so characteristic of Napoleon's policy.

CHAPTER XXXV.

The First Consul the Admiration of Foreigners at Paris—Eagerness of Foreigners to see Bonaparte—Bonaparte's Dislike of them—The Princess with Five or Six Husbands—The Prince de Rohan and the Pensioned Husband—The Duchesse de Sagan and the Duchesse de Dino—The Princess Dolgorouki—Prince Galitzin—Lord and Lady Conyngham—Lord Whitworth and the Duchess of Dorset—Lord Yarmouth—Prince Philip von Cobentzel—Madame Demidoff—Napoleon desires me to show the Objects of Art to the Distinguished Foreigners at Paris.

THE First Consul said one day to Junot, "You and your wife see a great many foreigners, do you not?" Junot replied in the affirmative; and in truth, English and Russians, the latter especially, constituted the chief part of our society. Junot had just bought a country house at Bièvre, where we frequently had large parties; and the First Consul had given us for the baptismal gift of my little Josephine the house in the Champs-Elysées, which enabled us to receive our guests with convenience, and creditably to fulfil the duties of the post Junot occupied, as well as those to which he was bound as the oldest friend and servant of that astonishing man on whom the eyes of the whole world were at this time fixed.

To such an extent was this admiration of Napoleon carried, that it sometimes happened that Englishmen came to France only for a few hours, went to the parade of the troops in garrison, saw the First Consul, and returned to England. Junot enjoyed this tribute of interest. I have sometimes seen a dinner interrupted for half an hour, while the company listened with avidity to his account of his favourite General's glorious early years. The ladies were not outdone in curiosity respecting the previous life of Napoleon; they asked even more questions than the men.

We had for neighbours in our new habitation a Russian family, whose enthusiasm for the First Consul surpassed that of his most ardent admirers. This was the Diwoff family; the Countess Diwoff, in particular, had such an exclusive passion for him, for his glory, for his most trifling actions, that Junot and I did not hesitate to admit her to the intimacy she demanded, and which the proximity of our respective residences increased; so that I always found pleasure in spending an evening with my *little sister*, as she insisted on my calling her, though thirty years older than myself, and the more so as her many parties included all the foreigners of distinction in Paris.

One of Napoleon's peculiarities, perhaps but little known, was his extreme aversion, during the Consulate and the first years of the Empire, for the society of foreigners and of that of the Faubourg Saint Germain, but amongst the travellers with whom France was then inundated were a few whose names he held in consideration, and a very limited exception was made in their favour. He had generally some bitter remarks to make upon persons of notoriety, whose reputations had preceded them in France.

No one was more the object of these remarks than the Princesse Louis de Rohan, alias *Princess Troubetskoi, Duchess of Sagan, Duchess of Courland*—I scarcely know by what name to call her, filled as the history of her life is with divorces. Her beauty at this period could not be questioned; but it was not to my taste. I may be deemed fastidious, and I will plead guilty; but I could never like those snowy charms, destitute of all animation—that swan-like transparent skin—those eyes, whose only expression was pride; a pride for which it would be difficult to assign a cause, unless it was intended as a compliment to the memory of her grandfather, Biron. I could discover no beauty in that neck, certainly fair, and dressed in the most shining satin, but stiff, formal, and devoid of feminine grace. This is an attraction which, however, she ought to have possessed, for she ruined herself in husbands—a singular article to set down among the expenses of a pretty woman, but it was nevertheless true.

A clause in the last marriage contract stipulated that M. Louis de Rohan should have a pension of 60,000 francs in case of a divorce demanded by the Princess; but if the demand was made on his part it was to be but 12,000. M. de Rohan, therefore, left matters to the will of Providence, or rather to the will of his wife, contenting himself with the enjoyment of present possession, without disturbing himself about the future. Various strictures of the Princesse de Rohan upon the Court of the Tuileries, and especially upon his sisters, had reached the First Consul, who in consequence, perhaps, concerned himself more with her than he would otherwise have done. One evening he enlarged upon the absurdity of founding pretensions on rank and riches, in a country altogether Republican, and where all such distinctions were confounded in perfect equality.

"Mr. Fox," said he, "will always hold the first place in an assembly at the Tuileries, and Mrs. Fox would in France always take precedence of the Princesse de Rohan, because the reputation of her husband is reflected upon her. As for Madame de Courland, as she is called, I really do not understand upon what high merit she founds her right to treat with rudeness a people who do not desire her company, and are well versed in her pedigree."

This sally showed me the danger of injuring those who have not attacked us. There can be no doubt that the First Consul, desirous as he was of preserving with the young Emperor the friendly relations he had held with his father, would have been particularly gracious towards a lady who was partly his subject, had not her own proceedings drawn his ill-will upon her. The airs of the Princess were especially ill-judged at a period when France, so great in herself, saw assembled within her bosom all the greatest and most illustrious denizens of England, Germany, Italy, and Russia.

When the Princess trespassed on the rules of politeness, which continually happened, the source of her high pretensions was naturally looked into, and her genealogy was found to be but of seventy years' standing ;—sufficient, it is true, to confer nobility on a really illustrious extraction, but by no means adequate to support an hereditary title to arrogance.

The Duchess of Courland, her mother, united with a haughty carriage considerable amenity of speech and manner, and pleased me much. She had been beautiful—more so, indeed, than her eldest daughter. I was not acquainted with her daughter, whom they called *Eccellenza ;* but I think the beauty of the Duchesse de Dino,* the youngest daughter, incomparably preferable to that of her eldest sister ; there was more fire, more feeling, more intellectual vivacity in one of her black eyes than in the whole person of Madame de Sagan. At the time I am speaking of, however, she was a child, and could not enter into rivalry with her sister.

* The Duchesse de Dino was married to a nephew of Prince Talleyrand in 1809, and died in 1862. Her career in the political world is well known.

What an admirable picture is Gérard's of the Duchesse de Dino! It is the most enchanting of the children of the desert. Her turban, her robe, the sky which surrounds her, all is in harmony with the Oriental character she assumes; the picture, like all others from Gérard's hand, is admirably poetical.

Madame Dolgorouki, of whom I have before spoken, had the power of being extremely agreeable if she had had the inclination, but this was unfortunately wanting. She found us more lenient in our judgment upon her than her own countrymen, one of whom, Prince George Galitzin, declared a mortal enmity against her. I have known few men so witty, but he was too satirical to be liked. Without absolute misanthropy, he was no friend to human nature, which was neither good nor amiable enough to please him, but such characters as the Princess Dolgorouki he persecuted incessantly. The Prince was for ever in pursuit of some of her absurdities, her pride, her literary pretensions, her passion for splendid attire; he drew admirably, and possessed the difficult art of making the most exact resemblances in caricature.

Who does not remember with sensations of tenderness and pleasure the charming Pole, Madame Zamoiska? How attractive was her mild, amiable, and intelligent countenance! The sweetness of her disposition, the grace of her manners, and the symmetry of her figure! Her husband, though colder in manner than is usual with the Poles, was agreeable and much liked in society.

The lovely Lady Conyngham, since so celebrated in England, was then in the first bloom of that beauty which acquired such general and just admiration, though I must confess that a countenance so devoid of expression could never interest me. In contemplating the Venus de Medici, I know that the almost divine vision before me is but a marble statue, and look for no smile responsive to mine; but in a living and intellectual being I have a right to expect something more than mere regularity of feature—some emanation of mind; the face of the beautiful Marchioness, however, exhibited none.

She was extremely elegant, dressed well, and carried her solicitude for her complexion to the extent of saving it by spending the day in her bed, from which she rose only in time to prepare for a ball or other evening engagement. Lord Conyngham was a striking contrast to his wife. The Duchess of Gordon, who, in her masculine language, often hit upon a witty truth, once said of him: "Lord Conyngham! Oh! He is a perfect comb—all teeth and back."

The English Ambassador, Lord Whitworth, appeared to have been selected by his Government expressly for qualifications likely to prove disagreeable to us. His fine figure and handsome face could not atone to French society for his haughtiness, in which his wife, the Duchess of Dorset, seconded him to admiration. Their manners speedily rendered both so unpopular in the circles they frequented that their stay at Paris must have been anything but pleasant to themselves; his lordship, however, knew it would not be of long duration. There were other Englishmen in France of greater distinction, for originality at least, if for no superior attribute.

Amongst these was Lord Yarmouth, now Marquis of Hertford, respecting whom a greater diversity of opinion was entertained as well by his own countrymen as ours; but one qualification which he indisputably possessed was a clearness and acuteness of intellect rarely met with in the most subtle Venetian or Gascon. The faculties of Lord Yarmouth's mind were incomparably more penetrating than those of his countrymen generally, whose capacities, however extensive, are for the most part slow of conception.

Young as he then was, an indifferent opinion of his fellow-creatures was but too visibly imprinted on his features; his countenance, his smile, expressed utter coldness, or a sardonic and cynical criticism of all that was passing around him. The world of fashion was not to his taste; but when he was induced to *put on harness*, as he termed it, he made himself perfectly agreeable to those with whom he associated. He was passionately fond of gambling, and played nobly and generously.*

One of the new-comers, who was generally well received, was the Count Philip von Cobentzel, Imperial Ambassador to the French Republic. I never knew a man whose excellent sense and judgment, courteous manners, and goodness of heart, were more perfectly in harmony with talents of the highest order, or more absolutely out of keeping with his countenance and the whole exterior man. His person was less comic than his cousin's, when the latter received couriers in black silk breeches and puffed hair—but scarcely less unusual.

In contrast to Count Louis's slovenliness and perpetual action, Count Philip, a little man, was neatness and precision personified. Amongst his striking peculiarities may be reckoned his well-tied queue, and his front hair carefully turned up above the forehead, which gave him a perfect resemblance to *the ace of spades*, a nickname which was accordingly given to him; his dress, always strictly suited to the season, of the make of Maria-Theresa's Court, and most incongruous with the fashions of the day; his clear shrill voice, like that of a good old active, gossiping woman; and the odd constraint of his gait, shuffling between the quick pace, most natural and convenient to him, and the slow motion which he considered most becoming to an

---

* Thackeray's portrait of the Marquis of Steyne (in "Vanity Fair") will be recalled by this passage.

ambassador. With all these eccentricities he was an excellent man, of observant habits and retentive memory, and chatted freely and very agreeably with such persons as pleased him.

He was once the subject of a humorous incident. At a ball at my house, about two o'clock in the morning, the Duchess of Gordon took Count Philip by the hand and led him down the whole length of an English country-dance, at that time the favourite amusement, and introduced about four times at every ball. The Duchess bustled about not the less actively for her respectable rotundity, dragging after her the illustrious diplomatist, not in the habit of moving his slender legs with such impetuosity.

The Count, who enjoyed a joke, but did not relish being its object, was conscious of the ludicrous spectacle in which he was figuring; the unrestrained joviality of his partner, however, got the better of his vexation, and he good-humouredly attended her up and down the dance, making one of his formal bows whenever he asked her hand, acquitting himself on the whole with good grace, and laughing heartily afterwards at the mad prank in which the Duchess had made him share. The singular effect of a couple so oddly assorted, not only with each other, but with the young and merry group amongst whom they mixed, might well make an impression which time has not effaced from my mind.

While passing in review the persons who in 1802 enlivened the society of Paris, I must not omit my beloved friend Madame Demidoff, who created a great sensation there by the luxury and splendour of her establishment, which exceeded all that had yet been witnessed in Paris since the Revolution. Her husband, who was then a different being from when we last saw him on his road to die in Italy, but neither more amusing, good-humoured, nor agreeable, gave *fêtes* and balls, as he afterwards did at Florence; but in 1802 my amiable Elizabeth was present to do the honours of his house, and the fine salons of the Hôtel de Praslin were continually opened to a joyous multitude, happy not only in the gaiety of the scene, but in the charm, so seldom experienced in such crowded assemblies, of a friendly and kind reception. Madame Demidoff did not, however, bestow her affections indiscriminately; it was not everyone that she loved, but there was a magic in her simplest word or look which charmed all who approached her.

"I am very glad to see you," said she, in her soft sweet voice, smiling, and inclining her head with a grace peculiarly her own. And these simple words, addressed to a stranger whom she saw, perhaps, for the second or third time, comprised all that the most cordial hospitality could offer; but when anyone she loved, myself for example, approached, "How happy I am to see you!" said she; and the pressure of her hand and animation of her countenance plainly spoke her sincerity. Madame Demidoff was not pretty, and yet she was universally pleasing; because she possessed charms which are superior even to beauty—unaffected grace and suavity. Who that has seen her waltz can forget her sylph-like movements? unequalled in ease and suppleness by any other person I ever knew, except Madame Lallemand.

During the visits of these distinguished foreigners in Paris much attention was directed to the treasures of art it contained, as well as to the specimens it afforded of the national industry and skill. I had hitherto, from various causes, more particularly from my attendance upon my dear mother during her long illness, been prevented from becoming acquainted with the extent of these splendid objects, and accordingly embraced eagerly the opportunity now afforded me of making many excursions in the company of artists and scientific men, in order to gratify my taste for the arts. When the First Consul heard of this he reproached me for not including our foreign visitors in the parties. "You are the wife of the Commandant of Paris; it would be an agreeable way of doing the honours of the city to show your friends that we are worth the trouble they take in visiting us."

CHAPTER XXXVI.

Our Russian and English Friends—M. von Cobentzel's Travelling Costume—French Institute—Messieurs Denon and Millin—David the Painter—The Steam-pumps of the Brothers Perrier—Mirabeau and Beaumarchais—The Museum of the Louvre—The Committee of Public Instruction—M. Denon and the Old Paintings—Original Drawings of the Great Masters—The Gallery of Apollo—Visit to M. Charles, the Philosopher—The Camera Obscura and M. von Cobentzel's Secretary—The Cabinet of Medals—Vigilance of the Police under M. de Sartines—The National Library—Its Rich Contents—Charitable Institutions—The Barriers round Paris—Mademoiselle Chameroi — Scene at Saint Roche — Napoleon's Anger—The Archbishop of Paris.

IN compliance with the expressed wish of the First Consul, several English and Russian friends were invited, to their great satisfaction, to join our excursions to view the objects of art; and M. von Cobentzel, hearing that strangers were admitted, begged to be included among the elect, and was not refused. The recollection of his travelling costume affords me, even now, a portion of that hilarity with which my young mind first scanned it. He arrived at my house at twelve o'clock, accoutred like Baptiste the younger, in the *Orator Thwarted*, with the exception of the helmet, the absence of which was fully redeemed by a little turned-up three-cornered hat, and all this preparation was for a ride, not to the Valley of Montmorency, but to the Rue de Richelieu, or the Louvre.

He proved, however, the best and most agreeable of companions on such occasions, for he was remarkably well informed, and could converse with interest on all scientific subjects. Among our most intelligent and most polite guides were Millin, Denon, the Abbé Sicard, who was at the head of the Institution of the Blind; M. Lenoir, of the Museum of the Petits-Augustins; and Reigner, Director of the Armoury.

David was also one of our most useful cicerones. Although he and Robert did not very readily understand each other's vernacular tongue, they were both versed in the language of science, which needed no interpreter between them. I indulged a few moments of pride in the triumph of French talent over foreign prepossession. The name of David produced at first rather a singular effect; but the mist of prejudice speedily dispersed in presence of the head of our regenerated school, and David was not only received, but sought after by all that was noble or enlightened in Paris, even from the most distant lands. It was, however, in his own gallery that the victory was completed. His Belisarius was there to be retouched, which is not the less a fine picture for being somewhat inferior to Gérard's. There is poetry in the old soldier recoiling with surprise and pity at the sight of his aged General, blind, and soliciting alms. It must, I think, have been this picture which inspired Le Mercier's admirable cantata, for I can call it nothing else, which Garat has so finely set to music.

We visited the *Gobelins** and other manufactories of

---

* It has been generally said that this establishment was first instituted by Colbert, the Minister of Louis XIV. This, however, is a mistake. *Jean Gobelin* had a manufactory on the same site as the present, about the year 1400, and chose this spot, as well as many other dyers, owing

Paris, and extended our excursions to some leagues' distance, to Jouy, Virginie, Versailles, etc., and amongst other curiosities saw the steam-engine of Chaillot, called the Perrier waters, which Paris owed to the skill of two brothers of that name in 1778.

A circumstance not generally known, relating to the Perrier waters, is the controversy between two highly celebrated men on the subject of the original company's proceedings. Beaumarchais and Mirabeau were the parties in this paper war, which degenerated into virulence and abuse for want of temper on both sides; not content with carrying it through the medium of the journals, pamphlets were circulated, which are now extremely scarce, and not to be met with at all in the shops. Mirabeau accused Beaumarchais of making a stock-jobbing affair of it. The fact is that, several proprietors having treated with the Government, the latter came into sole possession, and the pumps were placed under the direction of public functionaries.

One of our earliest visits was paid, as may be supposed, to the Museum of Paintings, which, independently of the curiosity so admirable a collection (then the finest in the world) must universally inspire, was moreover a novelty to the French themselves, as the gallery had been but a very short time adorned with those numerous *chefs-d'œuvre* that we had snatched from barbarism and indifference, and in many instances, as may be proved, from approaching and total ruin.

The establishment of the Museum of Painting and Sculpture, in the situation it now so admirably occupies, is

---

to the excellent quality of a small stream, the Bièvre, for the purposes of dyeing woollen goods. This man realized a fortune, and added considerably to his premises. Subsequently Colbert purchased the whole, and it then became a royal manufactory.

due to M. Thibeaudeau, who, in 1792, was a member of the Committee of Public Instruction, where his voice was as influential as it deserved to be; and the Convention, in compliance with the report of that Committee, ordered the establishment of a National Museum, and fixed the 10th of August in that year for its opening.

On the first opening of the Gallery of the Louvre for the reception of works of art, nearly five hundred and fifty paintings, by the first masters of every school, were deposited in it; but it was not till 1798 that the museum was enriched by that profusion of inestimable treasures of art, from Italy, Piedmont, Holland, and the Netherlands, which rendered it the first in Europe.

In the spring of 1800 they were opened to general inspection; but the restoration of such works as had sustained injury was not completed till 1801, when we were at length enabled fully to enjoy the rich fruits of our various conquests. Denon had himself restored many of the finest productions to more than their pristine beauty; these were yet in the Grand Salon of the Louvre, waiting to be placed in the gallery, where they were to make an incalculable addition to the value of the treasures already committed to his charge.*

The Gallery of Apollo had been opened to the public a few days previous to our visit, and contained a new treasure, consisting of original drawings, not only of French painters, but of all the Italian schools. There we contemplated the first ideas of Raphael, Carlo Maratti, Michael Angelo Buonarotti, Leonardo da Vinci, Correggio, Guercini, the

---

* The Institute had published notices of the paintings exhibited, and Denon, though a contributor to that catalogue, had himself compiled a similar one. Both contained curious details respecting the pictures and their adventures. The walls of the gallery then displayed twelve hundred and forty pictures by the first masters, and of all the schools.

three Caraccis, Julio Romano, Perugino, Tintoretto, and a number of other illustrious names. Denon told me that this gallery had always been dedicated to drawings, which, however, till the resurrection of our Museum, remained nearly in obscurity, though amounting in number to more than eleven thousand, principally by Lebrun, Jabach, Le Sueur, Lanoue, Poussin, and others, whose slightest efforts are deserving of attentive study.

There were, however, but few drawings of the Flemish, Dutch, and German schools. Amidst that profusion, where the eye, fatigued with the beauties and wonders of the Italian school, reckoned more than three hundred original drawings of each of the famous painters I have mentioned, but one could be found of Rembrandt's, one by Ruysdael, and three by Teniers, so fertile in the productions of his easel. At that time we had only one drawing by Van Huysum; Rubens alone produced seventeen or eighteen.

It is unnecessary to dwell on the rarities that enriched the Gallery of Apollo! Magnificent tables of the finest mosaic, ancient bronzes, Etruscan vases, etc.; and in the adjoining room how many precious curiosities were deposited!

The Museum of Armoury was not in existence at the time of our rambles, but was already commenced under the superintendence of M. Reigner, and we were shown at his house a number of singular curiosities: such as a small missal, enclosing a pistol; an ancient emblazonment, partly effaced, was still sufficiently distinct to indicate its having been formerly the property of a high dignitary of the Church. M. Reigner had already amassed a large collection of rare and curious arms, which his care had preserved from the revolutionary wreck. Many notable articles from the Château of Chantilly and the Royal wardrobe were in his possession.

The armour of Joan of Arc and Charles the Bold were also among these treasures of antiquity. Joan's armour was not complete, yet the weight of the remaining portions amounted to sixty-six pounds. This feminine panoply was of most singular construction, uniting the uttermost extremes of deficiency in safety and ingenuity to avoid fatigue. I know not whether Agnes Sorel was attired in similar armour, when on her white palfrey she occasionally followed her royal paramour to the field.

During a visit we paid to M. Charles, a scientific man, who had constructed in the upper story of his house a magnificent camera obscura, a ludicrous incident occurred.

M. von Cobentzel had solicited the addition of one of his private secretaries to our party, for the purpose of taking notes of all that passed under our observation; and he desired the poor secretary to go down to the court, walk twice across it, and when in the middle to take off his hat and make us his best bow. The unfortunate wight, who did not much like the part he was to perform, set out with all the reluctance of a jaded horse. To descend two or three hundred steps, then mount again, and afterwards return by the same circuitous route, and all for the simple purpose of making a genuflexion, was not indeed calculated to afford much diversion to the actor; but he would have been amply repaid could he have witnessed the intense delight of M. von Cobentzel. No sooner did he perceive his man at the extreme point of vision than he broke into the most joyous exclamations. As he advanced, the raptures increased; but when at length the secretary, faithful to his injunctions, stopped in the middle of the court, and made us his three obeisances, civilly taking off his hat, as every man who knows how to salute is in duty bound to do, oh! then M. von Cobentzel screamed with delight, as children do the first time they see the magic-lantern—

clapped his hands, danced, and returned the salutations of the secretary, addressing him in German; in truth, it must be confessed, in extenuation of his absurdity, that it was not a little amusing to see before us, at the distance of a hundred and fifty or a hundred and eighty feet, a little figure offering to our view, not a resemblance, but the very identity of a person who, but the moment before, was of our party.

The Cabinet of Medals and Antiques was much less frequently visited during the Consulate than at the present day.* Millin, its guardian, was truly proud to usher us

---

* A slight history of the formation of the Cabinet of Medals will not be uninteresting here. The Cabinet was not always in the royal library. It was commenced at the Louvre. Francis I., who appears to have been the first King of France who interested himself in such subjects, collected some gold and silver medals of the Middle Ages, not to form a cabinet, but as ornaments for his apparel, and for that purpose had them set in rich gold and silver filigree. He was followed by Catherine de Medicis, who brought an abundant store of such curiosities from Florence. Charles IX. increased his mother's collection by that of the learned Groslier. But the civil wars, the commotions excited by the League, produced an era of destruction that nothing could resist, and the medals were almost entirely pillaged and dispersed. The good King who succeeded would willingly have remedied all the evils of those disastrous times: he recovered some of the stolen gems, and summoned the learned Bagarris to Paris, to superintend the Cabinet of Medals he intended to form. But, alas! death intervened, and his son, a perfect cipher, did not concern himself with following up the plans of his predecessor. Bagarris quitted Paris, carrying with him the treasures he would have contributed.

The fine Cabinet of Medals and Antiques of the Louvre was at length instituted by Louis XIV., that is to say, by Colbert, who, far more deserving of the name of "great" than his vainglorious master, augmented that rich collection by whatever treasures his extreme economy enabled him to purchase: he despatched enlightened connoisseurs into Switzerland, Italy, and Greece, to select the most valuable specimens; but it would seem that a sinister fate has invariably attended an institution which should be distinguished in the annals of science alone. In 1662 the Duc d'Orleans, father of the celebrated Mademoiselle, bequeathed

into his own domain, as that portion of the National Library confided to his care may be properly called. Such historical memorials of the earliest ages and of all nations offered an interesting field of investigation, and half the pleasure we derived from it may fairly be attributed to our learned instructor. The medals, when we saw them in his keeping, were not yet arranged with all the care which had been bestowed on them before the disgraceful robbery* a

---

to the King all the rarities, medals, and manuscripts in the Château de Blois, where he resided; and Bruneau, the well-informed keeper of the collection, was appointed by Louis conservator of the medals of the royal cabinet. In November, 1666, this unfortunate man was assassinated and robbed in the Louvre itself; and the circumstances of the crime made it apparent that the medals were the object of the assassins. The precious deposit was, in consequence, transferred to the royal library, which was then, as it is now, in the Rue Vivienne.

An antiquary named Vaillant enriched the Cabinet of Medals by an ample harvest brought from Africa, Persia, and the most distant countries. In 1776, under the reign of Louis XVI., it acquired the immense collection of M. Pélerin, comprising many rare and precious articles, and amounting to no less than thirty thousand medals.

* In M. de Sartines' days the police was of another complexion; but, without travelling so far back, such an event would not have occurred under Comte Dubois' administration.

During M. de Sartines' lieutenancy of police in France he received a letter from the Minister of the same department at Vienna, stating that a great criminal had taken refuge in Paris, to the certain knowledge of the police at Vienna; and entreating M. de Sartines, in virtue of the friendly relations existing between the two Courts, to adopt every means for the arrest of the criminal, whose person and dress were described with the utmost minuteness. M. de Sartines issued his orders accordingly: his subordinates were set to work; neither garret nor cellar escaped their scrutiny; the most active search was continued upwards of a month. At length, after five or six weeks had elapsed, M. de Sartines writes to his brother of Vienna:

"SIR AND DEAR BROTHER,—Immediately upon the receipt of your letter, I hastened to make inquiries in every direction for the criminal you had described. The efforts of my people were for a long time fruitless, but we have at length succeeded in discovering him, and I

few years later, but the collection already boasted of upwards of sixteen hundred drawers.

---

have the pleasure of informing you that it is in your power to seize him immediately, for he is at this moment in Vienna, which he has never quitted; you will find him in such a faubourg, at such a number."

Every indication by which the fugitive could be traced was exactly given, even to a flower-pot standing on his chamber-window.

This story reminds me of another and very amusing one respecting M. de Sartines.

He had a friend for whom he entertained a fraternal attachment. Such friendships are sometimes dangerous; but, be this as it may, his affection was as warm as two compatriots might be supposed to entertain for each other in Monomotapia, with no other civilized being near. His friend, on the other hand, thought it advisable to play the Monomotapian in earnest, but in quite a different sense, as will presently appear. One day, in the course of conversation, the friend said:

"The police is a fine thing, to be sure! I am sure nothing useful ever comes to your knowledge! You learn only what you are intended to know!"

M. de Sartines grew angry. To doubt the alertness of his myrmidons was to dispute his omnipotence, for his credit at Versailles rested entirely on their unparalleled ingenuity in tracing the most difficult clues. He asked his friend, in a tone of defiance, whether he would not be much astonished to hear the most circumstantial detail of everything he had done or said for a whole week.

A secret reflection made the latter smile at the proposal.

"Well, let us try," said he: "I consent; but I wager a hundred louis that your hounds are at fault; and, remember, all you may accomplish will stand for nothing if a single hour is unaccounted for."

"That is a matter of course," said M. de Sartines.

The two friends shook hands upon it, and the execution of the enterprize was to commence the next day. On the second morning the scout who was charged with watching the friend, and whose new task allowed a holiday to the pickpockets and cut-purses of Paris, made his appearance before M. de Sartines and delivered his report; which specified that the party had risen at nine o'clock, had put on his slippers and dressing-gown, had sneezed, yawned, and coughed for a quarter of an hour, then had taken chocolate, read the *Mercure de France* and one of Freron's bulletins, had written a note, but it was not known to whom, because he had instantly put it into his pocket, where even an emissary

I cannot exactly recollect whether it was General Hitroff, aide-de-camp to the Emperor Alexander, then in Paris, and

of police could not follow; but it was a love-letter, that was ascertained, for the paper was perfumed, and the note folded in a particular manner. It was decidedly a love-letter. After this the friend had walked to the Tuileries, taken a few turns on the river terrace, then walked three times up and down a certain portion of the centre alley; had saluted Mademoiselle Arnould three times, Madame Dugazon once, Mademoiselle Gaussin twice; then had dined at M. le Premier's, because one cannot stay in the garden for ever saluting one's friends, however charming. After dinner he had been Madame le Premier's partner at cribbage, had won eight louis, and nobly lost them again at quinze. After this he had been to the Opera, had directed his glass to all the boxes, and scrutinized all the ladies—one especially. After the Opera he had supped with M. de Sartines. "It appeared," said the report, "that he must have made an indifferent dinner, for he supped like a half-famished man: he ate of five or six dishes," and, to do the spy justice, M. de Sartines found the delicacies of his table scrupulously recapitulated. "But, Monseigneur," said the last lines of the report, "my comrades and I found it equally impossible to discover what became of M. de —— on leaving your hotel; his carriage drove with such rapidity that no human being could keep pace with it."

"What, wretch!" exclaimed M. de Sartines, "you have been wearying me to death these two hours with insipid details about slippers, and dressing-gowns, and eating; and then you lose the scent at the very moment it should be most acute. Take care that you succeed better to-morrow; I must know how every minute of M. de ——'s time is employed."

"My dear friend," said he, the next day, "I have heard news of you, as I will prove at the end of the week. . . . Ah! ah! ah! This is the way you proceed! Stay, I will give you a bit of friendly advice: Do not seek the company of actresses so much. Yesterday, at the Tuileries, you were seen with the most fascinating ones; I do not like to see you the dupe of such infatuation. . . . And afterwards at the Opera! Take my advice—choose better company. . . . The real pleasures of the heart are not to be met with in so low a sphere. You understand me?"

"Yes, indeed," answered his friend, "and so much the more readily, that I have not waited to receive your advice before I followed it."

"Really?" said M. de Sartines, with a look of surprise.

"Really—yes."

one of the best-informed persons I have ever met with in the numismatic science, that accompanied us to the Cabinet

---

"Then you will make me your confidant?"

"Certainly not; it is your part to find out all you want to know; I am mute."

M. de Sartines, whose curiosity was excited by his friend's expressions, awaited with still greater impatience the next day's report; but was again disappointed. The slippers, the dressing-gown, the chocolate, all appeared in their turn; but from midnight to one o'clock M. de —— disappeared, as if by enchantment, and no trace of him could by any means be found. M. de Sartines flew into a passion, and told his scouts:

"I discharge you all, unless you bring me to-morrow such a report as I have required."

The persons thus menaced looked at each other as they left their master's cabinet.

"What is to be done?" said one to the leader.

"There is no alternative," replied he, and communicated his plan.

The following morning M. de —— had just put on his slippers, and thrust his arms into the sleeves of the dressing-gown so well described in the informers' reports, and was about to seat himself before a cup of that smoking and savoury coffee the precise quality of which had been recited; his lips had just relaxed into that triumphant smile of roguish malice when his valet announced three men who were earnestly desirous to see him. "They begged," said the valet, "as a particular favour, to be admitted."

M. de —— was not inaccessible; he ordered that they should be introduced, and then sent away his valet.

"M. le Comte," said the chief of the party in a supplicating accent, "you would not deprive brave men, all fathers of families, of their subsistence. We come to beg you will save our lives; for if we are dismissed from our vocation we shall no longer have bread, and no resource will be left us but to hang or drown ourselves."

So saying, all threw themselves on their knees.

"My good friends," cried M. de ——, hastening to raise them; "for Heaven's sake, what is the matter with you? How can I influence your fate? I do not understand you."

"Alas! your wager with M. de Sartines is the matter in question: we are to inform him of your proceedings from minute to minute. We are fully acquainted with them . . . but——"

M. de —— began to unriddle the mystery.

of Medals, or a Germanized Dane; but which ever it was, his presence gave rise to a warm discussion respecting one of the votive bucklers found in the Rhone, upon which opinions were very much divided; the foreigner maintaining that the design represented the continence of Scipio, while Millin defended the antiquity of his buckler, declaring it to mean the restoration of Briseis to Achilles, and this opinion agrees with that of Winckelman. It weighs forty-two marks, and is six feet and a half in circumference; another is forty-three marks in weight and six feet nine inches round. The Cabinet contains numerous similar pieces, but our scientific riches consisted chiefly in medals. We had many that were unique, and the nationality of such a treasure ought to have made cupidity itself tremble to covet it. The gold medallion of Justinian, which is justly at the head of the collection, is three inches in diameter. Another choice medallion engraved with a fine head of Pescennius Niger, is in silver. Next to this were medals of Romulus; Alexander, a tyrant in Africa; and the younger Antoninus. If this last medal has been stolen, it is an irreparable loss to art and to France, so indeed are all the others I have mentioned above.

"But, you understand, M. le Comte, it is impossible we can say that you are visiting Madame de Sartines at the hours when we are compelled to pretend that we lose sight of you . . . and yet we must speak. Either permit us to invent a falsehood, or change your direction."

M. de —— looked at the chief speaker, and smiled.

"Thou art a clever fellow," said he, throwing him a purse filled with gold. "There, divide that with thy comrades—I lose my wager."

He tried their discretion no further, as may be supposed, but admitted the accuracy of their next report, and acknowledged himself vanquished; while M. de Sartines, rubbing his hands, repeated:

"I was confident of it! How could you think, my dear fellow, that anything could be concealed from a lieutenant-general of police?" and afterwards added: "I could only wish you were more regular in your habits. Why, deuce take it, my good fellow, why can't you choose from good society?"

Amongst other parts of the National Library, we saw the Cabinet of Manuscripts, [at the head of which at that time was M. Langles] containing Chinese manuscripts, those of the Arabian Tales, the "Thousand and One Nights," so dear to all who have fertile and creative imaginations; an immense quantity of Hebrew, Tartar, Greek, and Latin manuscripts, and amongst them perfect copies of Propertius, Catullus, Tibullus, and Sappho, and a poem by Claudian, etc. It is well known that the library now occupies the *Palais Mazarin*, and that the largest of its five rooms was formerly the Cardinal's library. It is a hundred and forty feet long by twenty-two in width. The ceiling was painted by Romanelli.

The Cabinet of Engravings, water-colour drawings, title-deeds, and genealogies is also very curious; the collection of engravings made by the Abbé Marolles contains specimens from the year 1470, when the art was first invented, up to the present day. I would particularly recommend to the attention of visitors a collection of engravings or stamps made to illustrate an edition of Dante in the year 1481, only eleven years after the first invention of the art.

At the time we thus visited, like foreign travellers, this magnificent depôt of human truth and error, the number of its printed books, as we were informed by the persons at the head of the establishment, was upwards of three hundred thousand; of the manuscripts, fifty thousand; and the Cabinet of Engravings contained about three hundred thousand subjects in ten thousand portfolios. We visited also the libraries of the various public edifices, but after examining that which I had so much admired it was mere waste of time. It must certainly be admitted that, in whatever advances the interests of science, Paris is the most amply endowed city in the world.

All the charitable institutions, of which I had partly the

superintendence, by virtue of Junot's office as Commandant, of course occupied part of our attention, as well as other establishments calculated to excite curiosity; such as the Orphan Asylum, the Museum of Natural History, that temple of Nature, comprising an abridgment of the universe, which the solicitous care of Messieurs Thibeaudeau and Fourcroy rescued from the general destruction of the days of terror; and to which M. Chaptal, when he rose to a place in the Ministry, afforded his special protection, as belonging to the science he professed.

We dedicated one day to a survey of the Barriers, those proofs of the folly of M. de Calonne, and no less of M. de Brienne, however he may have afterwards repented it. Those Barriers, destined to promote the interests only of the farmers-general of the revenue, excited complaints all over the city. The new enclosure appeared to its inhabitants a species of prison, and even the unnecessary and ridiculous pains bestowed on the decoration of the Barriers could not reconcile them to their confinement; but as the good citizens cannot even scold without a laugh, ballads were composed on the subject—for what do we not turn into ballads? Among other epigrams, the following was produced:

"Le mur murant Paris rend Paris murmurant."

These excursions occupied altogether six weeks; the party constantly varying with the engagements of our friends, who had all occasionally other calls, some of business, others of pleasure; for my own part, I have preserved to the present moment an agreeable remembrance of those days which passed so rapidly, yet were so well filled.

About this time an event occurred which made much noise at Paris. Mademoiselle Chameroi, a famous dancer, had died in childbed, greatly lamented by Vestris. The

Curé of Saint Roche deemed the profession of the deceased and the mode of her death doubly scandalous, and refused her admission within the pale of the Church.

The people of Paris were not yet, as in 1816, replaced under the ecclesiastic sceptre; they were discontented; the Curé did but augment the evil by grounding his refusal on facts injurious to the memory of the unhappy deceased; the storm had begun to threaten, when it was dispersed by Dazincourt, who acted in this emergency with courage and firmness, and succeeded in preventing a scandal still greater than that which the Curé sought to avoid, for the people were beginning to talk of forcing the church doors. Dazincourt prevailed on them to carry the body to the church belonging to the Convent of the Filles Saint Thomas, where the functionary performed the funeral service, and the matter terminated.

Not so the First Consul's displeasure; his recent restitution of the clergy to their churches, and provision for their support, was accompanied by the implied condition that intolerance and fanaticism should be expunged from their creed; and a sort of hostile declaration on their part, following so closely upon the recovery of their immunities, extorted a frown, and excited him to let fall some of those expressions which never escaped him but when he was violently agitated.

"They were foolish to insist," said he, in the presence of a large company; "if the Curé of Saint Roche was determined to create scandal, they should have carried the corpse straight to the cemetery, and induced the first wise and tolerant priest who passed near to bless the grave; there are still many good ones—the Archbishop of Paris, for instance! He is a worthy clergyman. What a venerable old age is his! That man may say within himself:

"'I have attained this advanced age without having

injured anyone: I have never done anything but good.' And do you know why? Because he acts upon the moral precepts of the Gospel. Whenever in his former diocese he wanted alms for the poor, and a ball or *fête* was given in the neighbourhood, he appeared among the company to plead the cause of charity, while their hearts were opened by mirth and pleasure: he knew that they were then most sensible to virtuous impressions, and his austerity did not take alarm at a dance tune. Yes, he is a worthy priest."

The Curé of Saint Roche was condemned to do penance, which was announced officially to his parishioners in the *Moniteur*. The latter article is in a peculiar style which betrays the hand, or at least the mind, of the First Consul; those who intimately knew him will recognize the turn of his phraseology in the following copy:

"*The Curé of Saint Roche, in a temporary forgetfulness of reason, has refused to pray for Mademoiselle Chameroi, and to admit her remains within the church. One of his colleagues, a sensible man, versed in the true morality of the Gospel, received the body into the Church of the Filles Saint Thomas, where the service was performed with all the usual solemnities. The Archbishop has ordered the Curé of Saint Roche three months' suspension to remind him that Jesus Christ commands us to pray even for our enemies: and in order that, recalled to a sense of his duty by meditation, he may learn that all the superstitious practices preserved by some rituals, but which, begotten in times of ignorance, or created by the over-heated imagination of zealots, degrade religion by their frivolity, were proscribed by the Concordat, and by the law of the 18th Germinal.*"

Poor Mademoiselle Chameroi was a charming dancer, and pirouetted delightfully;* but how would her reputation fall

* See vol. ii., p. 19.

off now, if compared with Mademoiselle Taglioni! The career of the Opera has effaced that of all the other theatres; their glories are extinct while it has risen higher—but in its company and decorations only; such beautiful ballets as *Psyche* and the *Danso-Mania*, *Flora* and *Zephyrus*, and many other charming compositions of the olden time, must no longer be looked for.

CHAPTER XXXVII.

The First Consul's Sponsorship—The Eldest Son of Madame Lannes, and my Daughter, the First Godchildren of Bonaparte—Cardinal Caprara and the Chapel of Saint Cloud—Napoleon's Ambassadors—Anecdote of the Prince Regent of England and General Andréossy, related by the First Consul—Madame Lannes, Madame Devaisne, Madame de Montesquiou, and Napoleon's Preferences—Lannes the Rolando of the French Army—My Daughter's Destiny—Ceremony of Baptism at Saint Cloud—Cardinal Caprara's Cap—Baptismal Gifts of the First Consul and Madame Bonaparte—Return of the Army from Egypt—Bianca, the Heroine of the Army—M. and Madame Verdier—Anecdotes—Marmont and his Wife—General Colbert—General Menou and M. Maret.

THE children to whom the First Consul stood sponsor with Madame Bonaparte (for he did not admit anyone else to share the office with him, except, indeed, very rarely, Madame Bonaparte the mother, and Madame Louis, his sister-in-law) were always baptized with imposing ceremony. Soon after the publication of the Concordat, several children, and amongst them my Josephine, the first god-daughter of Napoleon, and the eldest son of Madame Lannes, were waiting till the First Consul should appoint the time to be admitted to the sacrament of regeneration.

I received with pleasure an intimation to hold myself in readiness with my daughter, as in two days Cardinal Caprara, the Apostolic Nuncio, would perform the ceremony for these little ones in the Consular Chapel at Saint Cloud. I do not know whether Cardinal Caprara may be very well remembered at present; but he was one of the most crafty emissaries that ever obtained, even from the seat of Saint Peter, a temporary share in the commerce of diplomacy. Notwithstanding the decrepitude of his mien, the weak and subdued key of his musical voice, the humility of his deportment, and the stealthy inquisitiveness of his glance, that head concealed under its gray hairs and the scarlet cap of his order more subtlety, more cunning, more petty perfidy than can well be imagined.

The First Consul, at that time, liked him tolerably well, seeing in his various artifices only a source of amusement; for, as nothing could then exceed the frank simplicity of our diplomacy, the Nuncio's guarded reserve and insidious scrutiny were equally waste of time. General Lannes and Junot, ambassadors to Lisbon, General Beurnonville to Madrid, General Hedouville to St. Petersburg, Andréossy to London, Sebastiani to Constantinople; all these selections, made by Napoleon from the military ranks, sufficiently proved that the missions with which they were charged required no other enforcement than the will of him from whom they derived their credentials. It is true, the national vanity suffered a little from the proceedings of some of these personages, a rather diverting register of which is in existence, exhibiting sundry infringements of courtly etiquette; notwithstanding all which, this was, to my mind, the most glorious era of French diplomacy.*

---

* The First Consul once related an anecdote which he considered favourable to the Prince Regent's good taste, and it was very unusual for Napoleon to approve any word or act of the Prince of Wales, for whom he certainly felt no partiality, and was aware that the dislike was reciprocal.

General Andréossy had replaced M. Otto in London; the General was by no means deficient in politeness; he had been very well edu-

But where have I been wandering? From the keen, wily, artful Cardinal Caprara, all reverential obsequiousness, coughing in the chapel of Saint Cloud, in full canonicals, with his eyes, and great part of his cheeks, concealed behind an immense pair of green spectacles. A remedy, perhaps you imagine, for weakness of sight. No such thing; but

cated, but was unversed in the language of courts; he had entered the military service previously to the Revolution, and was then too young to have acquired, from intercourse with the best society of that day, those polished and deferential manners which are exacted by the highest ranks in all countries. England is, perhaps, of all the nations of Europe, the most rigorous in this exaction. He was frequently in company with the Prince of Wales, then the most amiable of heirs-apparent, the most liberal of men in all his notions. He frequently met the French Ambassador at the Duchess of Devonshire's and other tables, where the affability, easiness of access, and apparently compliant and obliging disposition of a personage so near the throne, could not fail of giving universal satisfaction; while the profound and ceremonious respect observed by all who approached the Prince, and of which his utmost condescension never tolerated a moment's transgression, imparted to his Royal Highness's popularity a tinge of aristocratic homage, the singular effect of which cannot be thoroughly understood by a stranger to English manners. General Andréossy, who was always politely saluted by the Prince of Wales, perceiving that his Royal Highness accosted with perfect familiarity several persons whom he (the General) considered greatly his own inferiors, imagined he might use his discretion as to etiquette, and chatted accordingly with the Prince in a style of easy indifference that soon became insupportable to one who prized above all things that extreme elegance and polished high-breeding of which he was the English model. Amongst his familiarities was a habit the General had contracted of calling him *mon Prince!* "Good God!" said he one day, to someone near him, "do pray tell General Andréossy to desist from calling me *mon Prince!* Why, I shall be taken for a Russian Prince." To comprehend the full point of this repartee, it must be recollected that both France and England were at that time inundated with foreigners, especially with Russians, the greater part of whom were called "my Prince," because their fathers, or perhaps their grandfathers, had been capital horsemen on the banks of the Borysthenes, or the Yaïk, the only qualification for nobility amongst the Cossacks.

fearing the penetrating look of the First Consul, that glance which was dreaded even by the most crafty, he intrenched himself behind a redoubt as the best means of escaping it. I have been told it was but a repetition of the part his Eminence had enacted at Florence during the negotiation of a treaty, in the course of the Italian wars; but Napoleon, who knew that the Cardinal was not weak sighted, rallied him so effectually, in the present instance, that the spectacles disappeared.

On the day appointed for the baptism, we all went to Saint Cloud with our children. Madame Lannes and I were the two most advanced in our maternity. Her eldest son, Napoleon, afterwards second Duc de Montebello, was only a few months older than my daughter. He was a good and lovely child, and possessed a degree of sensibility very rare at so tender an age; his mother doted on him, and not only punctually fulfilled all the maternal duties imperiously enjoined by nature, but entirely devoted herself to him with a self-denial highly meritorious in a young woman of such uncommon beauty and attractions. The First Consul professed a high esteem for her; and this was no slight distinction, for during the fourteen years of Napoleon's power I have known but two other females, Madame Devaisne and Madame de Montesquiou, to whom he gave proofs of similar respect; though he may have felt a warmer friendship for others, to say nothing of a more tender sentiment.

The conduct of Madame Lannes has on all occasions justified the preference shown her by Napoleon over the other ladies attached to his military Court, who were highly affronted at seeing her seated more frequently than themselves on the right of the First Consul at table, chosen for a party at cards, at a hunt, or an excursion to Malmaison. These decided marks of favour were no doubt partly ascribable to her husband, "that Rolando of the French army," as Napoleon called him, but those who, like myself, have intimately known Madame Lannes, can conscientiously certify that they were as much due to her own character as to the General's fame, and of this the Emperor gave her the strongest proof in nominating her as lady of honour to his second wife—to her who was the object of his tenderest solicitude, and who, in return, conferred on him nothing but misfortunes, fetters, and death.

My daughter at the period of her baptism promised all the loveliness and grace which her advancing years matured. I may be pardoned this effusion of maternal pride, for that beauty, those graces, and, I may add, those talents, and, dearest of all, those virtues, are buried within a religious cloister, and my child has bid adieu to the world.* Napoleon used to smile at the illusion I sought to pass upon myself at that period in dressing my child as a boy.

"What is your design?" inquired he one day, rather seriously, looking at my little girl, beautiful as a Cupid, in a little dark gray sailor's jacket and black beaver hat. "What object have you in putting that child into such a dress? Do you destine her for the superlative task of regenerating her sex, and restoring the race of the Amazons?" The inflexion of his voice, his smile, the expression of his eye, all indicated a degree of satire which made me cautious in my answer. "General," replied I, "I have no intention of making a Joan of Arc of my child. The bronze circle of a helmet and its chin-piece would be a very unsuitable mounting for those pretty cheeks, where the lily and rose strive for mastery." The First Consul looked again at my daughter. "It is true that little noisy pet of yours is very pretty," said he, recollecting the circumstances of her baptism, "and if she is

---

* Mademoiselle Josephine Junot in after-years returned to the world and married M. Amet.

not to wear a helmet or set a lance in rest, I suppose it will one day be her vocation to be POPESS."*

This was in allusion to an amusing little scene which took place at the time when with pride I carried my beautiful child in my arms to the baptismal font. She was then fifteen months old; the chapel, the numerous company, the clergy, and the bustle, so terrified the poor little creature that, hiding her pretty face in my bosom, she burst into tears. She had not yet seen Cardinal Caprara; his toilet, on occasions of ceremony, was not quickly completed.

He made his entrance at length from the sacristy, as red as a ripe pomegranate, resplendent in the blaze of many pastoral and cardinal rubies, and eminent in withered ugliness sufficient to scare infantine minds accustomed only to look upon gay smiles and merry faces. As soon as Josephine saw him I felt her cling closer to me and tremble in my arms, her rosy cheeks turning pale as death.

When the service was nearly ended, and the First Consul and Madame Bonaparte approached the font to present the infants for the ceremony of sprinkling, "Give me your child, Madame Junot," said the First Consul; and he endeavoured to take her, but she uttered a piercing cry, and, casting a look of anger on Napoleon, twined her little arms closer round my neck. "What a little devil! Well, then, will you please to come to me, Mademoiselle Demon?" said he to the little one.

The little Josephine, however, did not understand his words, but seeing his hands held out to take her, and knowing that her will, whether negative or commanding, was pretty generally absolute, she raised her pretty head, fixed her bright eyes on him, and answered in her childish prattle: "I will not." The First Consul laughed. "Well, keep

* This prediction was curiously borne out, the boy-girl mentioned above becoming for a time a Canoness.

her in your arms then," said he to me ; " but do not cry any more," he added, threatening the child with his finger, " or else——"

But his menaces were unnecessary. Josephine, now brought nearer to the Cardinal, was no longer afraid of him, but no doubt thought him something very extraordinary ; and her eyes, fixed on the Prelate, seemed to inquire what sort of animal he was. The Cardinal wore on his head the little black cap resembling those of our advocates, and which is the sign that sanctifies the purple, and the object of ambition to every man who enters the ecclesiastical profession. Its whimsical form, surmounting a face no less singular, captivated Josephine in the highest degree. She murmured no more, shed not another tear, suffered the First Consul to take, and even to embrace her, and imprint several kisses on her little round cherry cheeks without any other mark of dissatisfaction than wiping her cheek with the back of her little plump hand after every kiss.

But her large eyes were meanwhile riveted upon the person of the venerable Cardinal with an eager attention truly laughable. All at once, when no one could possibly guess what the little plague was meditating, she raised her round, fair, soft arm, and with her little hand seized and carried off the cap or *biretta* from his Eminence's head, with a scream of triumph loud enough to be heard in the courts of the castle.

The poor Cardinal, and all the assistants at the ceremony, male and female, were as much alarmed and surprised as diverted by this achievement. Josephine alone preserved her gravity. She looked at us all round with an inexpressibly comic air of triumph, and appeared determined to place the cap on her own head. " Oh no, my child !" said the First Consul, who had at last recovered from his laughing fit ; "with your leave—no such thing. Give me your plaything—for it is but a bauble, like so many others," added he, smiling—" and we will restore it to the Cardinal."

But Josephine was in no humour to surrender her prize; she would put it on my head, or on her godfather's own, but she had no notion of restoring it to the cranium to which it rightfully pertained, and when taken from her by force her cries were tremendous. "Your daughter is a perfect demon," said the First Consul to Junot; "by heavens! she has as stout a voice as the most masculine boy in France! But she is very pretty—she really is pretty." As he spoke he held her in his arms, and gazed on that captivating face, which in fact was "really very pretty." She looked at Bonaparte without resentment, and talked no more of leaving him; she even made a slight resistance when I took her from his arms.

"She is my *godchild, my child*," said he, pressing her father's hand. "I hope you rely on that—do you not, Junot?" Junot in such moments had not a word to offer; his heart was too full. He turned a moistened eye on the First Consul, and, when able to speak, said in a faltering voice: "General, I and all mine have long been accustomed to owe all the blessings of our existence to your bounty. My children will experience its effects, as their parents have done; and, like their parents, they will devote their blood and their lives to you."

The day after my eldest daughter's baptism Madame Bonaparte sent me a necklace, consisting of several rows of fine pearls of the size of large currants; the clasp was composed of a single pearl of the purest whiteness, to which the First Consul added a present of a different kind—no other than the receipted purchase-contract of our hotel in the Rue des Champs-Elysées, which had been paid by Napoleon's order as a baptismal gift. It cost two hundred thousand francs.

I have not taken sufficient notice of an important event that occurred about this time—the return of the Army of Egypt. I was already acquainted with many of Junot's friends; but every day now witnessed the arrival of troops of brothers-in-arms and companions in danger, whom Junot would run to meet, press their hands, embrace them with transport, and introduce them to me—so rejoiced was he to see them return safe and sound, after escaping the sabres of the Mamelukes and the perfidy of the English.

One day the servant announced that General Verdier awaited him in his cabinet, and that there was a lady with him. "By Jove!" exclaimed Junot, "that must be our dear gallant Bianca. I must run to see her. Laura, I bespeak your friendship for her; she is a charming woman." And away he flew. I had often heard of Madame Verdier, and knew that, having followed the army to Italy as a singer and actress under the name of Bianca, she had married General Verdier, and afterwards followed her husband in the Eastern campaign, where she never quitted his side. I had heard numerous traits of her admirable conduct, and had learned to esteem without knowing her; but the idea I had formed of the person by no means corresponded with the figure now introduced by Junot.

My imagination had portrayed a tall masculine form, jet-black eyes, raven hair, tawny skin, and, in short, the whole semblance of a *Chevalier* d'Eon: my surprise may therefore be conceived on seeing a small, well-made, pretty, graceful woman enter the apartment, with chesnut hair, complexion rather inclining to fair than brown, shy and pleasing manners, and a voice soft as music! Madame Verdier, in short, very rapidly gained my heart. Some portion of her history I knew almost from day to day, for she had traversed the desert in company with Junot, who had imparted to me his vivid remembrance of everything that passed during that journey. "What!" said I, taking her delicate little hands; "could this wrist lift a sword, fire a pistol, and guide a spirited Arabian horse?" "Oh yes, dear madame," answered she, with that soft inflexion of voice which in an Italian is harmony itself, "to be sure I used a sword! but, Holy Virgin! not to kill. But you know I must follow the General."

And from the naïveté of her tone it might have been supposed it was obligatory on all wives to follow their husbands to the wars. Then she recited her fatigues in the desert; spoke of the burning simoom, and of Junot's giving her the small remains of water he had preserved, and afterwards his cloak to shelter her from the abundant dew, and making her a seat of two crossed muskets.

"*Caro, Caro!*" And she held out to him her pretty little hand, which he shook as heartily as he would have shaken her husband's. "Madame Verdier must be one of your nearest friends," said Junot, addressing me. Then he told me that in crossing the desert her horse was once a little behind; and she was hastening to rejoin her troop, when she met an unfortunate soldier afflicted with ophthalmia, which had quite destroyed his sight. The poor creature was wandering in that sea of burning sands without guidance or assistance, and gave himself up for lost.

Madame Verdier approached and questioned him, and perceived with a shudder that his sight was totally lost. And no relief at hand! no possibility of procuring a guide! "Well, then, I will be your guide," said Madame Verdier. "Come here, my friend; give me your hand—there—now do not let go my horse; when you are weary you shall mount him, and I will lead you. We shall proceed more slowly, but God will protect us—no misfortune will overtake us." "Oh!" said the poor soldier, "do those sweet sounds that I hear fall from an angel's voice?" "An angel! Why, my friend, I am the wife of the brave General Verdier!" And the excellent woman said this with an accent of simplicity and nature that went to the heart.

Madame Verdier brought me that day an article which, with all my experience in perfumery, I have never since been able to procure—a large bottle of essence of roses. It was neither attar of roses nor that rose-water which we Europeans use for strengthening the eyes, but gave the perfume of an actual bunch of the living flower in its most odoriferous species. She told me that the Egyptian women use this delicious essence, to which no other perfume bears any resemblance, when bathing. It had none of the strength of the attar of roses, which affects the head so violently and attacks the nerves; it was mild, sweet, enchanting.

The Comtesse Verdier is no longer living, but the General is immortal.

Among the most remarkable of the acquaintances recommended to me by Junot were, the excellent M. Desgenettes—for whom I speedily felt a sincere regard, that subsequent years have not diminished—and General Davoût, since a Marshal, whose return had preceded that of the rest of the army by some months. He frequently visited both me and Madame Marmont, to whom I was much attached, for no sooner did she arrive from Italy, after my marriage, than Junot said to me:

"Laura, Madame Marmont is the wife of the man whom, next to the First Consul, I love best in the world. I cannot pretend to direct your affections, but if Madame Marmont should inspire you with sentiments similar to those I entertain for her husband, it will make me very happy." Fortunately I found her all I could desire in a friend; and our intimacy was based, on my side, on real affection. General Joseph Lagrange, General Menou,

M. Daure, the two brothers of Augustus Colbert, one of whom, now Lieutenant-General Edward Colbert, was about this time aide-de-camp to my husband: these names, and many others which memory has safely guarded, but which space will not permit me to record here, were then pronounced in my hearing with expressions of attachment and esteem.

Never did I see more convincing proof of Junot's goodness of heart than at this period of his life. His joy and emotion on again meeting his comrades were sincere and extreme. The First Consul was equally affected, but his feeling partook of that grief which the loss of a dear friend occasions; and though he never showed his dissatisfaction, I am sure he felt resentment and ill-will against General Menou. That officer owed it to the good offices of M. Maret, then Secretary of State, that he was not disgraced, and also his appointment at a later period to the government of the Transalpine Provinces.

CHAPTER XXXVIII.

Prolongation of Bonaparte's Consulate—*Senatus Consultum*—Remarkable Answer and Prophetic Words of Napoleon—Breakfast given to Madame Bonaparte at my House in the Rue des Champs-Elysées—General Suchet and his Brother—Present of a Hundred Thousand Francs—My Ball, at which the First Consul was present—Madame Bonaparte as Erigone—The Consulate for Life—The Wish of the Nation—Junot's Objections to the Measure—His Quarrel with Napoleon, and his Illness—The First Consul's Conversation with me at Saint Cloud—His Visit to Junot when Ill—Junot's Recovery.

It was in the spring of 1802 that the first appeal was made to Napoleon's ambition to reign, by his nomination as Consul for another ten years, after the expiration of the ten years fixed by the constitutional act of the 13th of December, 1799. Very little attention was at that time paid to this renewal or prolongation of power; and the *Senatus Consultum*, which appointed Napoleon Consul for life, conveyed the first warning to the French people that they had acquired a new Master.

It declared that "the French Republic, desirous of retaining at the head of her Government the Magistrate who had so repeatedly in Europe and in Asia conducted her troops to victory; who had delivered Italy; who had moreover preserved his country from the horrors of anarchy, broken the revolutionary scythe, extinguished civil discords, and given her peace; for it was he alone who had pacified the seas and the Continent, restored order and morality, and re-established the authority of the law: the Republic, filled with gratitude towards General Bonaparte for these benefits, entreats him to bestow on her another ten years of that existence which she considers necessary to her happiness."

The First Consul's reply is admirably conceived in the style of true simplicity and noble elevation, and is, besides, pervaded by a tincture of melancholy, the more remarkable as the expressions are for the most part prophetic: "I have lived but to serve my country," replied he to the Senate— "Fortune has smiled on the Republic; but Fortune is inconstant; and how many men whom she has loaded with her favours have lived a few years too long! As soon as the peace of the world shall be proclaimed, the interest of my glory and my happiness will appear to point out the term of my public life. But you conceive that I owe the people a new sacrifice, and I will make it," etc.

The important decree I have cited above was presented to the First Consul, and his answer returned on the 6th of May, 1802 (20th Germinal of the year x.). Junot, who felt for him that passionate attachment which makes everything a matter of ardent interest which affects the happiness or honour of its object, said to me: "We must celebrate at the same time this memorable event in the life of my General, which testifies the love of a great nation, and our gratitude to the First Consul and Madame Bonaparte for their generous favours. You must invite Madame Bonaparte to breakfast at our house in the Rue des Champs-Elysées, before it is completed. She must even see it in its present state; to wait till it is furnished would delay the project too long, and would, moreover, deprive us of a new opportunity of inviting her. Arrange the matter with

Madame Bonaparte, and I will undertake for the First Consul."

I waited then on Madame Bonaparte and preferred my request: she received it with extreme kindness. She was gracious whenever an opportunity allowed, and with a charm of manner that enhanced her favours. She accepted my invitation, therefore, conditionally.

"Have you mentioned it to Bonaparte?" said she. I told her that Junot was then with the First Consul making his request, and she replied: "We must wait his answer, then; for I can accept no *fête* or dinner without Bonaparte's special permission."

This was very true; I had myself been witness to a sharp lecture she received from the First Consul for having breakfasted with a lady for whom he himself entertained the highest esteem, Madame Devaisnes, only because he had had no previous notice of it. I believe he was actuated by prudential motives, and a knowledge of Madame Bonaparte's extreme facility in accepting everything offered to her; at the Tuileries it was difficult to approach her, as no one could visit there without authority; yet even there a few intriguing old ladies paid their respects to her regularly three or four times a week, with petitions, demands for prefectures, seats in the Senate, commands of military divisions, places under the Receiver-General; in short, nothing was forgotten in this long list, except the good sense which should have prevented such unbecoming interference.

The First Consul was aware that her favours were so unsparingly and indiscriminately distributed that she would sometimes make fifteen promises at a single breakfast, dinner, or *fête;* he was consequently extremely particular where he allowed her to go. He knew, however, that at our house she would meet only the same persons who visited at the Tuileries.

Junot was delighted at the kindness with which the First Consul had received his request; he had granted it, but with the singular addition of desiring that no other men should join the party except Duroc and Junot, while the women were to be twenty-five. The breakfast took place, but was not honoured by the presence of the First Consul. Madame Bonaparte and Madame Louis came without him. Madame Bacciochi and Madame Murat were also present, and all my young married comrades, if I may apply that term to the wives of Junot's brothers-in-arms.

Some were very agreeable, and all in the beauty of freshness and youth, so that no spectacle could be prettier than that our table exhibited, when surrounded on this occasion by from twenty-five to thirty young and cheerful faces, of which not more than one or two could be called ordinary. Madame Bonaparte was an astonishing woman, and must have formerly been extremely pretty, for though now no longer in the first bloom of youth, her personal charms were still striking. Had she only possessed teeth, she would certainly have outvied nearly all the ladies of the Consular Court.

The breakfast passed off very well. When it was disposed of, Madame Bonaparte chose to visit every part of the house, and in this amusement the morning passed rapidly away. At three Madame Bonaparte proposed a drive to the Bois de Boulogne. General Suchet and his brother accompanied us, and did not take their leave till we re-entered Paris. During the drive Madame Bonaparte conversed with me respecting our new establishment, and concluded by saying that she was commissioned by the First Consul to inform Junot and myself that he presented us with the sum of a hundred thousand francs for furnishing our house. "It is ready," added Madame Bonaparte; "Estève has orders to hold it at your disposal. For it is of no use, Bonaparte says, to give them a house unless it be made habitable."

Some time afterwards I gave a ball for my house-warming, when its newly-finished embellishments appeared to great advantage. The whole ground-floor was opened for dancing. The First Consul, whom the Republic had just called to the Consulate for life, did us the honour to be present. Madame Bonaparte had said to me the preceding day: "I am determined, in compliment to your ball, to dress in the very best taste; you shall see how charmingly I can perform my toilet."

She made good her promise. She personated Erigone; her head was adorned with a wreath of vine leaves interspersed with bunches of black grapes; her robe of silver llama was trimmed with similar wreaths; her necklace, earrings, and bracelets were of fine pearls. Hortense accompanied her mother, and was on that occasion, as on all others and in all places, graceful and fascinating. She danced like a sylph, and I seem to see her still, slender as an aërial nymph, and dressed after the antique in a short tunic of pink crape, embroidered in silver llama, her fair head crowned with roses.

I see her, as she always was, the life of the party; her gaiety, good-humour, and spirit of pleasing, imparting the same qualities to all around her. The young people grouped about her, looked at her, and loved her, as the crowd would now and for ever follow and love her. As for the First Consul, he insisted on seeing every part of the house, and Junot, at his desire, acted as his cicerone to the very cellars and garrets. He stayed only till one o'clock, but for him that was a very late hour, and we were proportionately grateful.

The *Senatus Consultum*, requiring rather than declaring the prolongation of the Consulate, did not appear sufficiently satisfactory; another was presented to the First Consul on the 31st of July, or the 1st of August. Junot went early that morning to the Tuileries, and had a long interview with the First Consul, and on his return assured me that Napoleon was still undecided whether or not he should accept the Consulate for life. It was two months after the requisition for the prolongation of the Consulate for ten years that the nation, sensible of the necessity of preserving to the utmost possible extent that protection under which France had seen her prosperity revive, demanded the Consulate for life. But Napoleon, great as was his ambition, desired that the will of France should justify it. An appeal was ordered, registers opened. The citizens were at liberty to sign or not without fear of proscription, for it is remarkable that Napoleon never revenged any political offence. Of this Moreau is a notorious proof.

"The life of a citizen belongs to his country," replied the First Consul to the deputation of the Senate; "as it is the wish of the French nation that mine should be consecrated to her, I obey her will." Surely he had a right to say that it was the will of the people, for of three millions five hundred and seventy-seven thousand two hundred and fifty-nine citizens who voted freely, three millions five hundred and sixty-eight thousand eight hundred and ninety gave their vote in the affirmative.

The opinions in which Junot had been educated were so entirely and purely republican that the *Senatus Consultum* declaring Napoleon Consul for life was by no means so agreeable to him as might have been expected from his attachment, at a time when indifferent observers saw in this event only the present and future welfare of France. One day when we dined with the First Consul at Saint Cloud, I remarked that Junot's countenance on returning to Madame Bonaparte's drawing-room, after half an hour's interview with Napoleon, was altered, and wore an expression of care.

In the carriage, on our way home, he was thoughtful and melancholy. At first I asked in vain what had affected him, but eventually he told me that, having been questioned by the First Consul as to the opinion of the better circles at Paris respecting the Consulate for life, he had answered that it was entirely favourable, which was the truth; and that the First Consul had observed thereupon, his brow becoming stern and gloomy as he spoke: "You tell me this as if the fact had been just the reverse. Approved by all France, am I to find censors only in my dearest friends?"

"These words," said Junot, his voice failing so much that I could scarcely hear him—"these words almost broke my heart. I become my General's censor! Ah, he has forgotten Toulon!" "But it is impossible that the expression of your countenance should have been the sole cause of his uttering such words." Junot was silent for some time, then, without turning towards me, said: 'No; I certainly spoke of our regret—I may use the word—on reading the new *Senatus Consultum*, which overthrows the Constitution of the year viii.—in reducing the Tribunate to a hundred and fifty members! The Tribunate is a body much valued by the friends of liberty and of the Republic; then the mode of election is absurd—those two candidates for the Senate; in short, all this has been found great fault with in the country, particularly what has been done for the Council of State." I asked Junot what he meant had been done for the Council of State.

"It has been recognized as a constituted body," said he; "I told the First Consul that this measure had been ill received in many of the provinces. I have been, as I always shall be, an honest and loyal man—I shall neither betray my conscience, the interests of my country, nor those of the man whom I revere and love above all things—but I believe that I am serving him better in speaking the truth than in concealing it. I then explained that any expression of dissatisfaction which he might have remarked upon my countenance was not to be attributed to his nomination as Consul for life, but to the unfavourable impressions very generally produced by the numerous *Senatus Consulta*, which for the last fortnight had daily filled the columns of the *Moniteur*. The nomination for life of the two other Consuls is also spoken of in terms that I do not like to hear applied to anything which relates to the First Consul. I have much friendship for one of them, and a high esteem for the other; but why should two magistrates be imposed upon the nation, which certainly has not raised its voice for them as for my General? In fine, my poor Laura, I spoke as I thought, and I begin to see that we have got a Court in earnest, because one can no longer speak the truth without exciting displeasure."

This journey to Saint Cloud caused Junot a fit of illness. His affection for the First Consul was so great that whatever tended to disturb it went directly to his heart. Some days afterwards I received an invitation from Madame Bonaparte to breakfast at Saint Cloud, and to bring my little Josephine. I went alone, because Junot was confined to his bed by indisposition. Napoleon, it is well known, never breakfasted with Madame Bonaparte, and never appeared in her room in the morning, except occasionally, when he knew he should meet some persons there to whom he was desirous of speaking without exciting observation.

This morning he came into the room just as we were rising from the breakfast-table, and on advancing towards us, at once descried in the midst of the group the charming figure of my little Josephine, with her pretty light hair curling round a face that beamed with grace and intelligence, though she was only eighteen months old. The First Consul, immediately on seeing her, exclaimed:

"Ah! ah! here is our god-daughter, the Cardinaless! Good-morning, m'amselle—come, look at me—there, open your eyes. Why, the devil! do you know that she is prodigiously pretty—the little thing resembles her grandmother—yes, faith, she is very like poor Madame Permon. And what a pretty woman she was!—she was really the most beautiful woman I ever saw." As he was saying this, he pulled the ears and nose of my little girl, who did not approve of it at all; but I had taken the precaution to tell her that if she did not cry at Saint Cloud we should stop at a toy-shop on our way home, and she should have whatever she liked. Napoleon, who did not know this promise, remarked how very good-tempered the child was, while I was secretly reminding her of the toy-shop ten times in a minute.

"That is what I like children to be," continued Napoleon, "not perpetually crying or fretting. There is that little Lætitia, who is as beautiful as an angel—well, she cries so violently that I make my escape as if the house was on fire."

As he was talking, the party had removed to the blue salon, which was Madame Bonaparte's morning-room.

A circular balcony upon which this room opened passed along the whole suite of apartments. The First Consul stepped out of the window, and made me a sign to follow. I was about to give the child to her nurse, but he prevented me, saying:

"No, no; keep your daughter; a young mother is never as interesting as when she has her child in her arms. What is the matter with Junot?" he added, as soon as we were out on the balcony.

"He has a fever, General, and it is so violent as to oblige him to keep his bed."

"But this fever is of some kind or other; is it putrid, malignant, or what?"

"Neither the one nor the other, Citizen Consul," I replied, with a little impatience, for I was provoked at the petulant tone of his questions; "but Junot is, as you know, very susceptible, and a pain which goes to his heart affects his health. You know, General, that such complaints are beyond the power of medicine."

"I see that Junot has been telling you of the sort of quarrel we had the other day. He made himself quite ridiculous."

"You will give me leave, Citizen Consul, not to confirm what you have just been saying with my assent; you are no doubt jesting. All that I can do is to affirm that, having probably misunderstood Junot, you have given him serious pain. That he has suffered severely has been manifest to me, because neither my cares nor this child's caresses have been able to calm his mind. Also I conclude, General, that, in reporting to me the conversation you are speaking of, he did not tell me the whole." This, as I afterwards learnt, was the truth.

The First Consul looked at me some moments without speaking—took my right hand, which held my little girl upon my left arm, then suddenly rejected it with a very singular movement; seized Josephine's little white and mottled arm, kissed it, gave a pretty hard tap upon her cheek, pulled her nose, embraced her, all in a minute, then disappeared like a flash of lightning. I repeated this little scene to Junot, whom, on my return, I found very ill. He was not only very irritable, but his temperament itself was opposed to his reasoning tranquilly upon anything that agitated him. His adventure at Saint Cloud had quite upset him.

This very morning he had suffered the application of

thirty leeches, and though the loss of so much blood ought to have weakened him, he was in no degree more composed, because his nerves were strongly agitated, and he had not slept for three days. However, about seven in the evening, after taking some mutton broth, he threw himself upon the sofa in my apartment, and fell fast asleep. The night soon drew on, I was left in darkness, and, fearing to wake my husband, I was resting in an armchair by his side, without any lights. My head began to nod; the strong and regular, but monotonous breathing of Junot gradually sent me to sleep also.

Suddenly I heard a quick step on the little staircase which led from the breakfast-room into the court. Accustomed to watching by a sick-bed, I was on foot in an instant, and heard Heldt, the first *valet-de-chambre*, running upstairs and calling, "Madame! madame!"

A light struck upon my still half-closed eyes, a well-known voice effectually roused me, and the First Consul appeared.

"Good-evening, Madame Junot; you did not expect me, I imagine; well, where is your dying patient?"

As he spoke, he entered the small cabinet which served as an anteroom between Junot's apartments and mine, and in which Andoche had just been sleeping.

"Well, M. Junot, what is the matter with you, then? Hey? What does this fever mean? Well, what are you crying for, great baby? Ay, I shall mimic you presently myself." Here he pulled his ears and his poor nose, pinched his cheeks, and lavished all his expressions of favour on him. Junot meanwhile was suffocating; I perhaps never knew him so deeply affected. He took the First Consul's two hands alternately, pressed them to his bosom, and looked at him with an expression of affection.

He could not speak. He next took the hand of the good Duroc—who had accompanied the First Consul candle in hand—that excellent friend, whom for some time he misunderstood, but who never ceased to be the truest and most valuable of his brothers-in-arms.

"I imagine you are no longer ill," said the First Consul, taking the chair I had been offering him ever since he came in. ".Hey! hot-brain?"

He was scarcely seated before he stood up again, and began walking round the room, saying:

"Ah! so this is what they call your palace; I should be glad to see it: they all tell me it is a marvel and a folly; but this room seems simple enough."

Hereupon he went into Junot's room and his cabinet, then returned and passed into my apartment. "Ah! ah! so this is the sanctuary," said he, in a tone of kindness, though rather banteringly. "But what the devil is this? Do these happen to be your grandmothers?"

"They are not even relations, General," I replied. "It is a piece of Junot's gallantry, who chose to ornament my room with portraits of all the celebrated females of antiquity and of the last century; he was willing that I should not be too humble in my character of a woman."

"Oh! he might have dispensed with the portrait-gallery for that purpose. But he was right not to admit into it the women of the present day, for all pretend to be celebrated; it is the folly of all countries."

He continued to walk on as he talked; while I looked at him with attention, and a smile which I could not wholly suppress. At first he did not remark this, but in the end guessed the cause, which was the singular style of his costume, always absolutely laughable, when he assumed the dress of a private citizen. From what cause I can scarcely tell, but all the illusion of glory which surrounded him could not make his appearance imposing when not attired in military uniform. It might arise from his being wholly unaccustomed to this undress; but at all events he was totally different in it, even in its very eccentricity, from other men. On this occasion his greatcoat was of superfine cloth, and his hat was a remarkably fine beaver, but it was still of the same unfashionable make, and was set on the head in the same peculiar manner, with the difference only from his former appearance, that his hair was not powdered, and the curls had disappeared.

"Well, M. Junot," said he, after having made the tour of my apartments, the only portion of the house yet furnished, "I hope this little journey round your domains has quite cured you?" Junot seized the hand which the First Consul presented to him, pressed it between both his, and wept without answering. At this moment he was neither the man of strong mind nor the courageous soldier, but a feeble child. "To prove that you are quite cured," continued the First Consul, "you will breakfast with me to-morrow at Saint Cloud. Good-night, my old friend. Adieu, *Madame la Commandante.*"

We attended him to the street door. No one knew that the First Consul was in our house; he had imposed silence upon Heldt, the only one of our servants who had seen him; and it is well known that Napoleon was not one of those persons who might be disobeyed. He was right in his privacy; the knowledge of his visit would but have created jealousies. He had crossed the Tuileries on foot, and at the entrance of the Champs-Elysées a chaise, or sort of cabriolet drawn by two horses, which Duroc generally used, was waiting for him.

Junot slept badly that night; his mind was so ardent that happiness and sorrow were equally inimical to his bodily health. He was, however, quite recovered the next morning, went to Saint Cloud, and returned perfectly enchanted. But a new storm was already threatening. Fouché, whose rank should have made him the friend, as he was the equal of his brother-in-arms, but who was, in fact, his most active enemy, and the more dangerous because unsuspected, took advantage of the extreme irritability of Junot's character, to which it was so easy to give a sinister colouring.

END OF VOL. II.

A LIST OF

SOME OF THE MORE IMPORTANT TITLES

CONFERRED BY

Napoleon,

EMPEROR OF THE FRENCH, KING OF ITALY,

PROTECTOR OF THE CONFEDERATION OF THE RHINE,
MEDIATOR OF THE HELVETIC REPUBLIC.

KING OF BAVARIA, 1806 (formerly Elector), Maximilian (Joseph).

KING OF ETRURIA, 1801-3 (Louis of Parma).

KING OF ETRURIA, 1803-7 (Charles of Parma).

QUEEN OF ETRURIA, 1801-7 (Marie Louise Josephine de Bourbon).

KING OF HOLLAND, 1806-10 (Louis Bonaparte).

QUEEN OF HOLLAND, 1806-10 (Hortense Eugénie de Beauharnais).

KING OF NAPLES [TWO SICILIES], 1806-8 (Joseph Bonaparte).

KING OF NAPLES [TWO SICILIES], 1808-14 (Joachim Murat).

QUEEN OF NAPLES [TWO SICILIES], 1806-8 (Marie Julie Clary).

QUEEN OF NAPLES [TWO SICILIES], 1808-15 (Caroline Bonaparte).

KING OF ROME, 1811-14 (Napoleon Francis Charles Joseph Bonaparte).

KING OF SAXONY, 1806 (from Elector), Frederick Augustus.
KING OF SPAIN [AND INDIES], 1808-13 (Joseph Bonaparte).
QUEEN OF SPAIN [AND INDIES], 1808-13 (Marie Julie Clary).
KING OF WESTPHALIA, 1807-13 (Jerôme Bonaparte).
QUEEN OF WESTPHALIA, 1807-13 (Frederica Catherine of Wurtemburg).
KING OF WURTEMBURG, 1806 (from Elector).

[NAPOLEON II., EMPEROR OF THE FRENCH, 1814.]
VICE-REINE OF ITALY, 1805-14 (Princess Augusta Amelia of Bavaria).
VICEROY OF ITALY, 1805-14, Eugène Beauharnais.
MADAME MÈRE, 1805, Madame Letizia, Mother of the Emperor.
PRINCE IMPERIAL, 1811, the King of Rome.

ELECTOR OF BADEN, 1803 (formerly Margrave).
GRAND-DUKE OF BADEN, 1806 (from Elector).
GRAND-DUCHESS OF BERG AND CLEVES, 1806-8, Caroline Bonaparte.
GRAND-DUKE OF BERG AND CLEVES,* 1806-8, Joachim Murat.
GRAND-DUKE OF BERG AND CLEVES, 1809-14, Charles Napoleon Louis Bonaparte (nephew of the Emperor).
DUCHESS OF GUASTALLA, 1806-14, Pauline Bonaparte.
DUKE OF GUASTALLA, 1806-14, Prince Camille Borghèse.
ELECTOR OF HESSE CASSEL, 1803 (from Landgrave).
GRAND-DUKE OF HESSE DARMSTADT, 1806.
PRINCE OF LUCCA AND PIOMBINO, 1805-14, Felix Pascal Bacchiocchi.
PRINCESS OF LUCCA AND PIOMBINO, 1805-9, Marie Anne Eliza Bonaparte.
DUKE OF NASSAU, 1806 (from previous title).

* A title now borne by Prince Alfred of England.

ELECTOR OF SALZBURG, 1803.

GRAND-DUCHESS OF TUSCANY, 1809-14, Marie Anne Eliza Bonaparte.

GRAND-DUKE OF TUSCANY, 1809-14, Felix Pascal Bacchiocchi.

GRAND-DUKE OF WARSAW, 1807-13, Frederick Augustus King and Elector of Saxony.

ELECTOR OF WURTEMBURG, 1803 (from Margrave).

GRAND-DUKE OF WURTZBURG, 1805.

PRINCE OF BENEVENTO, 1806-14, Charles Maurice de Talleyrand Perigord.

PRINCESS OF BOLOGNA, 1807, Josephine Beauharnais (daughter of the Viceroy of Italy, and afterwards Crown Princess of Sweden).

PRINCE OF ECKMÜHL, 1809, Marshal Davoût.

PRINCE OF ESSLING, 1810, Marshal Masséna.

PRINCE OF FRANKFORT, 1810, Eugène Beauharnais.

GRAND-DUKE OF FRANKFORT, 1806, Dalberg.

PRINCE OF LEYEN, 1806 (formerly Count Leyen).

PRINCE OF THE MOSKOWA, 1813, Marshal Ney.

DUKE OF NEUFCHÂTEL, 1806 } Marshal Berthier.
PRINCE OF NEUFCHÂTEL, 1806 }

PRINCE OF PONTE CORVO, 1805, Marshal Bernadotte (afterwards King of Sweden).

PRINCE OF VENICE, 1807, Eugène Beauharnais.

PRINCE OF WAGRAM, 1809, Marshal Berthier.

THE MARSHALS OR GENERALS HAVING LOCAL COMMANDS.

Spain (divided).
Portugal.
Holland.
Hanover.
Hanseatic Towns.
Prussia.

The Illyrian Provinces.
Poland.
Rome.
Naples.
Switzerland Home commands.

THE DIGNITARIES OF STATE APPOINTED BY NAPOLEON.

THE ARCH-CHANCELLOR OF THE EMPIRE, Cambacérès, 1804-14.
THE ARCH-CHANCELLOR OF STATE, Eugène Beauharnais, 1805-14.
THE ARCH-TREASURER OF THE EMPIRE, Le Brun, 1804-14.
THE HIGH CONSTABLE OF FRANCE, Louis Bonaparte, 1804-14.
THE VICE-CONSTABLE OF THE EMPIRE, Berthier, 1807-14.
THE GRAND ELECTOR OF FRANCE, Joseph Bonaparte, 1804-14.
THE VICE-GRAND ELECTOR OF FRANCE, Talleyrand Perigord, 1807-14.
THE HIGH ADMIRAL OF FRANCE, Joachim Murat, 1805-14.
THE REGENT OF FRANCE, The Empress Maria Louisa, 1814.
THE GRAND JUDGE { Regnier, 1802-13. Molé, 1813-14.
THE MASTER OF HORSE, Caulaincourt, 1804-14.
THE CHIEF RANGER, Berthier, 1804-14.
THE LORD HIGH ALMONER, Cardinal Fesch, 1804-14.
THE GRAND CHAMBERLAIN { Talleyrand Perigord, 1804-9. Anatole de Montesquieu, 1809-14.
THE GRAND MARSHAL OF THE PALACE { Duroc, 1804-13. Bertrand, 1813-21.
THE MASTER OF THE CEREMONIES, Ségur, 1804-15.
GOVERNESS TO THE KING OF ROME, Madame de Montesquieu, 1811-15.
MINISTER FOR FOREIGN AFFAIRS { Talleyrand. Maret. Caulaincourt. Champagny.

MINISTER FOR WAR { Berthier. / Clarke. }

MINISTER OF THE INTERIOR, Champagny.

MINISTER OF EDUCATION, Portalis.

MINISTER OF FINANCE, Gaudin.

TREASURER OF THE EXCHEQUER, Barbé-Marbois.

PRESIDENTS OF THE SENATE {
François de Neufchateau, 1804-6.
Monge, 1806-7.
Lacépède, 1807-8.
Saint-Vallier, 1808-9.
Garnier, 1809-11.
Lacépède, 1811-13.
}

PRESIDENT OF THE LEGISLATIVE BODY, Marquis de Fontanes.

THE PRESIDENT OF THE COUNCIL OF STATE, Cambacérès.

MINISTER OF MARINE, Décrès.

MINISTER OF POLICE { Fouché. / Dubois. / Savary. }

MASTER OF THE POSTS, Lavalette.

PRESIDENT OF THE INSTITUTE OF FRANCE.

VICEROY OF ITALY, Eugène Beauharnais, 1805-14.

THE CHANCELLOR OF THE KINGDOM OF ITALY, Melzi D'Eril, 1805-14.

THE OTHER MINISTERS AND COUNCILLORS OF STATE.

THE AMBASSADORS AND MINISTERS OF THE EMPIRE AND CONSULATE: Generals Macdonald, Duroc, Sebastiani, Lucien Bonaparte, Joseph Bonaparte, Lauriston, Lannes, Junot, Saint Marsan, Gardanne, Caulaincourt, Savary, Otto, Andreossy, Bourrienne, Tallien, etc.

THE RESTORATION OF ARCHBISHOPS AND BISHOPS OF THE CATHOLIC CHURCH.

THE TWENTY-SIX MARSHALS OF THE EMPIRE.

1804.

Soult, 35, Duke of Dalmatia.
Masséna, 48, Prince of Essling.
Davoût, 34, Prince of Eckmühl.
Ney, 35, Prince of the Moskowa.
Lannes, 35, Duke of Montebello.
Augereau, 47, Duke of Castiglione.
Murat, 37, King of Naples.
Mortier, 36, Duke of Treviso.
Jourdan, 42, Count.
Lefebvre, 49, Duke of Dantzic.
Bessières, 36, Duke of Istria.
Berthier, 51, Prince of Neufchâtel.
Bernadotte, 41, Prince of Ponte Corvo.
Moncey, 50, Duke of Conegliano.
Brune, 41, Count.
Kellermann, 69, Duke of Valmy.
Sérurier, 62, Count.
Perignon, 50, Count.

1807.

Victor Perrin, 43, Duke of Belluno.

1809.

Macdonald, 44, Duke of Tarentum.
Marmont, 35, Duke of Ragusa.
Oudinot, 42, Duke of Reggio.

1811.

Suchet, 41, Duke of Albufera.

1812.

Saint Cyr, 48, Count.

1813.

Poniatowski, 51 [Prince].

1815.

Grouchy, 49 [Marquis].

The figures following the names give the age of the Marshal on receiving the bâton, the dates above the names are those of creation.

THE DUKES OF

	BORN	DIED
ABRANTÈS, 1808, Andoche JUNOT	1771	1813
ALBUFERA, 1812 (da Valencia), Louis Gabriel SUCHET	1770	1826
AUERSTADT, 1807, Louis Nicolas DAVOÛT	1770	1823
BASSANO, 1811, Hugues Bernard MARET	1763	1839
BELLUNO, 1810, Claude Victor PERRIN	1764	1841
CADORE, 1810, Jean Baptiste Nonpere de CHAMPAGNY	1756	1834
CASTIGLIONE, 1809, Père François Charles AUGEREAU	1757	1816
CONEGLIANO, 1808, Bon Adrienne Jeanot de MONCEY	1754	1842
DALBERG, 18—, Emmeric von DALBERG	1773	1833
DALMATIA, 1808, Nicolas Jean de Dieu SOULT	1769	1851
DANTZIC, 1807 (not the First Creation of Nobility by Napoleon), François Joseph LEFEBVRE	1755	1820
DÉCRÈS, 1813 (Admiral Denis), DÉCRÈS	1765	1820
ELCHINGEN, 1808, Michel NEY	1769	1815
FELTRE, 1809, Henry James William CLARKE	1765	1818
FRIULI, 1809, Géraud Christophe Michel DUROC	1772	1813
GAËTA, 1809, Michel Charles GAUDIN	1756	1844
ISTRIA, 1809, Jean Baptiste BESSIÈRES	1768	1813
LODI, 1807, Count Francesco MELZI D'ERIL	1753	1816
MASSA, 1809, Claude Antoine REGNIER	1746	1814
MONTEBELLO, 1808, Jean LANNES	1769	1809
OTRANTO, 1809, Joseph FOUCHÉ	{1754 / 1763}	1820
PADUA, 1808, Jean Toussaint ARRIGHI	1773	1853
PARMA, 1806, Jean Jacques Regis de CAMBACÉRÈS	1753	1824

LIST OF SOME OF THE MORE IMPORTANT TITLES

THE DUKES OF (*continued*)   BORN   DIED

PLACENTIA, 1806, Charles François LE BRUN — 1739—1824

RAGUSA, 1808, Auguste Fréderic Louis Viesse de MARMONT - - - - 1775—1852

REGGIO, 1809, Nicolas Charles OUDINOT - 1767—1847

RIVOLI, 1808, André MASSÉNA - - 1758—1817

ROVIGO, 1808, Anne Jean Marie René SAVARY - - - - - 1774—1833

TARENTUM, 1809, Stephen James Joseph Alexander MACDONALD - - - 1765—1840

TREVISO, 1807, Edouard Adolphe Casimir Joseph MORTIER - - - 1768—1835

VALENGIN, 1806, Louis Alexandre BERTHIER 1753—1815

VALMY, 18—, François Christophe KELLERMANN (father of the Comte de Valmy of Marengo) - - - - 1735—1820

VICENZA, 1808, Armand Augustin Louis de CAULAINCOURT - - - - 1773—1827

THE COUNTS.

"Counts that were worth the Counting."
                         MADAME CAMPAN.

d'Aure.
Baraguay d'Hilliers.
Barbé-Marbois, 1806.
Barrois.
Baste.
Belliard.
Berthollet.
Bertrand.
Beugnot.
Bondy.
Bordesoulle.

Boudet, 1807.
Bougainville, 1808.
Boulay de la Meurthe, 1808.
Broussier.
Brune (Marshal).
Bruyères.
Cambronne.
Cambronne, 1815.
Carnot, 1815.
Caulaincourt, 1810.
Cessac, 1808 (Lacuée).

THE COUNTS (*continued*).

Champmol, 1808 (Cretet).
Chanteloup } 1808.
Chaptal
Charpentier.
Claparède.
Clausel, 1813.
Compans.
Corbineau, 1813.
Curial.
Danthouard.
Daru, 1811.
Defrane.
Dejean.
De Laborde, 1808.
Delfanti.
Deseve.
Desgraviers-Berthollet.
Dessaix.
Donzelot, 1807.
Duhesme, 1814.
Dumas.
Durutte.
Eblé.
d'Erlon (Drouet).
d'Espagne.
Fontanes, 1809.
Fournier-Servolesi, 1809.
Foy, 1811.
Franceschi.
Friant.
Gambier.
Garnier.
Gassendi, 1813.

Gazan, 1808.
Gerard, 1813.
Girard.
Gregoire.
Grenier.
Grouchy, 1809 (Marshal).
Gudin.
Guilleminot.
Guyot.
Harispe, 1813.
d'Hautpoul.
Hédouville, 1805.
Huber.
Hunebourg, 1808 (Clarke).
Jourdan, 1814 (Marshal).
Klein, 1808.
Lacépède, 1808.
Lacoste (Freval).
Lagrange, 1808.
Lamarque.
La Pagerie, Tascher de.
Laplace, 1808.
Lariboissière.
Lasalle, 1808.
Las Cases.
Latour Maubourg.
Lauriston, 1808.
Lavallette.
Lefebvre-Desnouettes.
Legrand.
Lemarrois.
Lemoine.
Lepic, 1815.

THE COUNTS (*continued*).

Lobau, 1810 (Mouton).
Loison.
Maison, 1813.
Mejean.
Mejean (Maurice).
des Michels.
Milhaud.
Miot de Melito.
Missiessy, 1811.
Molé.
Molitor, 1808.
Mollien, 1806.
Montalivet, 1809 (Bachasson).
Montbrun.
Montholon.
Morand, 1805.
Mouton-Lobau, 1809 (see Lobau).
Muraire, 1808.
Nansouty.
Ornano.
Oudinot, 1808 (Marshal).
Pagol, 1814.
Partouneaux.
Pelusium (Mongé).
Perignon, 1811 (Marshal).
Pino.
Portalis.
Rampon.
Rapp, 1809.
Regnault de Saint Jean d'Angely.
Regnier, 1809.
Reille, 1808.
Roederer.
Roguet.
Saint Croy.
Saint Cyr (Gouvion), 1808 (Marshal).
Saint Hilaire.
Saint Marsan.
Saint Vallier.
Sanson, 1808.
Sébastiani, 1811.
Ségur.
Sérurier, 1808 (Marshal).
Sieyes.
Songis, 1808.
Sorbier, 1808.
Sortin.
Souham.
Soulès, 1808.
Suchet, 1808 (Marshal).
Sussy, 1808 (Collin).
Truguet, 1814.
Unebourg, 1812 (General Vandamme).
Valée, 1814.
Valence (Timbrune).
Valmy (Kellermann).
[Vandamme — see Unebourg — not to be confused with Hunebourg.]
Verdier, 1808.

SOME OF THE BARONS CREATED BY NAPOLEON.

Albert, 1809.
Alix.
Almeras.
Ameys.
Aubrey.
Augereau.
Aulard.
Avy.
Bachelu.
Bailly de Monthion, 1808.
Bauduin.
Bechaud.
Berckheim.
Bernard.
Bigarré, 1810.
Bignon.
Blamont.
Bonami.
Bourdesoulle, 1813.
Breissard.
Cacault.
Cambronne, 1810.
Campredon, 1815.
Castex, 1808.
Caulaincourt.
Chamorin, 1809.
Chastel.
Chouard.
Cochorn.
Colbert.
Compere.
Corbineau, 1808.
Corvisart.
Costaz.
Couloumy.
Coutard, 1811.
Dalton.
Daumesnil, 1812.
Delantre.
Delonne.
Delort de Glion.
Delzons.
Denon.
Desgenettes, 1812.
Des Michels.
Desvaux.
Dode.
Dommarget.
Domon.
Donop.
Doumerc.
Dunesme.
Duperré, 1810.
Duprés.
Eblé, 1804.
Esclavin.
Excelmans, 1812.
Fain.
Fisché.
Fontane.
Fouché.
Gauthier.
Gérard.
Gifflenga.
Girard.
Grabowski.
Grandeau.
Grandjean.
Grandorge.
Grillot.
Guilleminot.
Guyon.
Guyot.
Guyot de la Cour.
Habert.
Haxo.
l'Heritier.
Heyligers.
Houard.
Huber, 1813.
Jacquard.
Janin.
Jaquinot.
Jeannin.
Keramelin.
Labédoyère.
Lacroix.
Lafitte.
Lahoussaye.
Lamotte, Paultre de 1808.
Lanabère.
Lanchartin.
Larrey.
Latour du Pré.
Laurency.
Le Camus.
Ledru.
Lefol.
Letort, 1808.
Levy.

Louis.
Mallet.
Marbot.
Marcognet, 1808.
Marion.
Maureillan (Poitevin).
Meneval.
Merle.
Mermet, 1809.
Mortemart.
Mouton-Duvernet.
Nagle.
Norvins.
Ouvrard.
Pajol, 1808.
Pampelone.
Pecheux.
Pelet (de la Lozère).
Penne.
Percy.
Pernetti.
Petit, 1813.
Piré.
Plauzonne.
Poltre (? Paultre de Lamotte).
Reiset.
Ricard.
Richmont.
Rioult d'Avenay.
Romeny.
Roussel.
Saint Charles.
Saint-Geniez.
Saint-Germain.
Senarmont.
Sicard.
Simmer.
Soult (brother of the Marshal).
Subervie.
Teste.
Tharreau.
Thiry.
Thomières.
Triaire.
Valée, 1811.
Valentin, 1809.
Van Marizy.
Vial, 1811.
Vichery.
Villata.
Wathier.

ALSO

THE KNIGHTS OF THE LEGION OF HONOUR.

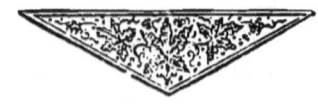

CONTEMPORARY RULERS.

FRANCE.—1774, Louis XVI. 1793, Louis XVII.—The Republic. 1802, The Consulate. 1804, Napoleon I. 1814, Louis XVIII. 1815, Napoleon. 1815, Louis XVIII.

MONACO.—1814, Honorius V.

ENGLAND.—1760, George III. (1812, Prince of Wales Regent.) 1820, George IV.

SPAIN.—1788, Charles IV. 1808, Ferdinand VII. 1808, Joseph (Bonaparte). 1814, Ferdinand VII.

PORTUGAL.—1777, Maria and Peter III. (1786, Maria only.) 1791, John Prince Regent (Retirement to the Brazils). 1816, John VI.

ITALY (Pope).—1775, Pius VI. 1800, Pius VII. 1823, Leo XII.

NAPLES (AND SICILY).—1759, Ferdinand IV. 1806, Joseph (Bonaparte). 1808, Joachim (Murat). 1815, Ferdinand I. (and IV).

SARDINIA.—1773, Victor Amadeus II. 1796, Charles Emmanuel II. 1802, Victor Emmanuel I. (until 1805). 1814, the same restored.

ITALY (King of). Napoleon I., 1805 to 1814.

ROME (King of). Napoleon II, 1811 to 1814.

ETRURIA (established 1801).—Louis I. 1803, Louis II.

TUSCANY (Grand-Duke).—1790, Ferdinand III. 1808, (Grand-Duchess) Eliza (Bonaparte-Bacchiochi). 1814, Ferdinand III.

TURKEY.—1789, Selim III. 1807, Mustapha IV. 1808, Mahmoud VI.

EGYPT.—Mehemet Ali.

ALGIERS.

PRUSSIA.—1786, Frederick William II. 1797, Frederick William III.

GERMANY (Austria).—1790, Leopold II. 1792, Francis II. 1806, Francis I.

HOLLAND (Netherlands).—1757, William IV. (to 1795). 1806, Louis (Bonaparte) to 1810. 1814, William Frederick.

POLAND.—1764, Stanislaus II. (Partition of Poland, 1795).

RUSSIA.—1762, Peter III., Catherine II. 1796, Paul I. 1801, Alexander I. 1828, Nicholas I.

SWEDEN.—1792, Gustavus IV. 1809, Charles XIII. 1818, Charles XIV.

NORWAY (with Denmark to 1814; with Sweden after 1814).

DENMARK.—1766, Christian VII. (1784, Frederick Prince Regent.) 1808, Frederick VI.

BAVARIA.—(Elector) Charles Maximilian, (King) Maximilian I.

HANOVER.—George III. (of England), George IV. (of England), William IV. (of England), Ernest (King of Hanover), 1837.

SAXONY.—(Elector until 1806) Frederick Augustus III. (and I.). 1827, Antony Clement.

WESTPHALIA.—1807, Jerôme (to 1813).

WURTEMBERG.—(Elector 1803, King 1805) Frederick II. (and I.). 1816, William I.

PERSIA.—1795, Aga Mohammed. 1797, Fatah Ali. 18 , Mohammed.

INDIA.—1772, Warren Hastings. 1785, Sir John Macpherson. 1786, Lord Cornwallis. 1793, Lord Teignmouth—(Lord Cornwallis, for a short time, followed by Sir Alured Clarke for a few weeks). 1798, the Marquess of Wellesley. 1805, Lord Cornwallis—(Sir George Barlow). 1807, Lord Minto. 1813, Earl of Moira. 1823, Lord Amherst.

CHINA.

JAPAN.

UNITED STATES.—1789, George Washington. 1797, John Adams. 1801, Thomas Jefferson. 1809, James Madison. 1817, James Munroe.

HAYTI AND SAINT DOMINGO.—1794, Toussaint. 1804, Dessalines. 1807, Christophe (Hayti). 1807, Petion (St. Domingo).

BRAZIL.—Pedro I.

MEXICO (see Spain).

CAMBACÉRÈS.

(*See* vol. iii., p. 256.)

"DURING the sitting of the Congress, the First Consul learnt that the Government couriers conveyed to favoured individuals in Paris various things, but especially the delicacies of the table, and he ordered that this practice should be discontinued. On the very evening on which this order was issued Cambacérès entered the *salon*, where I was alone with the First Consul, who had already been laughing at the mortification which he knew this regulation would occasion to his colleague : 'Well, Cambacérès, what brings you here at this time of night ?' 'I come to solicit an exception to the order which you have just given to the Director of the Posts. How do you think a man can make friends unless he keeps a good table ? You know very well how much good dinners assist the business of Government.' The First Consul laughed, called him a gourmand, and, patting him on the shoulder, said, 'Do not distress yourself, my dear Cambacérès ; the couriers shall continue to bring *you* your *dindes aux truffes*, your Strasburg *pâtés*, your Mayence hams, and your other tit-bits.'

"Those who recollect the magnificent dinners given by Cambacérès and others, which were a general topic of conversation at the time, and who knew the ingenious calculation which was observed in the invitation of the guests, must be convinced of the vast influence of a good dinner in political affairs. As to Cambacérès, he did not believe that a good Government could exist without good dinners ; and his glory (for every man has his own particular glory) was to know that the luxuries of his table were the subject of eulogy throughout Paris, and even Europe. A banquet which commanded general suffrage was to him a Marengo or a Friedland."--Bourrienne's *Memoirs of Napoleon*, vol. i., p. 440.

"Cambacérès never suffered the cares of Government to distract his attention from the great object of life. On one occasion, for example, being detained in consultation with Napoleon beyond the appointed hour of dinner—it is said that the fate of the Duc d'Enghien was the topic under discussion—he was observed, when the hour became very late, to show great symptoms of impatience and restlessness. He at last wrote a note which he called a gentleman usher in waiting to carry. Napoleon, suspecting the contents, nodded to an aide-de-camp to intercept the despatch. As he took it into his hands, Cambacérès begged earnestly that he would not read a trifling note upon domestic matters. Napoleon persisted, and found it to be a note to the cook containing only the following words, 'Gardez les entremets—les rôtis sont perdus.'

"When Napoleon was in good humour at the result of a diplomatic conference, he was accustomed to take leave of the Plenipotentiaries with, 'Go and dine with Cambacérès.' His table was, in fact, an important State engine, as appears from the anecdote of the trout sent to him by the municipality of Geneva, and charged 300 francs in their accounts. The auditor of the Imperial *Cour des Comptes*, having disallowed the item, was interdicted from meddling with similar municipal affairs in future."—Hayward's *Art of Dining*, p. 20.

"When I was sent to administer the Grand-Duchy of Berg, Cambacérès said to me, 'My dear Beugnot, the Emperor arranges Crowns as he chooses: here is the Grand-Duke of Berg (Murat) going to Naples; he is welcome, I have no objection, but every year the Grand-Duke sent me a couple of dozen hams from his Grand-Duchy, and I warn you I do not intend to lose them, so you must make your preparations.' I never once omitted to acquit myself of the obligation, and if there were any delay, his Highness never failed to cause one of his secretaries to write a good scolding to my house steward; but when the hams arrived exactly, his Highness never failed to write to my wife himself to thank her. This was not all: the hams were to come carriage free. This petty jobbery occasioned discontent, and it would not have cost me more to pay the carriage. The Prince would not allow it. There was an agreement between him and Lavalette (the head of the Posts), and my lord appeared to lay as much stress on the performance of this treaty as on the procuring of the hams."—*Beugnot*, tome i., p. 262.

www.ingramcontent.com/pod-product-compliance
Lightning Source LLC
Chambersburg PA
CBHW022148300426
44115CB00006B/400